Lynn,
Fond Best Wishes
in 2010 e.v.
I ove Ya!
XXOO Annie
Bones

CELESTIAL FORECASTER ®

2010

EVERYONE'S
DAILY ASTROLOGY GUIDE

FEATURING:

- Daily forecasts based on planetary alignments
- Monthly overview of significant aspects
- Lunar aspects guide
- Daily table of aspect influences
- Full year calendar,
- Built-in ephemeris and
- NEW famous birthdays

Loon Feather Publications
Box 47031 Victoria, B.C.
V9B 5T2 Canada
www.metaphysical.ca/forecaster
email: loonfeather@metaphysical.ca

Acknowledgements:

Thanks to all of you for continuing to make the Celestial Forecaster
a success. Your enthusiasm is what keeps the Forecaster going.
Thanks to Soror SSH for the great work editing,
and to Frater 72 for production.

Printing and Binding:	Data reproductions Corporation
Production & cover:	Frater 72
Editing:	Soror SSH
Inside Graphics:	Merx Toledo International
Front coat of arms	Merx Toledo International
ISBN:	978-0-9731518-7-9

TABLE OF CONTENTS

TIME ZONE ADJUSTMENTS

In the *Celestial Forecaster* we show Pacific Time and Eastern Time. Most poeple in North America are familiar with adjusting to one of those two zones. If you use **Central Time**, add two hours to Pacific Time. For **Rocky Mountain Time**, add one hour to Pacific Time. To get **Greenwich Mean Time**, add 8 hours to Pacific Time (PST) or seven hours to Pacific Daylight Time (PDT). If you live outside North America, you can refer to the Time Zone Map below.

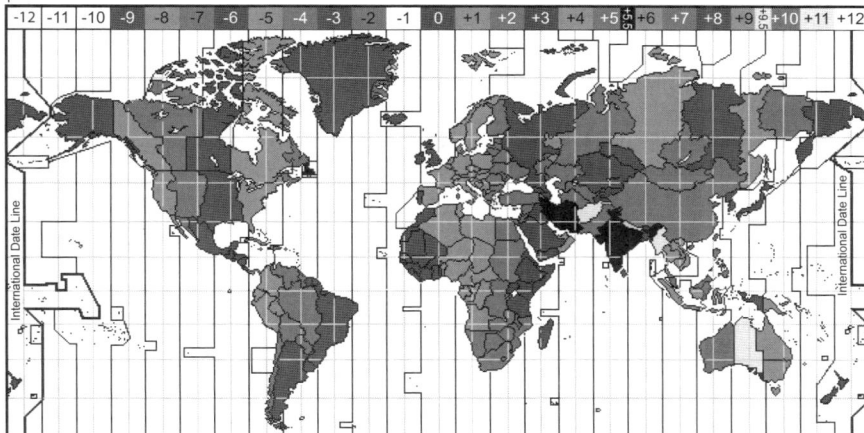

Definitions of Terms

Aspect: Planets are said to be "in aspect" with each other when their location in the sky forms particular angles with the earth which are deemed significant. The main aspects and angles used in this book are as follows:

✳ **Sextile (60°):** The sextile aspect is considered to be favorable, and opens up possibilities and opportunities to work energies out between the two planetary influences.

☐ **Square (90°):** The square aspect indicates a struggle or stress between two planetary influences. This aspect often brings obstacles, or difficulties in our ability to learn and understand. A positive way to address this aspect is to see it as a time when we need to work through our challenges. In these blocks or obstacles a great deal of energy is concentrated. If one acts with caution and care, the energy released by dealing with our challenges can be harnessed, and overcoming the obstacle becomes a personal triumph that leads to growth and the strengthening of character.

△ **Trine (120°):** The most advantageous and harmonious aspect. It is considered to bring the most positive effects. A trine aspect brings gifts, and talents are often realized and acted upon.

☍ **Opposition (180°):** The opposition is the furthest apart the two planets are able to be in their orbits. This aspect brings an acute awareness of the energies that two planetary influences have upon us. It can also bring an overwhelming effect, and handling the polarity often requires awareness and caution.

☌ **Conjunction (0°):** Conjunction is the act of joining, or the state of being joined. When two planets have reached the same degree in the sky this is called a conjunction. It represents the direct confrontation of these energies which will be positive or negative depending on the nature of the planets which are in conjunction.

The Orb: The orb is the area of influence before and after an exact aspect, measured in degrees. The smaller the orb, the closer we are to an exact aspect, and the more strongly we feel the planetary influences. Orbs are divided into two parts: applying and separating. **Applying** — the part of the orb when the planetary aspect is approaching the exact time of reaching its peak. **Separating** — the part of the orb when the planetary aspect is moving away from the peak point of the aspect. Orbs in this book have been calculated using an orb of 6° applying, and 3° separating for all aspects except the sextile, for which 4° applying and 2° separating have been used.

v/c **Void-of-course Moon:** As it travels through a zodiacal sign, the Moon is in aspect with a number of planets. The final major aspect it reaches in a sign marks the time when the Moon goes void-of-course (v/c), meaning it will undergo no further aspects while in that zodiac sign. The Moon will remain void-of-course until it enters the next zodiac sign. While the Moon is void-of-course is a time of less direction and more confusion, particularly on the emotional or mood level.

R **Retrograde:** This occurs when the orbit of a planet causes it to appear to move backward through the sky. It represents a time of moving back over old ground, and inverting influences. The section on Mercury retrograde (page 8) gives examples of how retrogrades work. The Sun and Moon, not being planets, do not go retrograde.

D **Direct:** After a period of retrograde motion, the planet ceases its backward motion and moves forward again through the zodiacal signs. It represents a time of release and forward movement, though the old ground that was just covered in retrograde fashion must be gone over again before any new progress can be made.

Glossary of Astrological Symbols

Aries	♈	Sun	☉	
Taurus	♉	Moon	☽	
Gemini	♊	Mercury	☿	
Cancer	♋	Venus	♀	
Leo	♌	Mars	♂	
Virgo	♍	Jupiter	♃	
Libra	♎	Saturn	♄	
Scorpio	♏	Neptune	♆	
Sagittarius	♐	Uranus	♅	
Capricorn	♑	Pluto	♇	
Aquarius	♒			
Pisces	♓			

How to Use this Book

To adjust for time zones other than Pacific or Eastern USA, use the *Time Zone Adjustments* table on page 5.

For planetary aspectarian and for the phases of the Moon: use the *Overview of Significant Aspects in 2010* found on pages 9 – 19.

For major daily influences at a glance: look at the *Table of Aspect Influences* on pages 20 - 23.

For exact zodiacal position of a planet: use the *Ephemeri*s on pages 266-272.

For daily commentary and analysis: see the main section pages 39-265, including:

Sun Signs: The glyph for the current sun sign is shown in the upper right margin on each page of the daily commentary.

Headers: The date headers at the top of each day show the date, the day of the week, and a selection of notable holidays.

Moon signs and void-of-course periods: Below the date header is the Moon's sign. The Moon's void-of-course period and entry to the next sign is shown chronologically with the day's planetary aspects. The numerous lunar aspects are included this year, and are interpreted in the new *Lunar aspects guide* on pages 25 - 37.

Aspects: Below the Moon's sign in the header is a list of the day's exact planetary and lunar aspects, together with their time of occurrence. Also listed are aspects whose orb of influence is just beginning, and the aspect's date of exact occurrence. Occasionally the aspect information is followed by quotes from famous people.

Mood Watch:: Each day features a *Mood Watch:* section. This commentary examines key lunar aspects of the day, and explains their likely influence on our moods. Like our moods, these lunar aspects are generally short-lived.

Aspect Analysis: Below the *Mood Watch:* section are shown the day's main planetary aspects, the dates their orb of influence occurs, and an in-depth aspect analysis.

Mercury retrograde periods: 2010

BEGINS (Mercury goes retrograde)

(Dec. 26, 2009   in Capricorn)

April 17   in Taurus

Aug. 20   in Virgo

Dec. 10   in Capricorn

ENDS (Mercury goes direct)

Jan. 15   in Capricorn

May 11   in Taurus

Sept. 12   in Virgo

Dec. 29   in Sagittarius

Mercury Retrograde through the Earth Signs, and through Sagittarius

Mercury represents how we process information and communicate. Mercury retrograde is a term that describes an orbital shift as it moves backwards through a sign. Technically it only appears to move backwards through the degrees of the zodiac from our geocentric view. Astrologically, this is a time of communication related setbacks, reiterations, or inconsistencies – particularly the first few days going into and out of the retrograde period. Mercury retrograde periods take place for an average of three weeks at a time, and will occur on the average of three times a year. This year brings four retrograde periods, with last year's final retrograde cycle overlapping into the beginning of this year.

Mercury retrograde is a time of going back over various topics, and repeating or correcting a lot of information. General misinformation and absentmindedness are the most common symptoms.

This year Mercury will go retrograde in the three earth signs of the zodiac: Capricorn, Taurus, and Virgo. In the final half of the last retrograde phase (Dec. 10 – 29), it will also be retrograde in the mutable fire sign, Sagittarius. As Mercury goes retrograde through the earth signs, communications of a material nature are easily misinterpreted. It is best not to underestimate (or overestimate) the material concerns of others when attempting to communicate. Mercury retrograde through the earth signs will bring a tendency to misplace physical items, and there may be a lot of miscommunication over necessities, money, practical matters, and the physical wellbeing of things.

Mercury retrograde in Capricorn brings miscommunications over large scale contracts, issues of control and time restraints. While Mercury is retrograde in Taurus, be cautious with banking matters and with keeping track of possessions; beware of the potential for disputes over the necessity for practicality and economic viability. While Mercury is retrograde in the Mercury-ruled earth sign, Virgo, be careful not to get caught up in disputes over health matters, accounting and budgets, and be sure to double check inventories. Expect some confusion over situations involving the maintenance of resources and re-sale goods.

While Mercury is retrograde in the fire sign, Sagittarius, communication mistakes will be apparent in such topics as philosophy, travel, sports, and exploration, and expect travel delays and misunderstandings.

Overview of Significant Events in 2010

Particularly noteworthy events

January 17	Jupiter enters Pisces
January 31	Saturn square Pluto
April 7	Saturn enters Virgo
April 26	Saturn opposite Uranus
May 22/23	Jupiter opposite Saturn
May 27	URANUS ENTERS ARIES
June 5/6	Jupiter enters Aries
June 8	Jupiter conjunct Uranus
July 21	Saturn enters Libra
July 23	Uranus-square-Pluto-non-exact
July 24/25	Jupiter square Pluto
July 26	Saturn opposite Uranus
August 13	Retrograde Uranus re-enters Pisces
August 21	Saturn square Pluto
Sept. 8/9	Retrograde Jupiter re-enters Pisces
Sept. 18	Jupiter conjunct Uranus

Monthly Overview

JANUARY

	Exact Occurrence Date	*Orbital Range* BEGINS	ENDS
4	Sun conjunct Mercury	Jan. 1	Jan. 5
5	Mercury conjunct Venus	Jan. 2	Jan. 6
7	**Last Quarter Moon in Libra**		
11	Sun conjunct Venus	Dec. 17, 2009	Jan. 24
13	Venus sextile Uranus	Jan. 9	Jan. 14
	Saturn goes retrograde	Jan. 13	May 30
	Sun sextile Uranus	Jan. 9	Jan. 15
14	**New Moon in Capricorn** – *Solar Eclipse*		

JANUARY (Cont'd)

Exact Occurrence Date		*Orbital Range*	
		BEGINS	ENDS
15	Mercury goes direct	Jan. 15	April 17
	Mercury-conjunct-Pluto-non-exact	Jan. 8	Jan. 20
	Mercury-square-Saturn-non-exact	Jan. 7	Jan. 21
17	JUPITER ENTERS PISCES	Jan. 17	June 5
18	Venus enters Aquarius	Jan. 18	Feb 11
19	Sun enters Aquarius	Jan. 19	Feb. 18
21	Venus trine Saturn	Jan. 17	Jan. 24
23	First Quarter Moon in Taurus		
24	Sun trine Saturn	Jan. 18	Jan. 27
26	Venus opposite Mars	Jan. 23	Jan. 28
29	**Full Moon in Leo**		
	Sun opposite Mars	Jan. 25	Jan. 31
31	SATURN SQUARE PLUTO	Sept. 14, 2009	March 9

FEBRUARY

2	**Candlemas / Imbolc / Groundhog Day**		
5	**Last Quarter Moon in Scorpio**		
6	Mercury sextile Uranus	Feb. 2	Feb. 7
	Jupiter sextile Pluto	Jan. 17	Feb. 15
7	Venus conjunct Neptune	Feb. 2	Feb. 10
10	Mercury enters Aquarius	Feb. 10	March 1
11	Venus enters Pisces	Feb. 11	March 7
12	Mercury trine Saturn	Feb. 8	Feb. 14
13	Mercury opposite Mars	Feb. 9	Feb. 14
	New Moon in Aquarius		
14	***Chinese New Year: Metal TIGER***	Feb. 14	Feb. 2, 2011
	Sun conjunct Neptune	Feb. 8	Feb. 17
	Venus sextile Pluto	Feb. 11	Feb. 16
15	Mars sextile Saturn	Feb. 2	March 30
16	Venus conjunct Jupiter	Feb. 10	Feb. 19
18	Sun enters Pisces	Feb. 18	March 20
21	**First Quarter Moon in Gemini**		
23	Sun sextile Pluto	Feb. 19	Feb. 25
27	Mercury conjunct Neptune	Feb. 23	March 1
28	**Full Moon in Virgo**		
	Sun conjunct Jupiter	Feb. 20	March 4

MARCH

Exact Occurrence Date

		Orbital Range	
		BEGINS	ENDS
1	Mercury enters Pisces	March 1	March 17
3	Venus conjunct Uranus	Feb. 26	March 6
4	Mercury sextile Pluto	March 1	March 5
7	Venus enters Aries	March 7	March 31
	Last Quarter Moon in Sagittarius		
	Venus trine Mars	March 2	March 9
	Mercury conjunct Jupiter	March 3	March 9
9	Venus opposite Saturn	March 4	March 11
10	Mars goes direct	March 10	Jan. 23, 2012
11	Venus square Pluto	March 6	March 13
14	*Daylight Saving Begins*		
	Sun conjunct Mercury	March 7	March 17
15	**New Moon in Pisces**		
	Mercury conjunct Uranus	March 12	March 17
	Mars-trine-Uranus-non-exact	Feb. 25	April 3
16	Sun conjunct Uranus	March 10	March 20
17	Mercury enters Aries	March 17	April 2
	Mercury trine Mars	March 14	March 19
18	Mercury opposite Saturn	March 15	March 19
20	**Vernal Equinox** - Sun enters Aries	March 20	April 19/20
	Mercury square Pluto	March 17	March 21
21	Sun trine Mars	March 14	March 24
	Sun opposite Saturn	March 16	March 24
22	Mars sextile Saturn	Feb. 2	March 30
23	**First Quarter Moon in Cancer**		
25	Sun square Pluto	March 19	March 28
29	Venus sextile Neptune	March 26	March 31
	Full Moon in Libra		
31	Venus enters Taurus	March 31	April 24
	Mercury sextile Neptune	March 29	April 2

APRIL

2	Mercury enters Taurus	April 2	June 9
3	Venus square Mars	March 28	April 6

APRIL (Cont'd)

Exact Occurrence Date   *Orbital Range*

		BEGINS	ENDS
4	Venus trine Pluto	March 30	April 7
	Mercury square Mars	March 31	April 28
6	**Last Quarter Moon in Capricorn**		
	Mercury trine Pluto	April 1	April 8
	Pluto goes retrograde	April 6	Sept. 13
	Mercury-conjunct-Venus-non-exact	March 26	April 11
7	SATURN ENTERS VIRGO	April 7	July 21
14	**New Moon in Aries**		
17	Venus sextile Jupiter	April 13	April 19
	Mercury goes retrograde	April 17	May 11
18	Sun sextile Neptune	April 13	April 20
19	Sun enters Taurus	April 19/20	May 20
21	**First Quarter Moon in Leo**		
23	Venus square Neptune	April 18	April 26
	Venus sextile Uranus	April 20	April 25
24	Venus trine Saturn	April 19	April 26
	Venus enters Gemini	April 24	May 19
25	Mercury square Mars	March 31	April 28
	Sun trine Pluto	April 19	April 28
26	SATURN OPPOSITE URANUS	March 10	Aug. 20
28	**Full Moon in Scorpio**		
	Sun conjunct Mercury	April 24	April 30

MAY

		BEGINS	ENDS
1	**Beltane / May Day**		
3	Mercury trine Pluto	April 23	May 23
4	Sun square Mars	April 23	May 9
5	**Last Quarter Moon in Aquarius**		
7	Venus sextile Mars	May 2	May 10
11	Mercury goes direct	May 11	Aug. 20
13	**New Moon in Taurus**		
7	Venus square Jupiter	May 11	May 20
	Sun sextile Jupiter	May 12	May 20

MAY (Cont'd)

| *Exact Occurrence Date* | *Orbital Range* | |
	BEGINS	ENDS
18 Venus square Saturn	May 13	May 20
Venus trine Neptune	May 13	May 21
Sun trine Saturn	May 12	May 21
19 Sun square Neptune	May 13	May 22
Mercury trine Pluto	April 23	May 23
Venus square Uranus	May 14	May 22
Venus enters Cancer	May 19	June 14
20 **First Quarter Moon in Leo**		
Sun sextile Uranus	May 16	May 22
Sun enters Gemini	May 20	June 21
22 JUPITER OPPOSITE SATURN	April 25	Aug. 31
23 Venus opposite Pluto	May 18	May 26
27 **Full Moon in Sagittarius**		
URANUS ENTERS ARIES	May 27	Aug. 13
29 Mercury-sextile-Venus-non-exact	May 21	Jun. 8
30 Saturn goes direct	May 30	Jan. 25, 2011
31 Neptune goes retrograde	May 31	Nov. 6

JUNE

	BEGINS	ENDS
4 Mars opposite Neptune	May 23	June 10
Last Quarter Moon in Pisces		
5 JUPITER ENTERS ARIES	June 5/6	Sept. 8/9
6 Mars enters Virgo	June 6	July 29
8 JUPITER CONJUNCT URANUS	April 25	Oct. 27
Mercury trine Saturn	June 4	June 10
9 Mercury square Neptune	June 5	June 10
Mercury enters Gemini	June 9	June 25
10 Mercury sextile Uranus	June 7	June 11
Mercury sextile Jupiter	June 7	June 11
11 Mercury square Mars	June 5	June 13
12 **New Moon in Gemini**		
Venus sextile Saturn	June 8	June 14
14 Venus enters Leo	June 14	July 10
Venus trine Uranus	June 9	June 17

JUNE (Cont'd)

Exact Occurrence Date		Orbital Range	
		BEGINS	ENDS
15	Venus trine Jupiter	June 9	June 17
	Mars trine Pluto	June 4	June 20
18	**First Quarter Moon in Virgo**		
19	Sun square Saturn	June 12	June 22
	Sun trine Neptune	June 13	June 22
21	**Summer Solstice**-Sun enters Cancer	June 21	July 22
	Sun square Uranus	June 15	June 24
23	Sun square Jupiter	June 16	June 26
24	Mercury square Saturn	June 21	June 25
	Mercury trine Neptune	June 21	June 25
25	Mercury enters Cancer	June 25	July 9
	Mercury square Uranus	June 22	June 26
	Sun opposite Pluto	June 19	June 28
26	**Full Moon in Capricorn** – *Lunar Eclipse*		
	Mercury square Jupiter	June 23	June 27
27	Mercury opposite Pluto	June 24	June 28
28	Sun conjunct Mercury	June 23	June 30

JULY

1	Mercury sextile Mars	June 28	July 2
4	**Last Quarter Moon in Aries**		
5	Uranus goes retrograde	July 5	Dec. 5
8	Venus opposite Neptune	July 3	July 11
	Mercury sextile Saturn	July 6	July 10
9	Mercury enters Leo	July 9	July 27
	Mercury trine Uranus	July 6	July 11
10	Venus enters Virgo	July 10	Aug. 6
	Sun sextile Mars	June 30	July 16
11	Mercury trine Jupiter	July 7	July 12
	New Moon in Cancer – *Solar Eclipse*		
13	Venus trine Pluto	July 8	July 16
18	**First Quarter Moon in Libra**		
21	SATURN ENTERS LIBRA	July 21	Oct. 5, 2012

JULY (Cont'd)

Exact Occurrence Date	*Orbital Range*	
	BEGINS	ENDS
22 Sun enters Leo	July 22	Aug. 22 / 23
Sun sextile Saturn	July 18	July 25
23 Sun trine Uranus	July 16	July 26
Jupiter goes retrograde	July 23	Nov. 18
Uranus-square-Pluto-non-exact	May 6	Aug. 11
24 JUPITER SQUARE PLUTO	May 28	Sept. 10
25 **Full Moon in Aquarius**		
26 Mercury opposite Neptune	July 22	July 28
Sun trine Jupiter	July 19	July 29
SATURN OPPOSITE URANUS	March 10	Aug. 20
27 Mercury enters Virgo	July 27	Oct. 3
29 Mars enters Libra	July 29	Sept. 14
30 Mercury trine Pluto	July 25	Aug. 1
Mars opposite Uranus	July 20	Aug. 4
31 Mars conjunct Saturn	July 19	Aug. 5

AUGUST

1 **Lammas / Lughnassad**		
2 **Last Quarter Moon in Taurus**		
JUPITER SQUARE PLUTO	May 28	Sept. 10
3 Mars opposite Jupiter	July 25	Aug. 8
Mars square Pluto	July 25	Aug. 8
6 Venus enters Libra	Aug. 6	Sept. 8
7 Venus opposite Uranus	Aug. 1	Aug. 9
8 Venus conjunct Saturn	Aug. 2	Aug. 11
9 Venus opposite Jupiter	Aug. 4	Aug. 12
New Moon in Leo		
Venus square Pluto	Aug. 4	Aug. 12
13 URANUS ENTERS PISCES	Aug. 13	March 11, 2011
16 **First Quarter Moon in Scorpio**		
JUPITER OPPOSITE SATURN	April 25	Aug. 31
20 Sun opposite Neptune	Aug. 14	Aug. 23
Venus conjunct Mars	Aug. 4	Oct. 8
Mercury goes retrograde	Aug. 20	Sept. 12
21 SATURN SQUARE PLUTO	June 21	Sept. 14

15

AUGUST (Cont'd)

| Exact Occurrence Date | Orbital Range | |
	BEGINS	ENDS
22 Sun enters Virgo	Aug. 22/23	Sept. 22
24 **Full Moon in Pisces**		
25 Sun trine Pluto	Aug. 19	Aug. 29

SEPTEMBER

1 **Last Quarter Moon in Gemini**		
3 Sun conjunct Mercury	Aug. 31	Sept. 4
4 Venus trine Neptune	Aug. 28	Sept. 8
8 **New Moon in Virgo**		
Venus enters Scorpio	Sept. 8	Nov. 7
8 JUPITER ENTERS PISCES	Sept. 8	Jan. 22, 2011
9 Mars trine Neptune	Aug. 31	Sept. 14
12 Venus sextile Pluto	Sept. 6	Sept. 15
Mercury goes direct	Sept. 12	Dec. 10
Mercury-trine-Pluto-non-exact	Sept. 5	Sept. 15
13 Pluto goes direct	Sept. 13	April 8, 2011
14 **First Quarter Moon in Sagittarius**		
Mars enters Scorpio	Sept. 14	Oct. 27
16 Mercury-sextile-Venus-non-exact	Sept. 10	Sept. 20
18 JUPITER CONJUNCT URANUS	April 25	Oct. 27
Mars sextile Pluto	Sept. 12	Sept. 21
21 Sun opposite Jupiter	Sept. 15	Sept. 23
Sun opposite Uranus	Sept. 15	Sept. 24
22 **Autumnal Equinox**		
Sun enters Libra	Sept. 22	Oct. 22
23 **Full Moon in Aries**		
25 Sun square Pluto	Sept. 19	Sept. 28
30 Sun conjunct Saturn	Sept. 23	Oct. 4
Last Quarter Moon in Cancer		

OCTOBER

1 Mercury opposite Jupiter	Sept. 28	Oct. 3
2 Mercury opposite Uranus	Sept. 28	Oct. 3
3 Mercury enters Libra	Oct. 3	Oct. 20
Venus conjunct Mars	Aug. 4	Oct. 8
4 Mercury square Pluto	Oct. 1	Oct. 6

16

OCTOBER (cont'd)

Exact Occurrence Date	Orbital Range	
	BEGINS	ENDS
7 **New Moon in Libra**		
8 Venus goes retrograde	Oct. 8	Nov. 18
Mercury conjunct Saturn	Oct. 4	Oct. 10
14 **First Quarter Moon in Capricorn**		
16 Sun conjunct Mercury	Oct. 8	Oct. 21
18 Mercury trine Neptune	Oct. 14	Oct. 19
19 Sun trine Neptune	Oct. 13	Oct. 22
20 Mercury enters Scorpio	Oct. 20	Nov. 8
Mars trine Jupiter	Oct. 13	Oct. 24
22 Sun enters Scorpio	Oct. 22	Nov. 22
Mars square Neptune	Oct. 13	Oct. 26
Mercury sextile Pluto	Oct. 20	Oct. 23
Full Moon in Aries		
24 Mars trine Uranus	Oct. 16	Oct. 28
25 Mercury conjunct Venus	Oct. 22	Oct. 26
26 Sun sextile Pluto	Oct. 22	Oct. 28
27 Mars enters Sagittarius	Oct. 27	Dec. 7
28 Sun conjunct Venus	Oct. 25	Oct. 30
30 **Last Quarter Moon in Leo**		
31 **All Hallows (Halloween) / Samhain / Witches' New Year**		

NOVEMBER

1 Venus sextile Pluto	Oct. 25	Nov. 4
4 Mercury trine Jupiter	Oct. 31	Nov. 6
5 **New Moon in Scorpio** – *Hecate's Moon*		
Mercury square Neptune	Nov. 2	Nov. 7
6 Mercury trine Uranus	Nov. 2	Nov. 8
Neptune goes direct	Nov. 6	June 6, 2011
7 *Daylight Saving Ends*		
Venus enters Libra	Nov. 7	Nov. 29
8 Mercury enters Sagittarius	Nov. 8	Nov. 30
13 **First Quarter Moon in Aquarius**		
14 Mars sextile Saturn	Nov. 8	Nov. 18
15 Sun trine Jupiter	Nov. 9	Nov. 18
17 Mercury sextile Saturn	Nov. 14	Nov. 19

NOVEMBER (cont'd)

Exact Occurrence Date	*Orbital Range*	
	BEGINS	ENDS
18 Sun square Neptune	Nov. 12	Nov. 21
Jupiter goes direct	Nov. 18	Aug. 29, 2011
Venus goes direct	Nov. 18	May 15, 2012
Sun trine Uranus	Nov. 13	Nov. 21
20 Mercury conjunct Mars	Nov. 11	Dec. 15
21 **Full Moon in Gemini**		
22 Sun enters Sagittarius	Nov. 22	Dec. 21
23 Venus-trine-Neptune-non-exact	Nov. 4	Nov. 26
25 Mercury square Jupiter	Nov. 20	Nov. 27
27 Mercury sextile Neptune	Nov. 24	Nov. 28
Mercury square Uranus	Nov. 23	Nov. 30
28 Last **Quarter Moon in Virgo**		
29 Mars square Jupiter	Nov. 20	Dec. 3
Venus enters Scorpio	Nov. 29	Jan. 7, 2011
30 Mercury enters Capricorn	Nov. 30	Dec. 18

DECEMBER

1 Mercury sextile Venus	Nov. 26	Dec. 12
2 Mars sextile Neptune	Nov. 27	Dec. 5
3 Mars square Uranus	Nov. 25	Dec. 7
5 **New Moon in Sagittarius**		
Mercury conjunct Pluto	Nov. 29	Dec. 16
Uranus goes direct	Dec. 5	July 12, 2011
6 Sun sextile Saturn	Dec. 2	Dec. 9
7 Mars enters Capricorn	Dec. 7	Jan. 15, 1011
8 Venus sextile Pluto	Nov. 30	Dec. 11
10 Mercury goes retrograde	Dec. 10	Dec. 29
Mercury sextile Venus	Nov. 26	Dec. 12
13 **First Quarter Moon in Pisces**		
Mercury conjunct Pluto	Nov. 29	Dec. 16
Mercury conjunct Mars	Nov. 11	Dec. 15
Mars conjunct Pluto	Dec. 5	Dec. 17

DECEMBER (cont'd)

| *Exact Occurrence Date* | *Orbital Range* | |
	BEGINS	ENDS
16 Sun square Jupiter	Dec. 10	Dec. 19
18 Sun sextile Neptune	Dec. 13	Dec. 20
Mercury enters Sagittarius	Dec. 18	Jan. 13, 2011
Sun square Uranus	Dec. 12	Dec. 21
19 Sun conjunct Mercury	Dec. 17	Dec. 20
20 Mercury square Uranus	Dec. 16	Dec. 22
Mercury sextile Neptune	Dec. 17	Dec. 22
21 **Full Moon in Gemini** – *Lunar Eclipse*		
Winter Solstice		
Sun enters Capricorn	Dec. 21	Jan. 20, 2011
Mercury square Jupiter	Dec. 17	Dec. 24
26 Sun conjunct Pluto	Dec. 20	Dec. 29
27 **Last Quarter Moon in Libra**		
29 Mars square Saturn	Dec. 20	Jan. 1, 2011
Mercury goes direct	Dec. 29	March 30, 2011
Mercury-sextile-Saturn-non-exact	Dec. 26	Jan. 2, 2011

TABLE OF ASPECT INFLUENCES

JANUARY 2010

1	2	3	4	5	6	7	8	9	10	11	12	13	14	15	16	17	18	19	20	21	22	23	24	25	26	27	28	29	30	31

Aspect influences:
- ♄□♀
- ☿☌♀
- ♀✶♅
- ♃✶♀
- ♀△♄
- ☿☌♀
- ♀☍♂
- ☉☌☿
- ☿□♄
- ☉☌♀
- ☉✶♅
- ☉☍♂
- ☉△♄

FEBRUARY 2010

1	2	3	4	5	6	7	8	9	10	11	12	13	14	15	16	17	18	19	20	21	22	23	24	25	26	27	28

Aspect influences:
- ♄□♀
- ♃✶♀
- ♂✶♄
- ♀☌♆
- ♂△♅
- ☿✶♅
- ♀✶♀
- ♀☍♅
- ♀☌♃
- ☿☌♆
- ♀△♄
- ☿☍♂
- ☉✶♀
- ☉☌♆
- ☉☌♃

MARCH 2010

1	2	3	4	5	6	7	8	9	10	11	12	13	14	15	16	17	18	19	20	21	22	23	24	25	26	27	28	29	30	31

Aspect influences:
- ♄□♀
- ♄☍♅
- ♂✶♄
- ♂△♅
- ♀☌♅
- ♀△♂
- ♀☍♄
- ♀✶♆
- ♀□♀
- ☿□♀
- ☿✶♀
- ♀△♂
- ♀☌♃
- ☿☍♄
- ☿✶♆
- ♀△♅
- ☿☌♅
- ♀□♂
- ☉☌♀
- ☿☌♀
- ☉☌♅
- ♀☌♀
- ☉☌♃
- ☉△♂
- ☉☍♄
- ☉□♀

20

TABLE OF ASPECT INFLUENCES

APRIL 2010

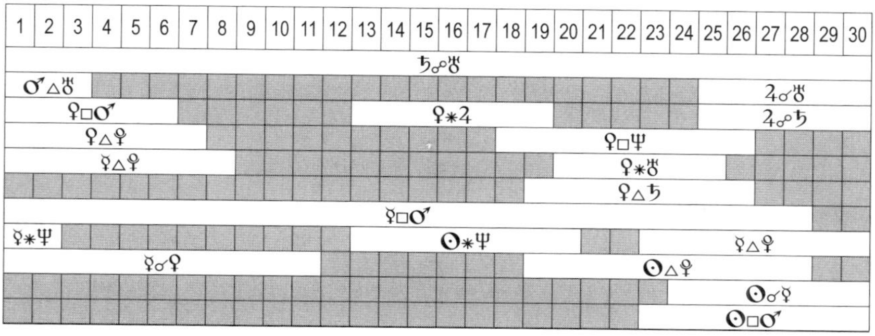
1 2 3 4 5 6 7 8 9 10 11 12 13 14 15 16 17 18 19 20 21 22 23 24 25 26 27 28 29 30
♄☍♅
♂△♅
♃☌♅
♀□♂
♀✶♃
♃☍♄
♀△♇
♀□♆
☿△♇
♀✶♅
♀△♄
☿□♂
☿✶♆
☉✶♆
☿△♇
☿☌♇
☉△♇
☉☌☿
☉□♂

MAY 2010

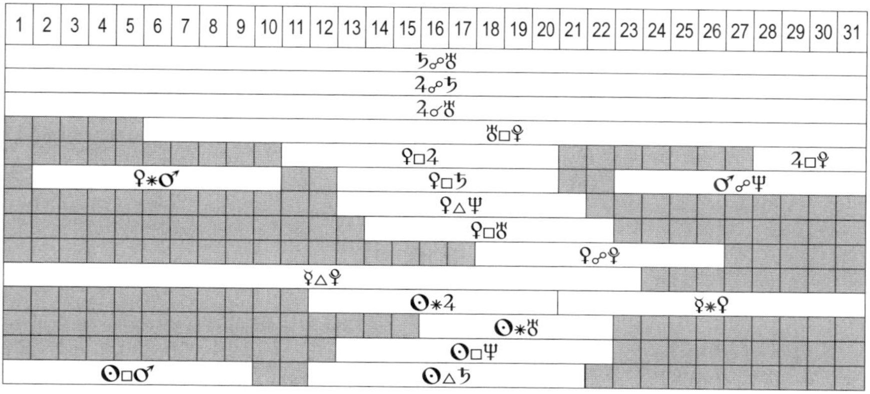
1 2 3 4 5 6 7 8 9 10 11 12 13 14 15 16 17 18 19 20 21 22 23 24 25 26 27 28 29 30 31
♄☍♅
♃☍♄
♃☌♅
♅□♇
♀□♃
♃□♇
♀✶♂
♀□♄
♂☍♆
♀△♆
♀□♅
♀☍♇
☿△♇
☉✶♃
☿✶♀
☉✶♅
☉□♆
☉□♂
☉△♄

JUNE 2010

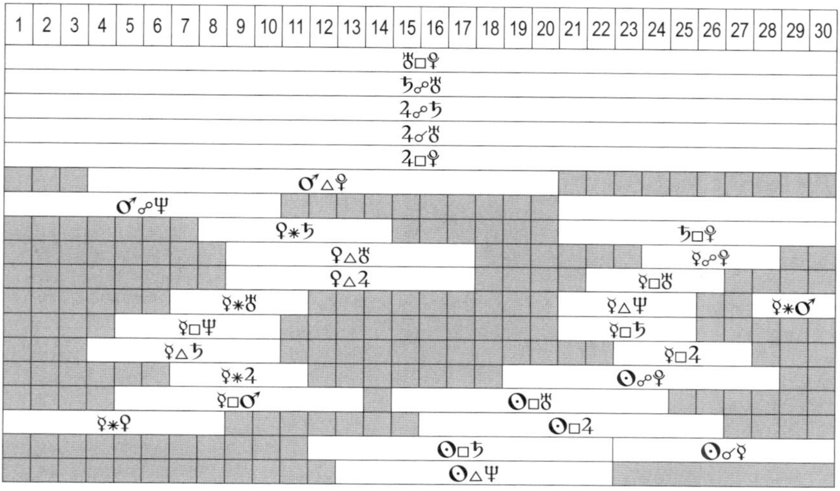
1 2 3 4 5 6 7 8 9 10 11 12 13 14 15 16 17 18 19 20 21 22 23 24 25 26 27 28 29 30
♅□♇
♄☍♅
♃☍♄
♃☌♅
♃□♇
♂△♇
♂☍♆
♀✶♄
♄□♇
♀△♅
☿☍♇
♀△♃
☿□♅
☿✶♅
☿△♆
☿✶♂
☿□♆
☿□♄
☿△♄
☿□♃
☿✶♃
☉☍♇
☿□♂
☉□♅
☿✶♀
☉□♃
☉□♄
☉☌☿
☉△♆

TABLE OF ASPECT INFLUENCES

JULY 2010

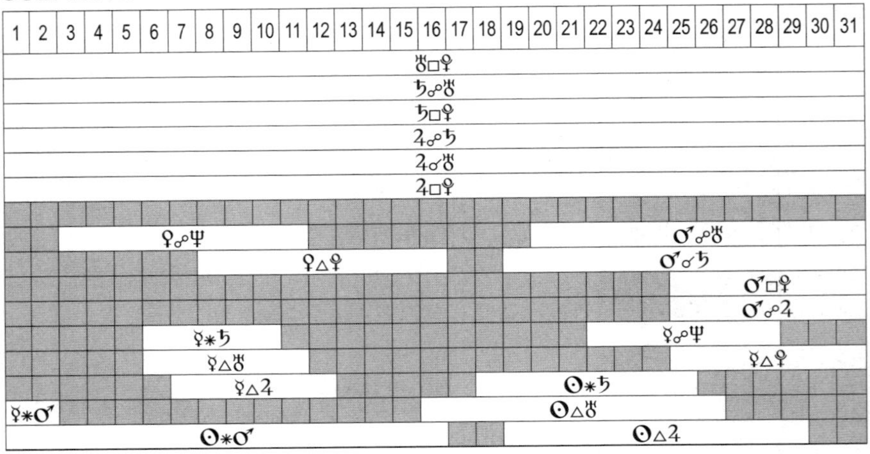

1	2	3	4	5	6	7	8	9	10	11	12	13	14	15	16	17	18	19	20	21	22	23	24	25	26	27	28	29	30	31

Aspect influences (July 2010):
- ♅□♀
- ♄☍♅
- ♄□♀
- ♃☍♄
- ♃☌♅
- ♃□♀
- ♀☍♆
- ♂☍♅
- ♀△♀
- ♂☌♄
- ♂□♀
- ♂☍♃
- ♀⚹♄
- ☿☍♆
- ♀△♅
- ♀△♀
- ♀△♃
- ☉⚹♄
- ☿⚹♂
- ☉△♅
- ☉⚹♂
- ☉△♃

AUGUST 2010

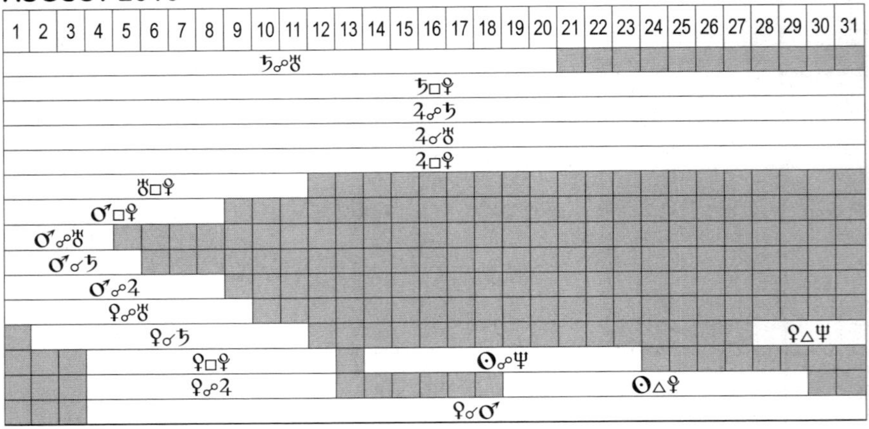

1	2	3	4	5	6	7	8	9	10	11	12	13	14	15	16	17	18	19	20	21	22	23	24	25	26	27	28	29	30	31

Aspect influences (August 2010):
- ♄☍♅
- ♄□♀
- ♃☍♄
- ♃☌♅
- ♃□♀
- ♅□♀
- ♂□♀
- ♂☍♅
- ♂☌♄
- ♂☍♃
- ♀☍♅
- ♀☌♄
- ♀△♆
- ♀□♀
- ☉☍♆
- ♀☍♃
- ☉△♀
- ♀☌♂

SEPTEMBER 2010

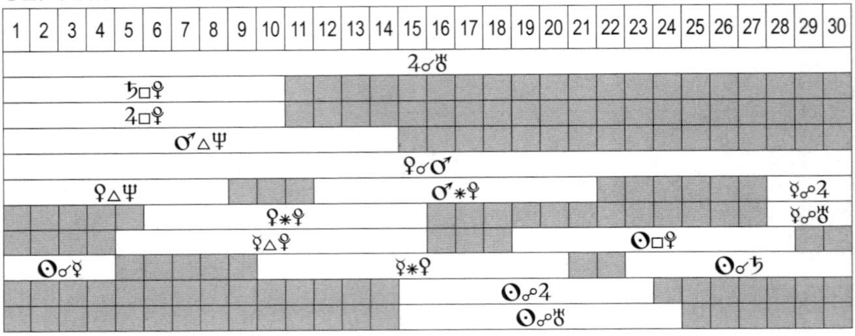

1	2	3	4	5	6	7	8	9	10	11	12	13	14	15	16	17	18	19	20	21	22	23	24	25	26	27	28	29	30

Aspect influences (September 2010):
- ♃☌♅
- ♄□♀
- ♃□♀
- ♂△♆
- ♀☌♂
- ♀△♆
- ♂⚹♀
- ☿☍♃
- ♀⚹♀
- ☿☍♅
- ☿△♀
- ☉□♀
- ☉☌♀
- ☿⚹♀
- ☉☌♄
- ☉☍♃
- ☉☍♅

22

TABLE OF ASPECT INFLUENCES

OCTOBER 2010

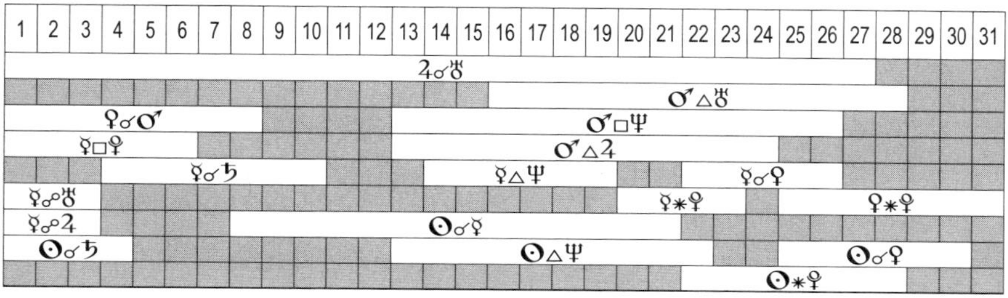

1 2 3 4 5 6 7 8 9 10 11 12 13 14 15 16 17 18 19 20 21 22 23 24 25 26 27 28 29 30 31
♃☌♅
♂△♅
♀☌♂
♂□♆
☿□♀
♂△♃
☿☌♄
☿△♆
☿☌♀
☿☍♅
☿✶♀
♀✶♀
☿☍♃
☉☌☿
☉☌♄
☉△♆
☉☌♀
☉✶♀

NOVEMBER 2010

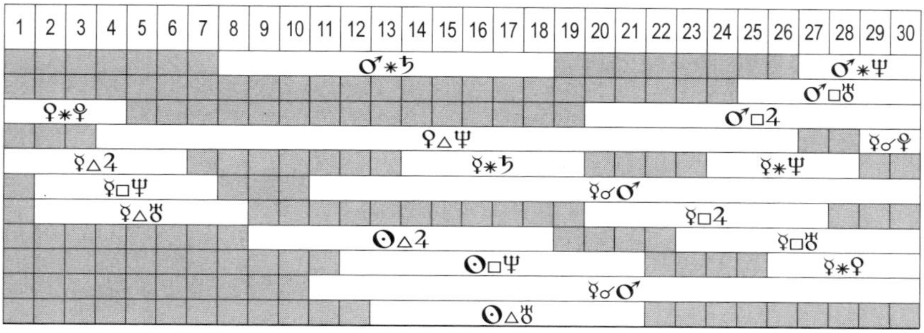

1 2 3 4 5 6 7 8 9 10 11 12 13 14 15 16 17 18 19 20 21 22 23 24 25 26 27 28 29 30
♂✶♄
♂✶♆
♂□♅
♀✶♀
♂□♃
♀△♆
☿☌♀
☿△♃
☿✶♄
☿✶♆
☿□♆
☿☌♂
☿△♅
☿□♃
☉△♃
☿□♅
☉□♆
☿✶♀
☿☌♂
☉△♅

DECEMBER 2010

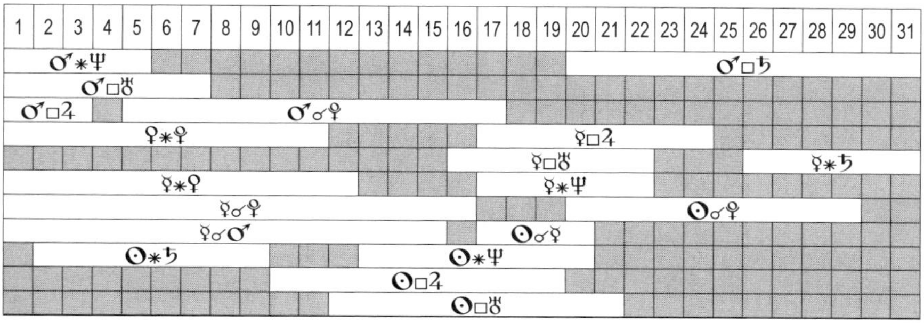

1 2 3 4 5 6 7 8 9 10 11 12 13 14 15 16 17 18 19 20 21 22 23 24 25 26 27 28 29 30 31
♂✶♆
♂□♄
♂□♅
♂□♃
♂☌♀
♀✶♀
☿□♃
☿□♅
☿✶♄
☿✶♀
☿✶♆
☿☌♀
☉☌♀
☿☌♂
☉☌☿
☉✶♄
☉✶♆
☉□♃
☉□♅

Phases of the Moon

Times in Pacific Time (for Eastern add 3 hours)

	☾ 3rd Qtr	● New	☽ 1st Qtr	○ Full	
January	7th 2:40AM Libra	14th 11:11PM Capricorn	23rd 2:52AM Taurus	29th 10:17PM Leo	
February	☾ 5th 3:49PM Scorpio	● 13th 6:51PM Aquarius	☽ 21st 4:41PM Gemini	○ 28th 8:32AM Virgo	
March	☾ 7th 7:42AM Sagittarius	● 15th 2:00PM Pisces	☽ 23rd 3:59AM Cancer	○ 29th 7:25PM Libra	
April	☾ 6th 2:37AM Capricorn	● 14th 5:28AM Aries	☽ 21st 11:19AM Leo	○ 28th 5:18AM Scorpio	
May	☾ 5th 9:15PM Aquarius	● 13th 6:04PM Taurus	☽ 20th 4:29AM Leo	○ 27th 11:12AM Sagittarius	
June	☾ 4th 3:12PM Pisces	● 12th 4:14PM Gemini	☽ 18th 9:30PM Virgo	○ 26th 4:30AM Capricorn	
July	☾ 4th 7:34AM Aries	● 11th 12:34PM Cancer	☽ 18th 3:11AM Libra	○ 25th 6:36PM Aquarius	
August	☾ 2nd 9:52PM Taurus	● 9th 8:07PM Leo	☽ 16th 11:15AM Scorpio	○ 24th 10:04AM Pisces	
September	☾ 1st 10:20AM Gemini	● 8th 3:29PM Virgo	☽ 14th 10:51PM Sagittarius	○ 23rd 2:16AM Aries	☾ 30th 8:51PM Cancer
October	● 7th 11:45AM Libra	☽ 14th 2:26PM Capricorn	○ 22nd 6:36PM Taurus	☾ 30th 5:45AM Leo	
November	● 5th 9:52PM Scorpio	☽ 13th 8:33AM Aquarius	○ 21st 9:26AM Gemini	☾ 28th 12:36PM Virgo	
December	● 5th 9:36AM Sagittarius	☽ 13th 5:58AM Pisces	○ 21st 12:12AM Gemini	☾ 27th 8:18PM Libra	

LUNAR ASPECTS GUIDE
MOON TO SUN ASPECTS

In general, the Moon aspects to the Sun bring us a greater awareness of our feelings with regard to the season through which we are passing.

Moon sextile Sun

Moon sextile Sun brings optimism, or a brighter spirit, towards whatever seasonal activities are occurring and our moods are more likely to be encouraged by the endearing qualities of the season. This aspect helps our moods to accept and be at peace with the relevant seasonal factors, getting in tune with the seasonal pace. It assists us in making the shift from the early stage of emotional experience to the next stage of emotional development. In general, Moon sextile Sun brings positive vibrations, and acts as a catalyst in the ebb and flow of the emotions. It brings the promising potential for acceptance and reassurance and, where such moods are absent, there is the driving hope to reach a happy medium. Moon sextile Sun brings inspiration to our dreams and gives us a sense of where we are going next.

Moon square Sun (First and Last Quarter Moons)

Moon square Sun represents the First and Last Quarter stages of the Moon. It is the middle road, the half-way mark between the waxing and waning process of the Moon. It is the pinnacle of the in-between stage, and it represents the crux of what we hope to establish in our emotional process as it is affected by the Moon. The square aspect represents struggle or challenge; this tends to be the point where we exercise our emotions with diligent effort. The square of the Moon to the Sun is a time when we tend to make extra adjustments with our emotional process, and we take extra steps towards the place we have determined that our emotions are headed. This is characterized by the sign the Moon is in, and how we respond, individually, with the qualities of that sign. Moon square Sun summons some very lively and busy emotional responses in the course of our dreams.

First Quarter Moon (Waxing Quarter Moon) Halfway in between the New and Full Moon, the First Quarter Moon has built up some momentum in our emotional process. This is a positive, upbeat, anticipatory time. The sign that the Moon is in will denote the types of focuses and themes that will preoccupy us, and these are the things we will be building up and strengthening in our emotional core. As the waxing Moon reaches this First Quarter mark, this is a good time for maintaining and nurturing positive emotional vibrations.

Last Quarter Moon (Waning Quarter Moon) Halfway in between the Full and New Moon, the Last Quarter Moon breaks down the emotional momentum that was built up during the Full Moon period of the previous week. This is a time of letting go, of finishing or completing certain aspects of the emotional process. The waning Moon allows us to process and let go of emotionally taxing sensations, and from there we begin to be less weighted down by our feelings. When we struggle with letting go, it is highlighted through this stage of lunar development. As the waning Moon reaches this Last Quarter mark, this is a good time for weeding out and cleaning up emotional negativity, and for letting go of unnecessary emotional baggage.

Moon trine Sun

Overall, Moon trine Sun brings good vibes; it allows us to create or to access congenial, hopeful, and positive moods. Moon trine Sun always reminds us of the aspects of the current season that are inspiring and uplifting. Whenever the trine aspect occurs, the Moon and Sun will both (usually) be in the same element together: a fire, water, air, or earth sign. This brings synchronization and focuses the energy of our moods on positive and cohesive emotional responses. Moon trine Sun brings beautiful harmony to the mood of the day. In general, this aspect brings sunny, cheerful moods, and a positive outlook on life. Moon trine Sun influences dreams with positive vibrations, and it brings sparkling delights and gifts of happiness.

Moon opposite Sun (Full Moon)

The Full Moon represents the fruition of our emotional process. Moon opposite Sun magnifies the emotional or spiritual qualities of the season. This is a time when we access and harness a great deal of emotional energy. It's a great time to establish positive affirmations, and to celebrate the bountiful fullness of the season. Often, the Full Moon time brings a whirlwind of activity, and this represents the crescendo or climax of our emotional process as it is affected by the Moon. This climax of the Moon's luminous reflections of the Sun brings the greatest amount of light to our emotional experience, and this is a very good time to count your blessings and enjoy the wonders of your life. Moon opposite Sun brings astonishing images and rich, fulfilling, experiences to the dream world.

Moon conjunct Sun (New Moon)

The New Moon represents the beginning; a starting point, where our feelings begin their development, and where our pre-established feelings are renewed, confirmed, or re-established. This is a dark time of night, as the Moon joins forces with the daytime Sun. Through this time, our emotional process is often internalized, where it is replenished with a sense of newness. Here, newer feelings may emerge with a certain affirmation or assurance. It is here that we muster new hope, new faith, and there is a subtle – but certain – expression of re-birth in our emotional understanding. This is the time to tap into the wiser parts of the soul, to allow our older feelings to be recycled and renewed, and to open up to, and give room for, new feelings as they begin to emerge. It is also important to remember to rest, to let emotions just be, without adding complexity to them. Moon conjunct Sun brings insightful, regenerative, and profound images to the dream world.

MOON TO MERCURY ASPECTS

Moon sextile Mercury

Moon sextile Mercury brings the potential for inspiring news and communications. This lunar aspect brings clear and succinct communications which will assist us to keep business running along smoothly. It's a good time to reiterate plans, schedules, and messages and to handle communications very thoroughly. Moon sextile Mercury inspires our moods with informative talk and information but, when Mercury is retrograde, it would be wise to follow up any new information with careful research. This time brings the potential for inspiration through thoughts and ideas, and all this is possible despite the travails of Mercury retrograde periods. Moon sextile Mercury brings the potential for some intelligent brainstorming between people, and this will be a very good time to run your ideas by others. It brings intellectually stimulating dreams and reveals a lot about your thoughts and ideas.

Moon square Mercury

Moon square Mercury often brings a challenging time for communications. This may be a time when it is difficult to reassure others, and moods may be challenged by intellectual debates and discussions. It may be difficult to get the message across in the way it was intended. It may also bring uncommunicative moods, or we may find that it is difficult to describe our moods. This lunar aspect is the least ideal aspect for communications under the influence of Mercury retrograde. Moon square Mercury tends to bring moods or emotional responses which are thwarted by complex communications and difficult subjects, and defensive moods may become argumentative. This is a good time to use caution with our words and to consider the impact that harsh statements may have on others. Moon square Mercury adds mental nervousness to the course of our dreams, and may contribute to nightmarish feelings and thoughts about our dreams.

Moon trine Mercury

Moon trine Mercury brings moods in harmony with communications. This is an excellent time to talk, relay thoughts, and communicate with greater ease. Moon trine Mercury brings the gift of thoughtfulness, making communications very harmonious. This aspect brings pleasantly talkative and mindful moods, leading to discussions that may clarify misinterpreted facts. It will assist us to communicate more clearly during Mercury retrograde periods. Moon trine Mercury brings a superb time for us to communicate amicably and effectively. As a general rule, this is the time to promote positive thoughts. As the day closes, Moon trine Mercury brings a helpful time to rest the mind, but for those who are awake, this may seem like an excellent time to think matters through more easily. Moon trine Mercury brings positive thoughts to our dreams.

Moon opposite Mercury

Moon opposite Mercury brings a deeper sense of awareness – or curiosity – while we are communicating. This lunar aspect inspires a surge of thoughts and discussion, and it may be necessary to comprehend a lot of things at once. This is a time when we tend to be overwhelmed or overloaded by communications or the communication process. Our feelings are more readily challenged by our thoughts. Sometimes this lunar aspect gives us the feeling that there is a great deal more to be communicated. Beware of exhausting arguments. Moon opposite Mercury brings an intense need to communicate, to reiterate on complex messages, and to set the record straight when Mercury retrograde periods have brought havoc to our communications. Moon opposite Mercury brings complex nervous responses and complex thoughts with regard to what we are feeling or sensing.

As for dreams, this aspect brings very nervous or restless kinds of dreams which may seem overwhelming and possibly loaded with too much information.

Moon conjunct Mercury

Moon conjunct Mercury brings mental clarity and acuity, inspiring thoughtful and communicative moods – this is a great time to catch up on journals, research, and correspondence. Moon conjunct Mercury brings a pensive time, and our moods will be as clearly succinct as our thinking. It engages us in mindful and resourceful planning. Moon conjunct Mercury invites us to take some time to explain various matters very carefully, especially when Mercury is retrograde. This aspect reminds us of our need to pay attention to what is being communicated, and to stay on top of communications. It allows us to drop nervous tension in our sleep, and lets those who can't sleep think clearly and relevantly through their mental processes. Moon conjunct Mercury affects our dreams and moods with the desire to connect to brilliance and intelligent ideas.

MOON TO VENUS ASPECTS

Moon sextile Venus

Moon sextile Venus brings moods inspired by beauty and there are opportunities for our moods to tune into the power of love and affection. This aspect brings moods inspired by kind and attractive feminine influences, finding us easily captivated by the law of attraction. Moon sextile Venus brings the potential for very pleasurable, affectionate, and beautiful feelings to occur. It holds the potential to bring moods that will be responsive to love, affection and gentle kindness. It also brings the potential for positive vibes between loved ones, but a definite effort to create those positive vibes will have to be made. Moon sextile Venus brings pleasant dreams touched by infinite beauty.

Moon square Venus

Moon square Venus brings moods challenged by matters of love and attraction. It's also bound to bring some challenging weather between loved ones, and this may be a good time to avoid making idealistic promises that could possibly go unfulfilled. Our moods are likely to be strained by the effort to maintain beauty and comfort. Moon square Venus tests our affections and our ability to feel and express love, and may cause unpleasant moods due to a lack of kindness or love wherever it is needed. This lunar aspect may be a difficult time for us to find the kind of affections we need, but it's best to patiently persevere through love related challenges. Moon square Venus brings dreams that may seem particularly unpleasant, and dreams that may leave us feeling abandoned, torn asunder, or separate from the things to which we are attached.

Moon trine Venus

Moon trine Venus is the most receptive and advantageous time to spread loving energy. This lunar aspect generally brings moods which will be pleasant and easily prone to affection. Moon trine Venus brings gentle, beautiful, and harmonious moods and vibrations. It often blesses our moods with kindness, and increases our fondness and appreciation for beauty. Moon trine Venus brings the strong urge for love, and loving energy won't be too hard to find. This lunar aspect helps to smooth over chaotic energies with loving and kind moods. Moon trine Venus puts us in the mood for love and for all those things that bring us comfort, inspiring especially beautiful, alluring, and relaxing dreams.

Moon opposite Venus

Moon opposite Venus brings moods that will make us acutely aware of our affections – both the giving of, and the desire for, all kinds of affection. This aspect will draw relationships and love related situations into focus, and it may be especially difficult to try to please everyone, especially our loved ones. Moon opposite Venus may bring overwhelming or obsessive desires for beauty and pleasure. This aspect implies that our moods may be dominated by feminine expression or demands. Lady Justice is blind, but that doesn't mean that her logic is not sound. Sometimes, Moon opposite Venus brings obsessive or agitating moods with regard to love. Here, we often find that our affections have been spread too thin. We may feel overwhelmed by compelling attractions. This lunar aspect brings dramatic moods and dreams about our needs for affection and beauty.

Moon conjunct Venus

Moon conjunct Venus brings gentleness, kindness, and love to our moods. It puts us directly in touch with those things we are attracted to. This lunar aspect can bring deeply affectionate and sometimes very intense loving moods. Different levels and expressions of affection occur, depending on the sign in which the Moon and Venus are conjunct. Moon conjunct Venus brings moods that will be instantly drawn to beauty and love wherever it exists. This is a good time to seek pleasure and to appreciate beauty to the fullest. Moon conjunct Venus brings dazzling beauty and pleasure to the scope of our dreams.

MOON TO MARS ASPECTS

Moon sextile Mars

Moon sextile Mars tends to bring energetic moods which are motivated by force and activity, and inspired by high energy levels. Incisive action and the affirmation of will infuse our moods. Moon sextile Mars brings moods that may point to the need to take action, but this inclination is not always acted upon. Generally, Moon sextile Mars brings positive energy, strength and courage to our moods. It brings strong impulses and urges, and our dreams will seem triumphant, although somewhat martial and headstrong in attitude.

Moon square Mars

Moon square Mars suggests our moods will be challenged by invasive forcefulness, our patience levels will be tested, and it may be difficult to get amicably motivated.

This aspect brings offensive and maddening challenges to our moods where abrupt energies and unbalanced temperaments will seem like bullying martial forces. Moon square Mars – this is a recipe for accidents, fights, headaches – and many people will find that they are being especially defensive as well as impatient. This lunar aspect may lead to difficulty or conflict when one is attempting to take initiative to do things, and it often tests our temper, strength, and willpower. Moon square Mars usually brings challenging moods with regard to masculine energies. While we sleep, cruelty or mad aggression may be evident in our dreams.

Moon trine Mars

Moon trine Mars brings moods that will be gifted with lots of vibrant, positive energy and our moods are often in harmony with masculine energies and courageous activities. This aspect invites optimism that inspires action. For some, this aspect brings vibrant emotional and physical energy, positive strength and might. It's an advantageous time to build on our strength, get motivated, and to get things rolling. Moon trine Mars harmoniously energizes our dreams, often making us stronger than we ever imagined.

Moon opposite Mars

Moon opposite Mars brings moods which are opposed to offensive kinds of pressures. Some may find that they are opposed to, or overwhelmed by, masculine force. In general, it brings moods at odds with some disharmonizing force. Forcefulness and brazen activity are highlighted, and Moon opposite Mars brings exceedingly energetic and feisty moods which are sometimes offensive. A surge of emotional heat may lead to anger for some. This lunar aspect is known for its extreme force, and may stimulate alarming kinds of offensive and defensive behavior. Some folks may be overwhelmed or affronted by the activities and actions occurring around them. Without a doubt, Moon opposite Mars motivates us, and brings a sharp awareness of martial forces and masculine energies. Some folks may appear to be obsessed by or preoccupied with aggressive forces. This may also be an accident prone time. Moon opposite Mars may bring pushy, impatient, or overly defensive moods, and it can bring bloody battles to the forefront of our dream world.

Moon conjunct Mars

The sign where the Moon and Mars are conjunct will have a strong bearing on the type of energy conjured by this lunar conjunction. Moon conjunct Mars activates our moods with a feeling of get-up-and-go, stirring our moods with energy and adrenaline that may seem refreshingly positive for some and overly aggressive for others. While Moon conjunct Mars occurs, our moods are active, hot, and eager to take action. Energized moods may lead to incredulous force. Moon conjunct Mars may bring moods activated by complex and reactionary kinds of aggression. Sometimes, this conjunction puts us in touch with our anger issues. Moon conjunct Mars impresses our moods with the need to take action on some level, and to get in touch with our true will. It's bound to stir up raw energy and action in our dreams.

MOON TO JUPITER ASPECTS

Moon sextile Jupiter

Moon sextile Jupiter brings the potential for our moods to be inspired by a sense of joviality, prosperity, travel, and adventure. It also brings moods inspired by opportunity, generosity, and extravagance. This lunar aspect invites moods which are generally hopeful and optimistic, inspired by promising prospects and propositions. It brings the potential for a warm and generous spirit, and sets the tone of the day with the potential for positive, upbeat feelings, and a sense of wellbeing and prosperity. Moon sextile Jupiter brings adventurous dreams.

Moon square Jupiter

Moon square Jupiter may cause our moods to be less generous than usual. We may find we are less willing to extend ourselves beyond our limits. Moon square Jupiter often brings moods challenged by matters of expenses and wealth. This lunar aspect may bring some apprehension with regard to the need to prosper, and this often leads to prudent or unreceptive moods. Jupiter's influence represents joy, and some folks may be prone to depression as they struggle with their ability to find joy or to express it. Many people may be irritated by rising costs or hidden expenses. We may find difficulty in handling large productions. Sometimes, our moods are challenged by travel related expenses, inconveniences, and delays. Our dreams may appear like a gambler's losing streak. Moon square Jupiter brings moods that are challenged by overextension — or perhaps, overexertion — especially in the dream world. The events in our dreams are often reflected by the fear of loss.

Moon trine Jupiter

Moon trine Jupiter brings moods that will be very generous, joyous, and gregarious, and it tops our experience with optimistic and prosperous moods. This aspect is an excellent time to appreciate good fortune, and to enjoy parties, fund raisers, and social affairs. Good luck, happiness, and positive vibes, often ensure a sense of wellbeing, bringing a healthy desire to prosper. Moon trine Jupiter harmonizes our moods with an outgoing spirit and an enthusiastic sense of adventure. Generally speaking, this aspect brings especially pleasant moods, and our dreams are bound to lead us into a pot of gold.

Moon opposite Jupiter

Moon opposite Jupiter brings moods that may be overwhelmed by abundance and rapid growth. People may be put off by, or suspicious of, extreme generosity. Moon opposite Jupiter brings deeply involved moods, especially with regard to our livelihoods, our fortunes, and our sense of wellbeing. This aspect brings an acute awareness of the need to excel and to prosper, and there may be something very tempting calling out to us at this time. Our moods could seem overwhelmed by overextension, either on a financial or a psychological level. Moon opposite Jupiter brings a bit of a roller coaster ride on the collective wheel of fortune, which in turn brings a lot of excitement with regard to our expenditures and our sense of wellbeing. Beware of a tendency towards compulsive gambling. In some cases, this lunar aspect puts us in touch with the feeling of greed, as Jupiter brings the compulsory need to gain, profit, and get ahead of all the financial commotion. Moon opposite Jupiter brings a tendency to overindulge, and there may be a lot of defensiveness over expenditures. In the dream world, we may get lost, or find that we have gone too far out on a limb, leaving us with the feeling of overextension.

Moon conjunct Jupiter

For those who are willing to tap into it, this lunar aspect impresses our moods with rich and prosperous feelings. Moon conjunct Jupiter brings abundant enthusiasm. Moods are especially extravagant and optimistic, connecting us with a sense of joy, wealth, joviality, prosperity, and wellbeing. This is a good time to count your blessings. Moon conjunct Jupiter puts us in touch with our visions and our hopes. It's a great time to enjoy feasts and epicurean delights. This is also an excellent time to exercise, travel, and to explore new territory. With this lunar conjunction, our dreams are often gratifyingly joyous and prosperous in nature.

MOON TO SATURN ASPECTS

Moon sextile Saturn

Moon sextile Saturn opens up our moods to employment opportunities. This is a great time to instill discipline and a sense of duty, to teach, and to work. Moon sextile Saturn inspires discipline and focus, but this usually only starts to occur when some effort towards work is made. In other words, just do the work, and the inspiration to carry on will follow. Our moods tend to be expressed a little more seriously, or with greater expectation towards seeing results. Here, seeing others apply discipline can often inspire us to do the same, making this a great time to set an example, and to focus on getting things done rather than putting them off. The Moon sets the tone of the mood, the sextile aspect brings raw potential and opportunity, and the influence of Saturn gets things done. Moon sextile Saturn brings serious dreams that inspire a sense of duty and discipline.

Moon square Saturn

Moon square Saturn brings moods which are tested by deadlines, responsibilities, and limitations. It often causes challenges with our ability to concentrate, stay focused and handle pending deadlines. Sometimes, Moon square Saturn infringes on the comfort zones of our moods which may seem overshadowed by a foreboding kind of seriousness. Moon square Saturn brings another dimension to our moods, as many folks will be troubled by the burdensome responsibility of difficult work, adding a feeling of being restricted. Moon square Saturn sometimes brings moods challenged by authority. Sometimes, time is warped, or we may find ourselves wishing that time would go by a little faster. While we sleep, Moon square Saturn slips into the night and into our dreams, bringing moods often irritated by the need for discipline; with any luck, this is a time to rest and not to worry. Moon square Saturn may bring troublesome dreams about our struggles over having control, or not having it. Sleeplessness is usually filled by obsessions over career challenges, troublesome work, or burdensome responsibilities. Hang in there – stay on course with your efforts.

Moon trine Saturn

Moon trine Saturn often inspires an amicable work mood. It is a superb time to practice disciplines and to work on things that require perfect timing, allowing for a greater sense of control, precision, and focus. Moon trine Saturn brings harmonious moods with regard to our approach to discipline, or to work in general, and this usually results in more effective teamwork. It also brings moods that are likely to be in harmony with our responsibilities and, as a result, basic duties and tasks may be carried out much more smoothly than expected. This favorable aspect assures us that time is the healer. Moon trine Saturn brings dreams that allow us to feel in control, and to go beyond our limitations, possibly accomplishing the impossible.

Moon opposite Saturn

Moon opposite Saturn is a very challenging time for our moods to stay the course of our work, and it may seem tedious to fulfill our responsibilities. These are times when we may feel overworked. Moon opposite Saturn brings moods which may appear opposed to — or overwhelmed by — restrictions and limitations. This will be a good time to keep work schedules light and to anticipate serious or reluctant moods with regard to work tasks. This is usually not an easy time to hold people's attention for very long, or to get them to perform tasks beyond their usual pace. Difficult jobs will seem that much harder and may take longer than usual to do. Moon opposite Saturn brings a serious tone to our dreams and we may tend to over-extend ourselves, even in the dream world. In general, this aspect puts us in touch with our limitations and reminds us of the mortal side of ourselves.

Moon conjunct Saturn

Moon conjunct Saturn brings serious moods in general, and there is often a strong sense of determination present. We also tend to be guarded, cautious, and work oriented. This conjunction occurs once a month, and it is therefore a good time to reiterate on personal goals and achievements. Moon conjunct Saturn brings moods that will be inclined towards discipline and responsibility, and will appeal to our protective instincts as well. It brings moods that awaken us to the awareness of our limitations. The act of completion is an important part of the Moon/Saturn conjunction, and this is a good time to recognize what level of completion has been achieved in the various stages of our lives. It's also a good time to count blessings as well as setting goals.

MOON TO NEPTUNE ASPECTS

Moon sextile Neptune

Moon sextile Neptune brings peaceful moods, responsive to spiritual expression. It can bring a calmness that allows us to pace ourselves comfortably, and our moods will be pleasant for the most part. This aspect brings moods inspired by spiritual perspectives. This time holds the potential for us to experience more accepting and flexible kinds of moods. Here, forgiveness is possible. Whenever it's convenient, this is a good lunar aspect to seek the comfort of a sanctuary and to enjoy some tranquility. Moon sextile Neptune brings moods that are influenced strongly by our beliefs. It inclines our moods towards simplicity or the path of least resistance. People tend to respond more intuitively to many situations. Moon sextile Neptune brings spiritual hope and reassuring beliefs. It assists us by bringing peaceful rest and calming dreams.

Moon square Neptune

Moon square Neptune brings struggles with regard to our beliefs and in spiritual matters. Our moods may be challenged by passivity, resignation, or perhaps even laziness, and they are often nebulous or vague. Moon square Neptune brings difficult spiritual forces into the picture, challenged by inactivity and passiveness. Moon square Neptune brings moods which may seem troubled by a lack of spiritual harmony, or possibly by addictions, temptations, and a lack of resistance. This aspect brings less tolerance of the beliefs of others and quite a bit of spiritual doubt. People may be questioning the burdening imposition or inconvenience of some beliefs. This is a time when people may be more susceptible to illusion. In general, Moon square Neptune brings disquieting moods, and many folks may have an insatiable urge to find a peaceful sanctuary away from the complexities of emotional clamor. This lunar aspect brings spiritually disturbing moods and dreams, and it may haunt our dreams with deceptive misconceptions.

Moon trine Neptune

Moon trine Neptune blesses our moods with spiritually uplifting vibrations. It settles our moods with a calm, cool acceptance of the way things are and brings the blessing of peacefulness. Moon trine Neptune brings our moods into perfect harmony with the spiritual energies around us, bringing tranquil and passive energy that is positive in nature. People will be inclined to kick back, relax and to accept their beliefs as they stand. This aspect adds calmness to the astrological atmosphere, and helps to smooth over the sting of any conflicting aspects that are simultaneously occurring. It also brings positive inspiration to our moods and is a superb time to apply, or enjoy, artistic expression. This is a great lunar aspect to share in spiritual ceremonies and customs with others. Moon trine Neptune brings relaxing and enchanting dreams filled with blessed tranquility and divine pleasures.

Moon opposite Neptune

Moon opposite Neptune brings moods that will be strongly stimulated by spiritual encounters and experiences, often challenging, and overwhelmed by doubt. This lunar aspect invites weakness with regard to our addictive tendencies. Moon opposite Neptune brings an especially strong awareness of our spiritual needs, but our feelings tend to be at odds with our beliefs. This lunar aspect brings moods that may be opposed to, or overwhelmed by, spiritualism. Moon opposite Neptune brings a strong and compelling awareness of the art, poetry, music, and spiritual beliefs that shape and form who and what we are in spirit and at heart. This lunar aspect awakens our spiritual nature and impresses upon us the need to apply our faith. It could be challenging for some folks to feel comfortable or spiritually in tune with others. Moon opposite Neptune may bring escapist tendencies and the potential for overindulgent moods, and we may be more easily susceptible to life's little deceptions. This aspect brings remarkable and impressionable subliminal images to our dreams.

Moon conjunct Neptune

Moon conjunct Neptune connects our moods with our beliefs and our spirituality. It brings a stronger spiritual awareness of life and there is the general feeling of connectedness among people. Moon conjunct Neptune brings moods that will be responsive to the need for tranquility and peacefulness, and our moods are able to merge easily with spiritual awareness. It brings us closer to a sense of spiritual oneness with the universe, and the common bonds that connect us are felt beyond the physical realms. This lunar conjunction brings peaceful and comforting dreams.

MOON TO URANUS ASPECTS

Moon sextile Uranus

Moon sextile Uranus brings lively and outgoing expressions of mood as well as the potential for wild and disorderly moods. As a general rule, it inspires us to let loose and feel free. When Moon sextile Uranus rolls around, our moods are more prone towards, or sympathetic to, reckless activity or behavior. It helps us to embrace the unusual and to find freedom from the mundane. Moon sextile Uranus brings freedom-loving rebelliousness and our dreams are likely to be explosive and colorful, reflecting a feeling of liberation.

Moon square Uranus

Moon square Uranus is often very challenging, as unexpected outbursts and radical surprises create chaotic moods complicated by explosive conflict. This aspect often brings disruptive disorder; moods may be intensified by undisciplined forces and by radical attitudes. During this time, many people tend to be less forgiving, particularly around unusual behavior and unconventional tones of expression. Moon square Uranus brings chaos – the kind of chaos which requires extra clean up work. It also brings confused and difficult dreams. To some folks, these dreams may seem more like explosive nightmares.

Moon trine Uranus

Moon trine Uranus brings crazy, fun-loving, and unusual kinds of moods and focuses. There's a feeling of wild and reckless abandon, and all is in harmony with the forces of chaos. Moon trine Uranus brings a sense of freedom and our moods will be carefree, or blithely reckless, but not with malicious intent. This lunar aspect can also inspire brilliance and spontaneous inventiveness. Moon trine Uranus brings very exciting and liberating dreams often in harmony with chaos and disorder.

Moon opposite Uranus

Moon opposite Uranus brings discordant sounds, disruptive energies, and explosive distractions. This lunar aspect ignites a strong urge for freedom from oppression, and makes us acutely aware of – and sensitive to – disruption of any kind. Our moods are agitated with an overwhelming feeling of chaos and disorder. Explosively contradictory moods shaken up by extreme or disruptive actions and expressions of thought are common. Moon opposite Uranus brings alarming dreams and unsettled feelings.

Moon conjunct Uranus

Moon conjunct Uranus brings moods that may seem out of the ordinary. It aligns us with the need for freedom, and we may find ourselves being somewhat counterproductive.   Beware of the tendency towards irrational or unusual behavior; rules may be broken. Moon conjunct Uranus may bring a feeling of acceptance for disorder, or it may inspire us to tackle disorder with unabashed determination. Either way, chaotic fortitude will be the energy of our mood. This lunar aspect animates our moods and our dreams with turbulent emotions.

MOON TO PLUTO ASPECTS

Moon sextile Pluto

Moon sextile Pluto brings moods inspired by vigilant efforts in the face of intensity and strife often affected by life's unchangeable circumstances. Our moods may be preoccupied with the need for trouble-shooting and problem solving. Moon sextile Pluto brings moods inspired by the opportunities that are shaped by fate and intensified by powerful and variable situations. This aspect allows us to be receptive to the inevitable factors of life, and many folks will feel as though they can tolerate just about anything. Moon sextile Pluto brings moods that are influenced by the deeds of superpowers, and gives us the incentive to look for solutions to the troubles they generate. It also brings positive moods geared towards the necessity to find ways to change our apparent destiny. Moon sextile Pluto brings dreams that are open to helping us work out our individual struggles.

Moon square Pluto

Moon square Pluto brings moods challenged by the unforeseeable factors of life, by matters of fate and by perplexing transformations. This may be a difficult time to collaborate with people of another generation or those of a different cultural background. Our moods may be challenged by our hidden fears, particularly with regard to those irreversible processes of life. We may find that our moods are oppressed by dramatic losses, hopelessness, and troublesome realities. Moon square Pluto brings dramatic complexity to our moods, which very often ends up affecting everyone. It can bring troublesome and sometimes fearful moods and dreams.

Moon trine Pluto

Moon trine Pluto brings moods that will be inspired by transformation and permanent change. It gives us the strong incentive to tackle problems and find solutions and brings harmonious and therapeutic strength to our moods, especially with regard to matters of fate and the unchangeable factors of life. It also brings moods that will be attuned to the influences of superpowers. This lunar aspect promotes accordance among generations, and those with difficult realities will feel more in tune with the sympathies of others. Moon trine Pluto brings moods enriched with the acceptance of hardships and allows us to confront hardship with a lot less difficulty. This lunar aspect helps the process of healing wounds, and it brings moods that will lean amicably towards therapeutic methods of easing pain. Moon trine Pluto inspires a profound sense of renewed hope and brings a cathartic, as well as therapeutic, breakthrough in our dreams.

Moon opposite Pluto

Moon opposite Pluto makes us conscious of the troubles and the transformations occurring in our lives, especially those likely to be opposed by the influences of superpowers. This aspect causes moods which will be strongly affected by the generation gaps or the cultural gaps that exist between different folks. It also may be the cause of relentless kinds of obsessions, bringing moods that will inspire awareness of life's more intense qualities and hardships. There's a potential for dramatic, rocky moods. Moon opposite Pluto may be the cause of some sleepless energy for various folks, and there may be some overwhelming intensity to the scope of our dreams.

Moon conjunct Pluto

Moon conjunct Pluto brings intensity and extraordinary perspectives to our moods. It leads to an awareness of the influence of superpowers and how these forces affect everyone. Moon conjunct Pluto also brings moods which will be at one with a sense of acceptance of those things which we cannot change. It puts us in touch with world events, and our moods may be surprised by the peculiar ways in which destiny evolves. Moon conjunct Pluto puts our moods and dreams in tune with the relevance and importance of world events, which are busily shaping our individual lives and our lifestyles forever.

Table of Planetary Dignities

Planet	Sign of Rulership	Sign of Detriment	Sign of Exaltation	Sign of Fall
Sun	Leo	Aquarius	Aries	Libra
Moon	Cancer	Capricorn	Taurus	Scorpio
Mercury	Gemini, Virgo	Sagittarius, Pisces	Aquarius, Virgo	Leo, Pisces
Venus	Taurus, Libra	Scorpio, Aries	Pisces	Virgo
Mars	Aries	Taurus, Libra	Capricorn	Cancer
Jupiter	Sagittarius	Gemini	Cancer	Capricorn
Saturn	Capricorn	Cancer	Libra	Aries
Uranus	Aquarius	Leo	Scorpio, Aquarius	Taurus, Leo
Neptune	Pisces	Virgo	Cancer	Capricorn
Pluto	Scorpio	Taurus	Pisces	Virgo
Moon's North Node			Gemini	Sagittarius
Moon's South Node			Sagittarius	Gemini

Table of Planetary Associations

Planet	Day	Incense	Metal	Body Part
Sun	Sunday	Frankincense	Gold	Heart
Moon	Monday	Jasmine	Silver	Eyes
Mercury	Wednesday	Storax	Mercury	Nerves
Venus	Friday	Rose, Benzoin	Copper	Skin
Mars	Tuesday	Tobacco	Iron	Muscles
Jupiter	Thursday	Cedar	Tin	Diaphram
Saturn	Saturday	Myrrh	Lead	Bones
Uranus				
Neptune				
Pluto				

CAPRICORN

Key Phrase: "I USE"

Cardinal Earth Sign

Symbol: The Goat

Ruling Planet: Saturn

December 21st, 2009

through January 19th, 2010

Aspects and events currently in effect:

Saturn square Pluto (Sept. 14, 2009 – March 9, 2010)
– see January 31
Jupiter conjunct Neptune (Oct. 30, 2009 – Jan. 7, 2010)
– see January 7
Sun conjunct Venus (Dec. 17, 2009 – Jan. 24, 2010)
– see January 11
Mercury retrograde in Capricorn (Dec. 26, '09 – Jan. 15, '10)
– see intro on Mercury retrograde periods

January 1st Friday

New Year's Day

Moon in Cancer / Leo

	PST	EST
Moon opposite Mercury	12:33 AM	3:33 AM
Moon trine Uranus goes v/c	7:42 AM	10:42 AM
Moon enters Leo	6:42 PM	9:42 PM

Sun conjunct Mercury begins (see January 4)

Birthday: Vern "Mini-Me" Troyer 1969

Mood Watch: The New Year is initiated with the Moon in the sign it rules, Cancer, where our dreams are stirred by the necessity for a stable home, a peaceful retreat, and the assurances of love. In the morning, the Moon goes void-of-course, creating mildly chaotic moodiness and spacey tendencies. Themes of maternity, motherly love, and nurturing energies carry into the day. Yesterday's Full Cancer Moon was December's Blue Moon – a Partial Lunar Eclipse. As the Full Moon wanes, emotions may be murky, evasive, preoccupied, or confused at times. There is certainly an emotional hangover affect that comes with this combination of circumstances. With Mercury currently retrograde in Capricorn, this is a difficult time to communicate, especially about emotions. Comforting and familiar remedies may ease the blues. By evening, the Moon enters Leo, and our moods will pick up with a focus on personal needs and resolutions, family activities, and entertainment.

January 2nd Saturday

Moon in Leo	PST	EST
Moon sextile Saturn	1:54 AM	4:54 AM
Mercury conjunct Venus begins (see January 5)		

Birthday: Isaac Asimov 1920

Mood Watch: The first weekend of the year is kicked off by the vibrant energy of the waning Leo Moon, currently waning out of last Thursday morning's peak fullness. Leo Moon energies place an emphasis on strength of will, a sense of purpose, and personal needs. Moods may appear egocentric, feisty, self-involved, or preoccupied. Waning Leo Moon is a good time to break the mold of beastly old habits and support positive behaviors for the body, mind, and spirit. Things that enhance one's appearance and attitude will be the attraction of the day. The things we identify with the most have a way of complimenting our moods, bringing out that magnetic attraction mechanism within each one of us. Leo Moon is an excellent time to engage in activities with friends and family, especially while building on themes of personal improvement, excellence, and satisfaction.

January 3rd Sunday

Moon in Leo / Virgo	PST	EST
Moon conjunct Mars	12:08 AM	3:08 AM
Moon opposite Neptune	10:13 AM	1:13 PM
Moon opposite Jupiter goes v/c	1:55 PM	4:55 PM
Moon enters Virgo	6:53 PM	9:53 PM

Birthday: J.R.R. Tolkien 1892

Mood Watch: Seize the day – the earliest part of it will be the best! The waning Leo Moon continues to bring us magnetic energy and willpower. Use the morning energy wisely; as the Moon opposes Jupiter this afternoon/early evening, it also goes void-of-course. There is an acute awareness of expenditures, as folks may appear to be less generous or adventurous. Our moods tend to be self-oriented, attention demanding, proud, and playful. For a number of hours it may be difficult to find some good service. With this void-of-course Moon, people tend to be preoccupied to the point of utter distraction. When the waning Moon enters Virgo tonight, our moods shift into a much more analytical process. A great deal of reflection takes place as our moods focus on cleanliness, organization, and, purification. Virgo Moon is a good time to conserve energies.

January 4th Monday

Moon in Virgo	PST	EST
Moon trine Pluto	12:29 AM	3:29 AM
Sun conjunct Mercury	11:05 AM	2:05 PM
Moon trine Venus	4:05 PM	7:05 PM
Moon trine Mercury	5:49 PM	8:49 PM
Moon trine Sun	7:01 PM	10:01 PM

Birthday: Dyan Cannon 1931

Mood Watch: Sun in Capricorn and Moon in Virgo emphasize the need for practicality. Our moods may appear conservative or withdrawn. However, this couldn't be a better time to get organized and to take to physical tasks with ease. All of today's lunar aspects are trines. This implies easiness of attitudes and interactions with others, despite the fact that the waning Virgo Moon has a reserved and analytical nature. Virgo is ruled by Mercury and since Mercury is currently retrograde until January 15, the communication process is challenging at best. Nonetheless, today's multiple trine aspects of the Moon bring positive moods!

Sun conjunct Mercury (occurring Jan. 1 – 5) This conjunction will occur half a dozen times this year – it is a common occurrence due to the closeness of Mercury to the Sun. It will create a much more thoughtful, communicative, and expressive year ahead for Capricorn people celebrating birthdays from January 1 – 5. This is your time (birthday folks) to record ideas, relay important messages, and pay close attention to your imaginative thoughts as they are touched by Mercury, creating the urge to speak and be heard. Birthday Capricorns, your thoughts will reveal a great deal about who you are, now and in the year to come.

January 5th Tuesday

Moon in Virgo / Libra

	PST	EST
Mercury conjunct Venus	2:39 AM	5:39 AM
Moon opposite Uranus goes v/c	9:25 AM	12:25 PM
Moon enters Libra	8:59 PM	11:59 PM

Birthday: Robert Duvall 1931

Mood Watch: The morning starts out promising; however, as the waning Virgo Moon goes void-of-course, chaos ensues and our moods may appear overshadowed by doubt and skepticism. This tends to slow down progress. People may seem inattentive, or worse yet, argumentative. Our moods may be distracted by the disagreeable way we find ourselves interacting. This long void-of-course Virgo Moon phase is accentuated by communication mix-ups that are precipitated by Mercury's current retrograde process (Dec. 26, 2009 – Jan. 15, 2010). Don't become ensnared by mindless insults or mental complexities. Tonight's Libra Moon brings the balance of peace.

Mercury conjunct Venus (occurring Jan. 2 – 6) Today's conjunction of Mercury and Venus takes place in the serious and methodical sign, Capricorn, bringing a very convincing – or perhaps even manipulative – quality to our communications. These two planets conjunct in Capricorn bring a strong, sometimes challenging tone to the communication of love, particularly for those Capricorn folks celebrating a birthday during the time of this conjunction. Any words of love or adoration uttered now will come across with serious intent – and with clear reception – particularly if this expression of love is very sincere and genuine. Mercury conjunct Venus in Capricorn brings a demanding tone to discussions among loved ones, and it may create an urgent quality in negotiations over such prized items as art and valuables. Communications are received best when they are delivered with considerable care. Be sure to let those whom you love know it; sometimes it's what isn't said that disquiets the heart. Hold no expectations in the expression of love, and take no offense if your attempts to express love are poorly interpreted. Know that there is a need to communicate love occurring now, and that the most simple and direct way to express love might be best. This conjunction will come close to reoccurring March 26 – April 11, coming within a couple of degrees to an exact conjunction in the sign of Taurus on April 6. It will reoccur for a final time this year on October 25.

January 6th Wednesday

Moon in Libra	PST	EST
Moon square Pluto	3:00 AM	6:00 AM
Moon conjunct Saturn	4:54 AM	7:54 AM
Moon square Mercury	4:40 PM	7:40 PM

Birthday: Rowan Atkinson 1955

Mood Watch: Overnight, the square of the Moon to Pluto may bring themes of power struggles – or nightmares – to our dreams. The waning Libra Moon emphasizes the need for harmony, peace, and justice among friends and loved ones. This morning, Moon conjunct Saturn demands a serious tone in our moods and some concentrative effort may be necessary to get things rolling. Libra Moon always emphasizes the need for balance. It's usually not difficult to see the imbalances in our lives – the real trick is to address those imbalances somehow. Libra Moon is here to remind us to make an effort towards achieving harmony. Be careful not to misinterpret others while the Moon is square to Mercury, especially while Mercury is still retrograde (until Jan. 15). Early evening will be a particularly important time to avoid misinterpretation by communicating carefully.

January 7th Thursday
LAST QUARTER MOON in LIBRA

Moon in Libra	PST	EST	
Moon square Venus	12:36 AM	3:36 AM	
Moon square Sun	2:40 AM	5:40 AM	
Moon sextile Mars	3:35 AM	6:35 AM	
Moon trine Neptune	4:34 PM	7:34 PM	
Moon trine Jupiter goes v/c	10:08 PM	1:08 AM	(January 8)
Jupiter conjunct Neptune ends (see below)			
Mercury-square-Saturn-non-exact begins (see January 15)			

Birthday: Nicolas Cage 1964

Mood Watch: The **Last Quarter Moon in Libra** (Moon square Sun) reminds us of the need to continue working on the imbalances in our relationships, much of which is probably caused by Mercury retrograde (Dec. 26, 2009 – Jan. 15, 2010). Libra's adage is simple: "I balance." This is the time to let the emotional pressure be released, and to handle matters with friends and loved ones carefully and congenially. The Last Quarter Moon aspect confirms the need to make amends with others and unite peacefully. If some aspect of your connection to a friend or loved one disrupts your sense of peace, reach within for the answers. A balanced response will soon follow, but don't expect instant answers. However, we can expect a somewhat kicked back and pleasantly tranquil time later today while the Moon is trine to Neptune.

Jupiter conjunct Neptune ENDS today (peak occurrence dates: May 27, 2009, July 10, 2009, and December 21, 2009). Jupiter conjunct Neptune in Aquarius has brought limitless possibilities for spiritual advancement in humankind. Due to the retrograde patterns of Jupiter and Neptune last year, this rare-occasion aspect reached its peak three times during its occurrence period which ends today. This has been a time of extraordinary expansion with inventions and technology (Jupiter in Aquarius), and it's been a time when we've taken on a more expansive viewpoint of life's mysteries, the arts, and our belief in humanity and the role of science (Neptune in Aquarius). This conjunction has brought major changes with regard to commerce and our world economy; all of this is a reflection of the integration of our beliefs. This is the month just one year ago when Barack Obama took office as President of the United States of America and, interestingly enough, this new President has the gift of Jupiter in Aquarius in his own birth chart. He took office the same month Jupiter entered Aquarius, January 2009. The application of knowledge (Aquarius) is a fine attribute for addressing the need for economic growth and recovery (Jupiter).

January 8ᵗʰ Friday

Moon in Libra / Scorpio	PST	EST
Moon enters Scorpio	2:01 AM	5:01 AM
Moon sextile Pluto	8:33 AM	11:33 AM
Moon sextile Mercury	6:26 PM	9:26 PM
Mercury-conjunct-Pluto-non-exact begins (see January 15)		

" The truth, of course, is that there is no journey. We are arriving and departing all at the same time. " - David Bowie (born January 8, 1947)

Birthday: Elvis Presley 1935

Mood Watch: The Libra Moon phase is now passing and it represents a time of adjustment. Out of that adjustment, the swift entry of the waning Scorpio Moon brings sensational color to our moods. As a general rule, we can count on Scorpio Moon to give us the impetus to face the nitty-gritty elements of life. Here the theme of birth, death, and regenerative force keeps us busy. The intensity of this time requires due diligence. Scorpio Moon brings out our perceptive abilities, and this is often a time when people are sensitive to various emotional factors that are surfacing. This is a great time to focus on the healing and regenerative qualities of life.

January 9ᵗʰ Saturday

Moon in Scorpio	PST	EST	
Moon square Mars	9:24 AM	12:24 PM	
Moon sextile Venus	1:18 PM	4:18 PM	
Moon sextile Sun	2:17 PM	5:17 PM	
Moon trine Uranus	9:29 PM	12:29 AM	(January 10)
Sun sextile Uranus begins (see January 13)			
Venus sextile Uranus begins (see January 13)			

Birthday: Jimmy Page 1944

Mood Watch: The start of the day brings a touch of anxiety – or anguish – with

Moon square Mars. However, positive forces are at work with the rest of today's lunar aspects, and there's no reason to hide under the covers. The waning Scorpio Moon is an excellent time to release emotional build ups. Exhilarating activities bring intense vibrancy to our experience, and there's nothing wrong with taking the time to rest between the exertions. It's the season to stay on top of large events such as winter storms, but it's also an important time to rest and relax whenever possible. Scorpio Moon invites intensity, and this is always good as long as we apply it in tolerable increments. Keep bundled up in cold weather and maintain a smooth pace.

January 10th Sunday

Moon in Scorpio / Sagittarius	PST	EST
Moon square Neptune	12:22 AM	3:22 AM
Moon square Jupiter goes v/c	7:02 AM	10:02 AM
Moon enters Sagittarius	10:11 AM	1:11 PM
Moon sextile Saturn	7:07 PM	10:07 PM

Birthday: Rod Stewart 1945

Mood Watch: This morning may be a difficult time to get in touch with a sense of advancement or prosperity, particularly since the Moon goes void-of-course when it squares Jupiter. Be especially careful to watch for thieves. Take extra measures to protect valuables. Also, take note that there may be an absence of generous feelings in the air. After a few hours of small but melodramatic mood adjustments, the Moon enters Sagittarius. Moods will be a great deal more adventurous and optimistic. While the Sagittarius Moon wanes, this is a good time to internalize visions and to apply positive thinking. This evening's Moon sextile Saturn is an opportunistic time to set goals as well as establishing time frames for achieving goals.

January 11th Monday

Moon in Sagittarius	PST	EST
Sun conjunct Venus	1:05 PM	4:05 PM
Moon trine Mars	5:48 PM	8:48 PM

Birthday: Samuel Liddell MacGregor Mathers 1854

Mood Watch: The waning Sagittarius Moon with the Sun in Capricorn inspires optimistic moods in the working environment. This Moon brings positive energy, agility, and resilience. Here we rebound from the stressful areas of life where we've had to be patient, persistent, and diligent. The general optimism of this Moon is highlighted by this evening's action packed Moon trine Mars aspect. Positive vibes bring strong urges to take action. Positive energy is a terrible thing to waste. Get the week started wisely; use positive vibrations to set the right tone.

Sun conjunct Venus (occurring Dec. 17, 2009 – Jan. 24) The Sun and Venus are conjunct in Capricorn. This conjunction particularly affects the love lives of those Capricorn people celebrating birthdays from December 17, 2009 – January 24, 2010. These birthday folks are being filled with the need to have or to express love as best as they can, and this is the year for them to address the love matters in their lives. There is an attraction which draws us to beauty, romance, and love when Venus connects with the natal solar degrees. The issue of love is unavoidable, and these birthday folks' love needs become evident whether they wish to acknowledge them or not. It is through the attraction magnet of Venus that the personality (Sun sign) is assured of that with which they choose to identify, be affected by, and attracted to. Sometimes sheer magnetism is unavoidable and an event or relationship cannot be chosen – it just happens. This can encompass not only love matters, but also other areas such as the arts, aesthetics or appreciation of beauty. This will be a year of love, birthday Capricorns. This conjunction will occur again October 25 – 30, affecting the birthday Scorpio people of that time, and it will reach its exact peak on October 28.

January 12th Tuesday

Moon in Sagittarius / Capricorn	PST	EST
Moon square Uranus	7:52 AM	10:52 AM
Moon sextile Neptune	10:52 AM	1:52 PM
Moon sextile Jupiter goes v/c	6:43 PM	9:43 PM
Moon enters Capricorn	8:54 PM	11:54 PM

Birthday: The Amazing Kreskin 1935

Mood Watch: The morning begins with fiery, masculine fervor. As the Moon travels in the realm of the mutable fire sign, Sagittarius, it also squares to Uranus. Morning struggles with chaos imply that there is a creative process going on in the volatile depths of our fiery moods. Within a couple of hours, Moon sextile Neptune brings the opportunity to smooth over the heightened energy with a bit more gentleness and tranquility. Much of the day will continue at an acceptable pace as our moods explore insightful ideas with hopefulness. When the Moon goes void-of-course this evening, inspired but tired minds will appear spacey. Moon in Capricorn grounds our feelings, and even subdues them to the point where feelings are no longer an issue.

January 13th Wednesday

Moon in Capricorn	PST	EST
Venus sextile Uranus	1:47 AM	4:47 AM
Moon conjunct Pluto	4:23 AM	7:23 AM
Moon square Saturn	6:10 AM	9:10 AM
Saturn goes retrograde	7:57 AM	10:57 AM
Moon conjunct Mercury	8:35 AM	11:35 AM
Sun sextile Uranus	10:41 AM	1:41 PM

Birthday: Patrick Dempsey 1966

Mood Watch: We may as well face it – today is a day of toil. Lunar aspects demand our full attention and extra effort, particularly while Mercury is preparing to go direct (see tomorrow), and there is a tendency for disruptive misunderstandings and communication mix ups. Time may seem to stand still, or fly away all too quickly, while there are goals and deadlines tugging at our conscience. The waning Capricorn Moon undergoes its darkest stage before tomorrow's solar ecliptic New Moon, and the moods in the air are anticipatory and persevering. Don't be fooled by dark energy; Capricorn Moon gives us what it takes to persist.

Venus sextile Uranus (occurring Jan. 9 – 14) Venus in Capricorn is sextile to Uranus in Pisces. Radically serious kinds of love and aesthetics can be very uplifting at this time, particularly while extreme types of tests are occurring and being stretched beyond the limits in love related matters. Eccentric love may erupt with this aspect. This is the time to work on pent up frustrations with loved ones and to reconcile differences by loving and accepting variation, giving freedom and slack to our loved ones. This aspect will reoccur on April 23.

Saturn goes retrograde (Saturn retrograde: Jan. 13 – May 30) Saturn represents discipline, responsibility, and the tenacity required to get the job done. Sacrifices may be necessary in order to complete important projects, and discipline and perseverance are essential. While Saturn, currently in Libra, is retrograde, it will return to Virgo April 7 – July 21. Saturn retrograde in Libra (Jan. 13 – April 7) requires extra work to maintain the due process of the justice system, as well as the maintenance of relationships and friendships. While Saturn is retrograde in Virgo (April 7 – May 30), staying on top of health matters, as well as managing accounting and bookkeeping, will be big priorities. For some folks, this will be a time of completion, of ending the treadmill of old cycles, and of learning to let others take responsibility for themselves. During Saturn retrograde, there will be a lot of work to do, retracing steps in the areas of life that need restructuring. It may be difficult, although not impossible, to begin new endeavors that require structure and the investment of time or commitment. We may be haunted by incomplete projects, and unsolved problems of the past could dominate the stage. Being careful of what we commit to at this time may prevent the need to drop other unfulfilled commitments midstream. If we haven't already dropped a few unnecessary responsibilities, we may have to do so soon. Learn how to delegate your tasks fairly to those who can handle them. Keep a steady check on quality control while Saturn is retrograde today through May 30.

Sun sextile Uranus (occurring Jan. 9 – 15) This occurrence of Sun sextile Uranus particularly affects those Capricorn folks celebrating birthdays January 9 – 15. These birthday people are being given an opportunity to blow off some chaotic steam, and to reach for qualities of freedom that may have been absent in their recent past. This will be your time to make radical breakthroughs, birthday Capricorn; your natal Sun is currently sextile Uranus for a good reason – to find a liberating balance in the midst of the chaos, and to use the chaos in your life to your advantage. Once you've done this, you'll be ready to take the next step. Right now, there is no holding back, so go for it; discover your freedom. The victory of creative change will bring a more optimistic outlook on life. This aspect will repeat on May 20, affecting the lives of Taurus/Gemini people whose birthdays fall between May 16 – 22.

January 14th Thursday
NEW MOON in CAPRICORN – Solar Eclipse

Moon in Capricorn	PST	EST	
Moon sextile Uranus	8:09 PM	11:09 PM	
Moon conjunct Sun	11:11 PM	2:11 AM	(January 15)

Birthday: LL Cool J 1968

46

Mood Watch: The **New Moon in Capricorn** (Moon conjunct Sun) brings down-to-earth determination to our moods. New beginnings occur on the physical plane with the Moon and the Sun in Capricorn. New Moon in Capricorn urges us to create fresh goals and to set new heights for ourselves. Today's New Moon also brings a solar eclipse, and for some there may be a tendency to feel melancholy or lonely, which makes this an opportune day to cheer people up with an open and positive attitude. Be sure to dream big when it comes to setting goals and finding ways to break the patterns of negative feelings. The Capricorn Moon brings a powerful defiance in the face of adversity, and we must not let dark feelings affect our sense of pragmatism and dignity. Go easy on people and use your protective emotional shields to combat the harsh attitudes of others. Expect services to run slowly at times, and take note that co-workers may appear lazy. Beware of the tendency for employers and leaders to expect too much, or to be disappointed in the way business goes today. No matter what – be positive!

An **Annular Solar Eclipse in Aquarius** brings an emphasis on the needs of humanity and the systems by which they operate. This may be a time of technological glitches or accidental breakthroughs. There may also be some form of inspiration or liberating change as a result of longer and harder looks at the way systems operate. For some, the act of thinking comprehensively may be overshadowed by the solar eclipse energy, particularly now that Mercury is currently pulling out of a retrograde cycle (see tomorrow – Mercury direct). This is a good time to pace ourselves through the motions of this shadowy time.

January 15th Friday

Moon in Capricorn / Aquarius

	PST	EST
Moon conjunct Venus goes v/c	1:02 AM	4:02 PM
Mercury goes direct	8:52 AM	11:52 AM
Moon enters Aquarius	9:17 AM	12:17 PM
Moon trine Saturn	6:43 PM	9:43 PM
Mercury-conjunct-Pluto-non-exact (see below)		
Mercury-square-Saturn-non-exact (see below)		

Birthday: Don Van Vliet (Captain Beefheart) 1941

Mood Watch: This morning the shadowy aftermath of yesterday's New Moon / Solar Eclipse in Capricorn is still penetrating our moods; nevertheless, the dark Moon now waxes. Although we may have a more positive outlook on the day, it may be difficult to get motivated this morning with the void-of-course Capricorn Moon. Mercury is stationary and it begins now to go direct (see below), and this adds a stagnant quality to our ability to reciprocate clearly. However, innovative thinking begins to improve the mood as the Moon enters Aquarius. Throughout the day, the Aquarius Moon inspires us to work creatively on our troubles. It gives us a better outlook on humanity. This evening's Moon trine Saturn is a beneficial time to reestablish our disciplines, goals, and limitations.

Mercury goes direct (Mercury direct: January 15 – April 17) Since December 26, 2009, Mercury has been retrograde in the sign of Capricorn, commonly causing communication mix-ups. The retrograde Mercury in Capricorn has been causing communication mix-ups that revolve around issues of control, stability, and inaccurate timing. Now we can breathe a greatly needed sigh of relief as Mercury, the planet governing the realms of communication, becomes stationary and will soon begin to move forward in the late degrees of Capricorn. Take note that our faculties and manner of communicating will definitely improve within the next few days. Although perhaps not today – when the stationary Mercury often freezes communication efforts – but very soon our communications will run more smoothly; this will be a good time to begin clearing up various misunderstandings that have occurred over the past few weeks. For more on Mercury retrograde patterns throughout this year, see the introduction on *Mercury retrograde periods*.

Mercury-conjunct-Pluto-non-exact (occurring Jan. 8 – 20) Since the retrograde Mercury will go direct today, this is as close as we'll come to an exact conjunction of Mercury and Pluto in Capricorn. Mercury conjunct Pluto raises issues of power. The areas of our lives that have required challenge, struggle, sacrifice and transformation now bring us to a place where we can talk about them. With Mercury and Pluto in Capricorn, a very strong sense of duty is instilled in the delivery of messages. This is a time when people instinctively know their own fate. Mercury conjunct Pluto in Capricorn allows us to voice our hardships, and to contemplate and deliberate over the powerful occurrences that challenge and change our lives. While Mercury conjuncts with Pluto and is also square to Saturn (see below, Mercury-square-Saturn-non-exact), many may be faced with the troubles of job loss or career related struggles. There will be a great deal of intensity in our conversations at this time, especially with regard to the fate of the world and our ongoing efforts to end hardship and suffering. Mercury and Pluto in Capricorn will reach a peak conjunction later this year on December 5, and again while Mercury is retrograde, on December 13.

Mercury-square Saturn-non-exact (occurring Jan. 7 – 21) The retrograde Mercury is going direct today, and even though this aspect does not reach an exact peak, like the conjunction of Mercury and Pluto (*see above*), it is still occurring nonetheless. Mercury in Capricorn square Saturn in Libra may be a difficult time to ask for favors, or to make requests of others in a way that they don't feel as if they're being used or taken advantage of. It may be a challenging time to communicate instructions or to inform someone of the end of something. It may also be challenging to sell someone on a product, or to successfully request a raise or promotion. Whatever the desired effect may be, it is wise to use caution when attempting communications during Mercury square Saturn. The retrograde Saturn is in Libra, creating limitations and structural changes in matters of law, justice, marriage, and relationships. This aspect makes it difficult to put a message out there and be taken seriously, or sometimes, we are taken *too* seriously. Some people may become very tongue-tied and feel quite off track. Mercury square Saturn will reoccur on June 24, with Mercury in Gemini and Saturn in Virgo.

January 16th Saturday

Moon in Aquarius	PST	EST
Moon opposite Mars	3:12 PM	6:12 PM

Birthday: Kate Moss 1974

48

Mood Watch: Moon in Aquarius emphasizes the need to apply knowledge in order to take shortcuts through the congested systems of humanity. The newly waxing Moon in Aquarius focuses our moods on idealistic, inventive and humanitarian expression. Aquarius brings out the need to face ourselves and learn about who we are. Later today Moon opposite Mars brings offensive and defensive moods, and people may have a tendency to overreact to things. Restlessness has set into our moods. Early evening may be a good time to work out and get some exercise. Be particularly careful around traffic, as people's driving habits may seem offensive, aggressive, or thoughtless.

January 17th Sunday

Moon in Aquarius / Pisces	PST	EST	
Moon conjunct Neptune goes v/c	12:22 PM	3:22 PM	
JUPITER ENTERS PISCES	6:10 PM	9:10 PM	
Moon enters Pisces	10:18 PM	1:18 AM	(January 18)
Moon conjunct Jupiter	10:21 PM	1:21 AM	(January 18)
Jupiter sextile Pluto begins (see February 6)			
Venus trine Saturn begins (see January 21)			

" An investment in knowledge pays the best interest."
– Benjamin Franklin (born January 17, 1706)

Birthday: Michelle Obama 1964

Mood Watch: The newly waxing Aquarius Moon inspires the unexpected. Unusual moods bring creative thinking. As the Moon conjuncts with Neptune, it also goes void-of-course. Today's moods may seem somewhat nebulous or complex, particularly while technological glitches distract us and throw us off track at times. A hunger for true knowledge necessitates some extra research. As the Moon enters Pisces, passive moods bring a calming affect. Waxing Pisces Moon is a good time to enjoy the arts. A quiet sanctuary may also appeal.

Jupiter enters Pisces (Jupiter in Pisces: Jan. 17 – June 5) An imaginative – but also nebulous and uncertain – era of economic advancement begins today with the planet of luck and fortune, Jupiter, newly entering the constellation Pisces. Jupiter in Pisces brings mysterious, open-minded, and faith driven solutions to economic problems. Building up prosperity and wealth just ain't what it used to be, and it's here that folks will aspire to find genuine joy in the *illusion* of wealth. This does not mean that we should squander a new chance to build our prosperity by abusing a fresh line of credit; that's largely what got many folks into trouble in the first place. This is the time to persevere through financial shifts with a bubbling wealth of joy and appreciation for what we do have here in North America, which is still one of the richest regions of opportunity and growth on the planet. Jupiter in Pisces is the place where fortune is found in artistic talent and wise counsel.

Those who recognize the spiritual nature of wealth know that our ongoing economic shifts and volatile changes do not have to rob us of our understanding of what truly makes us prosperous. Jupiter in Pisces often brings jubilation to the arts. From these challenging economic times come exceptional and unique music, art, dance, creative writing, and poetry. It is no surprise that the beer and wine

49

industry will do well during this time. Jupiter in Pisces expands our focuses in the areas of escapism, drug use, and metaphysical outlets to overcome depression.

There will also be a lot of attention paid to our institutions of faith, our cultural and moral beliefs, and our need to maintain charitable contributions which ignite a sense of hope and boost the morale of the many less fortunate folks around us. The imbalances and atrocities that have befallen our economic food-chain have been largely the result of greed and poor lifestyle choices. Jupiter in Pisces brings joy and expansion through our abstract attempts to feel out, or intuit, the course of our true needs in the economy of the future. It is in this time of Jupiter in Pisces that we will empower our vision to bring a better economy through our ability to let go of the things we've lost and to embrace, or re-invent, an entirely new economic focus. Pisces is the last sign of the zodiac and it comes full circle in the realm of experience. At the end of any cycle there is usually a lot of unfinished business, but in order to make a smooth transition, we must learn to see the silver-lining of our sacrifices. Now is as good a time as any to continue to make informed decisions, but with Jupiter in Pisces, we will also have to use our intuition. Out of the old treadmill of our addictive indulgences, the mutable water sign of Pisces brings a resilient and adaptive character to our spirits, while Jupiter spreads joviality, inspiration, and a willingness to enjoy life despite economic hardship!

JUPITER IN AQUARIUS (Jan. 5, 2009 – Jan. 17, 2010)

A review of the past: Since January 5, 2009, Jupiter has been traveling through Aquarius, focusing the magic of great wealth and expense on such Aquarius-like things as education, vocational training, science, and technology.

Jupiter in Aquarius generated a variety of business endeavors associated with politics. Last year's January 20th presidential inauguration took place in the same month that Jupiter entered Aquarius, and it is interesting to note that Barack Obama, an August 4th born Leo, has Jupiter in Aquarius in his birth chart, at the zero degree point of entry. As Mr. Obama took his new office as president, he was also experiencing a "Jupiter return" and, as sure as Aquarius provides an unusual and eccentric outlook on human problem solving, the new president's take on fixing the crumbling economy required bold and extraordinary action. Aquarius looks at the whole picture and often sees outside the parameters of a problem, which is why Jupiter in Aquarius has its advantages – Jupiter, too, deals with rapid expansion and growth.

Before the Aquarian approach to gaining economic recovery and growth, many people's misfortune or mismanagement of financial affairs has been to the prosperous advantage of wealthy business tycoons and other shifty manipulators of the economic slump which began in 2007, and openly reared its ugly head in early 2008. Jupiter was in Capricorn (Dec. 18, 2007 – Jan. 5, 2009), and it was during that time that corporate industries began to plummet. It was also evident that big economic change was headed our way when, on December 11, 2007, Jupiter reached an exact conjunction with the power-monger, Pluto – on the Sagittarius/Capricorn cusp – bringing some seriously disruptive shifts to our economic powers and our overall perception of what it means to maintain and develop wealth.

The past year of Jupiter in Aquarius has been a time of innovative thinking and assessment. We must remember that Jupiter's domain focuses on gain, and those areas of life where fortunes continue to rise, not fall. Just as it is in any era of marked recession, where many have fallen, some do excel at unprecedented rates. As a general rule, Jupiter's influence brings enthusiasm, stimulates economy and focuses on prosperity. Even in difficult economic times, Jupiter puts us in touch with the necessity to find, to develop, or to create new skills and new means to generate prosperity. Jupiter is often the catalyst in raising the overall morale. Out of the drive to create competent caregivers and practical management strategies, comes the hope of maintaining and rebuilding a stable economic future. While Jupiter was in Aquarius, the key to successful gains came with the unusual and unconventional means of generating goods and services.

JUPITER IN PISCES

Jupiter now travels through the mutable domain of Pisces, bringing a sensitive and perceptive outlook to our economic systems. Jupiter gloats over wealth, skill, and abundance; the Neptune-ruled Pisces pierces through the illusion of wealth and creates a sound acceptance of what it will take to make us happy and content. Jupiter's social appeal represents prosperous growth, valuable talents, fascination, joy, joviality, and the spreading of happiness. When Jupiter traverses through Pisces, prosperity occurs with a consciousness raising purpose, with humility and faith, and with an enthusiastic effort to keep our dreams alive. Pisces puts us in touch with our dreams and Jupiter brings dreams of prosperity into fruition. Without our dreams, turning fantasy into reality is next to impossible.

Pisces people will be able to enjoy some abundant opportunities and joyous personal experiences while Jupiter crosses over their natal Sun. They will also have a strong influence on the wave of the economic future, undoubtedly through the arts. The other water signs of the zodiac, Cancer and Scorpio, will enjoy the fruits of Jupiter being trine to their natal Sun signs. This will bring the potential for travel or financial boons of some kind for Cancer and Scorpio people. Virgo folks would be wise to use their sensibilities and take precautions with their expenditures while Jupiter opposes their natal Sun. They may also find that the effort to handle massive volumes of business, or a large inheritance, may be overwhelming at times, especially for accountants. Gemini and Sagittarius people may discover that it will be especially difficult to keep up with expenses and opportunities in their lives while Jupiter squares to their natal Sun signs. They would be wise to proceed cautiously in business. Capricorn and Taurus people's natal Sun signs will be in the sextile position to Jupiter, and this will bring the potential for business or career opportunities in those areas of life where these people have already been working hard, or where they have made some genuine effort to succeed over time.

Jupiter will move swiftly through Pisces until June 5 when it enters Aries. Jupiter will go retrograde on July 23 (until Nov. 18) and will shift back into the tail end of Pisces on September 8/9, where it will remain in Pisces until January 22, 2011.

January 18th Monday

Dr. Martin Luther King Junior Day *(born January 15, 1929)*

Moon in Pisces	PST	EST
Moon sextile Pluto	6:15 AM	9:15 AM
Venus enters Aquarius	6:17 AM	9:19 AM
Moon sextile Mercury	10:48 AM	1:48 PM
Sun trine Saturn begins (see January 24)		

" An individual has not started living until he can rise above the narrow confines of individualistic concerns to the broader concerns of humanity.
" – Martin Luther King, Jr. (1929 – 1968)

Birthday: Robert Anton Wilson 1932

Mood Watch: The Pisces Moon brings a colorful and serene quality to our moods, and this adds a richly intuitive spirit to the atmosphere. Adaptable moods bring comfort where it is needed. Pisces Moon places an emphasis on our need for spiritual fortification. Many will seek to find some form of validation for their beliefs or their sense of intuition. Waxing Moon in Pisces is a great time to influence our moods with musical and artistic expressions.

Venus enters Aquarius (Venus in Aquarius: Jan. 18 – Feb. 11) Venus in Aquarius creates a fondness for invention, eccentric pleasures, and social life. It puts the focus of attraction and adoration on illuminating types of knowledge and on brilliant humanitarian causes and exploits. There is an especially strong attraction to invention – all types of invention – and to new technologies. It is likely to be a beneficial time for the love life of Aquarius people, whose affections and aesthetic pleasures can be enhanced now. By contrast, Scorpio and Taurus people may notice that love related focuses are causing tension in their personal lives – too many complex issues. Leo people, as a general rule, can never get enough love and affection, and they may be particularly aware of their own personal needs for love and beauty while Venus is opposing their natal Sun. Venus in Aquarius is a prime time to perfect and enhance our love of humanity, and to break down the barriers of useless and destructive prejudice and stereotyping.

January 19th Tuesday

Moon in Pisces	PST	EST	
Sun enters Aquarius	8:27 PM	11:27 PM	
Moon conjunct Uranus goes v/c	10:05 PM	1:05 AM	(January 20)

Birthday: Alexander Woollcott 1887

Mood Watch: Let the intuitive and creative process begin! Let the spirit of renewed faith cleanse our beliefs. This is the time to allow for new inspiration to come through in such Piscean kinds of things as art, music, poetic thought and prose, as well as spiritual reverie and meditation.

Sun enters Aquarius (Sun in Aquarius Jan. 19 – Feb. 18) Aquarius is ruled by the enigmatic planetary force of Uranus, the often strange villain who forges new clarity and hope through the storms of chaos and disruption. Freedom fighters will remind us always that we must find a solution to every great atrocity that dampens the human spirit. We must take measures to prevent tomorrow's health crisis and

AQUARIUS

♒

Key Phrase: "I KNOW"

Fixed Air Sign

Ruling Planet: Uranus

Symbol : The Water Bearer

January 19th through February 18th

to ensure the perpetuity of our species. Aquarius is the "fixed air" sign which represents the sum of human knowledge. It is an old world oppression that we must address in this Aquarian time – through knowledge we will succeed. This is a time for opening up new ideas and possibilities. Aquarians are usually very clever people who love a good challenge.

January 20th Wednesday

Moon in Pisces / Aries	PST	EST
Moon enters Aries	10:37 AM	1:37 PM
Moon sextile Sun	11:53 AM	2:53 PM
Moon sextile Venus	4:36 PM	7:36 PM
Moon square Pluto	6:31 PM	9:31 PM
Moon opposite Saturn	7:41 PM	10:41 PM

Birthday: George Burns 1896

Mood Watch: The early morning Moon is void-of-course in Pisces. Morning moods will be spacey and prone to fantasy and escapism. As the Moon enters Aries, our moods shift over to a more outgoing and competitive quality of expression. This afternoon will be the best time to get things done. Waxing Aries Moon is a great time to start new projects, particularly new routines that fall under the category of New Year's resolutions. That's right – New Year's resolutions! Remember those? This is just about the time when many folks begin to slip away from their individual pledges from the first of the month, and an advantageous time to take to the art of motivation. Waxing Moon in Aries invites us to initiate projects, to motivate ourselves and others, and to tackle dormant energies with an inspired new outlook.

January 21st Thursday

Moon in Aries	PST	EST	
Moon square Mercury	1:25 AM	4:25 AM	
Moon trine Mars	12:00 PM	3:00PM	
Venus trine Saturn	10:06 PM	1:06 AM	(January 22)

Birthday: Benny Hill 1924

Mood Watch: The Aries Moon has us on a roll now. The necessity to keep motivated is still in the air. This afternoon's Moon trine Mars aspect inspires us to take action in positive ways. Waxing Moon represents a time of increasing the awareness of our feelings. Winter restlessness stirs our hearts. The desire to start up new projects is also a symptom of the youthfully waxing Aries Moon. Overall, we can expect to get a lot of things accomplished on this Aries Moon Thursday. Aries Moon generates energy and gives many of us the impetus to tend to personal needs and projects requiring attention.

Venus trine Saturn (occurring Jan. 17 – 24) Venus in Aquarius trine Saturn in Libra brings very attractive humanitarian efforts to stabilize our relationships through balanced and responsible action. Here is where we easily devote ourselves to the thing(s) that attract us most, but with Venus in Aquarius, devotion alone is not enough – intelligence is required. While Saturn is in Libra, a commitment to trustworthiness, compromise, and teamwork becomes equally important. Where love and attraction have withstood the test of time, this aspect is bound to remind us of who, and what, matters most. Venus trine Saturn often brings the gift of responsive and enduring love. This aspect may assist in bringing some peace to the structure or the closure of a love relationship. It is also a good time to initiate or enhance a love vow or oath, and to apply the values of devotion and responsive caring intelligently. Love is a gift and a responsibility. Use this time affectionately and wisely; it often makes an impression. This aspect will occur again on April 24 with Venus in Taurus and Saturn in Virgo.

January 22nd Friday
Moon in Aries / Taurus

	PST	EST	
Moon sextile Neptune goes v/c	11:44 AM	2:44 PM	
Moon enters Taurus	8:40 PM	11:40 PM	
Moon sextile Jupiter	10:49 PM	1:49 AM	(January 23)

Birthday: Sir Francis Bacon 1561

Mood Watch: Energetic moods kick off the day right with the waxing Moon in Aries. However, as the Moon goes void-of-course our moods may seem reckless, distracted, or hasty. The void-of-course Aries Moon puts some people in pushy or aggressive moods. The day may bring a series of false starts. Naïve tendencies lead to head butting and impatience. The potential for angry, confused, or frustrated moods is strong. This may be the time to temper impatience – or high expectations – with guarded tolerance. Later tonight, as the Moon enters Taurus, our moods will become more grounded and practical.

January 23rd Saturday
FIRST QUARTER MOON in TAURUS
Moon in Taurus

	PST	EST
Moon square Sun	2:52 AM	5:52 AM
Moon trine Pluto	4:18 AM	7:18 AM
Moon square Venus	8:34 AM	11:34 AM
Moon trine Mercury	2:06 PM	5:06 PM
Moon square Mars	7:02 PM	10:02 PM

54

Venus opposite Mars begins (see January 26)

Birthday: Django Reinhardt 1910

Mood Watch: The **First Quarter Moon in Taurus** (Moon square Sun) brings the pressure to take care of essential needs. Taurus is the *fixed earth* sign, and the nature of Taurus Moon leads many folks to watch their pocketbook, and make sure they're getting the most value possible out of all expenditures. There is also a need to let the beauty of our surroundings be accented and appreciated. Somewhere in between the processes of earning and reaping rewards, a happy medium is struck. The Moon is *exalted* in Taurus, and positive harmony brings satisfaction.

January 24ᵗʰ Sunday

Moon in Taurus	PST	EST
Sun trine Saturn	7:37 AM	10:37 AM
Moon sextile Uranus	4:24 PM	7:24 PM
Moon square Neptune goes v/c	7:02 PM	10:02 PM

Birthday: John Belushi 1949

Mood Watch: The waxing Taurus Moon brings a positive time to get things done. Taurus Moon inspires the need for a comforting and pleasing atmosphere. The momentum of our efforts begins to pick up today as we work our way through physical tasks, and beautify and warm up our surroundings with a renewed outlook. Tonight, lazy and lackadaisical moods are expected, particularly as the Taurus Moon goes void-of-course.

Sun trine Saturn (occurring Jan. 18 – 27) This aspect particularly affects Capricorn and Aquarius people celebrating birthdays January 18 – 27. This is a positive time for these folks to get a handle on their lives, and it may be easier for them to take on their responsibilities with fewer complications and less difficulty in the year to come. These birthday people may notice more acceptable forms of control, responsibility and work occurring in their lives. Now is your time (birthday people) to successfully work on putting some structure into your life; the kind of structure you've needed and wanted awaits you in the coming year. It is possible that time (Saturn) is on your side to make that move you've wanted to make. This aspect will reoccur May 12 – 21, reaching its peak on May 18, affecting the birthday Taurus and Gemini people of that time.

January 25ᵗʰ Monday

Moon in Taurus / Gemini	PST	EST	
Moon enters Gemini	3:12 AM	6:12 AM	
Moon square Jupiter	6:09 AM	9:09 AM	
Moon trine Saturn	11:02 AM	2:02 PM	
Moon trine Sun	1:15 PM	4:15 PM	
Moon trine Venus	7:36 PM	10:36 PM	
Moon sextile Mars	10:34 PM	1:34 AM	(January 26)
Sun opposite Mars begins (see January 29)			

Birthday: Virginia Woolf 1882

Mood Watch: Gemini Moon playfully waxes and loves to play tricks on the mind. Don't overdo the caffeine and take it easy on the nervous system. When in doubt, apply humor. Jovial and positive lunar aspects bring optimistic moods, with the exception of Moon square Jupiter, which is likely to bring stagnant – or less than ambitious – energies first thing this morning. Most of the day will be positive in spirit. At last, we can begin to straighten out the facts as the Moon in the Mercury-ruled sign, Gemini, brings communicative moods that will assist us to find supportive and encouraging words. This is a good time to address some of the communication mistakes which may have cropped up during the last Mercury retrograde cycle (Dec. 26, 2009 – Jan. 15, 2010).

January 26th Tuesday

Moon in Gemini	PST	EST	
Moon square Uranus	8:05 PM	11:05 PM	
Venus opposite Mars	9:29 PM	12:29 AM	(January 27)
Moon trine Neptune goes v/c	10:30 PM	1:30 AM	(January 27)

Birthday: Stephane Grappelli 1908

Mood Watch: Talkative moods bring bustling chatter. The more our thoughts stir the pot of the general mood, the thicker this gumbo stew of busy thoughts becomes. The mutable air sign of Gemini engages us in the urge to communicate. There is a strong need to satiate our curiosities, and to indulge in our need to bounce our ideas off someone else. That's what the twin does, isn't it? One twin complements the other. Later tonight, the Gemini Moon goes void-of-course; this is a most important time to rest the mind, and to silence those restless thoughts.

Venus opposite Mars (occurring Jan. 23 – 28) Venus in Aquarius is opposing the retrograde Mars in Leo. The opposition of these planets can attract and repel at the same time, and there is a constant need to give and take with the act of compromise. If you are among those somehow caught up in this battle of the sexes, it is important to realize that losses can occur around attempts at moderation just as easily as with extremes. Venus in Aquarius creates an intelligent, open-minded, and eccentric expression of love and attraction. Mars in Leo brings out a self-motivated, proud, and sometimes territorial form of martial (or masculine) energy. This may bring a particularly challenging time for loved ones to agree with each other. It is wisest to observe and learn as much as possible. This is also a good time to take precaution with our beloved valuables as they may become more easily damaged or destroyed if they're not properly protected. By all means, go easy on your loved ones during this period of Venus opposite Mars. This is the only time this year that Venus will oppose Mars.

January 27th Wednesday

Moon in Gemini / Cancer	PST	EST
Moon enters Cancer	6:02 AM	9:02 AM
Moon trine Jupiter	9:35 AM	12:35 PM
Moon opposite Pluto	12:55 PM	3:55 PM
Moon square Saturn	1:18 PM	4:18 PM

Birthday: Wolfgang Amadeus Mozart 1756

56

Mood Watch: As the early morning void-of-course Gemini Moon enters Cancer, mixed moods turn to definitive emotional responses. The waxing Cancer Moon inspires hope, particularly as the Moon trine Jupiter aspect encourages us to explore and seek fortune. Some folks may be thrown off by the energy of Moon opposite Pluto, an aspect that makes us acutely aware of the differences in our cultures and the various generations of thought. This afternoon's Moon square Saturn aspect makes it difficult for some folks to concentrate on their work. As a general rule, Cancer Moon keeps us preoccupied by our feelings.

January 28th Thursday

Full Moon Eve

Moon in Cancer	PST	EST
Moon opposite Mercury	4:21 AM	7:21 AM
Moon trine Uranus goes v/c	8:48 PM	11:48 PM

Birthday: Jackson Pollock 1912

Mood Watch: Today our moods will be highlighted with emotional concerns, which are often worked out at home or in domestic settings where the nurturing spirit of Mother Moon brings responsive and sympathetic conscientiousness. Our instincts are strong on this heavily waxing Cancer Moon day. Deep feelings of compassion, desire, or perhaps loneliness may lead some people to seek some motherly advice. Later tonight, chaotic feelings are bound to set in as the Cancer Moon goes void-of-course while it trines Uranus. This would be a good time to try to get some rest, but don't be surprised if tyrannical feelings keep some folks awake on this void-of-course Full Moon Eve.

January 29th Friday

FULL MOON in LEO

Moon in Cancer / Leo	PST	EST	
Moon enters Leo	6:11 AM	9:11 AM	
Sun opposite Mars	11:43 AM	2:43 PM	
Moon sextile Saturn	1:07 PM	4:07 PM	
Moon conjunct Mars	9:20 PM	12:20 AM	(January 30)
Moon opposite Sun	10:17 PM	1:17 AM	(January 30)

Birthday: Oprah Winfrey 1954

Mood Watch: The **Full Moon in Leo** (Moon opposite Sun) captivates our moods with a wild and instinctual push. The Full Moon in Leo reaches its peak later tonight, leading to playful, imaginative, and creative expressions of mood. Most of us are easily drawn towards the need to find warmth and affection, or just plain attention. There may be an opportunity here to enhance and harmonize friendships and family situations in a fulfilling and enriching manner. Moon in Leo puts us in touch with those places, people, and things to which we feel loyal. Many folks may find themselves feeling somewhat courageous and confident about the new month ahead of us, especially since the Leo Moon puts us in touch with the Sun. Leo is ruled by the Sun and the pending holiday of Candlemas (Feb. 2) marks the mid-point of winter. This brings the welcoming warmth of the much more noticeable lengthening of days when the solar light uplifts our spirits in preparation for spring.

Sun opposite Mars (occurring Jan. 25 – 31) This aspect creates extra awareness of accidents, attacks, outbursts of energy, and possibly anger issues, especially for Aquarians celebrating birthdays January 25 – 31. Something strong and full of heat opposes these birthday folks in a way that may cause sensitivity and defensiveness towards bold activities. Mars strikes to warn these birthday folks that they must be on guard and act swiftly against life's offensive blows. Being defensive is natural, and actions may require a careful approach or the heat may backfire. Birthday Aquarians, you may be sensitive to the necessity to take action in your life. Use this energy to make positive change occur in your apparently busy and active year ahead. This is the only time the Sun will oppose Mars this year.

January 30ᵗʰ Saturday

Moon in Leo	PST	EST	
Moon opposite Venus	5:49 AM	8:49 AM	
Moon opposite Neptune goes v/c	10:27 PM	1:27 AM	(January 31)

Birthday: Z. Budapest 1940

Mood Watch: Life improves as the post Full Leo Moon emphasizes our need to do good things for ourselves, and to enjoy some good times with our friends and family. Leo Moon is a great time to acquire new clothes, or to do things that will improve our outlook on ourselves. Leo Moon is also a good time to seek entertainment and things that bring us pleasure. The post Full Leo Moon inspires leisurely endeavors, and many folks may feel comfortably lazy today after all the busy hubbub of the Full Moon weekend.

January 31ˢᵗ Sunday

Moon in Leo / Virgo	PST	EST
Moon enters Virgo	5:24 AM	8:24 AM
Moon opposite Jupiter	10:19 AM	1:19 PM
Moon trine Pluto	12:17 PM	3:17 PM
SATURN SQUARE PLUTO	1:25 PM	4:25 PM

Birthday: Minnie Driver 1971

Mood Watch: Practical matters now come to the surface. The waning Virgo Moon keeps us cautious, suspicious, and carefully poised. This is a good time to concentrate on the cleansing process of the soul. Virgo Moon emphasizes the need to focus on such things as spa activities, accounting, dieting, research and analysis. Sun in Aquarius and Moon in Virgo bring out the need to get the technical world of communications in order. It's also a time for rest and relaxation, as much as it can be expected with the harsh arrival of Saturn square Pluto (see below).

Saturn square Pluto (occurring Sept. 14, 2009 – March 9, 2010) This is a large and long winded aspect that challenges and awakens us to address big transformations. The last time Saturn square Pluto reached an exact peak was on November 15, 2009. Saturn and Pluto are both in cardinal signs (Libra and Capricorn) bringing lawfully sanctioned and physically enduring types of permanent change.

When Saturn was in the challenging *opposite* aspect to Pluto back in August/September 2001, we all felt the brunt of some serious trials through the events of 9/11 and all that followed. It was not until April 26, 2003 that the Saturn opposite Pluto aspect came to an end of its cycle. In August 2007 and April 2008, the favorable *trine* aspect of Saturn and Pluto occurred, bringing us a temporary reprieve of more easily handling the trials of permanent change, as well as some long awaited rewards of our hard work and persistence during the difficult trials and transformations that the Saturn opposite Pluto tests demanded back in 2001. Through the events of Saturn opposite Pluto, the security guidelines we've created for ourselves, and to which we've adhered as a result of those events, have created a new foundation to sustain us.

However, now the *square* aspect of Saturn and Pluto creates grave new difficulties that will force us to reconcile some age-old problems between the generations and cultures of the world. For the next nine months to come, and for some time in the aftermath of this event, the tests of hardship are challenging us to face some serious rounds of devastating change; these are permanent, unrelenting, and difficult types of change that will definitively mark this period as a new century turning point.

Now that Saturn and Pluto are spending this time in the unfavorable square position to one another, it is up to us to determine how we will survive and grow stronger through this current transformation process. This is a time for us to apply a careful approach to lawmaking, and for us to be cautious with our sense of control, particularly with regard to the current channels of power occurring in the world at large. It is through the square aspect that we will take great pains in our efforts to redefine our responsibilities and to shift our goals and priorities to suit the rapidly changing ways of the 21st century. The trials that we will encounter will dramatically shape our ideas of how power operates, and we will eventually acquire the knowledge and the survival tools to see us through this difficult time. Restrictive laws and corruption in corporate circles point to a struggle that is being played out on the world stage through this aspect. Saturn in Libra intensifies judicial affairs while Pluto in Capricorn transforms the ways in which we go about the attainment of power. Limitations are likely to be imposed on a variety of relationships while Saturn is in the square position to the harsh and unrelenting forces of Pluto. This aspect is likely to bring great change in our attitudes, especially with regard to how we adapt to the structure of our rapidly changing environment within the confines of its stringent laws.

Saturn, which is currently retrograde (see Jan. 13), will re-enter the tail end of Virgo on April 7. Saturn will go direct on May 30 as it completes its cycle in Virgo from April 7 to July 21. Then, Saturn won't return to Virgo until October, 2036. Saturn in Virgo has signaled a time which brought volatile changes in the American market. Its unstable economy began with faulty home mortgages in early 2008, and later brought a plummeting market in all forms of industry by late 2008. This set off a myriad of financial market milestones in various countries around the globe. Jupiter, the surveyor and proprietor of wealth and prosperity, was in Capricorn in 2008, shaking up numerous corporate standards and focusing our livelihoods on the necessity for practicality, determination, and brazen survival techniques. Saturn, the stabilizer of all things, emphasizes frugality while traversing in Virgo, and this has brought the epitome of prudent action which is taken out of sheer necessity, bringing with it the need for survival, clarity, stabilization, and in many cases, really good accountants! Saturn represents our perimeters of realism and it also represents our accountability, or responsibility, to the physical world.

Pluto represents long-term, historically binding transformation, plain and simple. Pluto entered Capricorn in 2008, and since it takes the longest period of time to go through one single zodiac sign, its new station in Capricorn will have strong, long-lasting results while it traverses through Capricorn until March 23, 2023. When Saturn tangos with Pluto, our lives undergo change in remarkable and notably demanding ways. As Saturn takes the challenging square position to Pluto, we are bound to steadily undergo riveting transformational change which reflects our sense of stamina as well as our sense of reason, or wisdom. This change occurs across the board in political, ethical, social, religious, theosophical, and moral arenas of thought and human conduct. As Saturn takes its position in Libra, laws and judicial standards will be constituted to reflect these changes in order to meet the long-term conditions that the 21st Century lifestyle will effectively establish.

Saturn square Pluto will continue to occur until March 9, when it breaks the square temporarily. This aspect will begin to occur again on summer solstice day, June 21, reaching the next exact square on August 21, and ending on September 14. Once this time has passed, a process of healing and adjusting can begin. Through the trials we can reclaim our strength and begin to come full circle in our understanding of what this process of Saturn square Pluto has meant.

February 1st Monday

Moon in Virgo	PST	EST
Moon trine Mercury	11:13 AM	2:13 PM
Moon opposite Uranus goes v/c	8:17 PM	11:17 PM

Birthday: Clark Gable 1901

Mood Watch:: A new month is upon us in positive ways. Early in the day, the Virgo Moon trines with Mercury, bringing interactive, upbeat moods. Mercury rules Virgo and this is a splendid time to organize and communicate in an adaptive and efficient manner. There is smooth sailing for those who must move their goods and property. Thrifty buyers are likely to find good deals at this time. We are now on the brink of Candlemas (see tomorrow) and the light of the season will begin to show itself more readily. Light inspires the flow of life as the halfway mark of winter gives many people renewed hope. Uranus is primed this evening to wake up and shake up our moods as it opposes the Moon, which will go void-of-course. Be careful not to get too destructive with the restlessness that abounds.

February 2nd Tuesday

Candlemas / Groundhog Day

Moon in Virgo / Libra	PST	EST
Moon enters Libra	5:42 AM	8:42 AM
Moon conjunct Saturn	12:49 PM	3:49 PM
Moon square Pluto	1:02 PM	4:02 PM
Moon sextile Mars	7:09 PM	10:09 PM
Mercury sextile Uranus begins	(see February 6)	
Venus conjunct Neptune begins	(see February 7)	
Mars sextile Saturn begins	(see February 15)	

Birthday: Stan Getz 1927

Mood Watch: After a brief encounter with morning doubts while the Moon is void-of-course in Virgo, the Moon enters Libra. Our moods enter into the need for balance, and our energies become more focused on creating harmony among friends and partners. Strong powers of concentration and focus are at work while the Moon conjuncts with Saturn. This afternoon's Moon square Pluto aspect brings the potential for conflicts between generations. This is no time to argue with authorities. Tonight's Moon sextile Mars aspect brings positive but restless moods that demand some bold action. Libra Moon is the time to enliven relationships.

Today is Candlemas, a celebration of the return of the light. Out of the darkness and into the light – this represents a time of blossoming knowledge and a time to acknowledge one's own growth. We are now one half of the way through winter season. This holiday is also known as **Imbolc**, the breakthrough of winter's darkness. The days to come bring prismatic sparkling color through crystals suspended from windows. The light awakens and stirs the seeds of hope, and touches us from within. The legendary Irish Saint, Bridget, dons a crown of candles. Light candles and celebrate the return of the light! Today is also Groundhog Day, when the absence or presence of the groundhog's shadow predicts the course of the final half of winter season.

February 3rd Wednesday

Moon in Libra	PST	EST
Moon trine Sun	6:14 AM	9:14 AM
Moon trine Venus	4:30 PM	7:30 PM
Moon square Mercury	6:05 PM	9:05 PM

Birthday: Norman Rockwell 1894

Mood Watch: Throughout today, the waning Libra Moon places an emphasis on the need to encourage partnerships, friendships, and professional groups to work harmoniously together. Moon trine Sun always reminds us of the aspects of the current season that are inspiring and uplifting. Moon trine Venus brings easygoing attitudes inspired by pleasures. Libra is the Venus ruled sign emphasizing harmony. The Libra Moon reminds us that love conquers all. Later today, Moon square Mercury might not be the best time to deal with complex mental processes, or to argue with people. Early in the day will be the best time to successfully apply teamwork and to get people together "on the same page" in a positive way.

February 4th Thursday

Moon in Libra / Scorpio	PST	EST	
Moon trine Neptune goes v/c	1:28 AM	4:28 AM	
Moon enters Scorpio	8:56 AM	11:56 AM	
Moon trine Jupiter	4:15 PM	7:15 PM	
Moon sextile Pluto	4:54 PM	7:54 PM	
Moon square Mars	9:56 PM	12:56 AM	(February 5)

Birthday: Alice Cooper 1948

Mood Watch: Overnight, the Moon goes void-of-course in Libra, and our early morning waking moods may seem somewhat indecisive. After a series of minor adjustments, the Moon enters Scorpio, and our moods will appear to be a great deal more interactive and determined. As the Moon enters Scorpio, we feel the need to face or drop emotional buildups which have accumulated up to this point. Scorpio Moon encourages us to confront important matters with a sense of urgency. Later on, positive and optimistic moods are generated through the Moon trine Jupiter aspect. Generous feelings are followed by opportunities; it's a time to address important matters with Moon sextile Pluto. Later tonight, Moon square Mars denotes emotional combat. There is a tug-of-war going on in some restless hearts. Beware of late evening moods that have the potential to escalate to accident prone or violent outbursts. Waning Scorpio Moon teaches us about the nature of intensity.

February 5th Friday

LAST QUARTER MOON in SCORPIO

Moon in Scorpio	PST	EST
Moon square Sun	3:49 PM	6:49 PM

Birthday: William Burroughs 1914

Mood Watch: The **Last Quarter Moon in Scorpio** (Moon square Sun) occurs later this afternoon, and it focuses our attention on issues of passion and compassion. It is likely the dark secrets of our life will be touched on somehow. This Moon urges us to release stored up tension, and to find release for our emotional baggage without imposing it on others. Physical workouts are excellent for this Moon, provided safety consciousness is maintained. Safety consciousness of any kind is particularly important during Scorpio Moon. Don't forget to keep an eye out for suspicious activity – beware of thieves, smooth talkers, and the potential for aggressive outbreaks. Scorpio Moon brings out the daring side of our moods.

February 6th Saturday

Moon in Scorpio / Sagittarius	PST	EST
Mercury sextile Uranus	12:02 AM	3:02 AM
Moon square Venus	4:13 AM	7:13 AM
Moon trine Uranus	5:36 AM	8:36 AM
Moon sextile Mercury	6:13 AM	9:13 AM
Moon square Neptune goes v/c	8:11 AM	11:11 AM
Jupiter sextile Pluto	9:50 AM	12:50 AM
Moon enters Sagittarius	4:04 PM	7:04 PM

Moon sextile Saturn   11:56 PM   2:56 AM   (February 7)

Birthday: Babe Ruth 1895

Mood Watch: Early morning brings busy and intense lunar aspects as the waning Scorpio Moon influences our moods with powerful demonstrations of showmanship. As the Moon goes void-of-course, it squares Neptune, and our moods are likely to be obscured by emotional and spiritual complexity. The void-of-course Scorpio Moon state of affairs will lead to dissatisfaction, confusion, uncertainty, impatience, distraction, and delays. Beware of the potential for theft. Later today as the Moon enters Sagittarius, our minor but irritating anguish begins to fade. The waning Sagittarius Moon brings inward hope and optimism. Tonight will be an excellent time to look inwardly with a philosophical perspective that sets the right tone for a clear and positive future.

Mercury sextile Uranus (occurring Feb. 2 – 7) Mercury is in Capricorn, placing a determined emphasis on our efforts to communicate. Uranus is in Pisces, stirring up chaos in the arts, religion, and perhaps even in our collective struggle with substance abuses. Mercury sextile Uranus gives us the opportunity to freely speak our minds and to address the turmoil that exists in our lives. This aspect will reoccur on June 10, with Mercury in Gemini and Uranus in Aries.

Jupiter sextile Pluto (occurring Jan. 17 – Feb. 15) Jupiter affects our sense of prosperity, our aspirations and hope, and our expansion into new realms of fulfillment and discovery. Pluto affects world powers and the transformational processes of societies, cultures, and generations. When Jupiter is in the sextile position to Pluto, it powerfully expedites our sense of advancement, giving us the opportunity to expand to great heights and address heavy issues with regard to power. This is a time when power often changes hands through inheritance and through earned achievement, which can only occur with insightful awareness of what is needed next to keep our economy and our livelihoods empowered. This aspect merely brings opportunity which must be acted upon, and one must be careful not to take on more than their life's responsibility and commitment levels can afford. This aspect brings the opportunity for a better understanding of the power shifts in the job markets as well as the direction of the next generation's economy. Jupiter is in Pisces expanding our belief systems and beefing up interests in the realm of the arts, while Pluto in Capricorn brings efforts to control or institutionalize the ever changing powers that are coming into fruition. This aspect last occurred on September 17, 2005 with Jupiter in Libra and Pluto in Sagittarius.

February 7ᵗʰ Sunday

Moon in Sagittarius	**PST**	**EST**	
Moon square Jupiter	1:01 AM	4:01 AM	
Moon trine Mars	4:21 AM	7:21 AM	
Venus conjunct Neptune	9:43 PM	12:43 AM	(February 8)

" This is a world of action, and not for moping and groaning in. "
            – Charles Dickens (1812 – 1870)

Birthday: Charles Dickens 1812

Mood Watch: The waning Sagittarius Moon of winter is the time to prepare for the days ahead, to focus on our visions, to shed old pretenses, and to gather our courage. This is the time to broaden our awareness through exploration, and to do so with enthusiasm and wit. Sagittarius Moon, although waning, is always a good time to encourage optimism. It is also a good time to work on the internal vision of the self. Don't forget the optimism!

Venus conjunct Neptune (occurring Feb. 2 – 10) Venus represents love, magnetism, and attraction, while Neptune (the higher octave of Venus) represents spiritual love and the melding of spiritual energies. Venus is conjunct with Neptune in the sign of Aquarius. Here the cohesive and melding forces of Venus and Neptune manifest with original, idealistic, and inventive expressions. Beauty and art (Venus) are linked with spirituality and belief (Neptune), much of it focused around humanitarian causes and issues (Aquarius). Science and technology are given more acceptable and aesthetic appearances with this aspect. Venus conjunct Neptune can be utilized to reach a higher vibration of feminine, spiritual love. This aspect allows beauty, femininity, and personal attraction to be connected with the higher spiritual vibrations of the universe. This is an ideal time to connect with one's own guardian angel and spirit guide. Venus conjunct Neptune, if utilized, will bring great wisdom. This is the only time this year the Venus and Neptune conjunction will occur, and it last took place on March 6, 2008.

February 8ᵗʰ Monday

Moon in Sagittarius	PST	EST
Moon sextile Sun	6:16 AM	9:16 AM
Moon square Uranus	3:57 PM	6:57 PM
Moon sextile Neptune	6:37 PM	9:37 PM
Moon sextile Venus goes v/c	8:58 PM	11:58 PM
Mercury trine Saturn begins (see February 12)		
Sun conjunct Neptune begins (see February 14)		

Birthday: Eliphas Levi (Alphonse Louis Constant) 1810

Mood Watch: The waning Sagittarius Moon is a time of introspection and it is here that our moods go through a visionary process. Sometimes we intuit our conclusions, but most of the time we draw conclusions by collecting facts. Sagittarius Moon gives us no boundaries to draw our conclusions. Here, intuition and science work together to give us a clear picture. This is a good time to explore new skills and talents.

February 9ᵗʰ Tuesday

Moon in Sagittarius / Capricorn	PST	EST
Moon enters Capricorn	2:44 AM	5:44 AM
Moon square Saturn	10:45 AM	1:45 PM
Moon conjunct Pluto	11:58 AM	2:58 PM
Moon sextile Jupiter	1:18 PM	4:18 PM
Mercury opposite Mars begins (see February 13)		

Birthday: Ziyi Zhang 1979

Mood Watch: Early this morning the Moon enters Capricorn, and our moods awaken to a serious phase of expression throughout the day. Capricorn Moon keeps our moods focused on important matters and the need to accomplish necessary duties and tasks. Early in the day the Moon squares to Saturn, and our ability to concentrate is compromised by complexities or a heavy workload. Despite the extra concentration required, Capricorn Moon moods give us the impetus to get the job done. Moon conjunct Pluto intensifies the mood with the necessity to face powerful issues. This afternoon's Moon sextile Jupiter brings positive opportunities, but in order to benefit we must *act* on those opportunities.

February 10th Wednesday

Moon in Capricorn	PST	EST
No Exact Aspects		
Mercury enters Aquarius	1:05 AM	4:05 AM
Venus conjunct Jupiter begins (see February 16)		

Birthday: Mark Spitz 1950

Mood Watch: There are no notable lunar aspects on this waning Capricorn Moon day. This is a good time to mean what you say and to follow through with flying colors. Avoid making idle promises. Actions speak louder than words; if you want someone to take you seriously, show them you mean business! Meanwhile, don't let anyone waste your time. Capricorn Moon moods require serious attention and keen emotional control.

Mercury enters Aquarius (Mercury in Aquarius: Feb. 10 – March 1) Today, Mercury enters Aquarius, the fixed air sign of the zodiac which represents humanity's knowledge. As the force of communication (Mercury) travels through the constellation of fixed thought and meditation (Aquarius), there are great opportunities for us to share and to empower each other through our knowledge. This is a splendid time to communicate ideas and investigate the latest in technology, science, and the world of invention. Mercury in Aquarius is also a special time to speak out on humanitarian issues and the rights of freedom. Eccentric talk and unusual subjects will fill the airwaves while Mercury is in Aquarius.

February 11th Thursday

Moon in Capricorn / Aquarius	PST	EST	
Venus enters Pisces	4:09 AM	7:09 AM	
Moon sextile Uranus goes v/c	4:38 AM	7:38 AM	
Moon enters Aquarius	3:24 PM	6:24 PM	
Moon conjunct Mercury	8:39 PM	11:39 PM	
Moon trine Saturn	11:18 PM	2:18 AM	(February 12)
Venus sextile Pluto begins (see February 14)			

Birthday: Sheryl Crow 1963

Mood Watch: This morning and afternoon marks a long void-of-course Capricorn Moon period. There may be a decline in productivity and our day may seem dull at first. Despite delays and minor setbacks, the call to duty keeps us steadily moving at a slug's pace. Later, as the Moon enters Aquarius, very deep, thoughtful, and introspective moods will captivate our imaginations. This is a great time for creative thought.

Venus enters Pisces (Venus in Pisces: February 11 – March 7) Venus, the planet of magnetism and love, will be focusing our attention on recreational endeavors. While Venus is in Pisces, music, poetry, the arts, psychic phenomena, and spiritual and religious practices will all be endearing and lively pursuits. As Venus crosses over their natal Sun sign, it will touch the personal realms of our Pisces friends with an awareness of the need for love and beauty in their lives. Venus is the feminine planet of love, and Pisces is an extremely feminine, dreamy, and spiritual placement for the love force of Venus. Matters of the heart will emphasize passivity, tenderness, sensitivity and the need for a gentle approach towards love's expression. The last time Venus entered Pisces was on January 3 and April 11, 2009, and it will return to Pisces again in late March 2011.

February 12th Friday

Moon in Aquarius	PST	EST
Moon opposite Mars	1:00 AM	4:00 AM
Mercury trine Saturn	5:34 PM	8:34 PM

" People are about as happy as they make up their minds to be. "
– Abraham Lincoln (1809 – 1865)

Birthday: Abraham Lincoln 1809

Mood Watch: The darkly waning Moon in Aquarius opens up our moods to a receptive and productive quality of expression. Deep contemplative thoughts require brilliant solutions to brighten the mood. Introspective wisdom comes to those who take the time to think things through. A scientific approach to the world around us reminds us that discoveries are made when we choose to experiment. Today will be a good day for research and experimentation.

Mercury trine Saturn (occurring Feb. 8 – 14) Mercury is in Aquarius where the emphasis of information is placed on science, technology and the need for knowledge and know-how. Saturn is in Libra where new laws are forged and there is a strong emphasis on the need to protect ourselves and our civil rights. Mercury in Aquarius trine Saturn in Libra brings favorable communication which tells us how, and where, to intelligently draw the lines for ourselves. This is a good time to make an impression, to teach, and to communicate to others those important matters that must be clarified. This is a great time to study or practice memorization skills. Timely information and news represents a gift or blessing. This aspect will reoccur on June 8, with Mercury in Gemini.

February 13th Saturday
NEW MOON in AQUARIUS

Moon in Aquarius	PST	EST
Mercury opposite Mars	2:25 AM	5:25 AM
Moon conjunct Sun	6:51 PM	9:51 PM
Moon conjunct Neptune goes v/c	8:32 PM	11:32 PM

Birthday: Peter Gabriel 1950

Mood Watch: The **New Moon in Aquarius** (Moon conjunct Sun) is a good time to begin new social and philanthropic endeavors, and to gain fresh knowledge

66

by learning something new about ourselves or our ever changing world. Moods created by this New Moon may be bold or daring, with a flair for experimenting with life. This is the time to open up to new feelings and a greater comprehension of science and technology of these changing times, adding to our power. However, it may be best to take it easy on the old brain cells after the Moon goes void-of-course this evening, as our moods and attitudes may seem spacey and incomprehensible at times.

Mercury opposite Mars (occurring Feb. 9 – 14) This aspect often causes people to lose their tempers while communicating. This is a time to be especially careful to watch what you say. This requires thinking before acting, for often this aspect brings heated arguments and debates over the actions or outspoken thoughts of others. Mercury opposite Mars makes it difficult for some to justify their actions, or explain why they take a certain stand in life. Communications may be misunderstood if one is too caught up in the action of what is going on. It is best to apply reason and not to take aggressive language personally, particularly if it isn't necessarily pointed at you. In other words, watch out for signs of hypersensitivity and do not fall victim to other people's inability to handle their own anger or aggression. Many may misinterpret communications as being hostile, or perhaps war related news takes an overwhelming tone at this time. Scientific and progressive minded talk (Mercury in Aquarius) about the devastating causes and results of war makes us especially aware of it's affects on families and certain individuals (Mars in Leo). The callous, listless, seemingly unfeeling tone in much of the talk going around makes some folks truly angry. For some, it's good to get their troubles off their minds and out on the table. For others, it's best not to go there. Everyone has their own way. This is the only time Mercury will oppose Mars this year.

February 14th Sunday

Chinese New Year: TIGER (Year 4708) – Metal Tiger
Saint Valentine's Day

Moon in Aquarius / Pisces	PST	EST	
Moon enters Pisces	4:23 AM	7:23 AM	
Moon conjunct Venus	12:53 PM	3:53 PM	
Moon sextile Pluto	1:58 PM	4:58 PM	
Sun conjunct Neptune	3:18 PM	6:18 PM	
Moon conjunct Jupiter	5:31 PM	8:31 PM	
Venus sextile Pluto	11:16 PM	2:16 AM	(February 15)

Birthday: Jack Benny 1903

Mood Watch: Early this morning the newly waxing Aquarius Moon enters Pisces, bringing the need for dreams, fantasies, art, music, poetry, and romanticism. This is an ideal Moon for Valentine's Day activities. The Moon conjunct Venus is the most ideal aspect for the expression of love. For optimal results on your romantic investment, utilize this perfect afternoon aspect with the gift of love – give flowers! Later, Moon sextile Pluto brings the opportunity for a profound transformation of our moods. This evening's Moon conjunct Jupiter is a particularly ideal lunar aspect for giving gifts and spreading generous and adventurous moods. Pisces Moon is a good time to celebrate love and affection. For those who are lacking affections, beware of the tendency to overindulge in strong drink.

Happy Chinese New Year! – Year of the Tiger (occurring: Feb. 14, 2010 *Metal TIGER* – Feb. 2, 2011 – next year's animal will be *Metal RABBIT*). Chinese New Year happens on the New Aquarius Moon in China, which means it usually occurs within a day of the Aquarius New Moon in North America. In the Chinese calendar, we have reached the year 4708, and this time marks the *Year of the Metal Tiger*. Every twelve years, the Year of the Tiger rolls around, and every sixty years, we come to the specific Tiger year known as the Metal Tiger. Metal Tigers of the 20th century were born from February 17, 1950 to February 5, 1951.

As for **Metal Tigers**, they can be quite mercurial. They can laugh and seem quite genuinely happy one moment, and the wrong trigger could easily send them into a tailspin of tantrums or tears the next moment. They can be suspicious and hesitant to trust others. They must be careful not to get burnt out too early in life. It is not healthy for Metal Tigers to hold grudges for too long. It is best if they learn to genuinely forgive and forget.

However, don't be fooled into thinking that the Metal Tiger is weak. In general, Metal people are forceful, strong, and determined. Metal in Chinese astrology represents the autumn and the fruition of the harvest. October 2nd born Libran, Groucho Marx, was a famous Metal Tiger comedian who was wildly unpredictable, both on stage and in his private life. Although he endured a lasting success in life, his low points – such as losing his life savings in the 1929 stock market crash – caused him a lifetime of insomnia. He suffered three failed marriages, and greatly resented his oldest brother, Chico, for squandering money on gambling, and complicating matters regarding the livelihood of the Marx Brothers' career. Overall, however, Groucho loved the chemistry that he, and his infamous brothers possessed and their collective legacy. Groucho was arguably the most successful Marx Brother in the entertainment field, with a career that spanned vaudeville to Broadway, then Hollywood and finally television. There are a rare few in America who have held successes in all four of those venues.

People born under the **Year of the Tiger** are very fiery in character. The personality of the Tiger may be likened to the qualities of the zodiac sign, Leo the Lion. Both of these large wild cats are totems of solar fire – after all, Leo is ruled by the Sun. Tigers must put their heart into what they do. The sun is the heart of the Universe; both the Lion and the Tiger draw their strength from the heart as well as the area of the solar plexus. In character, these archetypes are proud, courageous, active, and self-assured. The Tiger sign also carries many traits similar to the other fire signs of the zodiac, Aries and Sagittarius.

Tiger people are passionate, optimistic, charming, sometimes rebellious, and unpredictable. It is not wise to underestimate a Tiger's reactions to things – even though they can appear cool on the outside, their unpredictability can be startling at times. Tigers may choose to keep their hidden powers well veiled, but if ever tested or questioned, they will not hesitate to show their dynamic strengths. They love challenges and are quite fond of the art of competition.

Tigers are natural born leaders with a deep sense of pride and dignity. They can be very straightforward as well as uninhibited. Tigers enjoy protecting secrets and they often have a hidden agenda. They can also be stubborn and are not likely to give up easily. Tiger people need to learn to control their tempers or they can be easily thrown off by the consequences of overreacting. Tigers don't like to be penned up or stagnant for very long. If unproductive, they can be prone to deep depressions.

All Tigers need to master the art of pacing themselves. They need to rest between their exertions, but by all means they need to exercise and keep fit. Tiger people are generally very socially active. They often fill their homes with exotic treasures, and they take pleasure in originality, mystique, and having a lifestyle and interests that are out of the ordinary. Tigers can be rash or hesitant but if they learn how to relax, they can overcome their contradictory patterns, and they can be very successful as they rise above their nervousness with great pride.

If you know of Tiger people who do not fit these personality descriptions, bear in mind that systems such as Western or Chinese Astrology are multifaceted parts of an intricate and complex human makeup. Sometimes the vast combination of celestial traits in humans can bring surprising results, and sometimes, through sheer persistence of will – as well as environmental and cultural influences – people change completely from their inherent nature into something phenomenally different. This is why it is not wise to blithely accept every probability predicted in this book. You have the power to change what's around you! Meanwhile, don't underestimate the Tiger – what seems like a mild mannered pussy cat can easily spring into being a wild beast!

Famous Tiger People: Groucho Marx (metal 1890), Agatha Christie (metal 1890), Norma Shearer (water 1902), Queen Elizabeth II (fire 1926), Marilyn Monroe (fire 1926), Elizabeth Kübler-Ross (fire 1926), Diana Rigg (earth 1938), Cybill Shepherd (metal 1950), Tom Cruise (water 1962), Demi Moore (water 1962), Rosie O'Donnell (water 1962), Jodie Foster (water 1962), Penelope Cruz (wood 1974), Hilary Swank (wood 1974).

Sun conjunct Neptune (occurring Feb. 8 – 17) This occurrence of Sun conjunct Neptune particularly affects Aquarius people celebrating birthdays February 8 – 17 with intuitive inclinations and spiritual desires. Your visions (Aquarius birthday folks) will inspire great feats, and the higher, more spiritually refined parts of the soul are going to be speaking to you throughout the upcoming year. Listen! This may be a time to let go of personal attachments and outmoded desires that appear to be going nowhere. Your highly complex Aquarian idealism will work up your spiritual beliefs into a kind of peak performance level, even if you don't believe you have such a thing as spiritual beliefs. Birthday Aquarians, you will continue to encounter a kind of spiritual catharsis and, by the time you've come through this, you'll know what that means. This is all magnified by your ruling planet, Uranus, which has been traveling through the Neptune-ruled sign of Pisces since March 2003 and is about to exit Pisces to enter Aries on May 27. Integrate a listening pattern concerning the Great Spirit in your life; focus on the spiritual part of the self (or higher self) that rules over personal destiny and guides the true desires of the soul. Can you handle that, birthday folks?

Venus sextile Pluto (occurring Feb. 11 – 16) Just in time for Valentine's Day! Venus sextile Pluto means business when it comes to making proposals of love. Venus is in Pisces where the law of attraction is irresistible, easy going, and artistically uplifting. Pluto in Capricorn brings dutiful allegiance to matters of fate. Venus sextile Pluto implies that even in the midst of hardship, opportunities are arising with regard to the things we treasure and are attracted to, and also in matters of love and affection (Venus). These opportunities often are born out of fate or destiny (Pluto), or sometimes are a result of an unpredictable factor. For some, this aspect may be teaching them the lessons of acceptance, of learning to let go of attachments, as well as finding liberation through the transformative process of acceptance, particularly in matters of love. This aspect will reoccur on September 12, November 1, and again on December 8, with Venus in Scorpio.

February 15th Monday

Moon in Pisces

	PST	EST
Mars sextile Saturn	7:20 AM	10:20 AM

Birthday: Galileo Galilei 1564

Mood Watch: The newly waxing Pisces Moon awakens our senses to a vague sense of visionary awareness, and it initiates the potential for strong psychic intuition. All the while, a noticeable glimmer of light begins to penetrate our winter slumber; we've made it past Candlemas (Feb. 2) and the light seems much more prevalent. Something special and often incommunicable touches the heart in the newly waxing inspiration of Pisces Moon. This is the time to recognize an inherent gift that exists within, and to visualize the ways in which that gift can manifest.

Mars sextile Saturn (occurring Feb. 2 – March 30) Mars in Leo sextile Saturn in Libra is an active time for establishing personal strengths in the realm of careers, particularly careers that emphasize or influence law and justice. During this aspect, actions create opportunities, provided there is an application of discipline and timing. Those who are affected by this aspect may feel noticed now. Diligently practice your favorite sport, especially those physical activities that demand precision and perfect timing. Movement and the application of energy (Mars), plus responsibility and awareness of limitation (Saturn) allow the timely qualities of completion and new beginnings to occur. This would be the time to end a bad habit or to work to accomplish a goal. Due to the current retrograde motion of Mars and Saturn, during this occurrence period of Mars sextile Saturn, this aspect will reach a second peak on March 22, when Mars will be direct. It will also occur on November 14 with both planets direct.

February 16th Tuesday

Moon in Pisces / Aries	PST	EST	
Moon conjunct Uranus goes v/c	6:32 AM	9:32 AM	
Moon enters Aries	4:31 PM	7:31 PM	
Venus conjunct Jupiter	6:14 PM	9:14 PM	
Moon trine Mars	10:54 PM	1:54 AM	(February 17)
Moon opposite Saturn	11:38 PM	2:38 AM	(February 17)

Birthday: Sonny Bono 1935

Mood Watch: Chaos ensues as the void-of-course Pisces Moon awakens us to spacey moods while the Moon conjuncts with Uranus. Today may seem like more of a dreamy day than a productive one. Later today, as the Moon enters Aries, our moods are a great deal more interactive and straightforward. Aries Moon brings a sense of newness to life.

Venus conjunct Jupiter (occurring Feb. 10 – 19) The influence of beauty, love and attraction (Venus) blends and melds with the powers of production, expansion, and prosperity (Jupiter). In the sign of Pisces, these two planets are stirring up experiences which are very active and aggressive in nature. Pisces is associated with divine love, the arts, metaphysical sciences, entrepreneurship, and counseling. This is a time to enhance love relationships, and realize the precious value of love in its most limitless sense, since the influence of Jupiter reminds us that the resources of love in the universe are inexhaustible, and love's great bounty is designed to be shared. A love for expansion and the growth of skill (or personal economy) comes out with the conjunction of Venus and Jupiter. Love is infectious. These two planets were last conjunct on December 1, 2008 in the sign of Capricorn. This is the only time that Venus and Jupiter will be conjunct this year.

February 17th Wednesday

Moon in Aries	PST	EST
Moon square Pluto	1:59 AM	4:59 AM
Moon sextile Mercury	2:22 PM	5:22 PM

Birthday: Paris Hilton 1981

Mood Watch:: Aries Moon invokes the powers of initiation and newness as an essential part of regenerative force. This is a time to generate and promote inspiration and happiness. Aries is the sign of the warrior. The fight to sustain love on Planet Earth calls for many courageous battles, and now is an excellent time to actively initiate new projects and endeavors that will help to serve one's sense of well being. The Aries Moon of winter sometimes brings a restless spirit, and many folks may find themselves feeling somewhat agitated by the monotonous setbacks of winter. Aries Moon will either test our patience or inspire us to get out and do something productive.

PISCES

Key Phrase: "I Believe"

Mutable Water Sign

Ruling Planet: Neptune

Symbol : The Fishes

February 18th through March 20th PST

February 18th Thursday

Moon in Aries	PST	EST
Sun enters Pisces	10:23 AM	1:23 PM
Moon sextile Neptune goes v/c	7:51 PM	10:51 PM

Birthday: Yoko Ono 1933

Mood Watch: The Aries Moon brings moods that are notably more alert, high spirited, and a great deal more direct. Throughout the day and into the evening, our moods may be measured by the efficiency with which tasks and deeds are carried out, and by how much self-assurance and self-confidence can be felt in the course of our actions. Tonight's void-of-course Moon is the perfect time to settle down and relax.

Sun enters Pisces (Sun in Pisces: Feb. 18 – March 20) Out of Aquarius we take the extraordinary knowledge and experience of humanity, and in Pisces we purify that experience and seek further insight by getting in touch with divinity. Pisces is the last sign of the zodiac, representing the completion of a cycle. This mutable water sign is adaptive, and Pisceans can absorb all kinds of influence. However, if bogged down by oppressive influences, the Piscean becomes burnt out, oversensitive, and depressed; it's important to find ways to vent heavy feelings of oppression. Pisces people are very psychic as a general rule, and they are also quite artistic and imaginative. The Pisces time of year is a good time to get in touch with personal beliefs and divinity.

February 19th Friday

Moon in Aries / Taurus	PST	EST	
Moon enters Taurus	2:56 AM	5:56 AM	
Moon sextile Sun	4:20 AM	7:20 AM	
Moon square Mars	7:54 AM	10:54 AM	
Moon trine Pluto	12:09 PM	3:09 PM	
Moon sextile Jupiter	5:33 PM	8:33 PM	
Moon sextile Venus	11:47 PM	2:47 AM	(February 20)
Sun sextile Pluto begins (see February 23)			

" To know that we know what we know, and to know that we do not know what we do not know, that is true knowledge. "
— Nicolaus Copernicus (born February 19, 1473)

72

Birthday: Smokey Robinson 1940

Mood Watch: As the Moon enters Taurus, our moods answer to the call of practicality, and also to the desire and need for beauty. The Taurus Moon brings amicable, businesslike awareness. As the early days of Pisces unfold in the final throes of winter, the Taurus Moon inspires us to handle physical tasks. This is a good time to focus on making financial breakthroughs and to tackle money management with some clarity and purpose. The Taurus Moon puts us in touch with personal needs and the desire for comfort. This is an excellent time to work on beautifying your surroundings. Taurus Moon puts us in touch with our need for pleasure.

February 20th Saturday
Moon in Taurus

	PST	EST
Moon square Mercury	7:52 AM	10:52 AM
Sun conjunct Jupiter begins (see February 28)		

Birthday: Kurt Cobain 1967

Mood Watch: Taurus Moon keeps us focused on practical needs as well as the desire for luxurious quality. This morning's only aspect, Moon square Mercury, brings communication challenges. The Taurus Moon waxes, and our enthusiastic stubbornness to get the job done, despite faulty morning communications, will make the difference. This is a good time to focus on financial matters and to shop for necessities. The Moon is exalted in Taurus and our moods are often inspired by a sense of achievement or acquisition. The things to which we are attracted during a waxing Taurus Moon are the things that give us the most satisfying pleasure. What are you attracted to today?

February 21st Sunday
FIRST QUARTER MOON in GEMINI
Moon in Taurus / Gemini

	PST	EST
Moon sextile Uranus	2:05 AM	5:05 AM
Moon square Neptune goes v/c	4:14 AM	7:14 AM
Moon enters Gemini	10:48 AM	1:48 PM
Moon sextile Mars	2:33 PM	5:33 PM
Moon square Sun	4:41 PM	7:41 PM
Moon trine Saturn	4:47 PM	7:47 PM

Birthday: Anaïs Nin 1903

Mood Watch: Our early morning moods may be somewhat lazy with the Moon void-of-course in Taurus. However, soon enough the Moon enters Gemini. The **First Quarter Moon in Gemini** (Moon square Sun) brings the necessity for our moods to be changeable and adaptable. Our moods are easily affected by the busy buzz of intellectual focuses and pursuits. The emphasis of covering many details at once becomes the primary objective, but not necessarily the answer to our insatiable curiosity. The act of processing information becomes essential. Do not let gossip and idle chatter be the cause of disruption in your day – thoughtlessness is also a symptom of the Gemini Moon atmosphere. The Gemini Moon puts us in touch with how we feel about our thoughts. If you don't like how you feel about your thoughts, endeavor to alter your way of thinking. Omit thoughts which attempt to defeat your sense of purpose; encourage thoughts that uplift and inspire your spirit. Be careful not to overdo the caffeine.

February 22nd Monday

Presidents' Day, Washington's Birthday, USA

Moon in Gemini	PST	EST	
Moon square Jupiter	1:37 AM	4:37 AM	
Moon square Venus	12:04 PM	3:04 PM	
Moon trine Mercury	9:16 PM	12:16 AM	(February 23)

Birthday: Sybil Leek 1917, George Washington 1732

Mood Watch: Gemini rules the nervous system, a complex and essential part of our existence. What we do to affect the condition of our nerves is mind boggling. The waxing Gemini Moon energy puts our minds and our mouths into high gear. Nervousness creates tension. Nervous tension is a common mood symptom of the Gemini Moon, and it can be controlled by the way we think and by the quality of nutrition we absorb during tense times. Gemini Moon is a good time to feed the nervous system with vitamin rich foods. Be sure to avoid heavy sugars and caffeine overload. Calming meditations can ease a burned out brain. There are various techniques of easing busy thought processes. The afternoon's Moon square Venus aspect brings a challenging time to our sense of pleasure, and it's no time to barter for art. Later tonight's Moon trine Mercury aspect is a great time to fine tune the mind with positive and uplifting thoughts. Ease the tension; ease the mind.

February 23rd Tuesday

Moon in Gemini / Cancer	PST	EST	
Moon square Uranus	7:31 AM	10:31 AM	
Sun sextile Pluto	8:31 AM	11:31 AM	
Moon trine Neptune goes v/c	9:27 AM	12:27 PM	
Moon enters Cancer	3:29 PM	6:29 PM	
Moon square Saturn	8:53 PM	11:53 PM	
Moon opposite Pluto	11:52 PM	2:51 AM	(February 24)
Mercury conjunct Neptune begins (see February 27)			

Birthday: George Frederic Handel 1685

Mood Watch: There is a busy and chaotic quality to our moods on this Gemini Moon morning. Then the Moon goes void-of-course, and a mindless pattern of delays and distractions begins to take shape. Mindless activities are probably the safest, but if important afternoon business can't wait, be sure to mind the mindlessness. A Pisces Sun and a Gemini Moon bring a creative, bubbling well of mixed thoughts and ideas. Emotional images blend with the mind to create an intuitive understanding of our beliefs. Later today as the Moon enters Cancer, our moods are more inclined to focus on our emotional patterns. Moon square Saturn brings concerns over things like deadlines and limitations. Moon opposite Pluto puts us in tune with the power issues of our lives.

74

Sun sextile Pluto (occurring Feb. 19 – 25) Sun in Pisces sextile Pluto in Capricorn brings opportunities that appear both vast and demanding to Pisces born people celebrating birthdays between February 19 – 25. These birthday people are experiencing the sextile aspect of their natal sun to Pluto, giving them opportunities to take charge, to step into positions of power, and to accept and embrace permanent change in their lives. These are powerful transformations which provide opportunities to embody what has been learned from the personal trials of the past. Conquer, master Pisceans! Persist with diligence to resolve the conflicts of your life with self-respect and assurance. Your time to triumph is always available when your will to achieve is balanced by knowledge and hard work. This holds true for all signs of the zodiac. This aspect will reoccur on October 26 with the Sun in Scorpio, affecting some of the Libra and Scorpio born folks of that time.

February 24th Wednesday

Moon in Cancer	PST	EST
Moon trine Sun	1:00 AM	4:00 AM
Moon trine Jupiter	6:19 AM	9:19 AM
Moon trine Venus	8:05 PM	11:05 PM

Birthday: Billy Zane 1966

Mood Watch: The Sun and Moon are in water signs, commonly bringing wet weather throughout most of North America. The Moon is trine with the Sun, which also brings harmonious feelings with regard to the seasonal factors of this time. Cancer Moon keeps our moods focused on personal comfort zones, the nurturing spirit of motherly energies, and on the shifts taking place on the emotional level. This morning's Moon trine Jupiter aspect brings a feeling of optimism and hope. This evening's Moon trine Venus aspect brings joy and pleasure.

February 25th Thursday

Moon in Cancer / Leo	PST	EST	
Moon trine Uranus goes v/c	9:47 AM	12:47 PM	
Moon enters Leo	5:09 PM	8:09 PM	
Moon conjunct Mars	7:14 PM	10:14 PM	
Moon sextile Saturn	10:03 PM	1:03 AM	(February 26)
Mars-trine-Uranus-non-exact begins (see March 15)			

Birthday: George Harrison 1943

Mood Watch: There is a bit of havoc in our moods as Moon trine Uranus brings a rebellious spirit. The Cancer Moon goes void-of-course, making this a good time to rest the mind, and to avoid emotional distractions that might infringe on one's ability to concentrate. Mood fluctuation is inescapable and this tends to slow down overall progress considerably. All of this moodiness is a natural process, but it can cause forgetfulness, oversensitivity, or defensiveness. For those who have a busy agenda, a conscious effort to practice a little extra tenderness and forgiveness will go a long way and, believe it or not, it will save a lot of time. This evening, as the Moon enters Leo, our moods will be considerably more upbeat and prone towards entertainment.

February 26th Friday
Moon in Leo
No Exact Aspects
Venus conjunct Uranus begins (see March 3)

Birthday: Johnny Cash 1932

Mood Watch: Last night the Moon entered Leo, and it's a welcome change, as the long void-of-course Cancer Moon of yesterday may have worn some folks' patience down to a frazzle. Restlessness strikes the heart. It is no wonder that we awaken to wild and beastly moods. Such moods as these will get the chance to break out of their cage, as we gear ourselves up for a Full Moon eve (tomorrow). There may be an opportunity here to enhance and harmonize friendships and family situations in a fulfilling and enriching manner. This is a good time to stretch out your paws, seek warmth and light, enjoy affectionate hearts, and to reaffirm the strength of willpower. However, it would be wise to pace yourself today, as tomorrow brings yet another long and arduous void-of-course Moon phase. It will probably be a lazy Saturday.

February 27th Saturday
Full Moon Eve

Moon in Leo / Virgo	PST	EST
Mercury conjunct Neptune	6:02 AM	9:02 AM
Moon opposite Neptune	11:34 AM	2:34 PM
Moon opposite Mercury goes v/c	12:14 PM	3:14 PM
Moon enters Virgo	4:53 PM	7:53 PM

Birthday: Chelsea Clinton 1980

Mood Watch: The watchword for this playful tune of a Moon is "will." If one or more facets of your personal will is purposefully executed and gratefully achieved, you will have experienced a successful Leo Moon time. The Moon opposite Neptune aspect brings the potential for escapist tendencies, as well as a challenge to feel comfortable or spiritually in tune with others. Overall, the waxing Moon in Leo is a good time to assert some confidence, as it may well bring moods of self-assurance, amusement, and delight. However, the Moon goes void-of-course as it opposes Mercury, and our mouths are likely to get us in trouble if we don't keep a tight guard on our egos. The void-of-course Leo Moon time is a lazy time when our less ambitious qualities will tend to surface. The Moon is full tomorrow in Virgo, and the scrutinizing qualities of the Virgo Moon atmosphere will direct us toward a more impelling need to organize, purify, and apply some cleanliness to our existence.

Mercury conjunct Neptune (occurring Feb. 23 – March 1) This year's only conjunction of Mercury and Neptune inspires communications on the hypersensitive issues of people's belief systems. Aquarius represents humanity, and Neptune in the sign of Aquarius focuses on the essential need for belief in humankind; that is, we must believe in ourselves and our own capabilities in order to survive spiritually. Mercury in Aquarius focuses news, talk, and discussion on human rights issues. Many people, especially Aquarians, are deeply moved to speak about their convictions. This conjunction also presents a good time to learn from the news and talk concerning humanitarian issues and to pray, meditate on, and connect with that higher spirit that dwells within.

February 28th Sunday
FULL MOON in VIRGO

Moon in Virgo	PST	EST
Moon trine Pluto	12:50 AM	3:50 AM
Sun conjunct Jupiter	2:44 AM	5:44 AM
Moon opposite Jupiter	8:20 AM	11:20 AM
Moon opposite Sun	8:32 AM	11:38 AM

Birthday: Rae Dawn Chong 1961

Mood Watch: The **Full Moon in Virgo** (Moon opposite Sun) which reaches its peak this morning reminds us of the need to organize, analyze, and constructively criticize our health and cleanliness practices. Virgo also puts the focus on organization, filing, accounting, preparing taxes, and handling all of life's mundane necessities. Virgo Moon energy purges and purifies our surroundings with sound resourcefulness and simple logic. Virgo rules the intestines of the body and represents the process of elimination. Now is an excellent time to focus on eliminating toxins and purifying the body. This is also a good time to purge the useless, destructive, or outmoded habits of our life. Celebrate your existing health, and do something good for your body on this Full Virgo Moon.

Sun conjunct Jupiter (occurring Feb. 20 – March 4) This conjunction brings those Pisces folks celebrating birthdays February 20 – March 4 into an especially favorable position of their natal sun to Jupiter. This represents a time of gifts and expansion for these birthday folks, and there are good times in the works for these people. Financial or career advancement as well as skill building, exploration, travel, inheritance – and perhaps just plain happiness – becomes a bonus for these folks. Be sure to count your blessings, birthday Pisces; you may find there are a great deal more blessings opening up for you this year than you might have expected! As a general rule, this conjunction usually only occurs once a year.

March 1st Monday

Moon in Virgo / Libra	PST	EST	
Moon opposite Venus	4:32 AM	7:32 AM	
Mercury enters Pisces	5:27 AM	8:27 AM	
Moon opposite Uranus goes v/c	9:36 AM	12:36 PM	
Moon enters Libra	4:32 PM	7:32 PM	
Moon sextile Mars	5:45 PM	8:45 PM	
Moon conjunct Saturn	9:02 PM	12:02 AM	(March 2)
Mercury sextile Pluto begins (see March 4)			

Birthday: Harry Belafonte 1927

Mood Watch: The effects of a post-full Virgo Moon still ring with a buzz of information-sharing and questioning. Doubtfulness and scrutiny are symptoms of the fact that the Virgo Moon is void-of-course. As we prioritize our personal needs and achieve success by cherry picking our way through numerous tasks, often physical in nature, we also pull in our reins and act with a great deal more subtlety and poise. As the Moon enters Libra later today, we balance our doubting insecurities with the need to apply teamwork and a caring attitude. Logic prevails with a much more cooperative spirit.

Mercury enters Pisces (Mercury in Pisces: March 1 – 17) Today Mercury enters Pisces and this brings the emphasis of news, media, and communications on our beliefs, spiritual growth, cultural expression, and our tendencies towards escapism and drug use. Today through March 17, Mercury in Pisces brings out the mystic in all of us and adds quite a bit of color and flair to the imagination in relayed messages. This is also a good time to immerse oneself in creative writing and music or to open up the channels to the spirit world. Listen and learn from the priests, holy teachers, loved ones, and spirit guides of your choosing. Sometimes the voice of sense and reason needs to surrender to the simplicity of just listening in silence.

March 2nd Tuesday

Moon in Libra

	PST	EST
Moon square Pluto	12:45 AM	3:45 AM
Venus trine Mars begins (see March 7)		

Birthday: Lou Reed 1944

Mood Watch: Today's Libra Moon brings the stability of balance into our moods. We naturally focus on those areas of life that require the most attention, as well as the most diplomacy and tact. This is the time to share experiences with friends and working partners, to develop a sense of teamwork and togetherness. This past weekend brought a Full Virgo Moon, followed by yesterday's long void-of-course lunar phase. This is a good time to make adjustments and to work on balancing out the recent inconsistencies in our lives. The post Full Moon time is usually a time of winding down and resting, and while it's in Libra, there is a persistent need to contemplate decisions and work on important matters with loved ones. Besides the need for rest, it may be wise to get something important done today, as tomorrow brings yet another long void-of-course Moon phase that will require some patience and is likely to cause a lot of indecision.

March 3rd Wednesday

Moon in Libra / Scorpio

	PST	EST
Moon trine Neptune goes v/c	12:44 PM	3:44 PM
Moon enters Scorpio	6:12 PM	9:12 PM
Moon square Mars	7:09 PM	10:09 PM
Venus conjunct Uranus	8:07 PM	11:07 PM
Mercury conjunct Jupiter begins (see March 7)		

Birthday: Alexander Graham Bell 1847

Mood Watch: Libra Moon is a good time to discuss ideas with others and to make social arrangements. This is also a time for teamwork and cooperation. The best time to do these things would be the morning. By afternoon, the Libra Moon goes void-of-course as it reaches the trine position to Neptune. Although afternoon moods are likely to be pleasant and somewhat lackadaisical, there will also be a lot of indecision, and noncommittal attitudes are also likely to be present. This evening's Moon in Scorpio is a good time to seek solutions to pressing concerns. Instinctual, clairvoyant, and resilient expressions of mood will show us the way.

Venus conjunct Uranus (occurring Feb. 26 – March 6) It's no wonder that love matters seem wild or chaotic – this conjunction brings an element of shock value to the expression of love. Venus conjunct Uranus in Pisces creates the potential for lively encounters with spiritual love and affection, wherein there is sometimes an exceedingly wise, though often unusual, counsel of love. A radical or explosive attraction or fascination may occur with this conjunction, opening our senses to a more artistic understanding of chaos. For those who are strongly affected, mischievous, brilliant, and unusual modes of love and affection now occur. Hang in there. Chaos is often considered a true test of love. Be positive and open to the challenge of love with chaos. This is the only time during the year that Venus will be conjunct with Uranus.

March 4th Thursday

Moon in Scorpio

	PST	EST
Moon trine Mercury	2:53 AM	5:53 AM
Moon sextile Pluto	3:01 AM	6:01 AM
Mercury sextile Pluto	3:54 AM	6:54 AM
Moon trine Jupiter	12:57 PM	3:57 PM
Moon trine Sun	7:22 PM	10:22 PM

Venus opposite Saturn begins (see March 9)

Birthday: Miriam Makeba 1932

Mood Watch: The Sun and Moon are both in water signs and some folks may find this particular time a little emotionally taxing. Sun in Pisces and Moon in Scorpio often bring some tendencies towards escapism or melodramatic behavior. This is the time to face addictions and addictive behavior with brave fortitude. Hypersensitivity and emotional intensity may be some of the signs of today's mood setting. The midday aspect of Moon trine Jupiter brings jovial moods that are well worth sharing. Gentleness and kindness may be difficult to come into contact with, but there is no better way to find it than to apply it yourself.

Mercury sextile Pluto (occurring March 1 – 5) Communications and discussions are facilitated, with an opportunity to get your message across in negotiations with those in positions of power. Mercury is now in Pisces, ensuring the strong belief behind our topics of communication, while Pluto in Capricorn is forcing us to acknowledge our resources and to use them wisely. Vital information regarding treatments for illness or disease may frequent the news, and news in general may well have some critical impact. This is a good time to reach out to those of another generation and make an attempt to communicate something essential. This aspect will reoccur on October 22 with Mercury in Scorpio.

March 5th Friday

Moon in Scorpio / Sagittarius	PST	EST	
Moon trine Uranus	4:06 PM	7:06 PM	
Moon square Neptune	5:50 PM	8:50 PM	
Moon trine Venus goes v/c	8:32 PM	11:32 PM	
Moon enters Sagittarius	11:36 PM	2:36 AM	(March 6)

Birthday: Rex Harrison 1908

Mood Watch: The Sun and Moon are both in water signs and this represents a very fluid and insightful time of adaptability and transformation. Embrace safe and therapeutic outlets for emotional buildups. Waning Scorpio Moon is a good time to release emotional energy, and to face certain truths that may have been overlooked or avoided during the last Full Moon. Beware of addictive or violent tendencies. There is also the potential here for breathtaking art and creativity. Scorpio Moon is an excellent time to seek out and exercise talents and skills. The evening's Moon trine Venus aspect brings a void-of-course Moon, and although our moods will be preoccupied with pleasantries and affection, our moods may also be somewhat spacey and uncertain at times. Therapeutic exercises and a bit of pampering may be the best course of action this evening.

March 6th Saturday

Moon in Sagittarius	PST	EST
Moon trine Mars	12:23 AM	3:23 AM
Moon sextile Saturn	4:13 AM	7:13 AM
Moon square Mercury	5:54 PM	8:54 PM
Moon square Jupiter	8:59 PM	11:59 PM
Venus square Pluto begins (see March 11)		

Birthday: Elizabeth Barrett Browning 1806

Mood Watch: The Sagittarius Moon energy brings free spirited enthusiasm. That said, there are a couple of lunar square aspects to look out for tonight. Square aspects aren't always bad, but they do require some ingenuity to work through puzzling or sometimes difficult feelings. Quite often when we are feeling enthusiastic, there is a certain degree of anticipation or expectation. With a little bit of optimism, some extra effort towards communication, and with some extra patience or tolerance thrown in for good measure, this will be a time to enjoy. Apply some humor; it's always a safeguard for keeping up the ole morale of everyone involved.

March 7th Sunday

LAST QUARTER MOON in SAGITTARIUS

Moon in Sagittarius	PST	EST
Venus enters Aries	4:33 AM	7:33 AM
Moon square Sun	7:42 AM	10:42 AM
Venus trine Mars	11:15 AM	2:15 PM
Mercury conjunct Jupiter	5:45 PM	8:45 PM
Sun conjunct Mercury begins (see March 14)		

Birthday: Maurice Ravel 1875

Mood Watch: Like Maurice Ravel's famous concerto, *Bolero*, the journey of life is building towards a fantastic crescendo. Winter is in the process of ending its quiet slumber. The **Last Quarter Moon in Sagittarius** (Moon square Sun) is preparing us for that climactic experience. In order to get the most out of it, it's important to apply ourselves at every stage of this preparation process. This lunar quarter is a good time to internalize your new wishes and thoughts about the upcoming spring season. The best course of action centers on healing disruptive feelings and makes a sporting effort to let go of unsatisfactory habits. Sagittarius Moon focuses our attention on such things as fitness, philosophy and travel. Despite whatever hardships have soiled our travels, once we have cleared the path for our dreams to unfold, the Sagittarius Moon energies will inspire us to take bold and creative steps towards making life brighter and more positive. This is the time to broaden the mind and allow yourself to go further than anticipated in realizing your vision for the future.

Venus enters Aries (Venus in Aries: March 7 – 31) As Venus enters Aries the expression of beauty, love and attraction assumes a fascination for the warrior spirit. Venus represents magnetic draw and attraction, and now the planet of love and beauty focuses our attention on the force and fire of Aries related interests. This brings sheer love of and appreciation for such activities as competition, rights (or rites) of selfhood, and initiation into new endeavors. Venus in Aries brings out the warrior and conqueror quality in people, and a new sense of life and vitality will be evident. Venus in Aries emphasizes ardent, open and forthright expressions and proposals of love, especially from our Aries friends who may be blinded by the lust for beauty. New hobbies, crafts and talents will spring forth. Remember, Aries rules the head; there are numerous ways you can use your head before plunging head first into love matters. Try not to be too militant in the display of personal defenses and in the expression of true feelings of affection. New love is inspired with Venus in Aries.

Venus trine Mars (occurring March 2 – 9) Venus in Aries is trine Mars in Leo. Adventurous, outgoing, and bold expressions of affection will bring very energetic and romantic interactions between loved ones. Venus trine Mars brings love in action. When Venus and Mars are well harmonized by this ideal aspect, there is a greater opportunity for peace and healing in relationships, and often gifts are exchanged. These are gifts which help people to understand how masculine and feminine expressions are harmonized. This is the only time Venus trine Mars will occur this year.

Mercury conjunct Jupiter (occurring March 3 – 9) Mercury and Jupiter are conjunct in Pisces, and this brings an excellent time to explore the imagination. News and discussions (Mercury) revolve around our joys, our prosperity, and our wealth (Jupiter) – particularly relating to fulfilling our desires and abiding by our deep passions in life. This aspect creates expansive talk which spreads quickly with news about the economic state of affairs. Thoughts and information (Mercury) with regard to a prosperous and visionary breakthrough (Jupiter) will

81

be highlighted. It's a great time to boost the morale of others by complimenting them on their skills. As Mercury crosses over their natal sun, March born Pisces having birthdays during this time are being showered with a wealth of information, ideas, and opportunities which are worthy of their time and effort.

March 8th Monday

Moon in Sagittarius / Capricorn	PST	EST
Moon square Uranus	1:27 AM	4:27 AM
Moon sextile Neptune goes v/c	3:13 AM	6:13 AM
Moon enters Capricorn	9:14 AM	12:14 PM
Moon square Venus	12:31 PM	3:31 PM
Moon square Saturn	1:48 PM	4:48 PM
Moon conjunct Pluto	7:33 PM	10:33 PM

Birthday: Micky Dolenz 1945

Mood Watch: This morning there may be a few minor setbacks to disrupt our moods while the Moon is void-of-course in Sagittarius. Be careful of the tendency to get lost or to misinterpret today's schedule of events. As the Moon enters Capricorn, the determination to get things moving and to be in control empowers us to face our responsibilities and focus our efforts towards getting some work done. Once we've tackled the minor setbacks, the game plan to deal with the big stuff in life will seem a little less daunting. It might not be a bad idea to keep a steady pace going and to expect some complications while the Moon is square to Venus and later to Saturn. An extra workload is likely to interrupt many folks' attempts to find pleasure this afternoon.

March 9th Tuesday

Moon in Capricorn	PST	EST
Venus opposite Saturn	12:21 AM	3:21 AM
Moon sextile Jupiter	9:08 AM	12:08 PM
Moon sextile Mercury	3:28 PM	6:28 PM

Birthday: Bobby Fisher 1943

Mood Watch: Today will seem a great deal more productive than yesterday. The waning Capricorn Moon brings positive moods and the lunar aspects are promising. There is a great deal to comprehend and process as the Moon wanes in Capricorn, but the restrictive tendencies of emotional interruptions are often subdued for the sake of clarity and function. A time comes when we must set our emotions aside and deal with important matters and this is often the Moon to do the job. The best emotional responses will come to those who choose to be helpful and useful. A show of respect has great merit on a Capricorn Moon day.

Venus opposite Saturn (occurring March 4 – 11) Venus in Aries opposes Saturn in Libra and this brings daring, assertive, and sometimes impetuous expressions of love at odds with the even-tempered scrutiny of restrictive types of discipline. While there is a very strong need to attain a sense of beauty, there is also a constantly compelling and obsessive compulsion to press on with work and vital responsibilities. This may be a difficult time for some to feel in tune with loved ones, and career related disciplines may be impeding on recreational needs and desires. This may be particularly so because Saturn is currently retrograde (Jan. 13 – May 30). Love matters – and the things we are attracted to – are subjected to unavoidable trials and restrictions. There will be folks among us thrust into the challenges of facing jealousy, guilt, offensive outbreaks, anguish, oppression, defeat or despair. There are always lessons where our not so sheltered passions lie. We must be careful how our passions are stirred or handled. Hold steadfast to all principles of wisdom. Be careful not to bite off more than you can chew, especially with regard to irresistible attractions laden with restrictive laws. This is the only time Venus will oppose Saturn this year.

March 10th Wednesday

Moon in Capricorn / Aquarius	PST	EST	
Moon sextile Sun	12:41 AM	3:41 AM	
Mars goes direct	9:09 AM	12:09 PM	
Moon sextile Uranus goes v/c	1:59 PM	4:59 PM	
Moon enters Aquarius	9:43 PM	12:43 AM	(March 11)
Moon opposite Mars	10:18 PM	1:18 AM	(March 11)
Sun conjunct Uranus begins (see March 16)			
SATURN OPPOSITE URANUS begins (see April 26)			

Birthday: Sharon Stone 1958

Mood Watch: Productive moods keep us busy throughout the morning with the Moon in Capricorn. However, this afternoon the waning Capricorn Moon goes void-of-course, leaving the affairs of the morning somewhat pressed for time, disorganized, and fairly scattered. People may tend to take things too seriously, forgetting the necessity to lighten up and to keep matters running smoothly by avoiding heavy expectations. There's no point in getting bent out of shape over the heavy workload or the bad traffic – laziness abounds, and there is only so much progress that can occur today. Tonight, as the Moon enters Aquarius, a thoughtful approach to the day makes matters run a little more smoothly.

Mars goes direct (Mars direct: March 10, 2010 – Jan. 23, 2012) For those whose toughest challenges have been harnessing energies and conducting activities, here's the good news: Mars now moves *forward*. Since December 20, 2009, Mars, "the god of war," has been retrograde. Mars has been traveling back through Leo, focusing the course of war related activities on such things as prestige, brave showmanship, individual merits, and loyalty to the family as well as to country. Mars is now at the zero degree mark of Leo, ready to move forward through Leo all over again. This brings a very active life and atmosphere for our Leo friends, especially now that Mars moves forward through Leo instead of back, the action in the lives of Leo people will move forward also. Mars retrograde through Leo has been difficult for the square signs to Leo; both Taurus and Scorpio people may notice that they've had to work extra hard to be on top of their strength and their ability to act swiftly, but now their efforts, although still demanding, will seem less destructive and a lot more productive. This time may have seemed challenging for Aquarians, whose natal sun sign has been opposite to retrograde Mars, bringing abrupt actions and harsh opponents into their world. Although activities will still be busy and full, it will seem less encumbering to the Aquarian spirit as Mars moves forward in Leo. The masculine force and vitality of Mars holds the promise of action and represents the principle of will; this shows us that energy can be directed anywhere we choose. While Mars moves forward, the force of the will is less likely to backfire. Mars energy motivates us, summons our need for survival, enables us to act defensively, and awakens the urge to express rage at the apparent offenses of the world. It is best to maintain one's own masculine force with the greatest of dignity and integrity. To live with the vitality of Mars is to serve the life force that lives inside each of us. Mars will now assume a forward moving position around the sun from our geocentric perspective for a nice long time: until January 23, 2012.

March 11th Thursday

Moon in Aquarius	PST	EST
Moon trine Saturn	2:00 AM	5:00 AM
Moon sextile Venus	8:14 AM	11:14 AM
Venus square Pluto	9:35 AM	12:35 PM

Birthday: Lawrence Welk 1903

Mood Watch: Moon in Aquarius affects our moods with a sense of humanitarian openness, while a scientific sense of proceeding with caution reminds us to apply our knowledge in all dealings with others. This is a good time to try experimenting with one's way of life, and to apply new methods of living more boldly and freely. With the sun in Pisces, the characteristic dreamy quality of life, coupled with the Moon in Aquarius, makes for a very imaginative and interesting time. Opportunistic lunar aspects make for a promising day.

Venus square Pluto (occurring March 6 – 13) Venus in Aries is square to Pluto in Capricorn. The energetic, swift and intrepid qualities of our affections are likely to take a pretty good beating. Our concepts of beauty may be challenged as the corruption of superpowers prompts action which threatens or alters the beauty and pleasure in our lives. There may be environmental destruction that intrudes on our sense of natural aesthetics. Venus square Pluto often involves such difficulties as loss or death of a loved one, the obstacles of rejection, and general oppression for those aspects of life to which we are undeniably attached and which we hold dear. If something of this nature is occurring for you, it is best to recognize that love will triumph in every dimension, despite the pain of separation, or the disease and strife of the beloved. While Pluto is in Capricorn, the square of Venus in Aries may create the sense that loving efforts are unreciprocated. Some people may feel used, unappreciated, or disadvantaged. Be both strong and gentle in matters of love. Let the obstacles of love's pain become the building blocks of a better outlook, and a stronger love will supersede these current trials of the heart. Venus square Pluto will repeat on August 9, with Venus in Libra.

March 12th Friday

Moon in Aquarius
No Exact Aspects
Mercury conjunct Uranus begins (see March 15)

Birthday: Albert G. Mackey 1807

Mood Watch: Moon in Aquarius brings intelligent approaches to the forefront of our moods. This Moon guides us towards making a breakthrough. The waning Aquarius Moon draws our attention to the need for logic, knowledge, and scientific wisdom. The Pisces Sun carries us through the final days of winter despite the trepidation of storms, both internal and external. Our beliefs are always tested in the final throes of winter, particularly as the Moon wanes toward the new mark this Monday. As for now, imaginative and ingenious moods will make this a very productive and interesting day.

March 13th Saturday

Moon in Aquarius / Pisces	**PST**	**EST**	
Moon conjunct Neptune goes v/c	4:46 AM	7:46 AM	
Moon enters Pisces	10:44 AM	1:44 PM	
Moon sextile Pluto	9:20 PM	12:20 AM	(March 14)

Birthday: Mircea Eliade 1907

Mood Watch: Early this morning the Aquarius Moon goes void-of-course as it also conjuncts with Neptune. Beware of the tendency towards spacey attitudes, stupidity, and thoughtlessness. Technical equipment may prove to be unmanageable during the Aquarius void-of-course Moon. Later, as the Moon enters Pisces, deep spiritual reverie entices our moods to seek out fantasy and escapism. Imaginative moods may cause many folks to pursue various types of creative endeavors. Internal reflection brings spiritual rebirth. Note: **Tomorrow,** *Daylight Saving Time* **begins in North America**. Tonight at bedtime, don't forget to turn all clocks and timepieces *forward* one hour.

March 14th Sunday

DAYLIGHT SAVING TIME BEGINS
Turn clocks ahead one hour at 2:00 a.m.

Moon in Pisces	**PDT**	**EDT**
Sun conjunct Mercury	6:16 AM	9:16 AM
Moon conjunct Jupiter	2:16 PM	5:16 PM
Mercury trine Mars begins (see March 17)		
Sun trine Mars begins (see March 21)		

Daylight Saving Time: For the fourth year in a row, instead of the time changes occurring on the usual first Sunday in April and last Sunday in October, Daylight Saving Time will begin much earlier and end a bit later this year. Due to the United States' Energy Policy Act of 2005, Daylight Saving Time begins today and ends on Sunday, November 7.

Birthday: Albert Einstein 1879

Mood Watch: Today brings a New Moon eve when the Moon reaches its darkest phase. This is a time of introspection, intuition, and imaginative thought. The darkly waning Pisces Moon invites mystery, intrigue, and an attraction to the arts. As our moods go through an instinctual phase, it brings us to a place where we examine our beliefs. The waning Pisces Moon can help to keep us out of trouble if we use our intuition and listen to it very carefully.

Sun conjunct Mercury (occurring March 7 – 17) This conjunction will create a much more thoughtful, communicative and expressive year ahead for those Aries folks celebrating birthdays March 7 – 17. This is your time (birthday Aries) to record ideas, relay important messages, and pay close attention to your imaginative thoughts as they are touched by Mercury, creating the urge to speak and be heard. Birthday Aries, your thoughts will reveal a great deal about who you are, now and in the year to come.

March 15ᵗʰ Monday
NEW MOON in PISCES

Moon in Pisces / Aries	PDT	EDT	
Moon conjunct Sun	2:00 PM	5:00 PM	
Mercury conjunct Uranus	2:39 PM	5:39 PM	
Moon conjunct Uranus	4:38 PM	7:38 PM	
Moon conjunct Mercury goes v/c	5:00 PM	8:00 PM	
Moon enters Aries	11:32 PM	2:32 AM	(March 16)
Mars-trine-Uranus-non-exact (see below)			
Mercury opposite Saturn begins (see March 18)			

Birthday: Sly Stone 1944

Mood Watch: The **New Moon in Pisces** (Moon conjunct Sun) focuses our attention on the need to get in touch with our own beliefs, and to inspire those beliefs with devotion and renewed faith. Tendencies towards escapism may be strong today, particularly for those who are unwilling to let go of the past. The New Moon in Pisces inspires a new outlook on our moods. This is a time of emotional as well as spiritual purging. The spirit of what is now emerging and showing through our moods is a sense of renewed faith in something divine and omnipotent. The world of magic exists in the melding mutable water of the Piscean expression. This evening, as the Moon goes void-of-course, spacey moods will make it difficult to keep people's attention. Mindless entertainment may be the way to go on this lethargic Monday evening.

Mercury conjunct Uranus (occurring March 12 – 17) Mercury and Uranus are conjunct in Pisces, giving birth to radical, bright, inspired and intuitive ideas. This may raise some very interesting and unusual questions about what we choose to believe in. Consciousness raising talk is prevalent. Mercury conjunct Uranus magnifies the volume of shocking or question-raising news, and stirs the minds and mouths of rebels and non-conformists who are inspired to speak out. Everyone is crying for some kind of freedom! This is the only time this year Mercury and Uranus will be conjunct.

Mars-trine-Uranus-non-exact (occurring Feb. 25 – April 3) Today is as close as we come, within three degrees of a perfect trine between Mars and Uranus. Due to the retrograde pattern of Mars, which just ended on March 10, this aspect will never reach its peak. However, it does occur within close range, has been stirring up positive brazen activity since February 25, and is expected to continue, while it dissipates, through April 3. Mars is in Leo, right at the cusp of Cancer, where bravery in action is emphasized, while Uranus is at the tail end of Pisces, just four degrees away from Aries, stirring up emotional clamor and radical fascinations. The trine aspect brings positive action, capable of inspiring a healthy breakthrough, and pushing us well past the realm of uncertainty and doubt. This aspect will return, in full, on October 24, with Mars in Scorpio and Uranus in Pisces.

March 16th Tuesday

Moon in Aries

	PDT	EDT	
Moon trine Mars	12:28 AM	3:28 AM	
Moon opposite Saturn	2:54 AM	5:54 AM	
Moon square Pluto	9:54 AM	12:54 PM	
Moon conjunct Venus goes v/c	11:07 PM	2:07 AM	(March 17)
Sun conjunct Uranus	11:49 PM	2:49 AM	(March 17)
Sun opposite Saturn begins (see March 21)			

Birthday: Bernardo Bertolucci 1940

Mood Watch: It's March; the Moon is newly waxing in Aries. We're now counting down to the end of winter season and a restless fervor captures our moods. Aries Moon activity breaks the sleepy winter lull with a sudden propensity to cut through the grey areas of life. As a general rule, there is very little tolerance for vagueness or uncertainty going around. To be uncertain is to get pushed aside or perceived as being unworthy by the public. Stand up or stand out today, otherwise you might be overlooked. Unless, of course, you wish to lay low, at which point you're bound to be less noticeable.

Sun conjunct Uranus (occurring March 10 – 20) This one time annual occurrence of Sun conjunct Uranus especially affects Pisces people celebrating birthdays March 10 – 20. There may well be a healthy dollop of disruption and chaos in the lives of these folks. Radical breakthroughs that create a sense of freedom will be apparent. Sun conjunct Uranus causes strong rebellious tendencies. There is a stronger than usual Piscean desire to roll with change and take life at a different pace, to fight oppression and injustice, possibly even with an entirely off-the-wall approach to deal with calamity. Where there is knowledge to back this radical new approach, there's a way to achieve a sense of freedom with a good chance to make an impression in the year to come. This will be your year (birthday folks) to express yourselves and your innovative desires and ideas.

March 17th Wednesday

Saint Patrick's Day
Void-of-course Moon in Aries

	PDT	EDT
Mercury enters Aries	9:11 AM	12:11 PM
Mercury trine Mars	4:32 PM	7:32 PM
Mercury square Pluto begins (see March 20)		

" Put an Irishman on the spit, and you can always get another Irishman to turn him. "   - George Bernard Shaw (1856 – 1950)

Birthday: Nat King Cole 1919

Mood Watch: The basic mood-setting for today focuses on the need to stand out and be in control of events. Unfortunately, the Moon will be void-of-course for the entire day and night and there's nothing controllable about that. There is an eagerness about our moods as the Sun is on the brink of entering Aries. Today's moods will be filled with determination and inspiration. Sometimes the void Aries Moon causes too much inspiration, and the search for a good fight or release of raw aggression must come out. This may be a difficult time to ignore pushy aggressors; nonetheless, being aware of this behavior and attempting to avoid it by watching for the signs — before the oppressor gets out of hand — may well be in your favor today. With little cooperation in our moods, this is not a good time to be a social director. By all means, avoid overly feisty leprechauns.

Mercury enters Aries (Mercury in Aries: March 17 – April 2) Mercury now enters Aries, bringing a focus of communications on selfhood, initiation, new projects, and new ways of seeing and experiencing life. We are all perpetually in the process of being initiated into some aspect of selfhood, particularly given that we are constantly learning, acquiring new skills, growing and aging. Mercury in Aries brings some lively heat to our communications and discussions. Mercury is the messenger, activating information, and Aries is the warrior and the force of nature that takes on life with fearless vigor and aggression. Communications possess a quality of command and a pioneering spirit. Now through April 2, while Mercury is in Aries, talk, news and discussions will be actively focused on the challenging and demanding enterprises and battles that await us.

Mercury trine Mars (occurring March 14 – 19) Mercury at zero degrees Aries is trine to Mars at zero degrees Leo. This aspect is especially stimulating in a positive way when it comes to communications among family and friends. Thoughts, words and speech inspire activity, and the messages coming across often give us the incentive to get in on the action. Mercury trine Mars brings news and communications into a most favorable position when it comes to taking action. The trine aspect acts like a gift, and this is a superb time to communicate and to receive positive and uplifting information, which will inspire others to take affirmative action where needed. This is the only time Mercury and Mars will be trine this year.

March 18th Thursday

Moon in Aries / Taurus	PDT	EDT
Mercury opposite Saturn	4:04 AM	7:04 AM
Moon enters Taurus	9:30 AM	12:30 PM
Moon square Mars	10:45 AM	1:45 PM
Moon trine Pluto	7:34 PM	10:34 PM

Birthday: Manly Palmer Hall 1901

Mood Watch: Yesterday's endless void-of-course Aries Moon carries over into this morning, and many folks may find that they are somewhat impatient and full of attitude. As the Moon enters Taurus, a much more grounded approach to life fills our moods. Nevertheless, the Moon square Mars aspect may cause a few temper tantrums along the way. Taurus Moon attitudes are usually stubborn around themes of aggression. Once we've worked out the kinks in the atmosphere, the waxing Taurus Moon gives us the incentive to seek pleasurable and comfortable surroundings. Taurus Moon is an excellent time to enjoy beautiful things.

Mercury opposite Saturn (occurring March 15 – 19) This aspect occurred on this very day one year ago, the quintessential difference being that Mercury was in Pisces opposing Saturn in Virgo. Today Mercury is in Aries and Saturn is in Libra. This aspect brings a very strong awareness of the need to speak out on serious and important subjects. News, talk, discussions and media tend to revolve around matters of closure, deaths, endings, and the establishment of control. There may be an overwhelming tone of command or restriction in some of the more serious subjects being communicated. While Mercury opposes Saturn, be careful where you choose to draw the lines. Mercury is in Aries, where articulate precision is succinct, forthright, and uninhibited. Saturn is in Libra, where it emphasizes the perimeters and security of our relationships and other such Libra-like issues as the need to create balance and diplomacy in all serious dealings. We may be especially aware of the delicate subject of how rules and laws are affecting our wellbeing. This is the only time Mercury will oppose Saturn this year.

March 19th Friday

Moon in Taurus	PDT	EDT
Moon sextile Jupiter	12:35 PM	3:35 PM
Sun square Pluto begins (see March 25)		

Birthday: Glen Close 1947

Mood Watch: The newly waxing Moon in Taurus fixes our moods on the need to stay grounded and practical. Many of us will have our eyes set on new things we need or want to have in our life. For that very reason, this is an excellent time to indulge in some early spring cleaning. The final day of Pisces is here and that makes this the last day of winter. Today's Moon sextile Jupiter aspect puts us in tune with the need for prosperity, advancement, and good fortune. This is a good time to seek beautiful and pleasurable things that will enhance our experience of life. Now is the time to look for something that will get us in the mood for spring.

ARIES

Key Phrase: "I AM"

Cardinal Fire Sign

Ruling Planet: Mars

Symbol: The Ram

March 20th through April 19th

March 20th Saturday

Vernal Equinox
Moon in Taurus / Gemini

	PDT	EDT
Mercury square Pluto	1:16 AM	4:16 AM
Sun enters Aries	10:32 AM	1:32 PM
Moon sextile Uranus	11:31 AM	2:31 PM
Moon square Neptune goes v/c	12:40 PM	3:40 PM
Moon enters Gemini	5:29 PM	8:29 PM
Moon sextile Sun	6:02 PM	9:02 PM
Moon sextile Mars	7:09 PM	10:09 PM
Moon trine Saturn	7:56 PM	10:56 PM

Birthday: Spike Lee 1957

Mood Watch: Count on Taurus Moon to get us in the mood to address the physical issues in our life. The Moon is exalted in Taurus and this is an excellent time to welcome the new season. The morning is the best time to make use of the good vibes, as this afternoon's void-of-course Moon brings the potential for a great deal of laziness, and there may be a tendency for things to be misplaced. After the hard drive to achieve results, tonight would be a good time to kick back and relax. The Gemini Moon inspires curious and talkative moods.

Mercury square Pluto (occurring March 17 – 21) Mercury in Aries is square to Pluto in Capricorn. Selfishness will make it difficult to communicate with those of another generation. This is a particularly difficult time to deal with burdensome issues and discuss them in a manner that relieves tension. Mercury square Pluto often brings harsh and sometimes fatal news. Talk revolves around the corruption of superpowers and the setbacks caused by this corruption. This may be an especially difficult time to discuss matters involving permanent change. This aspect will reoccur on October 4 with Mercury in Libra.

Sun enters Aries (Sun in Aries: March 20 – April 19/20) Today, the event classically called **Vernal Equinox**, also known as Spring Equinox, marks the start of a new season and the beginning of the zodiac. This is the time when the daylight hours are equal in length to the hours of the night. Spring arrives when the earth is tilted so the Sun is directly over the equator. In the northern parts of the world, the first day of spring is on or about March 20. In the northern hemisphere we are on the side of the Equinox that returns toward the light, as opposed to Autumnal Equinox when the Sun enters Libra, the opposite of Aries. With Daylight Savings Time already underway since March 14, we now celebrate the continued lengthening of the days.

The Sun in Aries inspires courageous and bold new beginnings, as well as instilling confidence and forcefulness. Many Aries folks have an inherent desire to not only survive, but to exceed, and to make a lasting impression. Aries is the cardinal fire sign that doesn't give up easily. Some Aries folks love to start up businesses, but continue into other ventures once the business has been established and requires the dull monotony of upkeep and maintenance. The Aries character typically expresses quality of leadership in the fiery realm of the cardinal signs, and is ruled by the active and vital planet, Mars. Aries boasts of being the first, and works earnestly to defy all who would mock, criticize, or misunderstand their drive to reach a certain self-appointed plateau of excellence. Sun in Aries serves as a good time to initiate new projects and apply diligence with inspired ability. The youthful vigor that is characteristic of Arians is reflected in the season, and this springlike sprouting and growth is inspiration for us all.

March 21ˢᵗ Sunday

Moon in Gemini	PDT	EDT
Moon sextile Mercury	7:50 AM	10:50 AM
Sun trine Mars	10:54 AM	1:54 PM
Sun opposite Saturn	5:37 PM	8:37 PM
Moon square Jupiter	8:32 PM	11:32 PM

Birthday: Matthew Broderick 1962

Mood Watch: Yesterday was a partly winter and partly spring day. The day of Spring Equinox, which encompasses both Pisces and Aries, could be called a "win-spri" day. Today, however, the sun is in Aries for the entire day and that makes this the official first *full* day of spring. How much of it will be acting like spring remains to be seen, as the travails of unexpected weather patterns continue to baffle us in these years of global warming. The Gemini Moon keeps our minds busy throughout the day. It may be best to avoid arguing over money this evening while the Moon is square to Jupiter. This aspect usually challenges our sense of progress.

Sun trine Mars (occurring March 14 – 24) This occurrence of Sun trine Mars particularly affects those Pisces and Aries people celebrating birthdays from March 14 – 24. There will be loads of energy to work with, and a strong need to activate the personality and accomplish goals. There are special gifts of triumph for those Pisces and Aries birthday folks who activate their dreams and desires, allowing them to easily utilize existing energy. This is a time to exercise the will and the internal sense of primal might, to stir the personal agenda into a state of action. Heated matters will come to the surface in an advantageous manner. Through the act of making things happen, personal achievement will shine forth like a blessing in the year to come for these birthday folks.

Sun opposite Saturn (occurring March 16 – 24) This annual occurrence of Sun opposite Saturn particularly affects those Pisces and Aries people celebrating birthdays from March 16 – 24. These birthday folks are undergoing personal challenges with regard to patience, leaving them strongly aware of who and what is in control. These people are mindful of the crucial factors of time, limitations, and timing. Work demands may be overwhelming, and these Pisces and Aries folks will have to apply discipline and determination in order to achieve success. Work that requires self motivation may be the most challenging part of applying discipline while Saturn is in Libra. Pisces and Aries birthday folks, this is a most important time in your life to persist! Endure! Keep up the Great Work! Take heart, as this may well be your year to accomplish something astounding.

March 22nd Monday
Moon in Gemini / Cancer

	PDT	EDT	
Moon sextile Venus	2:53 AM	5:53 AM	
Moon square Uranus	5:48 PM	8:48 PM	
Moon trine Neptune goes v/c	6:48 PM	9:48 PM	
Mars sextile Saturn	8:51 PM	11:51 PM	
Moon enters Cancer	11:16 PM	2:16 AM	(March 23)

Birthday: Chico Marx 1887

Mood Watch: Learn to flip the coin of duality by taking in, hearing and witnessing both sides of the equation. Choose your thoughts integrally and wisely, and on the flip side of the coin, learn to laugh at the comedy of spontaneous confusion in a knowledge driven society full of layered ignorance and unsorted data. Our Gemini Moon moods will play around with new data and allow for new ideas. Get to know your wiser self by choosing your cosmology well. New feelings and moods will continually arise because the Gemini Moon has the cauldron of our emotions stirred by our thoughts. Tonight, as the Moon goes void-of-course, avoid idle chatter and gossip. Let the tranquil qualities of Moon trine Neptune bring peace.

Mars sextile Saturn (occurring Feb. 2 – March 30) Mars sextile Saturn brings an especially opportunistic time to practice control or discipline. However, since Saturn is still retrograde (Jan. 13 – May 30), it may be best to wait until November 8 – 18 to *start* a new enterprise, when Mars sextile Saturn occurs with no impeding retrograde action. This aspect is now reaching its peak for the second time during this occurrence period. For a review of Mars in Leo sextile Saturn in Libra, *see February 15*. The third and final peak of Mars sextile Saturn occurs on November 14 with Mars in Sagittarius.

March 23rd Tuesday
FIRST QUARTER MOON in CANCER
Moon in Cancer

	PDT	EDT	
Moon square Saturn	1:19 AM	4:19 AM	
Moon square Sun	3:59 AM	6:59 AM	
Moon opposite Pluto	8:37 AM	11:37 AM	
Moon square Mercury	9:54 PM	12:54 AM	(March 24)

Birthday: Chaka Khan 1953

Mood Watch: The **First Quarter Moon in Cancer** (Moon square Sun) urges us to share our feelings and take care of emotional needs, particularly in our home. Home focused activities bring warm expressions of contentment. With First Quarter Cancer Moon the emotional current tends to be magnified. Nutritional foods and trustworthy company are important components of today's activities. Treating ourselves and others in a nurturing way becomes the key to enhancing or cleansing our emotional perspective. Be careful not to push the buttons of sensitive people and use words wisely while considering the feelings of yourself and others.

March 24th Wednesday

Moon in Cancer	PDT	EDT	
Moon trine Jupiter	2:02 AM	5:02 AM	
Moon square Venus	12:12 PM	3:12 PM	
Moon trine Uranus goes v/c	9:38 PM	12:38 AM	(March 25)

Birthday: Harry Houdini 1874

Mood Watch: Throughout the day, the waxing Moon in Cancer brings out our maternal instincts, and focuses our moods and feelings on the desire to nurture emotional needs. This may be a typical time of moodiness, and the need to complain is just a symptom of wanting to be heard and understood. This is especially true with Moon square Venus complicating our sense of pleasure and affection. Moon in Cancer brings a wave of protective and instinctual impulses. For some, motherly cares and concerns come into play. There might well be a steady stream of emotional ups and downs, confirming that we are indeed affected by the tides. Go with the flow and apply some good motherly advice.

March 25th Thursday

Moon in Cancer / Leo	PDT	EDT
Moon enters Leo	2:39 AM	5:39 AM
Moon sextile Saturn	4:20 AM	7:20 AM
Moon conjunct Mars	5:14 AM	8:14 AM
Moon trine Sun	10:56 AM	1:56 PM
Sun square Pluto	8:45 PM	11:45 PM

Birthday: Elton John 1947

Mood Watch: Leo Moon moods are energetic and openly focused on identity. The sun and moon are both in fire signs, and archetypes abound with tales of the self, bursting with character and ego. A waxing Moon in Leo uplifts our moods with entertainment, magnetism and stimulation. It's good time to do something special for yourself and to reinforce your own integral outlook on the importance of living life according to willpower. Get in touch with a sense of personal vitality and call it your own.

Sun square Pluto (occurring March 19 – 28) This aspect particularly affects late-born Pisces and early-born Aries people celebrating birthdays this month from March 19 – 28. Pluto squaring the natal Sun of these people brings disruptive changes and many challenges to overcome, such as the pain of loss and the severity of transformation. Trying to hold onto the regrets and the pain of the past will only bring greater destruction later. This is the time to persevere through the obstacles of hardship. Yet, the hardships that are taking place now will resurface in time, so do take note of the struggles going on in the lives of the people who are directly affected by Pluto's tests. Realize this trend will be repeated, and so necessitates finding methods of release and attitude changes in order to survive the anxiety and stress. Take it one day at a time and do not let fear and worry rule this condition. Move steadily through the required transformation, as stagnation and fear will only bring extended suffering. This aspect will reoccur again this year on September 25, affecting some of the Virgo and Libra people of that time.

March 26ᵗʰ Friday

Moon in Leo	PDT	EDT
Moon trine Mercury	8:04 AM	11:04 AM
Moon trine Venus	6:36 PM	9:36 PM
Venus sextile Neptune begins (see March 29)		
Mercury-conjunct-Venus-non-exact begins (see April 6)		

Birthday: Joseph Campbell 1904

Mood Watch: Positive lunar aspects make this waxing Leo Moon day a positive one. Our moods are intrigued by the need for fun, entertainment, family activities, and personal hobbies. Sun in Aries and Moon in Leo brings spark, drive, and energy to our moods. Ambitious and eager moods entice many folks to stay active. This is a great time to apply some willpower and to work towards feeling good about the self. Where there is a sense of pride in personal efforts and achievements, there is a strong sense of self worth. This is the time to celebrate selfhood. Leo Moon reminds us that it is ultimately up to each individual to empower personal integrity for the self – what follows naturally is the encouragement of others.

March 27ᵗʰ Saturday

Earth Hour Eve (check local & international news reports for details)

Moon in Leo / Virgo	PDT	EDT
Moon opposite Neptune goes v/c	12:03 AM	3:03 AM
Moon enters Virgo	3:58 AM	6:58 AM
Moon trine Pluto	12:39 PM	3:39 PM

Birthday: Sarah Vaughan 1924

Mood Watch: Sensibility occurs as the Moon enters Virgo, and our moods enter into a health-conscious phase. Whether we pay attention to the signs of our bodies or not, they are there. Waxing Moon in Virgo emphasizes the need for purity and perfection. This quality of mood is also inclined to meticulous thought and deep contemplation. Virgo Moon is a superb time to clean and purify our surroundings, and to organize, simplify, and weed out superfluous emotional baggage. Youthful, innocent, virginal purity and beauty stand out and attract many folks today during this early stage of spring season.

March 28th Sunday

Full Moon Eve

Palm Sunday

Moon in Virgo	PDT	EDT	
Moon opposite Jupiter	6:29 AM	9:29 AM	
Moon opposite Uranus goes v/c	11:55 PM	2:55 AM	(March 29)
Venus square Mars begins (see April 3)			

Birthday: Julia Stiles 1981

Mood Watch: This morning's Moon opposite Jupiter brings moods that are inclined towards the call for advancement, adventure, and prosperity. Virgo Moon contentment can occur when we tend to personal needs without being overly critical of the self. The heavily waxing Virgo Moon emphasizes the necessity for cleanliness, order, and precision. There may also be a lot of emphasis placed on perfectionism and quality control. The Virgo Moon of springtime is an excellent time to do some spring cleaning. Virgo Moon reminds us of the necessity to eat well and digest our food well, too. Take precaution – the supermarkets are hitting us with a wide array of seasonal treats, and too many chocolate Easter bunnies, or the senseless gluttony of holiday spirits, can easily lead to indigestion on a nearly full Virgo Moon.

March 29th Monday

FULL MOON in LIBRA

Moon in Virgo / Libra	PDT	EDT
Moon enters Libra	4:22 AM	7:22 AM
Moon conjunct Saturn	5:29 AM	8:29 AM
Moon sextile Mars	8:05 AM	11:05 AM
Moon square Pluto	1:07 PM	4:07 PM
Venus sextile Neptune	1:24 PM	4:24 PM
Moon opposite Sun	7:25 PM	10:25 PM
Mercury sextile Neptune begins (see March 31)		

Birthday: Pearl Bailey 1918

Mood Watch: The **Full Moon in Libra** (Moon opposite Sun) brings events that revolve around such things as law, the justice system, friends, and marital partners. Relationships are a balancing act. Friends will share their strengths as well as their weaknesses. Troubled times can strengthen even the weakest links in friendship. Refuse to contribute to the weakness of a friend; nurture friendship with patience, understanding, and encouragement. Use this Full Libra Moon energy to empower your relationships. Diplomacy, peace and goodwill can be achieved among loved ones, but a definite effort is required.

Venus sextile Neptune (occurring March 26 – 31) Venus in Aries brings love, attraction, beauty, and the nature of feminine expression into prominence. Neptune in Aquarius is a time to awaken human spirituality and to excel in creative expression through music, art, writing, etc. Spread this healing power around for all to share! Realize profound beauty, and the depths of which true love is capable. Make the most of it as this will be the only time this aspect will occur year.

March 30th Tuesday

Passover

Moon in Libra	PDT	EDT	
Moon opposite Mercury	11:28 PM	2:28 AM	(March 31)
Venus trine Pluto begins (see April 4)			

Birthday: Celine Dion 1968

Mood Watch: Yesterday's Full Libra Moon is now waning but still very full in spirit. Libra Moon focuses our attention on research and court related matters, as well as specialty foods and culinary delights. Libra Moon emphasizes the pleasures of the learning and teaching processes. This is a good day to focus on business as usual, to take the time to show some appreciation for good friends, and to enjoy the contents of your latest favorite book. Libra Moon is also a time to apply teamwork and to arrange for –and catch up on – social affairs.

March 31st Wednesday

Moon in Libra / Scorpio	PDT	EDT
Moon trine Neptune	1:52 AM	4:52 AM
Moon opposite Venus goes v/c	5:13 AM	8:13 AM
Moon enters Scorpio	5:41 AM	8:41 AM
Moon square Mars	10:18 AM	1:18 PM
Venus enters Taurus	10:34 AM	1:34 PM
Moon sextile Pluto	2:50 PM	5:50 PM
Mercury sextile Neptune	8:22 PM	11:22 PM
Mercury square Mars begins (see April 4)		

Birthday: Al Gore 1948

Mood Watch: Swiftly, the post-full Libra Moon goes void-of-course this morning and then it enters Scorpio. The intensity of the blustery spring season always seems to deepen as the Moon enters Scorpio. It's an active day of lunar aspects and planetary shifts. Changeable moods are occurring rapidly as we strive to complete month end tasks. The busy quality of this time reminds us of the necessity to take a few deep breaths and to stay on top of the drama and aggressiveness that abound. Waning Scorpio Moon is a good time to focus on healing energies and on the improvement of personal skills and creativity.

Venus enters Taurus (Venus in Taurus: March 31 – April 24) Venus in Taurus is the time of an extraordinary attraction to beauty. Here in Taurus, Venus is at home nurturing us with sensual pleasure and enhancing our appreciation of nature and earthly bounty, as well as our appreciation for quality and specialty craftsmanship. Venus in Taurus brings out aesthetic awareness, and places a greater emphasis on the love of having valuable items, wealth, and abundance. Venus attracts and draws, and Taurus emphasizes the need for material acquisition, attainment, and beauty. Taurus people will be touched by the need for love and affection in their lives as Venus crosses over their natal Sun. Now is the time to acquire, polish, clean, and beautify things that give a sense of truly having something. To create beauty around oneself is to enhance one's sense of wellbeing. Simple pleasures are the best – an effort to enjoy the beauties of life is not necessarily expensive.

Mercury sextile Neptune (occurring March 29 – April 2) Mercury in Aries sextile Neptune in Aquarius brings bold, independent messages that inform us of opportunities for spiritual growth in humanity. This is an opportunistic time to cautiously attempt communication with regard to beliefs and spiritual matters. Mercury is in Aries, adding a fiery urgency to the question of how to face such Neptune related subjects as spiritual strength, guidance, and inspiration. Address addiction problems with helpful instruction. Mercury sextile Neptune allows us to verbalize and share beliefs in a way that encourages people. This aspect will reoccur on November 27 with Mercury in Sagittarius. Due to Mercury's final retrograde period this year (Dec. 10 – 29), this aspect will also return December 20.

April 1ˢᵗ Thursday

April Fool's Day

Moon in Scorpio	PDT	EDT
Moon trine Jupiter	11:34 AM	2:34 PM
Mercury trine Pluto begins (see April 6)		

" Any fool can criticize, condemn and complain and most fools do. "
– Benjamin Franklin (1706 – 1790)

Birthday: Susan Boyle 1961

Mood Watch: The Moon wanes in Scorpio and this is a time of eagerness and passion. Moon trine Jupiter brings a joyous outreach for success and wellbeing. Interactive and profound moods delight our senses with the desire to participate in all kinds of activity. Happy **April Fool's Day**, also known as *All Fools' Day*. This is a holiday of uncertain origin, but just about everybody knows it as the day for practical joking. Before the adoption of the Gregorian calendar in 1564, April 1ˢᵗ was observed as New Year's Day by many cultures from the Roman to the Hindu. This holiday is considered to be related to the festival of the Vernal Equinox, when the Sun enters Aries, on or about March 20ᵗʰ.

April 2ⁿᵈ Friday

Good Friday

Moon in Scorpio / Sagittarius	PDT	EDT
Moon square Neptune goes v/c	5:53 AM	8:53 AM
Mercury enters Taurus	6:05 AM	9:05 AM
Moon enters Sagittarius	9:53 AM	12:53 PM
Moon sextile Saturn	10:34 AM	1:34 PM
Moon trine Mars	3:47 PM	6:47 PM

Birthday: Giovanni Casanova 1725

Mood Watch:: For a brief time this morning, the Scorpio Moon goes void-of-course. Intense morning moods put our emotions into a guarded expression, and it's always wise to be careful and watchful for potential dangers. Old wounds or emotional afflictions require some sort of healing process. As the Moon enters Sagittarius, adventurous moods abound. The waning Sagittarius Moon brings insight. Introspective moods are also present with this Moon. This is a good time to travel, or to contemplate future trips and exploration.

Mercury enters Taurus (occurring April 2 – June 9) Mercury moves into the sign of Taurus, and communications will focus on manifesting sales and generating economic growth. It is a good time to clarify matters involving valuables, and to focus on documents, contracts, speeches, and business procedures. Mercury is the messenger, the speaker and the director of the subject matter at hand. Mercury is also classically known as "The Merchant," "The Trickster," and "The Thief." In the fixed earth sign of Taurus, Mercury inspires the inclination to buy, sell, trade, and barter. Issues of ownership and, undoubtedly, a "steal of a deal" will appear in the arena of barter. Resourceful thinking and information processing can lead to the extra buck. This is a time to accurately record practical matters and events, and to communicate about finances.

April 3rd Saturday

Moon in Sagittarius	PDT	EDT
Venus square Mars	4:25 AM	7:25 AM
Moon trine Sun	11:24 AM	2:24 PM
Moon square Jupiter	7:02 PM	10:02 PM

Birthday: Doris Day 1924

Mood Watch: Sun in Aries and Moon in Sagittarius bring a very fiery, active, and creative time. From Greek mythology, the Centaur is the symbol of Sagittarius. Centaurs are a race of creatures that are half human and half horse. They are famous in children's books for being stargazers, foretellers of the future, and they are also considered to be benevolent and wise, loyal to the very end. Throughout the course of the day, we are touched by the need to look ahead and to apply the wisdom and moral self-discipline to overcome the troublesome limitations of a treacherous and uncertain new century. Even when life's continuing difficulties seem insurmountable, the wisdom of the centaur reminds us to hold an optimistic outlook, no matter what. This evening's Moon square Jupiter brings moods challenged by the depletion of resources. Use the force of the Centaur's positive energy. Visionary images have great morale lifting influences; it's a step towards prosperity.

Venus square Mars (occurring March 28 – April 6) Venus in Taurus square Mars in Leo emphasizes the difficulties we may encounter (square aspect) over the maintenance of our treasured possessions, and the things we love (Venus in Taurus) – and the need to apply courageous action (Mars in Leo). Venus square Mars creates tension and obstacles between the forces of love and the forces of defense. The archetypal images of Venus and Mars are largely that of feminine and masculine counterparts, and this aspect may bring stress between people in love relationships. The pain of separation or the sorrow of unrequited love may be a symptom of this time, as the rocky boat of romance is due to have some notable ups and downs. On the other hand, the difficulties of these tests may strengthen the power of love and, although it is sometimes very difficult to endure love related conflicts, it is also a necessary process to ensure the authenticity of our love experience.

April 4th Sunday

Easter

Moon in Sagittarius / Capricorn	PDT	EDT	
Moon square Uranus	1:31 PM	4:31 PM	
Moon sextile Neptune goes v/c	1:58 PM	4:58 PM	
Moon enters Capricorn	6:07 PM	9:07 PM	
Moon square Saturn	6:30 PM	9:30 PM	
Venus trine Pluto	8:11 PM	11:11 PM	
Mercury square Mars	9:20 PM	12:20 AM	(April 5)

Birthday: Robert Downey, Jr. 1965

Mood Watch: The waning Sagittarius Moon brings idealistic and optimistic moods this morning and throughout the first part of the day. However, this afternoon the Moon goes void-of-course for a number of hours, and by then our moods will be distracted by detours, or by feeling lost. Our idealism may appear all too unrealistic and downright spacey. As the Moon enters Capricorn, our moods will be much more determined, and fixed on success. Capricorn Moon tempers the peculiar way we've been feeling today with a sound dose of reality. Tonight is the time to prioritize goals and to strategize a workable game plan for the week ahead.

Venus trine Pluto (occurring March 30 – April 7) Venus in Taurus is trine to Pluto in Capricorn. Practical beauty, the value of nature, and efforts to make the planet greener are enhanced and made stronger as we wade through the hardships of a vast landscape of irreversible change and transformation. Now is the time to let our ecological wishes be known, as those who are in positions of power are a little more likely to acknowledge the value of land preservation for the sake of delicate ecosystems. Beauty can be found in all aspects of existence. Venus trine Pluto represents a love or fascination for the workings of fate and power. This aspect often allows a breakthrough to occur for those who are under stress from hardship. There is hope yet that we will acquire an appreciation for the not-so-glamorous aspects of existence. This is also an aspect that allows for adoration and loving energy to flow more easily between generations, despite all the differences that have separated us in these fast changing times. This aspect will reoccur July 13, with Venus in Virgo.

Mercury square Mars (occurring March 31 – April 28) Mercury in Taurus is square to Mars in Leo. Efforts to barter or communicate, and attempts to be practical may seem complicated by stubbornness (Mercury in Taurus), particularly when it comes to taking action with family, friends, or the self (Mars in Leo). This is not a good time to lose one's temper. Be especially careful to watch what you say, preferably thinking before you speak; words can be easily taken the wrong way. This aspect stimulates arguments and mental blocks concerning people's actions, and it may lead to verbal abuse and destruction among family and friends. Refrain from making risky comments, and be careful not to misinterpret information as being hostile or personal. Remember, during this complex time of Mercury square Mars, not to shoot the messenger. This aspect occurs for a longer than usual period due to Mercury retrograde (April 17 – May 11). It will also reach a second peak, during this occurrence period, on April 25, while Mercury is in the prime of its upcoming retrograde period.

April 5th Monday

Moon in Capricorn	PDT	EDT
Moon trine Mercury	2:02 AM	5:02 AM
Moon conjunct Pluto	4:42 AM	7:42 AM
Moon trine Venus	5:38 AM	8:38 AM

Birthday: Algernon Charles Swinburne 1837

Mood Watch: The Capricorn Moon is a splendid Moon to get motivated, particularly with this morning's Moon trine Venus aspect, enticing us to seek enjoyment while concentrating on various tasks. Perhaps a hint of spring weather is also putting us in good spirits this Monday. Sun in Aries and Moon in Capricorn generally bring serious moods that require a sense of triumph. Capricorn says: "I Use," and this requires resourceful and determined effort. Are you making good use of your time? This is sure to bring progress. However, some folks may feel more like they're being used than useful. Creative efforts to determine the usefulness of your labors will allow you to find out what's in it for you. Make use of life by putting something into it, and make sure you're getting something useful in return.

April 6th Tuesday

LAST QUARTER MOON in CAPRICORN

Moon in Capricorn	PDT	EDT
Moon square Sun	2:37 AM	5:37 AM
Mercury trine Pluto	3:48 AM	6:48 AM
Moon sextile Jupiter	6:42 AM	9:42 AM
Pluto goes retrograde	7:35 PM	10:35 PM
Mercury-conjunct-Venus-non-exact (see below)		

Birthday: Baba Ram Dass 1931

Mood Watch: The **Last Quarter Moon in Capricorn** (Moon square Sun) is here. This Moon emphasizes issues of control – whether that means taking control or letting go of it where needed. The waning Capricorn Moon reminds us not to give up, to persist as the mountain goat does, and to find a way to overcome the steep and rocky roads. Capricorn Moon gives moods a serious undertone of needing and wanting to take hold of our goals and create results. Saturn ruled Capricorn emphasizes time and the timeliness of important events. This may be a time to address impending deadlines. Life is so serious with Capricorn Moon in its last quarter state; it reminds us that in order to be in control we must let go of that which we can't control. Attached to success? How important is success to you? Persistence wins overall where there is a stubborn drive to excel.

Mercury trine Pluto (occurring April 1 – 8) Mercury in Taurus trine Pluto in Capricorn brings resourceful thoughts and communications that will have powerful results. This aspect brings hope like a gift, and the myth of Pandora's Box shows us that hope regenerates our senses and fills us with the potential for triumph over difficulties. Mercury in Taurus gives a very practical and logical quality to our communications. This is a good time to share tales of triumph, spreading those miraculous stories that remind us of the potential of winning against all odds. This positive aspect aids communication about struggles with fate, major financial

100

losses, and fatal illnesses. Mercury will be retrograde in Taurus (April 17 – May 11) causing this aspect to reoccur on May 3. This could be the year for us to receive a lot of beneficial news from the world's superpowers, as this aspect will reoccur on three other occasions, May 19, July 30, and finally, September 12 (non-exact).

Pluto goes retrograde (Pluto retrograde: April 6 – Sept. 13) Processes governed by Pluto take the longest time to go through since, from our perspective, Pluto appears to move the slowest of all the planets because it's the furthest away from us. Pluto goes retrograde today and when it resumes a forward moving course late this summer, it will have traveled only a few degrees in the sky, which is average for a Pluto retrograde period. This means the types of hardships that have been created and brought to our attention in the past five months must be addressed all over again, and that we must acknowledge the evolution of humankind's current condition in order to survive the changes that are occurring on Earth.

Pluto deals with the changes that occur in attitude according to the overall group consciousness of each of the generations. Each generation has its own insight as to what hardship represents. This is a time to make life better by consciously transforming fear into determination and despair into belief in oneself, no matter what condition of fate surrounds you. The destructive habits, prejudices, sufferings and haunts of previous generations must be acknowledged and addressed – and of course – altered to enable us to tackle the world of the future. We will all face greater challenges and tests of epic proportions, and outdated concerns must be dealt with so that we may find solutions to the new problems in front of us.

With Pluto's changes we must face tragedies, diseases, losses (particularly monetary), shattered dreams, and altered or unexpected doses of reality. Pluto retrograde forces us to look within; this is a good time to confirm our greatest strengths by directing abusive patterns into constructive and useful disciplines which will reshape and bring hope to the emerging outlook on life.

Pluto represents the forces of power and control, which are always in a state of flux due to our mortal tango with fate. Pluto will retrograde back to the two degree mark (the Cusp) of Capricorn, and although it doesn't actually return to the Sagittarius constellation, it is still making the transition from Sagittarius related changes. Reality and normality are illusions that Pluto sweeps away as its final salute to Sagittarius opens up the last visionary glimpses of our transformational understanding of global awareness, and as it increases our foresight of worldwide struggles. Pluto retrograde is a time of readdressing universal human problems that take decades to fix.

Pluto, newly in the sign of Capricorn (since Jan. 25, 2008), will now influence such Capricorn related focuses as corporate growth, architectural feats, monumental achievements, industrial capitalization, environmental control, and many unprecedented forms of success and goal attainment. It is through the retrograde process that Pluto in Capricorn will shape and re-examine our views and perspectives on the large scale changes occurring on our planet.

Mercury-conjunct-Venus-non-exact (occurring March 26 – April 11) Today's near conjunction of Mercury and Venus only comes within a couple of degrees, and it takes place in the down-to-earth, material conscious, realm of Taurus. This is often a time when intimate and loving thoughts are best reciprocated in an atmosphere of luxury, comfort, and beauty. Where these things are not present, there is much talk about the desire for them. This is not a good time to have strong expectations in the expression of love, nor is it a time to take offense if your own attempts to express your love are poorly interpreted. This conjunction last occurred in Capricorn on January 5. It also occurs on October 25.

April 7th Wednesday

Moon in Capricorn / Aquarius

	PDT	EDT
Moon sextile Uranus goes v/c	1:18 AM	4:18 AM
Moon enters Aquarius	5:51 AM	8:51 AM
Moon trine Saturn	5:52 AM	8:52 AM
Saturn enters Virgo	11:51 AM	2:51 PM
Moon opposite Mars	3:02 PM	6:02 PM
Moon square Mercury	8:47 PM	11:47 PM

Birthday: Billie Holiday 1915

Mood Watch: Very early this morning, there may be some slightly stubborn moods that can stifle our sense of motivation while the Moon is void-of-course in Capricorn; but before we know it, the Moon enters Aquarius, and our moods will be more thoughtful and innovative. The Aquarius Moon atmosphere enlivens our outlook in unusual and dynamic ways. Moon trine Saturn gives us the incentive to concentrate on timely matters and to take control of morning tasks. Today's Moon opposite Mars aspect brings loads of action into what will be the busiest part of the day. Later on, Moon square Mercury leads to complicated thought processes and noncommunicative moods. Aquarius Moon challenges us to overcome the impossible with brilliant solutions.

Saturn enters Virgo (Saturn in Virgo: April 7 – July 21) The retrograde Saturn is re-entering Virgo for the last time in this cycle as it traverses through the late degrees of Virgo today through July 21. Saturn first entered Virgo on September 2, 2007 and it has seen us through some very large transitions, particularly with a world wide economic crunch and a number of shifts in leadership. Saturn in Virgo demands prudent and carefully analysis with regard to setting up perimeters and implementing rules. Discipline and the act of setting limits are emphasized in such Virgo related things as accounting, budget control, health care, the control and study of mental diseases, and the world of computers and communications technology. Virgo represents the development of structure through communications, and the preservation of the power and unique qualities of cultural and artistic pursuits.

Saturn in Virgo emphasizes disciplinary measures and carefully planned budgets, the very thing we've been forced to do through the arrival of the 21st century's first recession. So far, Saturn in Virgo has meant serious business for the survival of competitive companies, and consequently, a mutable landslide of jobs and occupations have undergone massive change or even extinction.

Saturn is there to remind us of the work required to deal with the harsh realities of life. When the work is done, our efforts are often rewarded with a sense of real accomplishment, as long as we act responsibly on the things in life that really matter to us and that are actually posing a threat or needing attention. Virgo says: "I analyze." While Saturn travels through Virgo, structure and discipline, when applied to analysis and forethought, bring magnanimous results. Here, there is no room for Virgo's ability to question or to cast doubt. Here, it is skill, persistence, and indefatigable management that will support grand feats of accomplishment during Saturn's last sweep through Virgo.

April 8th Thursday

Holy Day of Thelema (Nuit)

Moon in Aquarius	PDT	EDT
Moon square Venus	12:49 AM	3:49 AM
Moon sextile Sun	8:52 PM	11:52 PM

" Every man and every woman is a star. " - LIBER AL vel LEGIS, 1904

Birthday: Julian Lennon 1963

Mood Watch: The Aquarius Moon engages our moods with a sense of scientific foresight. Our moods are inspired by intelligence and enlightenment. Aquarius Moon gives us the incentive to tackle puzzling problems, and the waning Aquarius Moon often leaves us contemplative over the types of problems that could only be described as "manmade". If there's some form of logic that got us into a mess, there is indeed another kind of logic that will get us out of it. The Aquarius Moon gives our moods the extra push to seek out the knowledge that is necessary to succeed.

April 9th Friday

Holy Day of Thelema (Hadit)

Moon in Aquarius / Pisces	PDT	EDT
Moon conjunct Neptune goes v/c	2:43 PM	5:43 PM
Moon enters Pisces	6:48 PM	9:48 PM

" Let the rituals be rightly performed with joy & beauty ! " - LIBER AL vel LEGIS, 1904

Birthday: Charles Baudelaire 1821

Mood Watch: Out there in space, most of the planets of our universe currently travel through fire, earth and water signs, but only two planets, the Moon and Neptune, both conjunct today, travel through an air sign. Less air related influence often means that there is less attention being paid to the intellectual world and more attention to desires, physical things, and emotions. Waning Aquarius Moon puts us in the mood to think things through, and it sparks the imagination with idealistic – and sometimes impractical – schemes. Questions are often asked in hypothetical terms, and the reality or fact of a matter cannot be fully comprehended. It is up to the more air-influenced and air-oriented people among us to responsibly tend to the unyielding urgencies of the need for intelligence. As the Aquarius Moon goes void-of-course, the tendency towards mindlessness leads to numerous inconveniences. It may even seem like the Grand Architect of the Universe forgot to consult the Grand Engineer, the Grand Builder, and the Grand

Financier. But seriously, folks, the important thing to remember with Aquarius is: have some love and respect for humanity, despite the incompetence and lack of common sense that often comes with it. Tonight's Pisces Moon enlivens our moods with mystical reverie and tranquility.

April 10th Saturday

Holy Day of Thelema (Ra-Hoor-Khuit)

Moon in Pisces	PDT	EDT
Moon sextile Pluto	5:43 AM	8:43 AM
Moon sextile Mercury	2:37 PM	5:37 PM
Moon sextile Venus	8:32 PM	11:32 PM

" There is success ! "   - LIBER AL vel LEGIS, 1904

Birthday: Linda Goodman 1925

Mood Watch: The Piscean Moon fortifies our moods with a fascination for the mystical arts. Neptune rules Pisces, and today it is the only planet in an air sign. Intelligence is inspired by mystery, and mysterious themes are at work. Music, dance, art, poetry, and all those things that enliven the senses are the kinds of things that call out to our moods on this springtime Saturday. As the Moon wanes in Pisces, there is also a tendency towards escapism and the need for fantasy. In the right context, there is no harm in flights of the imagination. In fact, significant discoveries are born out of our need to explore new realities.

April 11th Sunday

Moon in Pisces	PDT	EDT
Moon conjunct Jupiter	10:12 AM	1:12 PM

Birthday: Louise Lasser 1939

Mood Watch: The theme of the mystical arts carries over into today's activities with the waning Moon in Pisces. The only aspect today, Moon conjunct Jupiter, brings an obsessive focus on the need for joy, happiness, and prosperity. The darkly waning Pisces Moon can sometimes be the source of our depressions, our need for escapism, or for our tendencies towards substance abuse. Moon conjunct Jupiter in Pisces brings a strong desire for advancement, enlightenment, and expansion. Here is a positive opportunity for us to empower our beliefs and our convictions. This is the time to dream, and to dream BIG. The Moon will reach the new mark in Aries this Wednesday. Take the next few days to guide your dreams with the positive reinforcement of your beliefs. The New Aries Moon will help you get started with the process of actualizing your big dream(s).

April 12th Monday

Moon in Pisces / Aries	PDT	EDT
Moon conjunct Uranus	2:39 AM	5:39 AM
Moon opposite Saturn goes v/c	5:51 AM	8:51 AM
Moon enters Aries	6:32 AM	9:32 AM
Moon square Pluto	5:02 PM	8:02 PM
Moon trine Mars	6:14 PM	9:14 PM

Birthday: Tiny Tim 1930

Mood Watch: This morning will have its time altering difficulties and illusions with the Pisces Moon going void-of-course as it opposes Saturn. Fortunately, our spacey and reluctant moods will shift quickly as the Moon enters Aries. There is eagerness in our moods, and an aggressive desire to launch into new patterns of life. This evening's Moon square Pluto brings intensity, particularly in areas of life that seem too powerful to expediently change. A positive breakthrough of activity comes later this evening with Moon trine Mars, and at this point our moods will be much more responsive, lively, and inspired.

April 13th Tuesday

Moon in Aries
   No Exact Aspects
   Venus sextile Jupiter begins (see April 17)
   Sun sextile Neptune begins (see April 18)

Birthday: Thomas Jefferson 1743

Mood Watch: There are no significant exact aspects occurring at this time while the darkly waning Moon builds a powerful sense of anticipation. The Aries Moon is currently in the *balsamic* phase, and this is a time of internal reflection, particularly with regard to the need for courage, self-assurance, integrity, and determination. Aries brings out the warrior spirit, as well as a competitive drive to excel and be successful. At best, our moods will be enthusiastic, courageous, and carefree. At worst, we can expect moods that will be headstrong, hot tempered, or unwittingly rude. Springtime restlessness is in the air.

April 14th Wednesday

NEW MOON in ARIES

Moon in Aries / Taurus	PDT	EDT
Moon conjunct Sun	5:28 AM	8:28 AM
Moon sextile Neptune goes v/c	12:21 PM	3:21 PM
Moon enters Taurus	3:55 PM	6:55 PM

Birthday: Julie Christie 1941

Mood Watch: The **New Moon in Aries** (Moon conjunct Sun) invokes the powers of initiation; it is the essential part of regenerative force to take the initiative and to start anew. This is the time when the new parts of the self begin to emerge, and our moods are encouraged by confidence, motivation, courageousness, and fiery intent. Now is the time to generate and promote inspiration and happiness. In general, the spirit of our moods brings a strong sense of newness and a great deal of activity. For a time the Aries Moon will be void-of-course, and this is always a good time to beware of the potential for accidents. Later on today, the Moon enters Taurus and our eager Aries Moon attitudes will be softened by the cool sentimentality of the earthy qualities of Taurus. Inspiration comes with the desire to attain the material goods and services that make us feel content, beautiful, and luxurious.

April 15th Thursday

Moon in Taurus	PDT	EDT
Moon trine Pluto	1:59 AM	4:59 AM
Moon square Mars	4:35 AM	7:35 AM
Moon conjunct Mercury	2:54 PM	5:54 PM

Birthday: Emma Thompson 1959

Mood Watch: Early this morning, as we work off the steam of aggression and tension while the Moon is square to Mars, we have successfully overcome the most hostile energy of the day. What lies beyond enlivens our senses with the soothing pursuit of beauty and pleasure. The newly waxing Taurus Moon brings material focuses, a bustling energy in the marketplace, and a firm sense of enterprising gaiety. Later today, Moon conjunct Mercury brings talkative and interactive moods that allow us to negotiate for the comforts, delights, and practical needs that give us a sense of having something tangible. Taurus Moon stimulates our sensibilities as well as our sensual yearning.

April 16th Friday

Moon in Taurus / Gemini	PDT	EDT	
Moon conjunct Venus	3:38 AM	6:38 AM	
Moon sextile Jupiter	6:18 AM	9:18 AM	
Moon square Neptune	7:48 PM	10:48 PM	
Moon sextile Uranus	8:00 PM	11:00 PM	
Moon trine Saturn goes v/c	9:56 PM	12:56 AM	(April 17)
Moon enters Gemini	11:08 PM	2:08 AM	(April 17)

Birthday: John Millington Synge 1871

Mood Watch: The waxing Moon in Taurus reminds us to pay attention to the unfinished business of the physical world. Since there is no end to physical tasks, it is always best to harness the bull energy when it comes around. Taurus Moon in the spring often puts the focus on spring cleaning and yard sales. This is the time to clean, shine, wax, polish and upgrade the value of those things. Moon in Taurus puts us in touch with the value of not only "things," but also the soothing esthetic value of comfort, atmosphere, and beauty that enchants us all.

April 17th Saturday

Moon in Gemini	PDT	EDT	
Moon sextile Mars	12:46 PM	3:46 PM	
Venus sextile Jupiter	1:43 PM	4:43 PM	
Mercury goes retrograde	9:07 PM	12:07 AM	(April 18)

Birthday: William Holden 1918

Mood Watch: The waxing Moon in Gemini opens us to communication and the handling of details. People will tend to communicate what has been on their minds. However, Gemini is ruled by Mercury, and today Mercury will go retrograde (see below), creating complexity and confusion around our attempts to communicate. Gemini Moon focuses our attention on those areas of life where we have mixed feelings, and there is a tendency to mull over those things that have not settled just right in our minds. Take a deep breath and avoid hasty decisions. It will take awhile to adjust to the perplexity of our easily misunderstood mental processes.

Venus sextile Jupiter (occurring April 13 – 19) Venus is in Taurus, the place of luxury, beauty, and sensual love play. Jupiter is in Pisces, bringing an intuitive and imaginative outreach for fulfillment and a joyful effort towards getting in touch with the things we love. Comfortable – as well as practical – attractions and pleasures (Venus in Taurus) lead us to possible opportunities in the arts, music, literature, counseling, and the metaphysical arts and sciences (Jupiter in Pisces). This is an excellent time to shower loved ones with gifts and compliments in a way that uplifts their spirits. This is the time to allow expansion to occur in love matters, and to take the next step towards enlivening and enhancing the beauty of life. A greater opportunity for increasing skills or augmenting your livelihood is available, especially if your focus remains on doing what you love most. This is the only time this aspect will occur this year.

Mercury goes retrograde (Mercury retrograde: April 17 – May 11) Mercury goes retrograde today in the sign of Taurus; it will travel back to the two degree mark of Taurus before going direct on May 11. Mercury retrograde in Taurus commonly causes problems and confusion when relaying information about possessions and properties. In Taurus, the retrograde Mercury often causes communication mix-ups with regard to valuables in general, especially things like business contracts, banking matters, and practical kinds of necessities such as scheduling and appointments. Despite rational and fair minded attempts to spontaneously articulate practical and down-to-earth subjects, Mercury retrograde in Taurus will often leave us dissatisfied and tongue tied. Establishing a clear understanding will be the most important part of engaging in various kinds of agreements. Expect to repeat yourself more than once or twice, and to be persistent as well as patient during this time. Whatever you agree on, if it's very important, *get it in writing*! For more information on Mercury retrograde, see the section in the introduction about *Mercury retrograde periods*.

April 18th Sunday

Moon in Gemini	PDT	EDT
Sun sextile Neptune	1:15 AM	4:15 AM
Moon square Jupiter	1:10 PM	4:10 PM
Venus square Neptune begins (see April 23)		

Birthday: Leopold Stokowski 1882

Mood Watch: Learn to flip the coin of duality by taking in, hearing and witnessing both sides of the equation. Choose your thoughts integrally and wisely, and on the flip side of the coin, learn to laugh at the comedy of spontaneous confusion in a knowledge driven society full of layered ignorance and unsorted data. It doesn't help that people may seem a lot less generous and outgoing while the Moon squares Jupiter. Our Gemini Moon moods will play around with new data and allow for new ideas. Get to know your wiser self by choosing your cosmology well. Avoid idle chatter and gossip. New feelings and moods will continually arise because the Gemini Moon has the cauldron of our emotions stirred by our thoughts, and also due to the recent commencement of Mercury retrograde (see yesterday).

Sun sextile Neptune (occurring April 13 – 20) This occurrence of Sun sextile Neptune creates an opportunistic time for those Aries and Taurus people celebrating birthdays from April 13 – 20. These folks are experiencing an opportunity to awaken in the realm of spirituality and creativity. There is an awareness of the self that goes deep here, and these birthday people are likely to appear distracted and difficult to reach while this phenomenon of great depth is occurring. This will be your year, birthday folks, to explore personal opportunities of spiritual growth. It may be a time to get away from it all, and find a sanctuary in which to meditate and open up to some valuable answers to old questions. These folks are in a place that gives them an opportunity to better understand the work of their path, but this is probably only true if they act on their own intuitive sensibilities, without the influences of others. That shouldn't be too hard for the enterprising and self-motivated Aries natures among us, as well as the (cusp born) practical minded Taurians. This will be your year (birthday people) to enhance and strengthen your intuition and primal instincts by tapping into them while they are easily available. This may also be the time to overcome additions and disruptive patterns. This aspect will reoccur on December 18 with the Sun in Sagittarius.

TAURUS

Key Phrase: "I HAVE"

Fixed Earth Sign

Ruling Planet: Venus

Symbol: The Bull

April 19th through May 20th

April 19th Monday

Moon in Gemini / Cancer	PDT	EDT	
Moon trine Neptune	1:30 AM	4:30 AM	
Moon square Uranus	1:48 AM	4:48 AM	
Moon square Saturn	3:14 AM	6:14 AM	
Moon sextile Sun goes v/c	3:20 AM	6:20 AM	
Moon enters Cancer	4:39 AM	7:39 AM	
Moon opposite Pluto	2:04 PM	5:04 PM	
Sun enters Taurus	9:29 PM	12:29 AM	(April 20)
Venus trine Saturn begins (see April 24)			
Sun trine Pluto begins (see April 25)			

Birthday: Tim Curry 1946

108

Mood Watch: In the earliest hours of this day, some long winded lunar aspects may make for a restless night. Our moods will seem disoriented while the Moon is void-of-course in Gemini, but fortunately, the Moon enters Cancer while it's still early, giving us some time to adjust to the moody quality this Cancer Moon morning brings. Waxing Cancer Moon is a good time to pay attention to your feelings, especially now that Mercury is retrograde (see April 17). When the mind is uncertain, our emotions tell us a lot about the mood.

Sun enters Taurus (Sun in Taurus: April 19/20 – May 20) Taurus is a Venus ruled sign whose attraction to beauty is second nature. As a general rule, Taurus energy promotes a strong desire to keep physically fit, and to keep possessions and personal effects shining and looking good. Taurus has a very matter-of-fact way of looking at life, and likes to keep the surroundings neat and functional, as well as aesthetically pleasing and socially acceptable. This is not to say that Taurus folks are orderly according to the rest of the world! They have a very sensitive and often sentimental side, and find it difficult to change and adapt swiftly when their lives seem to be in perfect order. Taurus loves stability and security. Taurus folks have a knack for smelling money and for finding the value in all things. Taurus says, "I have," and Taurus folks are interested in preserving and enhancing what they have attained and acquired in the course of their lives.

April 20ᵗʰ Tuesday

Moon in Cancer

	PDT	EDT
Moon sextile Mercury	2:18 AM	5:18 AM
Moon trine Jupiter	6:28 PM	9:28 PM
Venus sextile Uranus begins (see April 23)		

Birthday: Napoleon III 1808

Mood Watch: If someone reaches out to you, it sometimes means they trust you, or sometimes manipulative motivation is at work. When the Moon is in Cancer and someone is opening up to you, it is potentially dangerous to ignore them. Cancer Moon brings out our need for nurturing reassurance and, sometimes, motherly affection and advice are needed. It is an honor to be trusted by someone, and it is even more honorable when we do not break that trust. Sometimes we need to learn how to just listen, not judge, and give our advice only when it is asked of us. There are many ways to care, and since people are often complex, it may take awhile before we learn how to care in a way that is helpful. Don't buy guilt – it's far too expensive! Besides, today's lunar aspects are positive in nature and there is cause for joy and gratitude.

April 21st Wednesday

FIRST QUARTER MOON in LEO

Moon in Cancer / Leo	PDT	EDT
Moon sextile Venus	12:32 AM	3:32 AM
Moon trine Uranus	6:08 AM	9:08 AM
Moon sextile Saturn goes v/c	7:06 AM	10:06 AM
Moon enters Leo	8:42 AM	11:42 AM
Moon square Sun	11:19 AM	2:19 PM

Birthday: Queen Elizabeth II   1926

Mood Watch: For a little while this morning, it may be difficult to get into the swing of things as the Cancer Moon goes void-of-course, providing a tendency for moodiness and distraction. However, soon enough the Moon enters Leo, and the Cancerian moodiness fades into a courageous and charismatic attitude towards life. This much sunnier disposition comes with the expression of a **First Quarter Moon in Leo** (Moon square Sun), enhancing playfulness, self-indulgence, and the need for expression and adoration. Today's attractions tend to be towards those areas of life with which we identify the most. With the Sun in Taurus, the Moon in Leo is most likely expressed by the act of flashing around our best toys. Cool is always "in," and requires the assurance of the proper attitude.

April 22nd Thursday

Earth Day

Moon in Leo	PDT	EDT
Moon conjunct Mars	12:17 AM	3:17 AM
Moon square Mercury	4:42 AM	7:42 AM

"I really wonder what gives us the right to wreck this poor planet of ours"
- Kurt Vonnegut Jr. (1922 -   )

Birthday: Charles Mingus 1922

Mood Watch: This morning's Moon square Mercury brings abominable mental blocks. It doesn't help that Earth Day occurs with Mercury retrograde (April 17 – May 11), making this a difficult time to organize big events. Nevertheless, the significant raising of consciousness doesn't have to happen with large numbers. The significance starts locally with large convictions. The Leo Moon inspires us to connect with friends and family and to do what's right for the Earth. Leo Moon moods are enhanced by the act of amusing others. Make this day fun and entertaining by utilizing creative kinds of stunts, props, and ideas that will remind us all of the necessity to act responsibly for planet Earth. Of all the planets of our solar system, so far, Earth is the only inhabitable one. Leo Moon is a great time to act on personal convictions.

April 23rd Friday

Moon in Leo / Virgo	PDT	EDT
Moon square Venus	8:10 AM	11:10 AM
Moon opposite Neptune goes v/c	8:34 AM	11:34 AM
Moon enters Virgo	11:25 AM	2:25 PM

	PDT	EDT
Venus square Neptune	12:53 PM	3:53 PM
Moon trine Sun	5:39 PM	8:39 PM
Venus sextile Uranus	7:06 PM	10:06 PM
Moon trine Pluto	8:19 PM	11:19 PM
Mercury trine Pluto begins (see May 3)		
Sun square Mars begins (see May 4)		

♉

Birthday: Shirley Temple Black 1928

Mood Watch: This morning's Moon square Venus may bring unpleasant moods. This is swiftly followed by the confusion and doubt of Moon opposite Neptune gone void-of-course. Selfish or self-oriented types of moods will keep us busily aware of the fact that it will be difficult to get some decent service this morning. As the Moon enters Virgo, our moods will be inquisitive, adaptable, and at times, skeptical. Virgo Moon is a good time to clean up the environment and to purify the body with digestible and nourishing foods and supplements.

Venus square Neptune (occurring April 18 – 26) This may be a difficult – or extra busy – time to be drawn to or to meditate on spiritual matters or activities. Art with a spiritual approach may appear more phony than ethereal. Feminine expression may be set back by antiquated beliefs. Love matters could be rocky due to a conflict of beliefs. Venus is in Taurus, where the art of attraction often occurs on the physical plane, while Neptune is in Aquarius, formulating a new spiritual outlook for humankind. Venus influences beauty, attraction, and magnetism. Neptune is the higher spiritual vibration of the feminine spirit, the higher octave of Venus herself – the imperfect yet alluring mortal versus the perfect and irresistible goddess. When these two planets are in conflict, it is a time when women are being sent mixed messages about how to live up to a higher standard of the self. This aspect will begin reoccurring on December 28, when Venus will be in Scorpio, and it will reach its peak on January 4, dissipating on January 7, 2011.

Venus sextile Uranus (occurring April 20 – 25) Venus in Taurus is sextile to Uranus in Pisces. Natural beauty takes on a radical or unusual kind of expression. Venus sextile Uranus can encourage us to break useless tendencies and habits, and also may bring an opportunity for love related matters to transcend the restriction of unmet personal needs. Venus sextile Uranus last occurred on January 13, when Venus was in Capricorn.

April 24th Saturday

Moon in Virgo

	PDT	EDT	
Venus trine Saturn	12:43 AM	3:43 AM	
Moon trine Mercury	5:27 AM	8:27 AM	
Venus enters Gemini	10:05 PM	1:05 AM	(April 25)
Sun conjunct Mercury begins (see April 28)			

Birthday: Barbara Streisand 1942

Mood Watch: According to one source, environmentalists celebrate Earth Day on Vernal Equinox (March 20). Earth Day is officially on April 22 every year. However, many folks celebrate Earth Day events on the weekend. We may as well call this *Earth Week* since so much work and publicity are required to inspire the masses to jump on the Green Earth Bandwagon. Today's Moon is in the mutable earth sign of Virgo, inspiring us to research our earthbound facts, and to analyze the situation that planet earth has reached.

Venus trine Saturn (occurring April 19 – 26) When Venus interacts with Saturn it brings a very timely quality to relationships, and raises the questions of commitment and devotion with regard to our active love connections. Fortunately, the trine aspect brings probabilities that are more positive in nature when it comes to the law of attraction. Today's aspect of Venus trine Saturn implies that there is a good possibility here for a happy ending. Venus in Taurus trine Saturn in Virgo brings an earthy, practical, and stable expression of love and commitment to love. Venus in Taurus emphasizes the need for a practical, responsibly sound commitment to the person or thing that holds the greatest attraction. Here is where we easily devote ourselves to the thing(s) that attract us most. This aspect last occurred on January 21 with Venus in Aquarius and Saturn in Libra.

Venus enters Gemini (Venus in Gemini April 24 – May 19) Venus, the influence of love, magnetism and attraction now enters Gemini, the personification of duality. Love desires may be split and suffer from ambivalence and schisms. Gemini people will focus more intently on personal attractions and love related matters, while Sagittarius folks may be overwhelmed by love concerns as Venus opposes their natal Sun. Virgo and Pisces people are also likely to feel affection related challenges or difficulties in their lives as Venus squares their natal Sun positions. Librans and Aquarians will find things a little easier. With Venus in Gemini, there is an attraction to writing, speaking about, and recording extraordinary love experiences and stories. Gossip and talk about love matters will be especially prevalent. Venus in Gemini shows us the two sides of love – the giving and the taking. As attractions appear more diverse, concerns may arise among those with a jealous nature. Love related changes are rampant – to some it's a challenge, while for others, it's a breath of fresh air.

April 25th Sunday

Moon in Virgo / Libra	PDT	EDT	
Moon opposite Jupiter	1:02 AM	4:02 AM	
Mercury square Mars	3:39 AM	6:39 AM	
Sun trine Pluto	8:44 AM	11:44 AM	
Moon opposite Uranus	11:08 AM	2:08 PM	
Moon conjunct Saturn goes v/c	11:20 AM	2:20 PM	
Moon enters Libra	1:17 PM	4:17 PM	
Moon trine Venus	2:40 PM	5:40 PM	
Moon square Pluto	10:07 PM	1:07 AM	(April 26)

Jupiter opposite Saturn begins (see May 22)
Jupiter conjunct Uranus begins (see June 8)

Birthday: Ella Fitzgerald 1917

Mood Watch: This morning's Sun in Taurus, in accompaniment with the waxing Virgo Moon, brings practicality, resourcefulness, and a deep curiosity. Our Virgo Moon moods will encourage us to question, analyze, and doubt anything that can't be easily proved. As the Moon goes void-of-course, it is also conjunct with Saturn and this may be a particularly doubtful period. In fact, we may find that we are unable to keep track of time. As the Moon enters Libra this afternoon, our moods will appear more cooperative. Less doubt and more harmony brings some balance into our moods. Moon trine Venus brings pleasurable moods. Tonight's Moon square Pluto will be a good time to avoid troubling and dramatic types of subject matter.

Mercury square Mars (occurring March 31 – April 28) Due to Mercury retrograde (April 17 – May 11), Mercury in Taurus square Mars in Leo is reaching its peak for the second time since April 4. Insults and verbal abuse are common with this aspect. It could be awhile, at least until Mercury goes direct (May 11), before currently erupting conflicts caused by some people's words and actions are smoothed over. This aspect will repeat for a third time on June 11 with Mercury in Gemini and Mars in Virgo. For a recap on the story of what's going on with this phase of Mercury square Mars, *see April 4*.

Sun trine Pluto (occurring April 19 – 28) Positive, life altering changes are occurring, particularly in the lives of those Aries/Taurus cusp born people celebrating birthdays this year from April 19 – 28. These folks are currently undergoing the favorable trine aspect of Pluto to their natal Sun, bringing out experiences that involve transformation, and encounters with greater powers and with fate. For some of these birthday folks, the concept of receiving gifts and empowerment in the midst of fateful events may seem rocky and not particularly advantageous. Have no fear; this is a time to get in touch with your power, birthday Aries/Taurus! It is wise to remember Pluto moves slowly in our cosmos, and powerful encounters that seem deadly or harsh are actually a necessary process. Though unavoidable, matters involving fate can be positive, and the trine aspect does represent a gift being bestowed. Aries/Taurus birthday people, be grateful this is the trine aspect that brings power issues into your life in a more positive fashion with Pluto, and the work of destiny will bestow untold gifts this year. Sun trine Pluto will reoccur August 25, affecting the Leo and Virgo cusp born people.

April 26ᵗʰ Monday

Moon in Libra	PDT	EDT
Moon sextile Mars	7:09 AM	10:09 AM
SATURN OPPOSITE URANUS	4:23 PM	7:23 PM

Birthday: Carol Burnett 1933

Mood Watch: The waxing Libra Moon atmosphere is studious, congenial, and interactive. The day will have its ups and downs, but most people will try to make the best of it. It will help to apply a loving and patient attitude when the boat is rocked. This is a good time to avoid excesses, to seek objectives, and to give some ample time to others to make decisions, deliberate, and plan events. This is especially true while Mercury is retrograde (April 17 – May 11).

Saturn opposite Uranus (occurring March 10 – Aug. 20) This long winded aspect first reared its alarming and unconventional head on the USA election day – November 4, 2008. With this came the obvious radical change of the unprecedented election of an African American president. This aspect then returned twice in 2009, first on February 5, and secondly, on September 15, 2009. Now it returns full swing as it bids a final farewell in 2010. Just as it appeared with a loud and rebellious bang, changing the course of history and radically breaking our lines of limitation and restriction, Saturn opposite Uranus is not likely to go out quietly during this eventful time of its return.

Saturn has been in the Mercury-ruled planet, Virgo, off and on since September 2, 2007, and Uranus has been in the Neptune-ruled sign, Pisces, since March 10, 2003. Out of the maintenance of the structurally unsound elements of the past (Saturn in Virgo,) comes the belief altering disruption and explosive chaos of definitive change (Uranus in Pisces). The stark reality of this aspect suggests Saturn, which represents order and structure, is indeed the very opposite kind of energy in the very opposite position to its opponent, Uranus, which represents chaos and disorder. What are the results of this significant polarization? Which of the two masters' energy will outweigh the other? Saturn being control, and Uranus being disruption, one might surmise the very best to hope for would be an elaborate exercise in learning to control the uncontrollable. From storms, earthquakes, shifts of ocean currents, and volcanic activity come all kinds of earth shifts. Saturn is in the *mutable earth* sign, Virgo, affecting the accounting world and the unstable shifts of world economy. It indicates the mutability and the adaptability of the physical world, and the shifting of the physical realm will be unpredictable and chaotic while Uranus's opposing influence continues to bring immense and irreparable change.

Both Saturn and Uranus have a strong impact on societies as a whole, and this aspect has been dramatically affecting the world at large. It implies that there has been an acute awareness of explosive endings occurring on the planet. Saturn represents our guard or defense, which is being placed in a challenged state of awareness (the opposition) over the radically revolutionary surge of consciousness and chaotic urgency that Uranus's energy creates.

The Saturn-Uranus opposition occurred back in the mid-1960s, bringing with it a wave of authority-questioning skepticism, revolution, rebellion, civil unrest, and massive protests. The essential difference of that time versus the present lies in the fact that Saturn was in Pisces and Uranus was in Virgo, while now, the opposite holds true. The polarity of Pisces and Virgo emphasizes the struggle between belief (Pisces) and doubt (Virgo). This polarity examines the compelling power of intuition (Pisces) versus the temptation (or propensity) to question or analyze with skepticism (Virgo). It represents an unconditional acceptance (Pisces) opposed to a conditional lack of acceptance (Virgo). The Neptune-ruled sign, Pisces, does not usually seek to explain that which can only be categorized as nebulous or uncertain, whereas the Mercury-ruled sign, Virgo, requires explanation, and needs evidence to support every argument – in short, Virgo needs certainty before abandoning all doubt. What binds the traits of this polarity is summed up in one word: susceptibility. We are made susceptible to all kinds of unpredictable trouble the moment we begin to believe or to doubt anything. Uranus in Virgo during the 60s brought a revolution of doubt and resistance; whereas Uranus in Pisces, this time around, brings a revolution of belief, intuition, and spiritual rebellion.

The severe collapse of infrastructures and monetary systems, of rules and regulations, has required a great deal of clean up and restructuring. Saturn contains structure, while Uranus breaks structure that is no longer feasible for containment. However you slice it, revolution will be evident, and catastrophic natural disasters may also be evident. During this occurrence period, this aspect will reach a peak again on July 26, and by then Saturn will be in Libra and Uranus will be in Aries.

♉

April 27th Tuesday

Full Moon Eve

Moon in Libra / Scorpio

	PDT	EDT
Moon trine Neptune goes v/c	12:45 PM	3:45 PM
Moon enters Scorpio	3:29 PM	6:29 PM

Birthday: Ulysses S. Grant 1822

Mood Watch: This morning's heavily waxing Libra Moon brings a strong focus on harmony and the need to clear up life's little imbalances. This afternoon as the Moon goes void-of-course, an indecisive period affects our moods. Later today as the Moon enters Scorpio, we may begin to notice the thrilling excitement of various kinds of passion at work. The Full Moon Eve is upon us. There will be an emphasis today on facing challenges, finding solutions, keeping active, and on winning. It's a good time to be cautious, to watch for the signs of thievery, deception, and violence. Adventurous and daring moods may lead to trouble, but Scorpio Moon also brings intuitive and psychic abilities which can assist people in navigating their way through rough waters.

April 28th Wednesday

FULL MOON in SCORPIO

Moon in Scorpio

	PDT	EDT
Moon sextile Pluto	12:31 AM	3:31 AM
Moon opposite Sun	5:18 AM	8:18 AM
Moon opposite Mercury	5:48 AM	8:48 AM
Sun conjunct Mercury	9:43 AM	12:43 PM
Moon square Mars	11:20 AM	2:20 PM

Birthday: Terry Prachett 1948

Mood Watch: The **Full Moon in Scorpio** (Moon opposite Sun) reaches its peak early this morning and was certainly busy affecting us last night. With this Moon our moods are – for lack of a better word – intensified. As this lunar fullness builds to a crescendo of emotional dramas, our emotional patterns are being played out in interesting ways. Intense desires – and what provokes them – reveal a lot about who we are and what we need to appease the satisfaction-hungry inner child. Entertaining fun, and off-the-cuff kinds of play and humor are good medicine. The Full Scorpio Moon is a good time for garden lovers to transplant flowers and shrubs. Safe physical exercises and activities are excellent avenues of release.

Sun conjunct Mercury (occurring April 24 – 30) This conjunction will create a much more thoughtful, communicative and expressive year ahead for those Taurus folks celebrating birthdays April 24 – 30. This is your time (birthday Taurus) to record ideas, relay important messages, and pay close attention to your imaginative thoughts as they are touched by Mercury, creating the urge to speak and be heard. Birthday Taurus, your thoughts will reveal a great deal about who you are, now and in the year to come.

April 29th Thursday

Moon in Scorpio / Sagittarius	PDT	EDT
Moon trine Jupiter	8:04 AM	11:04 AM
Moon square Neptune	4:48 PM	7:48 PM
Moon sextile Saturn	5:07 PM	8:07 PM
Moon trine Uranus goes v/c	5:39 PM	8:39 PM
Moon enters Sagittarius	7:36 PM	10:36 PM

Birthday: Duke Ellington 1899

Mood Watch: Scorpio Moon puts us in touch with our passion. There is success in passion. Why let the great transformations of our lives go uncelebrated? Yes, for some, today may seem intense, tiring, and melodramatic in the face of a full, but waning, Scorpio Moon. Some of us may feel victimized or hard done by. There is no easy way to experience change, yet it happens all the time. Scorpio Moon is here to remind us of that fact. For a couple of hours in the evening, the Moon goes void-of-course. This is the time to be especially cautious of misleading kinds of moods and melodramatic behavior. As the Moon enters Sagittarius, optimism and a philosophical outlook will temper our moods and help us to make sense of it all.

April 30th Friday

Moon in Sagittarius	PDT	EDT
Moon opposite Venus	7:23 AM	10:23 AM
Moon trine Mars	6:16 PM	9:16 PM

Birthday: Willie Nelson 1933

Mood Watch: In preparation for a new month arriving, coupled with the fact that the Moon was just full in Scorpio, we currently find ourselves drawn to the things that lie just beyond our reach with the Moon, now waning, in Sagittarius. This morning's Moon opposite Venus aspect brings the desire for friendship, love, and reassurance. This evening's Moon trine Mars aspect inspires us to be outgoing and to take some action. Sagittarius Moon is the time for visionary work. It's simple; envision the thing you want, and meditate on it throughout the day. Use this Sagittarius Moon to empower your vision for the month ahead!

May 1st Saturday

Beltane / May Day

Moon in Sagittarius	PDT	EDT
Moon square Jupiter	3:34 PM	6:34 PM

Birthday: Judy Collins 1939

Mood Watch: Today's Sagittarius Moon ensures our moods will be geared towards finding a cohesive and acceptable perspective on matters. As the Moon squares to Jupiter, our morale may seem somewhat challenged, and many folks will be dismayed by the apparent skyrocketing cost of living. Nonetheless, this Moon inspires optimism. Sagittarius Moon invites us to apply some extra creativity in order to make sense of it all. Philosophical perspectives are hard-driving with the post-full Moon of Sagittarius.

Happy **May Day!** This is a traditional old world solar holiday, also known as **Beltane**. We have now reached the half-way mark – and the height – of the spring season. This holiday celebrates the dance of the Maypole and fertility, beauty, rapturous love, and the various kinds of youthful play and frolic appropriate to spring. May Day is a celebration of the fruition and beauty fond in nature. It represents the awakening of the passion and youthfulness in all of life. This time calls to us all to take joy in the fertilization of those parts of ourselves and our lives that need to be brought to fruition.

May 2nd Sunday

Moon in Sagittarius / Capricorn	PDT	EDT
Moon sextile Neptune	12:05 AM	3:05 AM
Moon square Saturn	12:10 AM	3:10 AM
Moon square Uranus goes v/c	1:08 AM	4:08 AM
Moon enters Capricorn	3:00 AM	6:00 AM
Moon conjunct Pluto	1:05 PM	4:05 PM
Moon trine Mercury	1:47 PM	4:47 PM
Venus sextile Mars begins (see May 7)		

Birthday: Bianca Jagger 1945

Mood Watch: The waning Capricorn Moon is not generally considered a good time to explore people's feelings. During Sun in Taurus and Moon in Capricorn, people tend to be staunch, distant, or preoccupied with their work. This may be the time to talk dollars and cents, to cover material matters, and to get some serious business done. This afternoon, Moon conjunct Pluto may be a time when people seem especially insensitive, or they may be somewhat manipulative and daunting with their attitudes. There are times when we must be frank about our situations, and the waning Capricorn Moon acts as a buffer to separate emotional turmoil from the need to face important decisions. Since Mercury is retrograde (April 17 – May 11), this afternoon's Moon trine Mercury aspect will be a splendid time to think matters through and to sort out complex details wherever necessary.

May 3rd Monday

Moon in Capricorn	PDT	EDT
Moon trine Sun	3:57 AM	6:57 AM
Mercury trine Pluto	5:02 AM	8:02 AM

Birthday: James Brown 1933

Mood Watch: The Moon in Capricorn carries on for the second day in a row, and many people may feel that they are making some progress in business. It is best not to push this progress too swiftly, as Mercury retrograde may have a bearing on communication mistakes, particularly in matters of business. This is a good time to be direct, but thorough, and take your time. Consider carefully the impact of your deeds as well as your words.

Mercury trine Pluto (occurring April 23 – May 23) This could be the year for us to receive a lot of beneficial news from the world's superpowers, as this aspect is occurring five times this year! While Mercury is currently retrograde (April 17 – May 11) there may be some easily misinterpreted information with regard to fateful transitions. Nonetheless, Mercury trine Pluto often brings positive results despite the roundabout way of communications that Mercury retrograde periods often bring. For a recap on the story of Mercury in Taurus trine Pluto in Capricorn, *see April 6*, when it first occurred.

May 4th Tuesday

Moon in Capricorn / Aquarius	PDT	EDT	
Moon sextile Jupiter	2:47 AM	5:47 AM	
Sun square Mars	6:08 AM	9:08 AM	
Moon trine Saturn	10:39 AM	1:39 PM	
Moon sextile Uranus goes v/c	12:07 PM	3:07 PM	
Moon enters Aquarius	1:52 PM	4:52 PM	
Moon square Mercury	10:35 PM	1:35 AM	(May 5)

Birthday: Audrey Hepburn 1929

Mood Watch: The Capricorn Moon starts off the day with strong urges to make the most of our time, particularly during Moon trine Saturn. This brings an excellent time to concentrate and to take steps forward. As Moon sextile Uranus occurs, the urge for freedom breaks the morning concentration, and for a couple of hours, the Capricorn Moon will be void-of-course, causing a bit of a time warp on our efforts to make progress. As the Moon enters Aquarius, our moods are much more inclined to find brilliant or possibly even unorthodox solutions to our problems. Aquarius Moon inspires the need to know, and to be in-the-know.

Sun square Mars (occurring April 23 – May 9) This aspect particularly affects those Taurus born people celebrating birthdays this year from April 23 – May 9. It creates the illusion that obstacles are constantly getting in the way of the actions (and will) of these people. Harnessing energy seems like a chore. This is a good time for these people to lighten up on their expectations of themselves for awhile, and not let such setbacks get in the way of enjoying life. Relax! In time, it will be easier once again to get your personal goals and your willpower into a state of action. This may be an accident prone time in the lives of these birthday folks. Since this year may bring the tendency for accidents and mistakes, this will be a good time for these birthday folks to learn a great deal about how to pace themselves and to work through the obstacles in order to perfect personal visions and goals. This is the only time this aspect will occur this year.

May 5th Wednesday

Cinco de Mayo
LAST QUARTER MOON in AQUARIUS

Moon in Aquarius	PDT	EDT
Moon trine Venus	4:11 PM	7:11 PM

Moon opposite Mars	7:22 PM	10:22 PM	
Moon square Sun	9:15 PM	12:15 AM	(May 6)

♉

Birthday: Ann B. Davis 1926

Mood Watch: The **Last Quarter Moon in Aquarius** (Moon square Sun) brings humanitarian focuses to the scope of our experience. A kind word or sympathetic ear has great healing power and oftentimes promotes peace. This Moon beckons to us to find solutions, however temporary, to human problems, and it connects us with the dichotomies and ironies of the human experience. This is a time when the work of genius is ever present, but often goes undetected. As Moon trine Venus occurs, our moods will be geared towards showing affection and seeking out pleasurable kinds of experience. This evening's Moon opposite Mars brings a rush of activity.

May 6th Thursday
Moon in Aquarius

	PDT	EDT	
Moon conjunct Neptune goes v/c	11:36 PM	2:36 AM	(May 7)
Uranus-square-Pluto-non-exact begins (see July 23)			

Birthday: Tony Blair 1953

Mood Watch: The waning Moon in Aquarius inspires intelligence, and brings an open interest in gadgets, novelties, books, politics, and scientific experiments. This is the time when many will be making social connections. The signs of the times are all around us, applying some very interesting twists and turns in the ventures and knowledge of humankind. On some level, the desire for freedom or personal breakthrough calls out to some folks. The restlessness of spring season stirs our hearts. Sun in Taurus and Moon in Aquarius is an important time to banish fear and test the realms with one's own sensibilities. There's enough love and beauty to go around for everyone.

May 7th Friday
Moon in Aquarius / Pisces

	PDT	EDT
Moon enters Pisces	2:34 AM	5:34 AM
Moon sextile Mercury	9:20 AM	12:20 PM
Moon sextile Pluto	1:02 PM	4:02 PM
Venus sextile Mars	2:54 PM	5:54 PM

Birthday: Johannes Brahms 1833

Mood Watch: As the Moon enters Pisces, we may find our moods more flexible to adapt to a wide range of emotional experiences. Tap into your creative and intuitive side. It is an important time *not* to get caught up in illusions. Just because people are feeling and acting a certain way doesn't necessarily mean that they are that way all the time. This morning's Moon sextile Mercury will help us to think and talk matters through. This afternoon's Moon sextile Pluto aspect may bring some dramatic twists to our outlook on people's gluttonous, theatrical, or unpredictable behavioral tendencies. Pisces Moon brings an instinctive and reflective understanding of the course of today's events.

Venus sextile Mars (occurring May 2 – 10) Mischievous, talkative, and outgoing

119

kinds of affection are evident while Venus in Gemini is sextile to Mars in Leo. Playfulness and multifaceted attractions will be evident through this aspect. It is here that feminine (Venus) and masculine (Mars) forces have an opportunity (the sextile aspect) to support each other. The Mars influence emphasizes the awareness and application of action, movement, involvement, and also harnesses strength and energy. Venus reminds us to draw towards ourselves the pleasures we desire. Here we have the incentive to apply action with love. This is the only time this aspect will occur this year.

May 8th Saturday

Moon in Pisces	PDT	EDT
Moon square Venus	11:39 AM	2:39 PM
Moon sextile Sun	3:09 PM	6:09 PM

Birthday: Melissa Gilbert 1964

Mood Watch: The waning Pisces Moon is a time to be aware of many people's need for escapism and overindulgence. Dreamy, somewhat spacey and artistic moods ebb and flow like the sea. This is a time when our moods tend to reflect on our beliefs. Moon square Venus may be a challenging time to come across pleasurable, affectionate, or comfortable moods. Later, Moon sextile Sun is sure to brighten our moods; Sun in Taurus and Moon in Pisces bring practicality and imagination together. The waning Pisces Moon is a great time to meditate and to seek a tranquil or relaxing environment. To contrast the meditative reverie, music and the arts play a big role in appeasing our imaginative and interactive moods.

May 9th Sunday

Mother's Day

Moon in Pisces / Aries	PDT	EDT
Moon conjunct Jupiter	5:31 AM	8:31 AM
Moon opposite Saturn	10:56 AM	1:56 PM
Moon conjunct Uranus goes v/c	1:11 PM	4:11 PM
Moon enters Aries	2:30 PM	5:30 PM

Birthday: Billy Joel 1949

Mood Watch: As the Moon conjuncts with Jupiter, our moods are met by the need for advancement. It could be the need to advance towards empowering a particular dream, or it could be the feeling of having – or needing – joy and optimism. Moon conjunct Jupiter in Pisces connects us with what we need most, spiritually, as well as materially, in order to claim a real sense of prosperity. On this **Mother's Day**, the early morning is the best time to show our gratitude to Mother, and to all those blessed motherly types of people who have influenced our maturation. Late in the morning/early afternoon, Moon opposite Saturn can create an oppressive weight to the seriousness of the mood. Many folks will feel compelled to work through their limitations despite the challenges of the work. Serious moods need to be met with perseverance and attentiveness. This afternoon, Moon conjunct Uranus brings a void-of-course Pisces Moon, and our moods will seem chaotic, spacey, and disruptive. Later, as the Moon enters Aries, our moods enter into a place of greater assurance and confidence.

120

May 10th Monday

Moon in Aries

	PDT	EDT	
Moon square Pluto	12:30 AM	3:30 AM	
Moon trine Mars	11:03 PM	2:03 AM	(May 11)

Birthday: Sid Vicious 1957

Mood Watch: On this Aries Moon Monday, there is an eagerness to get started, but with the Moon waning and the Sun in Taurus, we are swiftly reminded to pace ourselves, to approach the day with practicality. Waning Moon in Aries is a time when our moods may be influenced by the efficiency with which tasks are carried out, and by how much self-assurance and self-confidence can be mustered. Waning Moon in Aries challenges individuals to take charge and to take initiative in areas of life that require immediate action. This is the time to empower personal expertise with bold confidence. Today, acting on your volitions will bring satisfaction.

May 11th Tuesday

Moon in Aries / Taurus

	PDT	EDT	
Moon sextile Venus	4:27 AM	7:27 AM	
Mercury goes direct	3:27 PM	6:27 PM	
Moon sextile Neptune goes v/c	9:10 PM	12:10 AM	(May 12)
Moon enters Taurus	11:49 PM	2:49 AM	(May 12)
Venus square Jupiter begins (see May 17)			

Birthday: Irving Berlin 1888

Mood Watch: Waning Aries Moon is an excellent time to reiterate personal affirmations and to prepare for the reinventing process of the self. This means weeding out and dropping the old habits that are holding back the emergence of the new self. Most importantly, this is the time to abolish self doubt.

Mercury goes direct (Mercury direct: May 11 – Aug. 20) Since April 17, Mercury has been retrograde in the sign of Taurus, commonly causing problems and confusion when relaying information about possessions and properties. In Taurus, the retrograde Mercury often causes communication mix-ups with regard to valuables in general, and with business contracts, banking matters, and practical necessities such as scheduling and appointments. Now we can breathe a greatly needed sigh of relief as Mercury, the planet governing the realms of communication, becomes stationary and will soon begin to move forward. Take note that our faculties and manner of communicating will definitely improve within the next few days. Although perhaps not today – when the stationary Mercury often freezes communication efforts – but very soon, our communications will run more smoothly; this will be a good time to begin clearing up various misunderstandings that have occurred over the past few weeks. For more information on this recently completed phase of Mercury retrograde, see April 17. For more on Mercury retrograde patterns throughout this year, see the introduction on *Mercury retrograde periods*.

May 12th Wednesday

Moon in Taurus	PDT	EDT
Moon conjunct Mercury	4:45 AM	7:45 AM
Moon trine Pluto	9:14 AM	12:14 PM
Sun sextile Jupiter begins (see May 17)		
Sun trine Saturn begins (see May 18)		

Birthday: Dante Gabriel Rossetti 1828

Mood Watch: The darkly waning Taurus Moon sets the stage for the willful and unwavering attitude of the bull. Today's agenda is set straight with less-than-subtle tactics. Now that the Moon wanes darkly before it settles into newness (tomorrow evening), stubbornness and determination abound. With the Sun and Moon in Taurus, the wise old soul puts us in touch with a sense of value. Taurus Moon is a beneficial time to focus on getting finances in order. This is a good day for bargain hunters. Taurus Moon activity is like a magnet for discovering beauty and comfort.

May 13th Thursday
NEW MOON in TAURUS

Moon in Taurus	PDT	EDT	
Moon square Mars	8:41 AM	11:41 AM	
Moon conjunct Sun	6:04 PM	9:04 PM	
Moon sextile Jupiter	11:44 PM	2:44 AM	(May 14)
Venus trine Neptune begins (see May 18)			
Venus square Saturn begins (see May 18)			
Sun square Neptune begins (see May 19)			

Birthday: Arthur Seymour Sullivan 1842

Mood Watch: Today's first lunar aspect, Moon square Mars, may make for a difficult time to spring forth with action and to get matters running smoothly. Beware of the tendency for some folks to have minor bouts of frustration, anger, or impatience. However, the day is bound to improve as the **New Moon in Taurus** (Moon conjunct Sun) emphasizes the acquisition of new possessions, or it could mean there is a need to restore, replenish, and maintain the old ones. Personal contentment counts with new possessions. Search for the value of what you need and want. The Moon in Taurus is exalted and calls to us to enjoy the beauty that surrounds us. Taurus is ruled by Venus, the architect of the arts.

May 14th Friday

Moon in Taurus / Gemini	PDT	EDT
Moon trine Saturn	2:49 AM	5:49 AM
Moon square Neptune	3:50 AM	6:50 AM
Moon sextile Uranus goes v/c	5:27 AM	8:27 AM
Moon enters Gemini	6:18 AM	9:18 AM
Venus square Uranus begins (see May 19)		

Birthday: Cate Blanchett 1969

Mood Watch: For less than an hour, the newly waxing Taurus Moon goes void-of-course creating a quiet, lazy, lull of energy first thing in the morning. As the Moon enters Gemini, our moods emerge with the need to satiate curiosities. Spontaneous and random tidbits of information will draw our attention and highlight the need for correspondence and communication. This is a good time to bounce ideas off others. It has been a few days since Mercury has gone direct (May 11). Finally, a recognizable train of thought allows us to understand each other far better than we have been over the course of the past few weeks. This is the time to clear up loose-end details and misunderstandings. Gemini Moon brings an outgoing buzz to the springtime chatter.

May 15th Saturday

Moon in Gemini

	PDT	EDT
Moon sextile Mars	3:41 PM	6:41 PM

Birthday: Brian Eno 1948

Mood Watch: Spring energy is in the air, the Moon is waxing in Gemini, and this often brings talkative moods. Don't be fooled by those who are not talkative, they undoubtedly have a lot on their minds. Gemini Moon focuses our attention on those areas of life where we have mixed feelings, and there is a tendency to mull over those things that have not settled just right in our heads. Moon sextile Mars brings opportunities, as our moods will be bursting with fiery force and energy. This weekend is a good time to connect with social engagements.

May 16th Sunday

Moon in Gemini / Cancer

	PDT	EDT
Moon conjunct Venus	3:15 AM	6:15 AM
Moon square Jupiter	5:06 AM	8:06 AM
Moon square Saturn	7:18 AM	10:18 AM
Moon trine Neptune	8:24 AM	11:24 AM
Moon square Uranus goes v/c	10:05 AM	1:05 PM
Moon enters Cancer	10:46 AM	1:46 PM
Moon sextile Mercury	5:02 PM	8:02 PM
Moon opposite Pluto	7:25 PM	10:25 PM
Sun sextile Uranus begins (see May 20)		

Birthday: Pierce Brosnan 1953

Mood Watch: An eventful day of lunar aspects brings busy thoughts with this morning's waxing Moon in Gemini. For a brief period, the Moon goes void-of-course and then, swiftly, the Moon enters Cancer. A waxing Cancer Moon brings a focus on our defenses, and our security and comfort zones are also given a thorough check. The entire day's activities gear up our senses with deep emotional expressions, and focus our attention on nurturing and instinctual urges. It's a good time to brighten up the home and make it feel more comfortable. Sun in Taurus and Moon in Cancer brings out a strong desire for soothing, calming comfort.

May 17th Monday

Moon in Cancer	PDT	EDT
Venus square Jupiter	3:56 AM	6:56 AM
Sun sextile Jupiter	5:41 PM	8:41 PM

Birthday: Dennis Hopper 1936

Mood Watch: The Cancer Moon urges us to share our feelings and take care of our emotional needs. The Moon rules Cancer and Monday is considered a Moon day. Moodiness is expected, but it's nothing a caring attitude won't cure. Cancer Moon brings the truth of our feelings to the surface. The motherly touch does wonders.

Venus square Jupiter (occurring May 11 – 20) This aspect brings love and attraction (Venus) into difficulty or hard work (the square aspect) over material growth and our sense of jubulation (Jupiter). Venus in Gemini square Jupiter in Pisces brings a love for intelligent care and affection which may be challenged by the need to handle escalating economic obligations or social debts. Our experiences of beauty and affection may be tested by the difficulty of attracting or acquiring prosperity. Some might say that the act of appreciating beauty is a form of prosperity in itself, but at times like this, a great deal more effort and support is required. This aspect may create an obstacle to acknowledging the expenses incurred by our attractions and love-needs. It reminds us that something more than love's blindness is required in order for us to fully realize our riches and the value of what we care about most. This aspect will only occur once this year.

Sun sextile Jupiter (occurring May 12 – 20) Taurus people celebrating birthdays this year from May 12 – 20 are now being brought into a favorable natal Sun position to Jupiter. It's a time of opportunity and expansion for these birthday folks if they act on their desires and work towards their goals. Skills learned throughout this year will support their overall plans for career advancement and fortune building. It's a good time to make the most of it Taurus folks! This is the only time this aspect will occur this year.

May 18th Tuesday

Moon in Cancer / Leo	PDT	EDT	
Venus square Saturn	1:18 AM	4:18 AM	
Moon trine Jupiter	9:10 AM	12:10 PM	
Moon sextile Sun	10:06 AM	1:06 PM	
Moon sextile Saturn	10:37 AM	1:37 PM	
Moon trine Uranus goes v/c	1:35 PM	4:35 PM	
Moon enters Leo	2:07 PM	5:07 PM	
Venus trine Neptune	3:12 PM	6:12 PM	
Sun trine Saturn	5:26 PM	8:26 PM	
Moon square Mercury	10:01 PM	1:01 AM	(May 19)
Venus opposite Pluto begins (see May 23)			

Birthday: Perry Como 1912

Mood Watch: Lunar aspects are positive this morning as the waxing Cancer Moon brings intuitive and instinctual moods. This afternoon, the Cancer Moon briefly goes void-of-course and then enters Leo. The Leo Moon brings friendly, creative, and interactive moods. Personal needs, as well as the needs of family and friends, often stand out on a Leo Moon day.

Venus square Saturn (occurring May 13 – 20) Venus in Gemini is square to Saturn in Virgo. It may be difficult to engage in romance, particularly when communicating, as it might seem that something is always getting in the way of basic pleasures. Perhaps it is best not to get bent out of shape over some people's need to create restrictions in order to protect their own sense of security while love related troubles are being worked out. No matter how much one prioritizes a focus on love, it is still likely to be misinterpreted on some level during Venus square Saturn. Love related dramas may be taken too seriously. Give it your best – keep singing the praises of love and applying the law of attraction, but expect some challenges and limitations nonetheless. This is the only time this aspect will occur this year.

Venus trine Neptune (occurring May 13 – 21) Venus in Gemini is trine Neptune in Aquarius. This brings detail oriented feminine love right in harmony with ingenious kinds of spiritual expression. Artistic endeavors will shine with spiritual brilliance. This aspect brings calmness and tranquility that are vitally needed, particularly in love related matters. When coming from a place of love, it is easier to draw down a spiritual enhancement of that love with Venus trine Neptune. Enjoying beauty is a way to acquire gifts of the spirit world. This is a good time to actively engage in peaceful, pleasurable, and spiritual love. This aspect will reoccur on September 4 with Venus in Libra. It will also come to a near occurrence (non-exact) on November 23 with Venus in Libra.

Sun trine Saturn (occurring May 12 – 21) This aspect particularly affects Taurus and Gemini people celebrating birthdays May 12 - 21. This is a positive time for these people to get a handle on their lives, and it may be easier for them to take on the responsibilities of life. These birthday folks may notice more acceptable forms of control occurring in their lives. Now is your time (birthday people) to successfully work on putting some structure into your life; the kind of structure you've needed and wanted awaits you in the coming year. It is possible that time (Saturn) is on your side to make that move you've wanted to make. This aspect last occurred January 18 – 27, and it reached its peak on January 24, affecting the birthday Capricorn and Aquarius people of that time.

May 19th Wednesday

Moon in Leo	PDT	EDT
Sun square Neptune	11:14 AM	2:14 PM
Mercury trine Pluto	11:42 AM	2:42 PM
Venus square Uranus	12:40 PM	3:40 PM
Venus enters Cancer	6:04 PM	9:04 PM

Birthday: Malcom X 1925

Mood Watch: Leo Moon puts us in touch with personal and integral needs and desires. Today will be a good day to pursue a taste of personal pleasure.

Courageous moods abound. Take pride in the things you do!

Sun square Neptune (occurring May 13 – 22) This occurrence of Sun square Neptune especially affects those Taurus and Gemini people celebrating birthdays from May 13 – 22. Neptune, in the square position to these folk's natal Sun, brings a perception that obstacles are getting in the way of Spirit, the spiritual path, or the acknowledgment of one's beliefs. Beware of the potential for drug related problems or self delusion. The challenge for these folks is to overcome the doubts and confrontations that interfere with their beliefs. Over the next year, there will undoubtedly be some spiritual adjustments, and perhaps a change of belief is required for those encountering birthdays at this time. Taurus change? Never! Well, unless it suits them, of course. As for the cusp born Gemini folks – get used to it, my friends – Neptune is heading into Pisces next year (April, 2011), and your spiritual challenges will be evident for some time to come. This aspect will reoccur on November 18 with the Sun in Scorpio, affecting the lives and beliefs of some of our Scorpio friends.

Mercury trine Pluto (occurring April 23 – May 23) This could be the year for us to receive a lot of beneficial news from the world's superpowers, as this aspect is occurring five times this year! Due to Mercury's last retrograde cycle (April 17 – May 11), this aspect is reoccurring for the third time this year. For a recap on the story of Mercury in Taurus trine Pluto in Capricorn, *see April 6*, when it first occurred.

Venus square Uranus (occurring May 14 – 22) Venus, the planet that governs love and magnetism, is square Uranus, the planet of chaos and disruption. It may be difficult for love (Venus) to flourish in a spontaneous and carefree fashion. Venus in Gemini is square to Uranus in Pisces. Some folks are likely to become too easily affronted by radical or explosive kinds of magnetism. This influence may be testing the power of love to withstand the chaos of extremes and sudden change. This is the only time Venus will be square to Uranus this year.

Venus enters Cancer (Venus in Cancer: May 19 – June 14) Venus now enters the nurturing sign of Cancer, an appropriate place for the expression of love and affection. It invites those with rocky love relationships to patch things up, and to do so with more heart and less uncertainty. Venus in Cancer encourages our affections and affinities to be carefully placed and nurtured. When attractions occur, they will have a lasting impression and will seem very strong and emotionally sound. Venus in Cancer brings out a love for such things as the ocean, leisurely aquatic sports, motherly care and expression, and all varieties of nurturing. While Venus travels over their natal Sun, those folks born in the sign of Cancer will be especially aware of their love life and their needs for pleasure.

GEMINI   II

Key Phrase: "I THINK"

Mutable Air Sign

Ruling Planet: Mercury

Symbol: The Twins

May 20th through June 21st

May 20th Thursday
FIRST QUARTER MOON in LEO

Moon in Leo / Virgo	PDT	EDT
Moon conjunct Mars	1:51 AM	4:51 AM
Moon opposite Neptune	2:43 PM	5:43 PM
Sun sextile Uranus	2:47 PM	5:47 PM
Moon square Sun goes v/c	4:42 PM	7:42 PM
Moon enters Virgo	4:59 PM	7:59 PM
Moon sextile Venus	7:05 PM	10:05 PM
Sun enters Gemini	8:33 PM	11:33 PM

Birthday: Joe Cocker 1944

Mood Watch: The **First Quarter Moon in Leo** (Moon square Sun) brings playful moods. There is a strong desire to get out and enjoy the springtime. This is a good time to focus on personal needs and self motivation. Leo makes up in complexity what Virgo tries to simplify. Tonight, while the Moon shifts from Leo to Virgo, we will be particularly drawn to the desire to clean up and clarify whatever kind of egocentric jumble the first part of this day may have gotten us into. The important thing to watch out for, quite simply, is self-doubt. It is futile to question your nature to the extent that you are left without a sense of selfhood. Use the Virgo side of the Moon to reflect on the self, and not to scrupulously question it beyond recognition.

Sun sextile Uranus (occurring May 16 – 22) This occurrence of Sun sextile Uranus particularly affects those Taurus/Gemini folks celebrating birthdays May 16 – 22. These birthday people are being given an opportunity to blow off some chaotic steam and to reach for qualities of freedom that may have been absent in their recent past. This will be your time to make radical breakthroughs, birthday folks; your natal Sun is currently sextile Uranus for a good reason – to find a liberating balance in the midst of the chaos. Right now, there is no holding back, so go for it; discover your freedom. The victory of creative change will bring a more optimistic outlook on life. This aspect last occurred on January 13, affecting the birthday people of January 9 – 15, when the Sun was in Capricorn.

Sun enters Gemini (Sun in Gemini: May 20 – June 21) Gemini people love to think. They're often thinking of ways to change the picture and to make it brighter and more detailed. The mutable and adaptable mind must be free to roam with different concepts and ideas that haven't been fully integrated into the big picture. Gemini weaves tapestries of thought; great storytellers, Geminis are often articulate and eloquent speakers, captivating audiences with details and keen observations. Duality is the key factor that shapes the Gemini perspective, and there is always a need to explore the two sides of life.

May 21ˢᵗ Friday

Moon in Virgo	PDT	EDT
Moon trine Pluto	1:20 AM	4:20 AM
Moon trine Mercury	3:09 AM	6:09 AM
Mercury-sextile-Venus-non-exact begins (see May 29)		

Birthday: Thomas "Fats" Waller 1904

Mood Watch: The Sun is in Gemini and the Moon is in Virgo, and this brings an eagerness to communicate, deliberate, and carefully examine life's current events. Gemini loves a double take, and this solar and lunar positioning of Sun in Gemini with the Moon in Virgo will occur for a second time this year on June 18. As for now, our radars are running strong, and there is a positive buzz of conversation and thoughtfulness in the air. This is an excellent time to get organized and to engage in a bit of spring cleaning.

May 22ⁿᵈ Saturday

Moon in Virgo / Libra	PDT	EDT	
Moon opposite Jupiter	4:09 PM	7:09 PM	
Moon conjunct Saturn	4:13 PM	7:13 PM	
Moon opposite Uranus goes v/c	7:33 PM	10:33 PM	
Moon enters Libra	7:50 PM	10:50 PM	
JUPITER OPPOSITE SATURN	10:37 PM	1:37 AM	(May 23)
Moon trine Sun	11:17 PM	2:17 AM	(May 23)

Birthday: T. Boone Pickens 1928

Mood Watch: While the Moon is in Virgo, our moods are rapidly affected by the need to be resourceful and precautionary. Virgo Moon encourages us to take care of practical matters and to find the time to mull things over for awhile. Sun in Gemini and Moon in Virgo emphasize the necessity to set the details of life straight. Tonight's Moon in Libra sets a much more logical and thought oriented tone to the expression of our moods.

Jupiter opposite Saturn (April 25 – Aug. 31) Jupiter and Saturn are the two social planets of our solar system. Jupiter represents, joy, attainment, expansion, wealth, increase, and the place wherever growth happens, or wherever a surplus of supply is found. Saturn is the guard at the edge of time, and represents the work, discipline, timing, focus, restriction, limitation, and the responsibility that comes with the prosperous attainment of growth here on planet Earth. With each bountiful step of attainment, there is always the restriction imposed to maintain it, and the duty of labor required to keep it growing or expanding in value and quality. Jupiter in Pisces opposes Saturn in Virgo. Both of these social-monger planets are in mutable signs signifying a time of great shifts and changes, particularly since these planets (at the 27 degree mark) are both on the cusp of these signs. Jupiter is about to enter Aries (see June 5) and Saturn is about to enter Libra (see July 21).

Jupiter in Pisces brings a wealth of experimental exploits and expenditures based on faith and intuition, which leads to tenuous accounting, budgetary tasks and eventually, a sure regaining of growth. Saturn in Virgo emphasizes our need to draw the line with regard to what takes place in the accounting firms. Saturn in Virgo tests the boundaries of our health needs, and represents the need to defend, get to work on, or place limitations upon the things that matter most to us – those areas of life that we hope to see grow and prosper.

When Jupiter opposes Saturn, there is an acute awareness of our incessant need to spend at the same time we need to place some serious limitations on those expenditures. Does all this sound familiar with the global money crunch that has developed in the past couple of years? Now more than ever, this realization requires the application of prudence, care, and practicality. Nonetheless, through this aspect we can expect to see rapid growth, and the control of that growth, occur at an expedited pace.

There will be greater opportunities, for those folks who apply a discerning focus on their strengths and skills, to reinforce a sense of security and control with regards our economic focuses. Jupiter opposite Saturn is saying, be diligent and seize all opportunities with persistence, but also take joy and have faith in the work of assessing and seeking all avenues of resource and wealth. This is the time to be especially responsive and loyal to the important things in life that matter to everyone. It is through this process of loyal persistence to the things that matter that we can find peace where there is economic hardship, or wherever there is restriction due to budgetary measures. Opportunities are arising out of the act of analyzing and assessing what needs to be done, especially with regard to establishing prosperity. Work that is yet to be realized and assessed, as well as accepted and approved, can lead to a powerful resource of jobs and business. Jupiter opposite Saturn brings alarming breakthroughs towards social and economic security. During this occurrence period, this aspect will repeat on August 16 with Jupiter in Aries and Saturn in Libra.

May 23rd Sunday

Moon in Libra	PDT	EDT
Moon square Venus	2:40 AM	5:40 AM
Moon square Pluto	4:10 AM	7:10 AM
Venus opposite Pluto	8:15 PM	11:15 PM
Mars opposite Neptune begins (see June 4)		

Birthday: Scatman Crothers 1910

Mood Watch: For the most part, Sun in Gemini and Moon in Libra keep us keen, interactive, and willing to handle whatever comes along. There is an effort to put forth intelligent, congenial, and balanced moods. This is a good time to enjoy

129

epicurean delights and good company.

Venus opposite Pluto (occurring May 18 – 26) Venus in Cancer opposes Pluto in Capricorn. The love we feel for home – and those places from which we draw a nurturing spirit (Venus in Cancer) – will be diametrically opposed to those elements and conditions of life that transform our homes and home-life into something more career based (Pluto in Capricorn). Matters concerning love, beauty, and affection may be overwhelmed by powerful forces or unforeseeable twists of fate. These fateful forces may be intruding somehow on the objects or people we love and admire. This could include just about any kind of scenario – from being shattered over the loss of a loved one, to a terminal disease, to the process of learning how to fully accept and support some kind of total transformation of a loved one. Some people find it difficult to support loved ones through severe kinds of hardship, yet now is the time to offer support to them, despite the opposing forces that appear too harsh or overwhelming. This aspect may well bring on an acute awareness of the desire that some have for power, and the need to have power over loved ones. No one, no matter how powerful, can justifiably tell us what we love, who we love, or how we are to love. Deep in our hearts dwells the truth. When the going gets tough, look to your heart!

May 24th Monday

Victoria Day, Canada
Moon in Libra / Scorpio

	PDT	EDT	
Moon sextile Mars	11:31 AM	2:31 PM	
Moon trine Neptune goes v/c	9:01 PM	12:01 AM	(May 25)
Moon enters Scorpio	11:18 PM	2:18 AM	(May 25)

Birthday: Bob Dylan 1941

Mood Watch: Waxing Libra Moon brings the potential for positive progress to be made among friends and with marital partners. This is a good time to review decisions that have to be made, and to work towards making adjustments and compromises with others. Libra Moon activities emphasize the need for sound logic and clear objectives. There may be a strong need to research or to investigate the feasibility of our plans. There is also a need for us to understand the current laws and rules of the situations we face. Libra Moon requires balanced thinking and acting, as well as benevolent and civilized approaches to creating harmony and camaraderie in the midst of carrying out our objectives.

May 25th Tuesday

Moon in Scorpio

	PDT	EDT
Moon sextile Pluto	7:44 AM	10:44 AM
Moon trine Venus	11:10 AM	2:10 PM
Moon opposite Mercury	4:15 PM	7:15 PM

" Everyone has a vocation, talent is the call. " – Ralph Waldo Emerson (born this day, May 25, 1803)

Birthday: Annie Bones 1960

130

Mood Watch: The heavily waxing Moon of Scorpio gives us the confidence to look more intently at the fixed core of our emotional realm. Sun in Gemini and Moon in Scorpio bring curiosity and excitement. The waxing Scorpio Moon enlivens our senses and lights up our moods with anticipation. This morning's Moon sextile Pluto brings strong receptivity, and there is a firm resolve to overcome life's dramas, big and small. Moon trine Venus brings affectionate and fun loving moods. Later, Moon opposite Mercury inspires talk and thoughtful reverie. On a Scorpio Moon in spring, anything can happen!

May 26ᵗʰ Wednesday

Full Moon Eve

Moon in Scorpio	**PDT**	**EDT**
Moon square Mars	6:02 PM	9:02 PM

Birthday: Miles Davis 1926

Mood Watch: It's a Full Moon Eve and although the Moon will be in Sagittarius when it reaches its peak of fullness tomorrow, the Full Scorpio Moon energy of this evening takes place with ferocious intensity. It is quite common for crime, violence, and trouble to brew on a Full Moon Eve with the Moon in Scorpio, especially during Moon square Mars. Trouble is not the case for all people in all places, but it's frequently reflected in the news locally and throughout the world. The old saying, "when it rains, it pours," may apply to the troublesome events of tonight's heavily waxing Scorpio Moon. At times like this, all types of energy may seem to be building up like the steam in a pressure cooker. When the energy, which can build no more, finally gets a chance to blow, it is usually spectacular, beautiful, unbelievable, and dramatically demanding of our attention. This is the time to wade through the rough weather of our moods, with all the right equipment necessary to handle each situation with the power of our passion. Today is a good day for garden lovers to transplant shrubs and plants.

May 27ᵗʰ Thursday

FULL MOON in SAGITTARIUS

Moon in Scorpio / Sagittarius	**PDT**	**EDT**
Moon sextile Saturn	12:23 AM	3:23 AM
Moon trine Jupiter	1:39 AM	4:39 AM
Moon square Neptune	1:55 AM	4:55 AM
Moon trine Uranus goes v/c	4:13 AM	7:13 AM
Moon enters Sagittarius	4:16 AM	7:16 AM
Moon opposite Sun	4:07 PM	7:07 PM
URANUS ENTERS ARIES	6:44 PM	9:44 PM

Birthday: Isadora Duncan 1878

Mood Watch: The **Full Moon in Sagittarius** (Moon opposite Sun) brings new insights about life, and emotional energy runs very high throughout the day. For many, there is a tendency to go way out beyond the usual bounds and discover new territory as a matter of circumstance. How we chose to perceive and develop our understanding of this new territory has a lot to do with what stage in our life we have come to, and what kind of philosophy best suits our own individual needs. This is a particularly auspicious lunar time in which to interpret today's phenomenal occurrence of Uranus's entry into Aries (see below). Let your philosophical visions foretell the process of our revolutionary initiation into a powerful new trend for the 21st century!

Uranus enters Aries (Uranus in Aries May 27 – Aug. 13, 2010) For the next two and a half months, we will observe the initial entry of Uranus into the cardinal fire sign, Aries. On August 13, the retrograde Uranus will reenter Pisces and will not enter Aries again until March 11, 2011, where it will remain for the long run from March 11, 2011 to May 15, 2018.

This icy planet with its frozen gases is one of the three outer planets, and it has come to be associated by astrologers as the planet of insurrection. Radical and explosive change is associated with Uranus' influence. Its orbit around the Sun takes 84 years to complete, which gives Uranus an average of seven years through each sign of the zodiac.

RECENT ASTROLOGICAL HISTORY OF URANUS

Radical change is the status quo of Uranus' expression in our world. From 1988 – 1996 Uranus was in Capricorn shaking up the operations and standards of the old stoic institutions. From this we got strip malls and chain stores galore. Then from 1996 – 2003 Uranus graced the skies in Aquarius, the sign it rules, as radical change took place in humanitarian issues and in the world of invention and technology. The internet, cell phones and compact disks took the spotlight with massive production, and competition soared in the technology world.

Out of the creation of those strip malls and chain stores came the need to fill them up with innovative electronic gadgetry and tools for humanity. Technology has been mass produced to the point of inundating the market. Radical change has come in the Aquarian form of biological technology, scientific discoveries, biological warfare issues, and the mass marketing of pharmaceuticals.

Uranus has been in Pisces since March 2003 and soon, the planet of chaos and rebellion forges its path through the late degrees of Pisces for the last time (see Uranus enters Pisces Aug. 13). As for now, today through August 13 we will have the opportunity to observe the initial effects of Uranus in Aries. Uranus in Pisces has revealed much about our need to change and evolve. As production dropped off, companies downsized, and the recession moved in; the radical increase of a hunger for change has left us with technological chaos and far-reaching market fluctuations.

Uranus in Pisces has been testing our faith and our beliefs. It has ripped apart our false dreams and non-constructive patterns. All kinds of beliefs are tested: beliefs in science, in the existence of global warming, in the world's complex religious concepts, in our government, in our own capacities as an influence on the world, and the overall conduct of the world at large. The explosive and drastic energies of Uranus now move from the last sign of the zodiac, Pisces, into the initiator of new causes and new exploits – the pioneer's territory, Aries, the first sign of the zodiac.

URANUS IN ARIES

Uranus in Aries marks an era of new enterprise. If Uranus had a motto for this transition it would be, "out with the old and in with the new." This will mark a new era of energy and power systems. It will be a whole new era for robotics, engineering, digital technology, and international corporate business. There will be new policies set for world economy, global warming, and American commerce. We can expect to see a dramatic transformation occur as Uranus will go into an exact square to Pluto seven times over the course of a few years – from June, 2011 to March, 2015. This "square" will begin to occur in March 2011 between two of the most masculine outer planets. Uranus square Pluto will be the ongoing talk of many astrologers, claiming all kinds of extraordinary and dramatic changes in the 21st century. The changes will be permanent, trying, difficult, eye-opening, and unusual for us to fathom. There will be a total transformation of many kinds of establishments, and the complete annihilation of some time honored establishments.

Uranus is the higher octave of the god of war, Mars, and Aries is ruled by Mars. Uranus in Aries will be creating the need for explosive kinds of change in such Aries-like things as war tactics and war technology. Could this be the time for martial law? Uranus in Aries affects radical change in such fields as psychology, psychiatric studies, surgical procedures and techniques, the metallurgic sciences, exploration, artificial entities (robotics), engineering, firefighting, arms manufacturing, trade union policies, mechanical sciences, dentistry, and professional sportsmanship. Over the course of the next seven to eight years, we can expect to see the newest and latest versions of the extraordinary things to come in the 21st century.

Aries represents the exploration of new territory and Uranus represents radical breakthroughs in humankind. We might expect to see some unprecedented types of global change that will radically alter the operations of world politics. Since Uranus takes a long time to travel through a sign, we can expect to see some radical events that will alter our overall outlook on the development of the future. However, not all of these events will be unwelcome.

Uranus's traverses through the zodiac represent mankind's urges to take the big steps towards evolution. These changes are not easy to endure, but they do eventually allow us to overcome our ignorance and our prejudices. The biggest thing we can expect to notice is the shape of free enterprise. There will be a new world order of enterprises with Uranus in Aries. Since Aries is associated with competition and leadership, radical change of a competitive and authoritative nature can be expected.

HISTORY REPEATS

We might anticipate some hardships in the form of mass riots and protests, resembling the time of the late 1960s, when Uranus was in Libra, the polarized opposite of Aries. We might also expect some hardships that resemble the hard economic times of 1926 into the early 1930s when Uranus traveled through Aries in the 20th century. The Uranus square Pluto aspect was a reality at that time also. Uranus in Aries was square to Pluto in Cancer (1933 to 1934), a time of financial hardship for many people and a time when there was a pressing need to regenerate the morale and livelihood of so many hard hit Americans. We are bound to repeat history, but not in the same way as we did in the 1930s. This transformation requires a systems overhaul to suit the temperament of the future, and that is bound to bring the classic Uranus-like effects of chaos and disorder long before the newness of Aries concepts can take hold as workable and useful global systems.

Quite simply, Uranus represents the need for freedom and revolution, without which we would not evolve. Uranus clears away the obstacles that prevent us from evolving, while Pluto, the planet of the generations, sees us through our various stages of consciousness as the generations of humankind. We must learn the Tao of chaos and find a way to get used to the disarray of our future pandemonium. From this revolutionary process comes the freedom of movement that allows us to regenerate brilliantly. Uranus rules Aquarius and this is the Age of Aquarius. The lessons of this planet may seem volatile, but without it we would stagnate to the point of extinction.

May 28th Friday
Moon in Sagittarius
No Exact Aspects
Jupiter square Pluto begins (see July 24)

Birthday: Gladys Knight 1944

Mood Watch: Although the intensity of the Full Moon reached its peak last night, the full lunar energy of Sagittarius is still going strong. The urge to travel and move beyond certain boundaries is strong. The philosophical clarity of Sagittarius allows us to look at the bigger picture of where energy goes and how to make the most of our situation. Though all of this energy is still strong, it is now beginning to dissipate, and this is a good time to reflect on and push past all the intensity with a clearer and calmer vision.

May 29th Saturday

Moon in Sagittarius / Capricorn	PDT	EDT
Moon trine Mars	3:13 AM	6:13 AM
Moon square Saturn	7:38 AM	10:38 AM
Moon sextile Neptune	9:17 AM	12:17 PM
Moon square Jupiter goes v/c	9:40 AM	12:40 PM
Moon enters Capricorn	11:45 AM	2:45 PM
Moon square Uranus	11:50 AM	2:50 PM
Moon conjunct Pluto	8:49 PM	11:49 PM
Mercury-sextile-Venus-non-exact (see below)		

" There are costs and risks to a program of action, but they are far less than the long range risks and costs of comfortable inaction. "
– John F. Kennedy (1917 – 1963)

Birthday: John F. Kennedy 1917

Mood Watch: The early part of the day may be a bit of a struggle, particularly as the Moon squares to Saturn, which often brings deeply serious moods. Moon sextile Neptune tempers the mood with a calmer outlook on the day. However,

Moon square Jupiter may bring less generous and outgoing moods, especially while the Moon is also void-of-course. Spacey moods occur for awhile and some folks may get easily lost. Finally, the Moon in Capricorn sets the tone for the need to focus, concentrate, and to gain an edge. Moon square Uranus brings chaos, and the best way to combat this is to work towards the goal of overcoming the immediate obstacles. Later, Moon conjunct Pluto empowers our moods to face destiny with determination. Capricorn Moon is a good time to formulate goals and to steer clear of emotional complexities.

Mercury-sextile-Venus-non-exact (occurring May 21 – June 8) Mercury sextile Venus now comes within a couple of degrees of an exact sextile aspect. However, all too quickly, it begins to dissipate before it gets a chance to reach its peak. Nonetheless, the affects are active. Mercury is in Taurus, bringing money matters and other practical focuses to the forefront of our discussions. Venus is in Cancer, bringing the need for nurturing and conscientious kinds of love and attractions. This is a good time to seek opportunity with matters of love and the arts. This aspect will come into a non-exact position again on September 16 with Mercury in Virgo and Venus in Libra. This aspect will reach an actual peak on two other occasions this year, first, December 1 with Mercury in Capricorn and Venus in Scorpio, and secondly, December 10 while Mercury is retrograde.

May 30ᵗʰ Sunday

Moon in Capricorn	PDT	EDT
Saturn goes direct	11:09 AM	2:09 PM
Moon opposite Venus	12:23 PM	3:23 PM
Moon trine Mercury	4:55 PM	7:55 PM

Birthday: Benny Goodman 1909

Mood Watch: The waning Capricorn Moon is a time when our emotional expressions are kept to a minimum. Serious moods imply the need to face important matters, and emotional sentiments are rarely tolerated. This may seem oddly true while the Moon opposes Venus, imposing high demands for affection and beautiful things. Fortunately, the Moon in Capricorn is a splendid time for Saturn to go direct (see below), as Saturn rules Capricorn and it is especially auspicious for it to turn around at this time. Later, Moon trine Mercury is a good time to think matters through and to communicate. Eventually, the fruit of our labors brings real satisfaction.

Saturn goes direct (Saturn direct: May 30, 2010 – Jan. 25, 2011) Saturn, which represents time, restriction, responsibility, and disciplinary acts, has been retrograde since January 13 and will go direct today until January 25 next year. Saturn retrograde often requires us to backtrack on many previous, as yet unfulfilled obligations and disciplines. Since January, Saturn retrograde has been a time of implementing, testing and correcting various types of security measures in our lives, and many sacrifices were made in order for us to feel a sense of completion and accomplishment. Today Saturn goes direct at the 27 degree mark of Virgo and will remain in Virgo until July 21 when it enters Libra. This is a good time to regenerate the discipline of our senses, to end destructive habits, particularly

135

bad health practices, as well as to make new lifestyle choices and changes. As Saturn begins to move forward, this may be the time for Virgo folks to move forward towards positive endings and new beginnings as Virgo related focuses become society's priority. Certainly, one priority has been the act of restructuring the use of our revenue. Saturn in Virgo focuses on the power of research, statistics, accounting, communication and the dexterity of the mind.

May 31ˢᵗ Monday

Memorial Day, USA

Moon in Capricorn / Aquarius	PDT	EDT	
Neptune goes retrograde	11:49 AM	2:49 PM	
Moon trine Saturn	5:49 PM	8:49 PM	
Moon sextile Jupiter goes v/c	8:41 PM	11:41 PM	
Moon enters Aquarius	10:08 PM	1:08 AM	(June 1)
Moon sextile Uranus	10:22 PM	1:22 AM	(June 1)

Birthday: Walt Whitman 1819

Mood Watch: All systems are go for a day of accomplishments. The waning Capricorn Moon steadies our moods to take on the tasks of the day with brazen fortitude. This evening's Moon trine Saturn brings an excellent time to practice the art of perfect timing and precision. Tonight's Moon sextile Jupiter brings good moods; nonetheless, as the Moon goes void-of-course, the incentive to accomplish much falls by the wayside. The Aquarius Moon turns the page on our outlook on life. Humanitarian hopes and dreams take the stage for the new month ahead.

Neptune goes retrograde (Neptune retrograde: May 31 – Nov. 6) Like clockwork, every year the planet Neptune goes retrograde for about five months. Today Neptune goes retrograde in Aquarius. Neptune governs the spiritual dimensions and, when in Aquarius, it inspires a special interest in the spiritual development of humanity. Neptune harmonizes spiritual vibrations and represents intuition and higher feminine wisdom. While Neptune is retrograde, many of the spiritual issues that have come up in the last five to six months will reoccur. For the next five months, be aware of the frequency of escapist tendencies, and of the inclination to internalize deep-rooted spiritual matters. Being firm with your own spiritual center will allow for progressive spiritual growth. Be careful not to blindly disrupt the core of another's belief system, nor to become ensnared by someone else's blindness with regard to your own beliefs during Neptune's retrograde months.

June 1ˢᵗ Tuesday

Moon in Aquarius	PDT	EDT	
Moon trine Sun	9:14 PM	12:14 AM	(June 2)

Birthday: Marilyn Monroe 1926

Mood Watch: The Sun is in Gemini and the Moon is in Aquarius – this combination initiates this new month with an emphasis on the power of the mind and its impact on group awareness. Dynamic thinking spreads rapidly under this solar and lunar influence. Aquarius Moon inspires us to think more knowledgably, or to investigate more thoroughly, and it motivates gifted individuals to communicate something that leads others to think in extraordinary ways. Humanitarian efforts will have an impact, especially with so many significant astrological events coming into play this spring and upcoming summer. Keep your senses open to powerful messages designed to raise consciousness. Make a point of collecting and spreading some form of knowledge that uplifts people's morale and also plays with their imagination.

June 2nd Wednesday

Moon in Aquarius	**PDT**	**EDT**
Moon square Mercury	11:44 AM	2:44 PM

Birthday: Charlie Watts 1941

Mood Watch: Busy minds complicate our moods, particularly with the Moon square to Mercury. The waning Aquarius Moon inspires our desire to think brilliantly. It often puts people in touch with their need to be social, or their need to have solitude, depending on what they've been missing the most. Complex ideas intrigue us during the Aquarius Moon, and there is often some unusual tidbit of information that enlivens the mind's eye – that introduces us to some of the newer inventions and future trends.

June 3rd Thursday

Moon in Aquarius / Pisces	**PDT**	**EDT**
Moon opposite Mars	6:41 AM	9:41 AM
Moon conjunct Neptune goes v/c	7:55 AM	10:55 AM
Moon enters Pisces	10:34 AM	1:34 PM
Moon sextile Pluto	7:58 PM	10:58 PM

Birthday: Anderson Cooper 1967

Mood Watch: This morning's Aquarius Moon opposite Mars brings extremely active moods, and there may be a tendency for a lot of impatience, lack of tolerance, or annoyance over the audacious ignorance of others. This is especially true while the Moon is void-of-course. Moon conjunct Neptune reminds us of our beliefs and the need to reflect on the power of our spiritual wellbeing. Before you know it, the Pisces Moon ties us in directly with our belief process and how we maintain those beliefs through our actions. The waning Pisces Moon is like the mirror of the soul; we sense and feel things about ourselves that go beyond the scope of our descriptive powers. This is a good time to meditate, pray, and empower personal beliefs.

June 4th Friday

LAST QUARTER MOON in PISCES

Moon in Pisces	**PDT**	**EDT**
Mars opposite Neptune	10:52 AM	1:52 PM
Moon square Sun	3:12 PM	6:12 PM
Mercury trine Saturn begins (see June 8)		
Mars trine Pluto begins (see June 15)		

Birthday: Angelina Jolie 1975

Mood Watch: The **Last Quarter Moon in Pisces** (Moon square Sun) brings a dreamy sort of atmosphere. Waning Pisces Moon tends to keep us entranced by those areas of our life that bring depth and meaning. This is a good time to cleanse the spiritual cobwebs from our own lives. Reinforce personal fortitude with the strength to overcome addictions by using sheer willpower and belief.

Mars opposite Neptune (occurring May 23 – June 10) Individual integrity (Mars in Leo) is challenged by or opposed to (opposite) humanity's belief in science (Neptune in Aquarius). Mars activates and stirs up action, while Neptune calms and dissolves all concern. When in opposition these two planets create an acute awareness of our spiritual beliefs and the manner in which those beliefs are acted upon and absorbed. For some, this aspect can create a spiritual breakthrough, while for others, it may be that events are forging a strong spiritual awareness challenging personal beliefs. Sometimes we lash out at the world for draining so much of our energy. Perhaps this is a healthy sign that we need to re-structure our priorities, to take action towards finding a peaceful sanctuary where we can recharge our batteries. With Mars in Leo and Neptune in Aquarius, actions which relate to the self and the family are sometimes at odds with outside beliefs or beliefs imposed by society. Establishing a healthier attitude towards defending the self and one's own beliefs is the best remedy for the opposing outbursts that affect our spiritual wellbeing. This is the only time this aspect will occur this year.

June 5th Saturday

Moon in Pisces / Aries

	PDT	EDT	
Moon trine Venus	1:43 AM	4:43 AM	
Moon sextile Mercury	8:25 AM	11:25 AM	
Moon opposite Saturn	6:35 PM	9:35 PM	
Moon conjunct Jupiter goes v/c	10:48 PM	1:48 AM	(June 6)
Moon enters Aries	10:50 PM	1:50 AM	(June 6)
Moon conjunct Uranus	11:17 PM	2:17 AM	(June 6)
JUPITER ENTERS ARIES	11:28 PM	2:28 AM	(June 6)
Mercury square Neptune begins (see June 9)			
Mercury square Mars begins (see June 11)			

Birthday: Bill Moyers 1934

Mood Watch: The Moon is in Pisces today at the cusp of Aries, and this is the place where the great wheel of the zodiac begins and ends the cycle of the seasons. It is also here that Jupiter enters Aries (see below), and where Uranus hovers in this influential place of the Pisces/Aries cusp. Pisces Moon puts us directly in touch with the deep mystical ramifications of our spiritual evolution. Our moods will be fascinated, intrigued, and mystified by the sense that big changes really are occurring on the planet.

Jupiter enters Aries (Jupiter in Aries: June 5/6 – Sept. 8/9) Today Jupiter, the planet of joy, luck, and fortune, enters the constellation Aries. Since January 17, Jupiter has been traveling through the mutable water sign Pisces, bringing imaginative and emotionally responsive efforts towards economic growth and prosperity. Jupiter in the cardinal fire sign Aries begins an era of new enterprises, independent business, and bold risk taking. Jupiter in Aries brings a pioneering spirit to the

138

economic trends of our life. Jupiter is the planet where a sense of advancement is achieved and Aries, the first sign of the zodiac, emphasizes the need for leadership, independence, and enthusiastic confidence.

Here in Aries, Jupiter will boost our morale in an effort to regain our identity in the economic world. This will be seen in such Aries-like businesses as metalworking, engineering, arms manufacturing, mechanics, and the automobile industry. Take note how these occupations change and develop this summer. Since Jupiter will only be in Aries until September, we may see a lot of fresh up-starts that actually don't get off the ground, but for a time, there will be an enthusiastic effort to spend energy, time, and effort in the establishment of new enterprise. This is also the place where independence is asserted in business, as Jupiter in Aries demands enterprising advancement towards a sense of self-actualized fulfillment.

Aries has an integral, pioneering spirit that is hard to deny; however, not all new enterprising businesses of this time will be wise investments, since Aries also has an impulsive, reckless, and domineering quality that is sometimes overconfident and won't necessarily make wise decisions with large expenditures. In late July, Jupiter will be retrograde in the early degrees of Aries. This may bring complications in new business, but where there is prudent persistence, there will be the potential for new enterprise to make a breakthrough by next year, when Jupiter will stay the course through Aries.

Jupiter doesn't always represent money, business, and economy. It is the social pulse beat of our collective conscience which determines how and where we derive our sense of joy, happiness, and hope. Wherever we instill a sense of optimism and enthusiasm, there is often a growth pattern of interest which eventually expands into prosperous gain. Aries demands the freedom to act independently and competitively. The self-reliant Aries says, "I AM," and demands alert, incisive, and resourceful growth. The economic state of affairs is not likely to stagnate during this time of Jupiter in Aries, as it will certainly undergo a fiery, bold and courageous level of change and innovative establishment.

Aries people will be able to enjoy some abundant opportunities and joyous personal experiences while Jupiter crosses over their natal Sun. They will also have a strong influence on the wave of the economic future, undoubtedly through many forms of new enterprise. The other fire signs of the zodiac, Leo and Sagittarius, will enjoy the fruits of Jupiter being trine to their natal Sun signs. This will bring the potential for travel or financial boons of some kind for the early born Leo and Sagittarius people. Libra folks would be wise to use their sensibilities and take precautions with their expenditures while Jupiter opposes their natal Sun. They may also find that the effort to handle massive volumes of business or a large inheritance may be overwhelming. Cancer and Capricorn people may discover that it will be especially difficult to keep up with expenses and opportunities in their lives while Jupiter squares to their natal Sun signs. Aquarius and Gemini people's natal Sun signs will be in the sextile position to Jupiter, and this will bring the potential for business or career opportunities in those areas of life where these people have already been working hard, or where they have made some genuine effort to succeed over time.

Jupiter will go retrograde on July 23 at the 3 degree mark of Aries. While still retrograde, Jupiter will return to the tail end of Pisces on September 8/9. On November 18, Jupiter will go direct at the 23 degree mark of Pisces. During this cycle, Jupiter will complete its last trip through Pisces by January 22, 2011 when it returns to Aries for the full term. Jupiter will remain in Aries from January 22, 2011 until June 4, 2011 when it proceeds into Taurus.

June 6th Sunday

Moon in Aries	PDT	EDT	
Moon square Pluto	7:52 AM	10:52 AM	
Mars enters Virgo	11:11 PM	2:11 AM	(June 7)

Birthday: Alex Saunders 1926

Mood Watch: There is a desire to take action and press forward through the spirit of the day. Aries Moon calls to us and teaches us an important part of addressing the warrior self. This is a time when the force of energy compels us to act or react to the beat of those who are warrior beings. We are all warrior beings on some level. Vitality and energy are healthy signs of life that we all must maintain, nurture, and find within ourselves on a daily basis. Waning Aries Moon gives us the opportunity to exercise our vitality levels, and encourages us to drop emotional pressures that may be the source of some anger issues in our life.

Mars enters Virgo (Mars in Virgo: June 6 – July 29) Mars, "the god of war," enters the cautious and skeptical realm of Virgo. Tonight through July 29, Mars in Virgo creates heat, energy, and activity in the lives of Virgos. Mars in Virgo, in general, causes the heat of our activities to be focused on such Virgo-like tasks as communications, accounting, analyzing, and nitpicking perfection. Resourcefulness and cleverness are emphasized. Thoughtfulness and care are applied to war strategies. It is interesting to note that Barack Obama (whose Sun is in Leo) has Mars in Virgo (22 degrees) in his birth chart. He will undergo a "Mars return" from July 7 – 23. This will bring him extra vitality and strength. Mr. Obama's Mars in Virgo indicates that he is more inclined to meticulously analyze and discuss war related scenarios before acting on them.

June 7th Monday

Moon in Aries	PDT	EDT
Moon sextile Sun	7:30 AM	10:30 AM
Moon square Venus	6:43 PM	9:43 PM
Mercury sextile Jupiter begins (see June 10)		
Mercury sextile Uranus begins (see June 10)		

Birthday: Tom Jones 1940

Mood Watch: Springtime Gemini Sun and a waning Aries Moon can sometimes bring hastiness, impetuosity, and a brazen spirit. It's an *up, ready, and rarin'-to-go* kind of mood set. The challenging and demanding environment is bound to build up and blow off some heat. Our moods are geared toward working off energy and letting out aggression. Those candid and often satirical quips are usually not intended to hurt feelings; in some cases, it is just a childish attempt to raise a few eyebrows. Spring is in the air and the testosterone levels are running strong. It may be best just to push past it all and let the energy go.

Ⅱ

June 8th Tuesday
Moon in Aries / Taurus

	PDT	EDT
JUPITER CONJUNCT URANUS	4:27 AM	7:27 AM
Moon sextile Neptune goes v/c	6:12 AM	9:12 AM
Moon enters Taurus	8:41 AM	11:41 AM
Moon trine Mars	10:05 AM	1:05 PM
Mercury trine Saturn	4:12 PM	7:12 PM
Moon trine Pluto	5:07 PM	8:07 PM
Venus sextile Saturn begins (see June 12)		

" Youth is a quality, and if you have it, you never lose it. "
– Frank Lloyd Wright (1867 – 1959)

Birthday: Frank Lloyd Wright 1867

Mood Watch: Pushy morning moods may be the result of the void-of-course Aries Moon. Before morning's end, the Moon in Taurus brings practical sensibility. Taurus Moon wanes darkly making this a time of preparation and refinement. This Moon fixates our moods on the important focuses of the physical world. Spring cleaning practices call to us. There is also an emphasis on selling, buying, shifting and moving physical possessions. This means having to face a lot of emotional baggage attached to letting go of physical possessions. Taurus Moon often brings a sentiment of attachment to the things on which we fix our energy.

Jupiter conjunct Uranus (occurring April 25 – Oct. 27) Jupiter, which just entered Aries a few days ago (see June 5), represents prosperity, social advancement, opportunities towards growth – to name a few – while Uranus's influence symbolizes revolution, chaos, and disruption. This conjunction of these two highly influential planets will affect absolutely everyone, and it is likely to bring an economic shift that, for some, may seem especially alarming, as the course of great economic change will be inevitable. For some folks, this dynamic shift will be the beginning of a whole new economic revolution. Big chaos is still alive and well on the international market. This conjunction will bring unforgettable dealings in large corporations and many people may be consciously choosing to override the economic mistakes of the previous generations by radically investing in futuristic markets. At first, it may seem as if we've all been sold on a future vision, but hidden behind the scenes there is a strong incentive for big profiteers to stay ahead of international markets. The age of the corporate take over will come fast and furiously as many reluctant spectators will suddenly find themselves jumping on the bandwagon of new enterprises. This is especially true since Uranus just entered Aries (May 27).

Jupiter and Uranus are conjunct at the dynamic zero degree mark of Aries, implying not only large scale, chaotic changes in economics, but especially brilliant, bold, and risky investments. Aries opens us up to the necessity to act at the abyss of economic turmoil, and large scale markets are now on the brink of making large scale conversions in their manufacturing efforts. There are likely to be struggles regarding market control, and the volatile theme of unstable markets will continue to alarm us. These prognostications may sound like the contents of old newspapers, as we've heard and seen this all before. This theme of a battered and prolonged Jupiterian road to success is all part of an outer planet conjunction series.

There are three outer planets, Uranus, Neptune, and Pluto and when Jupiter is in conjunction with these purveyors of godhood and fate, there is bound to be an economic alteration of historical proportions. This century, Jupiter has been busily conversing with all three of the outer planets, starting with Jupiter conjunct Pluto in Capricorn, which occurred in December 2007; it silently kicked off the first impressive round of economic distresses. This is the point at which some of the most influential economic powers began to plummet, starting with the US housing market. Then in May, July, and December of 2009 Jupiter was conjunct with Neptune in Aquarius. This conjunction ended earlier this year (see January 7) and was responsible for a very necessary, quintessential boost for our morale in the midst of our economic plight. People needed faith in the financial system. People also needed faith in their dreams in order to persevere through the financial hardships that erupted in 2008.

In the autumn of 2003, Jupiter was in the *opposition* to Uranus, a time when the US - Iraq war was taking hold at a great expense to US taxpayers. Up to now, this revolutionary money machine has cost Americans more than three trillion dollars. Now that these two planets are conjunct, similar kinds of unprecedented expenses are poised to blow our minds.

The Jupiter – Pluto conjunction commenced the transformation of our economy. The Jupiter – Neptune conjunction established the spiritual tone of our economic revolution. Now, Jupiter conjunct Uranus represents the revolution itself. It is here we will begin to see the radical twists of our economic future. However, this conjunction is occurring in Aries, therefore we must expect some explosive false starts. There is bound to be brutal economic destruction this year. This conjunction of Jupiter and Uranus will reach another peak on September 18, however, at that time the two planets will be retrograde at the 28 degree mark of Pisces, and the theme of economic havoc and destruction is likely to be based on something that resembles an amazingly controversial pipe-dream.

It is not advisable to play the market until the Jupiter – Uranus conjunction has passed (after October 27). Some may argue this revolution is bringing nothing but opportunity. Jupiter always represents opportunity, and the necessity to find joy and exuberance in life. As a social planet, Jupiter represents our social duty to instill optimism and hope. Jupiter also represents the pursuit of happiness, and Uranus represents revolutionary and chaotic, irrevocable worldwide change. Opportunity is bound to occur through change, but it is wise to only gamble that which one can afford to lose. We can all afford to invest in hope and a positive attitude, but we cannot afford to surrender to disparity. Uranus's mysterious and abrupt evolutionary lessons are inevitable.

Mercury trine Saturn (occurring June 4 – 10) Mercury is in Gemini where talk is easily generated, and where news, media focuses, and information opens up many possibilities for the way we think. Saturn is in Libra where new laws are forged, and there is a strong emphasis on the need to protect ourselves and our civil rights.

Mercury trine Saturn brings favorable dialogue concerning where to draw the lines. Timely information and important news represents a gift or blessing. News concerning the end of a long and arduous task brings relief. This is a great time to study or practice memorization skills. Mercury trine Saturn last occurred on February 12, with Mercury in Aquarius.

June 9th Wednesday

Moon in Taurus	PDT	EDT	
Mercury square Neptune	3:38 AM	6:38 AM	
Mercury enters Gemini	10:39 PM	1:39 AM	(June 10)
Venus trine Uranus begins (see June 14)			
Venus trine Jupiter begins (see June 15)			

Birthday: Johnny Depp 1963

Mood Watch: The waning Taurus Moon encourages us to handle finances, money, and banking. The physical world stands out today. Through sheer determination and effort, Taurus Moon activities often bring an improved and more desirable atmosphere for us to relax in and enjoy.

Mercury square Neptune (occurring June 5 – 10) This aspect often brings difficulty in communications with the spirit world, and with understanding human spirituality and beliefs. As a result, talk and discussion concerning what we believe in may be greatly misunderstood. Neptune is in Aquarius, stirring up the issue of human divinity and the structure of humanity's beliefs in the confusing shifts of the Aquarian age. Deep subjects must not be treated lightly while Mercury squares Neptune. This aspect will reoccur November 5 with Mercury in Scorpio.

Mercury enters Gemini (Mercury in Gemini: June 9 – 25) When in Gemini, Mercury is known to increase our attention to detail and to cover a wide range of interesting topics. Mercury is at home in Gemini and it directs information – like food for the brain – in an interesting and captivating way. Mercury in Gemini is the best time to inspire a storyteller who is often looking for ways to make the story more interesting. Talk, discussion, stories, gossip, and the news media all generate flashes designed to captivate one's interest. Mercury in Gemini brings out the two sides of every story. Pay heed to the message if the storyteller happens to be telling *your* story while Mercury is in Gemini.

June 10th Thursday

Moon in Taurus / Gemini	PDT	EDT
Mercury sextile Uranus	3:26 AM	6:26 AM
Mercury sextile Jupiter	6:41 AM	9:41 AM
Moon sextile Venus	7:20 AM	10:20 AM
Moon trine Saturn	11:30 AM	2:30 PM
Moon square Neptune goes v/c	12:49 PM	3:49 PM
Moon enters Gemini	3:11 PM	6:11 PM
Moon sextile Uranus	3:36 PM	6:36 PM
Moon sextile Jupiter	4:14 PM	7:14 PM
Moon conjunct Mercury	5:31 PM	8:31 PM
Moon square Mars	6:41 PM	9:41 PM

Birthday: Judy Garland 1922

Mood Watch: A busy Taurus Moon morning filled with positive lunar aspects brings industrious moods. This afternoon's void-of-course lunar phase brings a spell of disorientation, and it's a time when distractions may cause us to misplace or lose things. As the Moon enters Gemini, an even flightier quality of busy moods brings an evening filled with chatter and thought provoking ideas. There's a lot on our minds at this busy time.

Mercury sextile Uranus (occurring June 7 – 11) Mercury is right on the cusp at zero degrees Gemini with Uranus newly in the sign of Aries (since May 27), focusing talk, information and news on unusual occurrences. Sensationalism may be played up in the news during this aspect. While Uranus is in Aries, chaos will be stirred up on such Aries-like focuses as new enterprises and mechanical engineering. Mercury sextile Uranus gives us the opportunity to freely speak our minds and to address the turmoil that exists in our lives. This aspect last occurred on February 6, with Mercury in Capricorn and Uranus in Pisces.

Mercury sextile Jupiter (occurring June 7 – 11) Mercury brings news and talk, while Jupiter brings wealth and prosperous advancement. The money flows where our attention goes. Communicating our thoughts (Mercury in Gemini) brings opportunities and the potential for success (the sextile aspect) in typical Piscean endeavors. These include the growth of community programs, places of worship, the expansion of the arts, spiritual enhancement, creative financing, charities, and entrepreneurship (Jupiter in Pisces). Opportunity exists for both the employer and the employee. Mercury sextile Jupiter brings joyful and mind expanding conversations. This aspect will only occur once this year.

June 11ᵗʰ Friday

Moon in Gemini

	PDT	EDT
Mercury square Mars	6:27 AM	9:27 AM

Birthday: Hugh Laurie 1959

Mood Watch:: The Moon wanes darkly and prepares our moods to anticipate newness. It always seems darkest before the light comes, so we may well expect to feel a bit bogged down by mixed feelings and the complex details of life. Gemini Moon is a good time for us to keep an open mind and to multitask our way through numerous situations without being overwhelmed by the compounding extraneous circumstances that tend to infringe on our sense of progress. As we prepare for tomorrow's New Moon in Gemini, this is a good time to organize, prioritize, and clean up loose papers, documents, notes, editing projects, and unfinished correspondences.

Mercury square Mars (occurring June 5 – 13) Mercury in Gemini square Mars in Virgo creates complicated thoughts and discussions over the active discernment and pressurizing doubts of others. Under the influence of this aspect, it is not a good time to lose one's temper. Be especially careful to watch what you say; words can be easily taken the wrong way. This aspect stimulates arguments and mental blocks concerning the actions of others. This is often a challenging time

144

to do memorization and to study for tests. Mercury square Mars makes it difficult for some to justify their actions or explain why they take a certain stand in life. Refrain from making risky comments, and be careful not to misinterpret information as being hostile or personal. Remember, during this complex time of Mercury square Mars, don't shoot the messenger! This aspect last occurred on April 25, and before that, April 4, with Mercury in Taurus and Mars in Leo.

June 12th Saturday
NEW MOON in GEMINI

Moon in Gemini / Cancer	PDT	EDT
Moon conjunct Sun	4:14 AM	7:14 AM
Venus sextile Saturn	8:18 AM	11:18 AM
Moon square Saturn	3:24 PM	6:34 PM
Moon trine Neptune goes v/c	4:34 PM	7:34 PM
Moon enters Cancer	6:51 PM	9:51 PM
Moon square Uranus	7:29 PM	10:29 PM
Moon square Jupiter	8:18 PM	11:18 PM
Sun square Saturn begins (see June 19)		

Birthday: Chick Corea 1941

Mood Watch: The **New Moon in Gemini** (Moon conjunct Sun) allows for new thoughts and ideas to flow, and new feelings about the way we are thinking will begin to emerge. New Moons are like clean slates. It's time to begin a process of strengthening and celebrating your energy and planning new vistas for growth, particularly in the area of emotional wellbeing. Pay attention to those newer thoughts, ideas and caprices in the wind. This would be a good time to initiate a round of creative writing, or to apply a new mental discipline in a manner which will eventually become more personally beneficial. Making an attempt to reach out to an old friend or to open up communications with a new circle will bring great insights to one's field of knowledge at this time.

Venus sextile Saturn (occurring June 8 – 14) Venus in Cancer sextile Saturn in Virgo brings the security of nurturing and reassuring expressions of love which are being amicably shared between lovers and friends. Venus emphasizes the vibrations of love, magnetism, and beauty, and while in Cancer, it brings an emphasis on the need for a peaceful retreat or a stable home environment. Saturn's influence emphasizes the awareness of time, responsibility, and dedication; while this planet is in Virgo, it inspires the need for a wholesome diet and good health practices, outdoor recreation, and relaxing hobbies. Saturn reminds us that beauty is temporary but with proper maintenance, it can also be preserved. This is the only time Venus sextile Saturn occurs this year.

June 13th Sunday

Moon in Cancer	PDT	EDT
Moon sextile Mars	12:11 AM	3:11 AM
Moon opposite Pluto	2:16 AM	5:16 AM
Sun trine Neptune begins (see June 19)		

Birthday: William Butler Yeats 1865

Mood Watch: Feelings are surfacing continuously with the Moon's travels through Cancer. Our instincts are hard at work as we take the time to nurture the heart, pamper the soul, and enjoy the best there is in a comforting home environment. In the privacy of the home, we can work out a number of kinks in our lives and are at liberty to display a wider variety of moods and feelings. This is the time to work through those feelings and let them tell us what we need to know about those emotional planes of existence. Listen to your intuition; our instincts are powerful survival tools in these days of chaotic change and challenge.

June 14th Monday

Flag Day, USA

Moon in Cancer / Leo	PDT	EDT	
Venus enters Leo	1:49 AM	4:49 AM	
Venus trine Uranus	10:20 AM	1:20 PM	
Moon sextile Saturn goes v/c	5:38 PM	8:38 PM	
Moon enters Leo	8:55 PM	11:55 PM	
Moon trine Uranus	9:35 PM	12:35 AM	(June 15)
Moon conjunct Venus	10:34 PM	1:34 AM	(June 15)
Moon trine Jupiter	10:45 PM	1:45 AM	(June 15)

Birthday: Harriet Beecher Stowe 1811

Mood Watch: Moon in Cancer is a good time to seek out a nurturing and comforting setting, but wherever this is not possible, the act of comforting others has its rewards and merits. Cancer Moon Mondays are notoriously moody. This evening as the Moon goes void-of-course, our moods may seem somewhat withdrawn and spacey. Later, Moon in Leo sets the tone for the need to reach out to a friend or someone in the family – or there may be a desire for some folks to focus on personal needs all on their own.

Venus enters Leo (Venus in Leo: June 14 – July 10) Venus in Leo brings out the more playful side of love. It also brings out the desire for more sophisticated and elaborate types of art and aesthetics. Venus represents the expression of love and affection; it is the influence of magnetism, beauty, and of feminine refinement. In the sign of Leo, Venus brings out desires and needs for personal attention. Magnetism is one of Leo's most endearing traits, and it is this magnetism that brings what Leos want most: loving attention. The entertainment industry will be highlighted as music, poetry, art, singing and acting are all enhanced with heartfelt expression. Leos will be more aware of their need for love. The love of looking good, having the best, and being the best is alluring to the ego. Wild lust will abound and the love of fantasies will be enhanced. Leo demands a lot of affection and, when Venus comes into play, the need for attention sometimes outweighs the need to reciprocate that attention. It is always wise not to have expectations in love matters and to be sure that the joys of exchanging love are balanced.

Venus trine Uranus (occurring June 9 – 17) Venus in Leo is trine Uranus in Aries. Playful and romantic kinds of love and attraction (Venus in Leo) will bring positive breakthroughs (the trine aspect) through radical self-expression (Uranus in Aries). This is a time of freedom fighters and rebel love, and youth is easily attracted to the spirit of rebellion. Dangerous love and taking chances become common occurrences. This aspect creates an attraction to the unusual, yet it allows a harmony to exist in love related matters while chaotic occurrences are taking place. Love at first sight is explosive at this time, but not necessarily long lasting. This aspect will start up one last time this year on December 28, and it will reach its peak next year on January 4, 2011 with Venus in Virgo and Uranus in Pisces.

June 15th Tuesday

Moon in Leo	PDT	EDT
Venus trine Jupiter	1:06 AM	4:06 AM
Mars trine Pluto	5:12 AM	8:12 AM
Moon sextile Mercury	1:41 PM	4:41 PM
Sun square Uranus begins (see June 21)		

Birthday: Jim Belushi 1954

Mood Watch: Waxing Leo Moon brings delight to our moods as a groovin' spirit builds throughout the day and into the course of this evening. The spirited harmony of Gemini Sun and Leo Moon brings a blend of spring and summer related focuses, and invites us to venture out into favorite hobbies, crafts, and gregarious kinds of fun. Leo Moon activities commonly revolve around friends or family, and sometimes both.

Venus trine Jupiter (occurring June 9 – 17) Valuable and inspiring gifts of love and affection come with this aspect. Love (Venus) is harmoniously placed with prosperity and opportunity (Jupiter). Venus in Leo trine Jupiter in Aries brings ardent and playful expressions of love and affection, which may lead to enterprising and elaborate displays of richness and prosperity. This is a great time to give gifts of love, and for many, it offers an expansive outlook of love's power. Getting ahead in life, in this case, has everything to do with appreciating and loving those areas of life in which we want to expand and prosper. A positive outlook can help make this happen. This aspect begins to appear again at the end of this year (occurring Dec. 27, 2010 – Jan. 7, 2011), reaching its peak on January 4, 2011 with Venus in Scorpio and Jupiter in Pisces.

Mars trine Pluto (occurring June 4 – 20) Mars is now in Virgo trine Pluto in Capricorn. Discerning, cautious, and practical action leads to positive, monumental, and powerful transformations. Actions taken now are more likely to have favorable results or to be influential with higher powers. This is a good time to resolve personal aggression directed towards the views and differences of another generation or established powers. This is also a good time for vital discoveries in the fight against diseases. Mars trine Pluto brings opportunity for favorable direct action that may well make a powerful and impressionable impact. Youthful or strong new influences will reach places of power. Mars, the god of war, and Pluto, the underworld god (or hell raiser), may actually be reaching some favorable kind of truce. This is the only time this aspect will occur this year.

June 16th Wednesday

Moon in Leo / Virgo	PDT	EDT	
Moon sextile Sun	3:27 PM	6:27 PM	
Moon opposite Neptune goes v/c	8:24 PM	11:24 PM	
Moon enters Virgo	10:41 PM	1:41 AM	(June 17)
Sun square Jupiter begins (see June 23)			

Birthday: Alice Bailey 1880

Mood Watch: People want to play and, all the while, they'll work to keep their tender egos intact. People want to entertain and be entertained! Children prance around and growl like wild animals, but Children are not the only ones growling! What can you do but let all this wild and crazy energy flow? The Sun is in Gemini and the Moon is in Leo - the twins are playing in the sun! As the Moon goes void-of-course tonight, our moods may appear a tad withdrawn, as many folks will be focused on personal needs. Later, Moon in Virgo brings resourcefulness and health conscious thoughts.

June 17th Thursday

Moon in Virgo	PDT	EDT	
Moon trine Pluto	5:53 AM	8:53 AM	
Moon conjunct Mars	7:53 AM	10:53 AM	
Moon square Mercury	11:36 PM	2:36 AM	(June 18)

Birthday: M.C. Escher 1898

Mood Watch: Waxing Moon in Virgo opens up our lines of communication and encourages stamina, efficiency, order, and cleanliness. Cultural pursuits and good conversations abound. This is a good time to get things done and to aid the body with nourishing and cleansing foods. Virgo Moon activities encourage resourcefulness and precision. Virgo Moon energy helps us to focus on our records, accounts, important documents, and also emphasizes the importance of memory and logic. Some of the best ways to access Virgo Moon energy is to banish and clean, wherever needed.

June 18th Friday

FIRST QUARTER MOON in VIRGO

Moon in Virgo	PDT	EDT	
Moon square Sun	9:30 PM	12:30 AM	(June 19)
Moon conjunct Saturn goes v/c	10:04 PM	1:04 AM	(June 19)

Birthday: Paul McCartney 1942

Mood Watch: There is a strong investigative curiosity at work with the Sun in Gemini and the Moon in Virgo. This is the **First Quarter Moon in Virgo** (Moon square Sun). Both of these Mercury ruled signs (Gemini and Virgo) emphasize the need to keep things flowing both on a logical and practical level of application, especially when passing on information. This particular Virgo Moon comes to us during a very busy time of spring when the "quickening" of summer is upon us.

148

June 19th Saturday

Moon in Virgo / Libra	PDT	EDT
Moon enters Libra	1:14 AM	4:14 AM
Moon opposite Uranus	2:03 AM	5:03 AM
Moon opposite Jupiter	3:55 AM	6:55 AM
Sun square Saturn	6:17 AM	9:17 AM
Moon square Pluto	8:31 AM	11:31 AM
Moon sextile Venus	12:03 PM	3:03 PM
Sun trine Neptune	5:21 PM	8:21 PM
Sun opposite Pluto begins (see June 25)		

Birthday: Paula Abdul 1962

Mood Watch: The Sun and Moon are in air signs and this puts a strong focus on lively conversation, interesting debates, and a search for balance in communications. Curious, vivacious, and affectionate interactions take the stage with loved ones and friends. Study and research are also highlighted. This is a good time to focus on teamwork and to discuss decision making with others.

Sun square Saturn (occurring June 12 – 22) This occurrence of Sun square Saturn especially affects Gemini and Cancer people who are celebrating birthdays June 12 – 22. These folks may be experiencing some personal challenges such as impatience, loss of control, a poor sense of timing, or difficulty identifying with current obligations. The challenge is therefore to overcome those obstacles that intrude on one's control of discipline and accuracy. These challenges will pass, and for those folks who have uplifting and positive things occurring in their lives, these (Saturn square natal sun) challenges may seem insignificant. Either way, you can bet these people are driven by their goals. These folks will have a good look at what really matters in life, and hopefully, they will honor and appreciate it. Saturn represents those things in life that we are willing to work for and maintain. Don't give up, birthday folks – conserve your energies and take losses and difficulties in stride! Through the tests, a stronger human being emerges to take on future tests with greater ability. This is the only time this aspect will occur this year.

Sun trine Neptune (occurring June 13 – 22) This occurrence of Sun trine Neptune particularly affects Gemini and Cancer people celebrating birthdays from June 13 – 22. These birthday folks are experiencing the favorable trine aspect of Neptune to their natal Sun, bringing gifts of spiritual encounters and awareness, as well as a calming effect on life. This serves as a good time (particularly for these birthday folks) to seek visions, apply prayer and meditation, and to explore spiritual avenues and beliefs that are being presented. Unfortunately, this calming and spiritually fortifying aspect may be somewhat overshadowed by the simultaneous affects of Sun square Uranus (see June 21), which is also bringing tyrannical chaos into these birthday folks' lives. Sun trine Neptune ensures that the compulsory passive and kindly qualities of Neptune's influence will lead these birthday people to be easily encouraged by spiritually uplifting practices and sanctuaries. Birthday folks, the trine of Neptune to your natal Sun will assist you in finding the calm space in the eye of the storm. This aspect will reoccur October 19 with the Sun in Libra.

June 20th Sunday

Father's Day

Moon in Libra	**PDT**	**EDT**
Moon trine Mercury	11:44 AM	2:44 PM

Birthday: Lionel Richie 1949

Mood Watch: The Sun and Moon in air signs will bring clever thoughts, and there is also an openness to educate and to focus on the learning process. Today's only lunar aspect, Moon trine Mercury, leads us to positive talk and interactions in the early part of the day. Waxing Libra Moon brings the potential for constructive progress to be made among friends and with marital partners. This is a good time to review decisions that have to be made and to work towards making adjustments and compromises with others, especially with Dad, and the hard working father figures in our lives. *Happy Father's Day*!

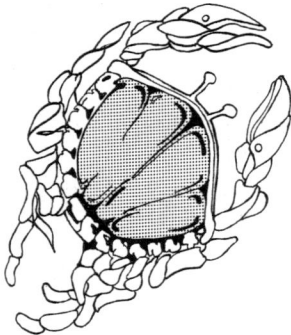

CANCER

Key Phrase: "I FEEL"

Cardinal Water Sign

Ruling Planet: Moon

Symbol: The Crab

June 21th through July 22nd

June 21st Monday

Summer Solstice

Moon in Libra / Scorpio	**PDT**	**EDT**	
Moon trine Neptune goes v/c	2:44 AM	5:44 AM	
Moon enters Scorpio	5:14 AM	8:14 AM	
Moon trine Sun	5:17 AM	8:17 AM	
Moon sextile Pluto	12:41 PM	3:41 PM	
Sun enters Cancer	4:28 AM	7:28 AM	
Sun square Uranus	5:27 PM	8:27 PM	
Moon sextile Mars	7:20 PM	10:20 PM	
Moon square Venus	9:22 PM	12:22 AM	(June 22)
Mercury square Saturn begins (see June 24)			
Mercury trine Neptune begins (see June 24)			
SATURN SQUARE PLUTO begins (see August 21)			

Birthday: Prince William 1982

Mood Watch: The waxing Moon in Scorpio brings a daring and bold quality to today's mood setting. Somewhere along the way in this busy day of aspects, Scorpio Moon gives us a reality check. This Moon often puts us in touch with the strength and depth of our courage. It's a good time to reinforce personal power. From that place of establishing courage, a strengthening awareness of personal integrity is activated. Happy Summer Solstice!

Sun enters Cancer (Sun in Cancer: June 21 – July 22) Within minutes of the time the Sun rises on the west coast, it also enters Cancer. Around this time, Summer Solstice enthusiasts are out celebrating old traditions and creating new ones while thanking the Sun for life and light. The dominion of the sign of Cancer is expressed by cardinal water, affecting people in deep and unconscious ways. Cancer people are extremely intuitive and often very psychic or perceptive. Cancers value their deep emotional attachments, their treasured memories and feelings. Cancer is a home oriented sign, and making the home a well-loved place calls out to us. Barbeques, home improvements, and other home based events are the focuses of many folks during the days of Sun in Cancer. This morning's commencement of Summer Solstice encompasses the solar qualities of Gemini and Cancer, and this phenomenon could be referred to as a "spri-sum" day (part spring/part summer). However, the sun enters Cancer early today, long before the sun rises on this first *full* day of the summer sun, and there is no denying that this will be a long day of solar light, also known as the longest day of the year. It is rather auspicious for the British monarchy to have a significant family member, an heir to the throne – Prince William – whose birthday falls on Summer Solstice. The concept of the archetype of the solar king has been avidly celebrated in many cultures throughout world history and in numerous mythology novels.

Sun square Uranus (occurring June 15 – 24) This occurrence of Sun square Uranus particularly affects Gemini and Cancer people celebrating birthdays June 15 – 24. Uranus is newly in Aries (see May 27), and the square of Uranus to these birthday folks' natal Sun brings a strong dose of unrestrained chaos and challenging events. This may be the year for you, birthday folks, to surrender to those aspects of life that are truly out of your control, and to concentrate more rationally on those facets of life over which you do have control. Sometimes the aftermath of Uranus's influence is an improvement, but with the square aspect at work, it is likely these people will feel personally challenged. Birthday people, if your life has no foundation, there is no point in holding on to the illusion of stability at this juncture of your sojourn. Albeit slowly, this aspect will pass. Try to be detached from chaotic events as they occur, and the outcome will seem less costly. It is vital not to give rapid change too much resistance, lest you be subject to the reversals of trying to fight chaos with logic at a time when resistance is futile. Project the picture of peace and it will be there for you at the other end. This aspect will reoccur December 18 with the Sun in Sagittarius.

June 22nd Tuesday

Moon in Scorpio
No Exact Aspects
Mercury square Uranus begins (see June 25)

Birthday: Todd Rundgren 1948

Mood Watch: The waxing Scorpio Moon entices our imaginations with an interest in the more intense situations and concerns of life. Summer excitement and drama are in full swing. Sun in Cancer and Moon in Scorpio classically bring an emotional time. The waxing Scorpio Moon awakens our sexual urges and intensifies our moods with passion. Even the least outgoing among us will participate in exhibiting one moment of unbridled passion or wild abandon, although this is often quite hidden under the surface. Scorpio Moon lends an air of mystery and intrigue to our lives, and it awakens our need to live life to the fullest.

June 23rd Wednesday

Moon in Scorpio / Sagittarius	PDT	EDT
Sun square Jupiter	6:20 AM	9:20 AM
Moon sextile Saturn	8:04 AM	11:04 AM
Moon square Neptune goes v/c	8:32 AM	11:32 AM
Moon enters Sagittarius	11:11 AM	2:11 PM
Moon trine Uranus	12:09 PM	3:09 PM
Moon trine Jupiter	2:52 PM	5:52 PM

Mercury square Jupiter begins (see June 26)
Sun conjunct Mercury begins (see June 28)

Birthday: Milt Hinton 1910

Mood Watch: This morning's Scorpio Moon is a time for deep encounters, strong feelings, and tough moments. As the Moon goes void-of-course, it squares to Neptune, bringing spacey but intense moods that could lead to delays, distractions, and minor setbacks. As the Moon enters Sagittarius, an explorative and outgoing confidence sets the tone of our moods. Positive, radical, and upbeat moods combine to make an eventful afternoon as the Moon trines to Uranus and later to Jupiter. The rare phenomenon of Jupiter conjunct Uranus (see June 8) is sinking in at the same time it's being well received. This is time to be courageous, bold, and joyous despite the chaos of explosive change.

Sun square Jupiter (occurring June 16 – 26) This occurrence of Sun square Jupiter will particularly affect those Gemini and Cancer people celebrating birthdays June 16 – 26. This aspect creates difficulties and obstacles to the personal joy and prosperous welfare of these birthday folks. Getting ahead financially or just staying on top of current trends may be personally challenging right now, requiring persistence and determination. The birthday people who are doing well financially may find this aspect is challenging their sense of what makes them happy, or that advancement in the world brings too much complexity and requires a lot of management. Though not all these people are living as prosperously as they may desire, they do have the ability to come through this and be much better for it. Obstacles create challenges, but do not necessarily dictate an end to efforts to improve our welfare. It is the Gemini and Cancer personality (Sun) that is being challenged (square aspect) in matters of advancement (Jupiter), requiring these people to make do with less assistance than they had anticipated. This may be a time to redefine and redirect personal goals. These birthday folks must reexamine what truly brings prosperity for them in their lives. This aspect will reoccur on December 16, affecting some of the Sagittarius birthday people at that time.

June 24th Thursday

Moon in Sagittarius	PDT	EDT
Moon square Mars	4:17 AM	7:17 AM
Moon trine Venus	9:21 AM	12:21 PM
Mercury square Saturn	9:23 AM	12:23 PM
Mercury trine Neptune	11:32 AM	2:32 PM
Mercury opposite Pluto begins (see June 27)		

Birthday: Jeff Beck 1944

Mood Watch: In the early hours of the morning, Moon square Mars brings anxious and complex moods, making it difficult to get motivated. Despite the insensitive haze of aggressive feelings, the waxing Sagittarius Moon inspires moods of optimism, enthusiasm, and courage. Moon trine Venus secures that optimism with a natural openness and attraction to love, pleasure, and treasured objects. As a general rule, today's good vibes help to smooth over the impact of Mercury square Saturn (see below). Fortunately, Mercury trine Neptune (also below) has quite a different effect on our communications. Spiritual messages will have more impact at this time, but there are always limitations on how we think or speak, as is typical of the Mercury square Saturn message.

Mercury square Saturn (occurring June 21 – 25) Mercury in Gemini square Saturn in Virgo creates tension in communications. Under the influence of this aspect, the battle to maintain accurate or precise information may be strongly evident. There may also be a tendency for "foot-in-mouth disease" as people may say the wrong things at the wrong time. It is wise to use caution when attempting communications during Mercury square Saturn, especially concerning matters of time and timing. It is also wise to be careful not to misinterpret health related information. While Mercury is square to Saturn, beware of the tendency for people to make uninformed assumptions about the conclusion or outcome of important matters. This will also be an especially difficult time to inform people of the ending of things, or to inform someone of a death or to speak at a funeral – not that this task isn't already difficult enough! Mercury square Saturn came close to reaching a peak on January 15 (non-exact), occurring for a time between January 7 – 21, when Mercury was in Capricorn and Saturn was in Libra.

Mercury trine Neptune (occurring June 21 – 25) Mercury in Gemini trine Neptune in Aquarius brings thoughtful discussions and intuitive knowledge. Communicate about spiritual needs with helpful counsel and receive gifts of renewed faith in your own beliefs. Accept that some messages are there to spiritually uplift you. This is a superb aspect for discussing personal philosophies and metaphysical subjects. Mercury trine Neptune brings gifts of encouraging news from Spirit. Mercury trine Neptune will reoccur on October 18 with Mercury in Libra.

June 25th Friday

Full Moon Eve

Moon in Sagittarius / Capricorn

	PDT	EDT	
Mercury enters Cancer	3:31 AM	6:31 AM	
Mercury square Uranus	9:35 AM	12:35 PM	
Sun opposite Pluto	11:54 AM	2:54 PM	
Moon square Saturn	4:19 PM	7:19 PM	
Moon sextile Neptune goes v/c	4:33 PM	7:33 PM	
Moon enters Capricorn	7:22 PM	10:22 PM	
Moon square Uranus	8:25 PM	11:25 PM	
Moon opposite Mercury	10:42 PM	1:42 AM	(June 26)
Moon square Jupiter	11:37 PM	2:37 AM	(June 26)

Birthday: George Orwell 1903

Mood Watch: Some challenging planetary aspects are piling up, as well as a number of lunar aspects on this Full Moon Eve. The heavily waxing Sagittarius Moon gives us the insight to move forward with unwavering attentiveness despite the demanding limitations and workload imposed by the influence of Moon square Saturn. It is important to instill faith and hope as the Moon is sextile to Neptune while it goes void-of-course. The evening brings spacey, disbelieving, and lost moods, but as the Moon enters Capricorn, a sobering sort of mood takes the stage. The Full Capricorn Moon is on the rise. The nitty-gritty of chaotic feelings will be pursued with due diligence and determination while the Moon squares to Uranus. Whatever kind of calamity tonight's nearly Full Moon brings, we will have many complicated things to say about it with Moon square Mercury, and we will find that there is a price to pay with Moon square Jupiter.

Mercury enters Cancer (Mercury in Cancer: June 25 – July 9) The shift in communications turns our attention from an emphasis on details and logic (Mercury in Gemini) to a focus on feelings and senses (Mercury in Cancer). This is a time when many people will appear to intuit their way through conversations. Thoughts may blend with mood as the emphasis on emotional expression takes the stage. As Mercury goes through the sign of Cancer, take special note of a tendency for people to talk more specifically about their feelings, defenses, and the need to be nurtured. Mercury in Cancer makes some people more intuitive to the thoughts of others, and this may be an easier time to interpret people's thoughts by observing their emotional body language. Through Cancer, thoughts and communications are shaped by the course of our complex world of emotions.

Mercury square Uranus (occurring June 22 – 26) This aspect creates excessive disruptions in communications. Mercury square Uranus brings communications, talks, discussions and news that may appear troubled and challenged by unusual or explosive circumstances. Mercury in Cancer emphasizes the need to communicate about emotional matters, while Uranus in Aries emphasizes the need to deal with the revolutionary process of enterprises, and with challenging or demanding new environments. The two focuses are creating a tension between people as they discuss their need for change and rapid adjustment. This aspect will reoccur November 27 with Mercury in Sagittarius and Uranus retrograde in Pisces. It will also occur on December 20 with Mercury retrograde in Sagittarius and Uranus in

Pisces.

Sun opposite Pluto (occurring June 19 – 28) Sun in Cancer opposes Pluto in Capricorn. Late born Geminis and early born Cancer folks having birthdays from June 19 – 28 are undergoing the effects of Pluto being in a lengthy opposition to their natal Sun sign. Birthday folks, with Pluto in opposition to your identity, this is the time to accept transition, however overwhelming the circumstances. Persist in recognizing the empowering differences each generation embodies. Gemini folks born near the Cancer cusp – here's the good news: it won't be that much longer for Pluto to be in opposition to your natal Sun position. Since 1995, Pluto has been opposite to Gemini, teaching Gemini people about the necessity of regeneration, and the shifting of the powers that be. Sun in Cancer opposite Pluto in Capricorn particularly affects early born Cancer birthday people, and they must begin to face the awakening challenges of transformation. These challenges may appear threatening and are often perceived as a painful process of loss and destruction. Late Gemini and early born Cancer birthday folks, do not get hung up on high expectations of life or you are likely to burn out. These lessons are meant to be, so open up to the need for endurance and perseverance during this time – use wisdom as your guide. Survival counts! Use your senses and your sensibilities well, but do not resist the forces of great change. Surviving all this means the best of life is yet to come, as you will grow to appreciate life in a delightfully transformed way. This is also true for your opposites, the late born Sagittarians and early born Capricorns, who are feeling the conjunction of Pluto to their natal Sun.

June 26ᵗʰ Saturday

FULL MOON in CAPRICORN – *Lunar Eclipse*

Moon in Capricorn	PDT	EDT
Moon conjunct Pluto	3:12 AM	6:12 AM
Mercury square Jupiter	4:08 AM	7:08 AM
Moon opposite Sun	4:30 AM	7:30 AM
Moon trine Mars	3:53 PM	6:53 PM

Birthday: Peter Lorre 1904

Mood Watch: The **Full Moon in Capricorn** (Moon opposite Sun) occurs early this morning. The Full Moon always suggests a time of celebration, and the earthy Capricorn expression focuses on the accomplishment of goals through the application of persistence and diligence. The gold is in your integrity and work. This is an excellent time to focus on accomplishing and setting important goals that will eventually bring satisfaction.

Partial Lunar Eclipse in Capricorn: A lunar eclipse occurs when the Earth moves between the moon and the sun, blocking the light that reflects off the moon's surface back to Earth. Some believe that eclipses bring darker than average moods. Some see this as mere superstition while others may base this belief on their personal experiences. A lunar eclipse with the Moon in Capricorn may bring earthquakes, or some other kind of earth shattering event. There may also be a death of a notable figure. Capricorn says: "I use;" this is a good time to beware of manipulative characters or those who might take advantage of unwitting victims. Every year there are at least two lunar eclipses and today brings the first one. The second lunar eclipse will occur on December 21.

Mercury square Jupiter (occurring June 23 – 27) Mercury in Cancer is square to Jupiter in Aries; this may be a tough time to communicate a sense of reassurance, particularly with regard to new enterprises. It may also be a difficult time to raise money for charities. During this aspect, it may be best to hold off on a job request, asking for a raise, buying a new business, or signing any binding contracts concerning long term investment and payment schedules. This aspect may bring discussions or complaints which revolve around the difficulties of getting funds or capital to grow, and it has a tendency to create expensive misunderstandings when it comes to large scale investments. This aspect will reoccur on November 25 with Mercury in Sagittarius and Jupiter in Pisces. It will also return on December 21 with Mercury retrograde in Sagittarius and Jupiter in Pisces.

June 27th Sunday

Moon in Capricorn	**PDT**	**EDT**
Mercury opposite Pluto	12:15 AM	3:15 AM

Birthday: Tobey Maguire 1975

Mood Watch: The still very full Capricorn Moon wanes, and the workload before us may appear demanding – and on a Sunday too! Despite this, the Capricorn Moon urges us to work hard and in a disciplined fashion. This intensely earthy Moon is a good time to apply some diligent and concentrated effort. There may be a troubling and somewhat overwhelming sense of pressure to do the impossible. The Capricorn Moon gives us the backbone to do what we must do. Steady does it.

Mercury opposite Pluto (occurring June 24 – 28) Mercury in Cancer opposes Pluto in Capricorn. Emotional perspectives of the intense and grotesque aspects of the news may be emphasized, causing horror, fascination, realization, and for some people, a kind of triumph as well. The news highlights power issues and the ensuing struggles for a breakthrough. This aspect will occur for a short time, but the long term effects for some folks may be unforgettable. Mind boggling awareness abounds now, as the need to comprehend awakening powerful issues comes through in our thoughts and discussions. This is the only time this aspect will occur this year.

June 28th Monday

Moon in Capricorn / Aquarius	**PDT**	**EDT**
Moon trine Saturn goes v/c	2:56 AM	5:56 AM
Sun conjunct Mercury	5:06 AM	8:06 AM
Moon enters Aquarius	5:53 AM	8:53 AM
Moon sextile Uranus	7:00 AM	10:00 AM
Moon sextile Jupiter	10:41 AM	1:41 PM
Mercury sextile Mars begins (see July 1)		

Birthday: Theodor Reuss 1855

Mood Watch: The Capricorn Moon has gripped our attention in serious and demanding sorts of ways, but now the Full Moon energy dissipates with the dawning of the Moon's entry into Aquarius. While the Moon has been full in Capricorn, a strong emphasis on accomplishing goals and taking work and career efforts seriously has claimed a great deal of our energy. As the Moon enters Aquarius, it invites us to seek knowledge and brilliant solutions to remedy our overwrought feelings. Aquarius Moon gives us a more scientific approach to life and allows us to examine more logical avenues of thought with an experimental flare.

Sun conjunct Mercury (occurring June 23 – 30) This conjunction will create a much more thoughtful, communicative and expressive year ahead for those Cancer folks celebrating birthdays June 23 – 30. This is your time (birthday Cancer) to record ideas, relay important messages, and pay close attention to your imaginative thoughts as they are touched by Mercury, creating the urge to speak and be heard. Birthday Cancer, your thoughts will reveal a great deal about who you are, now and in the year to come.

June 29th Tuesday

Moon in Aquarius	**PDT**	**EDT**
Moon opposite Venus	6:14 PM	9:14 PM

" You give birth to that on which you fix your mind " – Antoine de Saint-Exupéry (1900 – 1944)

Birthday: Antoine de Saint-Exupéry 1900

Mood Watch: It is appropriate that the quote above, by June 29th born Antoine de Saint-Exupéry, speaks of fixing the mind on the ways it can cultivate and deliver something very alive. The Aquarius Moon represents the fixed mind of our emotions, since Aquarius is the fixed air sign, and the Moon characterizes our moods through the whims of the heart. Today's only aspect, Moon opposite Venus brings a strong awareness of what we love most and how it is sometimes seemingly unattainable, or unripe for the picking when we find that we desire it most. Not only does Aquarius represent the unfathomable depth of the intellect, and all those ways it can be played out to satisfy our curiosity and our knowledge, it also represents humanitarian heroism. What isn't likely to be acknowledged by others today may be conceived internally. It can be cultivated with research and development, and it will be a pearl in the back of your mind that can be brought to others when they need it most. When we seek something with a fixed mind, we give birth to a new way of perceiving it, through the hearts and minds of others. The Moon wanes, and this is a good time to internalize knowledge and to focus the mind on the things that will be useful when the time comes to make an impact on something that's important to humanity.

June 30th Wednesday

Moon in Aquarius / Pisces	**PDT**	**EDT**
Moon conjunct Neptune goes v/c	3:03 PM	6:03 PM
Moon enters Pisces	6:10 PM	9:10 PM
Sun sextile Mars begins (see July 10)		

Birthday: Michael Phelps 1985

Mood Watch: Waning Aquarius Moon encourages us to let go of our grudges and sharp criticisms of others, and to honor humanity in a more positive way, with knowledge and wisdom. It also reminds us that when we fail, we must be forgiving of ourselves in order to progress in a more positive and forward moving direction. As the Moon conjuncts with Neptune and then goes void-of-course, our moods are prone to be abjectly spacey. Just when we are trying to get a handle on our sense of forgiveness and tolerance, more acts of stupidity test our faith in humankind. By the time the Moon enters Pisces, our senses are most inclined towards escapism. The waning Pisces Moon is a good time to set the day's troubles aside and enjoy a good fantasy novel or movie. Tomorrow brings a new day and a new month with our dreamy and imaginative Pisces Moon moods.

July 1st Thursday

Canada Day

Moon in Pisces

	PDT	EDT	
Moon sextile Pluto	2:11 AM	5:11 AM	
Mercury sextile Mars	5:19 AM	8:19 AM	
Moon trine Sun	2:15 PM	5:15 PM	
Moon opposite Mars	9:44 PM	12:44 AM	(July 2)

" *Ours is a sovereign nation, bows to no foreign will, but whenever they cough in Washington, they spit on Parliament Hill* " – Joe Wallace, 1964

Birthday: Liv Tyler 1977

Mood Watch: Throughout the day, waning Pisces Moon tests the weak links in the human spirit. It is often a time when we contend with our illusions, and struggle with our dreams while we review our beliefs. Repetitively escaping from troubles does not make them any easier, but at times like this, escapism is the highly likely theme. Most of the things we do must be put into perspective and into the proper context, but in dreams, anything is possible. Pisces Moon brings a very meaning-ful – but subtle – journey for the soul.

Mercury sextile Mars (occurring June 28 – July 2) Mercury in Cancer sextile Mars in Virgo brings heartfelt messages and carefully premeditated actions. Emotional responses to discussions are sure to keep our communications buzzing along swiftly. This aspect ensures that communications will move quickly. Mercury sextile Mars presents opportunities which can be received, recognized, communicated and acted upon. News or information may lead to immediate action. It's an advantageous time to apply one's word with a full backing of action for a very favorable outcome. This is the only time this aspect will occur this year.

July 2nd Friday

Moon in Pisces

	PDT	EDT
Moon trine Mercury	12:23 AM	3:23 AM

Birthday: Jerry Hall 1956

Mood Watch: The waning Moon in Pisces puts the emphasis of our moods on spiritual matters, in some cases moral and religious focuses; however, for those who don't care about such things, the wild abandon of parties and escapism also

158

takes the stage. Waning Pisces Moon may also cause some folks to become a little introverted and meditative. For some, this is a time to "clean house" with regard to the emotions and to banish away estranged feelings that create confusion or uncertainty. Applying acts that help to create peace and promote spiritual welfare can be very healing. Be careful not to overindulge in emotional calamity or the abuse of substances. While the Sun and Moon are both in water signs, this could easily end up being a very *emotional* day for many folks, and it is best just to let these feelings flow and not get caught up in placing harsh judgments on emotionally spurred behavior. Pisces Moon brings out our need to quench thirsts, connect with aquatic life forms, and release feelings through art and music.

July 3rd Saturday

Moon in Pisces / Aries	PDT	EDT
Moon opposite Saturn goes v/c	4:16 AM	7:16 AM
Moon enters Aries	6:45 AM	9:45 AM
Moon conjunct Uranus	7:54 AM	10:54 AM
Moon conjunct Jupiter	12:16 PM	3:16 PM
Moon square Pluto	2:31 PM	5:31 PM
Venus opposite Neptune begins (see July 8)		

Birthday: Montel Williams 1956

Mood Watch: For a time during the morning, the void-of-course Pisces Moon brings seriously spacey moods. As the Moon enters Aries, the competitive world surrounds us. Aries Moon brings out self-awareness and self-assertiveness, and focuses our attention on pushing forward with force and vigor, with strength and intent. This is not a time to get into a pushing match, though such behavior may be common. It may seem as if everyone is out to get something, and they must get there first. Gird your loins for battle and pace yourself today, and wherever there is a quiet refuge, be sure to disperse disruptive tension; work out energy in a constructive and non-aggressive environment to release hot-tempered tendencies.

July 4th Sunday

Independence Day, USA
LAST QUARTER MOON in ARIES

Moon in Aries	PDT	EDT
Moon square Sun	7:34 AM	10:34 AM

" No one can make you feel inferior without your consent. "
– Eleanor Roosevelt (1884 – 1962)

Birthday: Gina Lollobrigida 1927

Mood Watch: We now come to the **Last Quarter Moon in Aries** (Moon square Sun). In some cases, obstacles appear between one's emotions and one's sense of personal identity due to the square aspect. This Moon in Aries mood has very little trouble manifesting new energies. Last Quarter Moon requires disengaging from intense emotional energy. Dropping problems with the ego becomes the key to this moon. One cannot change the stubbornness and selfishness of others, but one can make a difference by setting the right example individually. Be true to yourself.

July 5th Monday

Moon in Aries / Taurus	PDT	EDT	
Moon square Mercury	12:38 AM	3:38 AM	
Moon trine Venus	6:51 AM	9:51 AM	
Uranus goes retrograde	9:49 AM	12:49 PM	
Moon sextile Neptune goes v/c	2:22 PM	5:22 PM	
Moon enters Taurus	5:30 PM	8:30 PM	

Birthday: Huey Lewis 1951

Mood Watch: A hustle and bustle quality of mood is at work, making this a good time to take charge where necessary. The Moon goes void-of-course later today – it's an accident prone period and a good time to stay out of the way of the more determined and pushy patriots among us. Tonight's Taurus Moon brings earthy, relaxed, and esthetically inclined moods.

Uranus goes retrograde (Uranus retrograde: July 5 – Dec. 5) Uranus, the outer planet representing revolution, chaos, explosive energy, and big changes, is right at the point where the zodiac ends and begins, the zero degree mark of Aries. Symbolically, this is the point where the orobus serpent bites its own tail and begins to consume itself, and it represents the amalgamation of the ending and beginning energies of the universe. Uranus is one of the slow moving outer planets that just entered Aries (see May 27), and it will now turn back through the zodiac towards the tail end of Pisces, where it will enter Pisces again this summer (see August 13). Outer planets move slowly, and this one will take five months to backtrack only five degrees before it moves forward once again. Uranus influences chaos and volatile or abrupt energies, and inspires the need for change and breakthroughs in the pursuit of freedom. When retrograde, the influence of Uranus teaches us to handle uncertainty, particularly internal chaos. Many aspects of chaos tend to be sporadically repeated until the boundaries of restriction loosen enough so we can move more freely. Uranus retrograde is a time when humanity as a whole must backtrack over their revolutionary practices in order to make breakthroughs in the long run. Uranus liberates, although for some people the retrograde process may seem to be excessively inhibiting, particularly if one's surroundings do not allow for much freedom. For rebels, contemplation and internalization bring greater inner strength. While Uranus is retrograde, be sure to set a standard for a certain degree of freedom in your life, so that you can stop and smell the flowers this summer and into the days of autumn. Don't let this valuable time of the year slide by without allowing your inner rebel to kick up his or her heels once in awhile. Freedom is a worthy thing to claim.

July 6th Tuesday

Moon in Taurus	PDT	EDT	
Moon trine Pluto	12:45 AM	3:45 AM	
Moon sextile Sun	9:34 PM	12:34 AM	(July 7)
Mercury sextile Saturn begins (see July 8)			
Mercury trine Uranus begins (see July 9)			

Birthday: His Holiness the 14th Dali Lama 1935

160

Mood Watch: As the Moon wanes in Taurus, it's an especially valuable time to enjoy beauty of some kind, or to improve upon one's appearance and surroundings. This fine day of the Sun in Cancer shines down on our summer. No matter what kind of weather appears, this serves as a good time to focus on enjoying the beauty around us and getting on with practical matters. Waning Moon in Taurus presents a good opportunity to clear up old depts, particularly the ones that have been weighing on the conscience. Taurus Moon is a beneficial time to address financial matters, to empower ways of earning and saving, and to reinforce the necessity to apply practical money management on a regular basis. There is also a need to tidy things up a bit in order to make life more functional and beautiful again.

July 7th Wednesday

Moon in Taurus	PDT	EDT	
Moon trine Mars	12:27 AM	3:27 AM	
Moon sextile Mercury	7:14 PM	10:14 PM	
Moon square Venus	8:05 PM	11:05 PM	
Moon square Neptune	9:51 PM	12:51 AM	(July 8)
Moon trine Saturn goes v/c	11:08 PM	2:08 AM	(July 8)
Mercury trine Jupiter begins (see July 11)			

Birthday: Ringo Starr 1940

Mood Watch: A waning Taurus Moon centers our moods on practical needs, esthetic surroundings, and the focuses of having, attaining, and paying for those material desires that persist to keep us working. The early part of the day indicates a good time to do business. Later, Moon sextile Mercury brings a favorable time to communicate. However, communications may be sidetracked in matters of affection, as the Moon square Venus aspect may present difficulties when trying to smooth matters over with loved ones, or when attempting to create a pleasurable mood. The evening's aspect of Moon square Neptune may introduce doubt or uncertainty – it's a time when our faith is tested. The evening closes on a serious note with Moon trine Saturn occurring as the Moon goes void-of-course. It's a good time to reaffirm personal goals and to try to get some rest.

July 8th Thursday

Moon in Taurus / Gemini	PDT	EDT	
Moon enters Gemini	12: 51 AM	3:51 AM	
Moon sextile Uranus	1:52 AM	4:52 AM	
Moon sextile Jupiter	6:14 AM	9:14 AM	
Venus opposite Neptune	4:54 PM	7:54 PM	
Mercury sextile Saturn	10:35 PM	1:35 AM	(July 9)
Venus trine Pluto begins (see July 13)			

Birthday: Kevin Bacon 1958

Mood Watch: The waning Moon in Gemini keeps our moods focused on activities involving writing, speech, lectures and talks. This Moon in Gemini allows our moods to release a lot of emotional tension through the process of communication. Talking our way through problems relieves stress and is very common activity with waning Gemini Moon. There is much to talk about as this has been an ominous time of celestial activity and change. Feeling overwhelmed may be a symptom of all this, coupled with the classical nervous energy generated by the cerebrally oriented Gemini Moon. If the mind is busy but scattered, fear not; this is a normal reaction to so much going on. The Gemini Moon energy helps us to internalize and process all the data.

Venus opposite Neptune (occurring July 3 – 11) Venus in Leo is opposing Neptune in Aquarius. What we are attracted to may be opposed to what we (or others) believe in. Selfishness conflicts with philanthropy. Wild and instinctual expressions of love and beauty are at odds with universal beliefs. This aspect brings an awareness of the dichotomy between fashion's feminine archetypes versus a natural or spiritual expression of femininity. The feminine spirit needs to be free and connect with a more divine image of womanhood; however, the goddess that lives within may seem distant or hard to reach. Nonetheless, the feminine parts of the spirit (Venus) are being made acutely aware of the divine parts of the spirit (Neptune) in one way or another. The opposition of Venus to Neptune may seem like an overwhelming time to try to make a spiritual connection with large groups of people, especially through the mediums of art, music, and theater. There may be a desire to create a spiritual refuge or retreat – an attractive, sensual, and aesthetically pleasing sanctuary. This opposition only occurs once this year.

Mercury sextile Saturn (occurring July 6 – 10) Mercury in Cancer is sextile Saturn in Virgo. Mercury in Cancer requires accurate but sensitive communications over vital subjects. Meanwhile, Saturn in Virgo demands prudent and carefully analyzed measures with regard to setting up perimeters and implementing rules. This tends to be a time when struggles and difficulties are discussed, and people draw collective conclusions on how best to handle their problems or responsibilities. This is an opportunistic aspect for communicating work skills, particularly with regard to home related tasks and chores. Make use of it while the opportunity is here. Mercury sextile Saturn will reoccur November 17 with Mercury in Sagittarius and Saturn in Libra. It will also begin to occur on December 26, when Mercury is retrograde, and it will come within 3 orbital degrees of this sextile aspect on December 29 (non-exact), where it will begin to dissipate due to Mercury ending its retrograde cycle on that day.

July 9th Friday

Moon in Gemini

	PDT	EDT
Moon square Mars	8:05 AM	11:05 AM
Mercury enters Leo	9:29 AM	12:29 PM
Mercury trine Uranus	4:44 PM	7:44 PM

Birthday: Nicola Tesla 1856

Mood Watch: The Gemini Moon wanes as it puts us in the mood to process nervous energies and introspective thought patterns. This morning's Moon square Mars aspect may be the cause of difficult or impossible types of activity. Some folks may be dealing with anger issues, while others may be particularly clumsy. Some folks may find their moods reflect an overly aggressive or anxious quality of expression. As the day progresses, busy thoughts keep our moods occupied and, in some cases, very talkative. The Gemini Moon keeps us in tune with a busy celestial period, and the thought provoking qualities of this Moon prepare us for the New Moon weekend, which is also a time of the solar eclipse (see Sunday).

Mercury enters Leo (Mercury in Leo: July 9 – 27) Mercury in Leo is an excellent time to effectively write or perform screenplays and comedy. When Leo the lion speaks, it's a penetrating sound! Mercury in Leo puts the focus of information, news and discussions on entertainment, personal interests, and connection with families. This is the time when many kids are turning to – or away from – family in an effort to find answers. They seek answers they can live with, answers about determining self-identity as well as survival skills. Mercury in Leo is a time when the mind establishes, reaffirms and maintains a self-created identity. Connections with Leos will come easily as expressed thoughts become more colorful and dramatic, and communications shift toward charismatic interplay. Self-expression and soulful fortitude will be more evident in our communications while Mercury is in Leo.

Mercury trine Uranus (occurring July 6 – 11) Mercury, emphasizing the transmission of news and information, is now in the favorable trine position to Uranus, representing disruption and chaos. This aspect brings news of disorder and calamity which (through the trine aspect) represents a gift, probably one of freedom or a break in the mundane routine. There are many premature or radical breakthroughs waiting in the wings, and Mercury trine Uranus often brings news of these discoveries. Mercury is in Leo trine to Uranus in Aries. Talk will be generated about radical changes that occur among friends and family. Catch phrases, or radical concept statements and ideas, are often born under this aspect, and are more easily absorbed. Mercury trine Uranus also allows for brilliant concepts to shine through and be worded in a way that radically makes sense. This is a good time to record thoughts and appreciate brilliant thinking. This aspect will reoccur November 6 with Mercury in Scorpio trine Uranus in Pisces.

July 10ᵗʰ Saturday

Moon in Gemini / Cancer	PDT	EDT	
Moon trine Neptune	1:46 AM	4:46 AM	
Moon square Saturn	3:16 AM	6:16 AM	
Venus enters Virgo	4:31 AM	7:31 AM	
Moon sextile Venus goes v/c	4:38 AM	7:38 AM	
Moon enters Cancer	4:39 AM	7:39 AM	
Moon square Uranus	5:36 AM	8:36 AM	
Moon square Jupiter	9:51 AM	12:51 PM	
Moon opposite Pluto	10:51 AM	1:51 PM	
Sun sextile Mars	9:13 PM	12:13 AM	(July 11)

Birthday: Jessica Simpson 1980

Mood Watch: Early this morning, the darkly waning Moon enters Cancer. This Moon commonly brings introspective exploration over emotional matters. Cancer Moon puts us in touch with the need to care for and nurture ourselves; of course, it's always darkest before the dawn, and this may seem like a time when it becomes necessary to weed out and eliminate bad habits and poor judgment that trigger negative emotional responses. This is prominently one of those times when we are reminded of the need to overcome temptation and do the right thing. The New Moon approaches (see tomorrow), at which point the process of mulling over useless or negative emotional tendencies becomes more of a rebirthing experience. Waning Cancer Moon is a beneficial time to dump useless emotional baggage, and to forgive ourselves and others for past offences. New Moon brings emotional clarity that allows us to open up more easily and to find trust in those areas where we place our hearts.

Venus enters Virgo (Venus in Virgo: July 10 – Aug. 6) Venus now enters the sign of Virgo, where love and attraction are highlighted with such Virgo-like traits as shyness, prudence, purity, and virginal beauty. While Venus is in Virgo, the expression of love and beauty will be analyzed and reflected upon, and love related activities are more often reserved or calculated than they are acted upon. Venus in Virgo is referred to as "the fall," a less ideal position for Venus and a time when disappointment in love matters may be felt by some folks. Keep faith in your affections, despite the cooling of passions.

Sun sextile Mars (occurring June 30 – July 16) Sun sextile Mars brings a surge of favorable energy and activity into our lives, particularly enlivening the lives of those Cancer people celebrating a birthday from June 30 – July 16. There are opportunities at work, which must be acted upon in order for all of this extra energy to pay off. There may also be a lot of anguish or pressure with regard to self-image, and the heat stirred up by this experience requires direction and assertiveness. Now is the time for Cancer birthday folks to take action, to get in shape, and to build up their energy and strength. This is the only time this solar aspect will occur with Mars this year.

July 11ᵗʰ Sunday

NEW MOON in CANCER – *Solar Eclipse*

Moon in Cancer	PDT	EDT
Mercury trine Jupiter	1:13 AM	4:13 AM
Moon sextile Mars	12:15 PM	3:15 PM
Moon conjunct Sun	12:39 PM	3:39 PM

Birthday: Lon Milo DuQuette 1948

Mood Watch: The **New Moon in Cancer** (Moon conjunct Sun) signals our moods to tune into newly emerging feelings about ourselves. The New Cancer Moon invites fresh experience and opens up our desires to take care of the child within, building up a brand new outlook on our home life. Cancer focuses on the nurturing strength of the mother. This is a good time to bring uplifting things to the home and brighten up one's outlook with optimistic moods and feelings.

Total Solar Eclipse in Cancer: This Solar Eclipse brings an emphasis on controversies rooted in our feelings and emotional core. For some, the ability to have clear feelings may seem overshadowed, but it must be remembered that this is only a brief shadow. Eclipses are believed to threaten the lives and liberty of leaders and special figures in society. The cardinal water sign of Cancer in the ecliptic

164

state often influences hurricanes, floods, storms, and drought. This is the time to reassure those who are undergoing emotional dramas and to be patient with emotional outbursts. Every time there is a Solar Eclipse, there is always a Lunar Eclipse within two weeks. This Eclipse duo will have another Eclipse pair at the opposite time of year. Although this may not feel like a particularly easy time for starting anew, the Solar Eclipse touches our lives with a fluid and accepting kind of assertiveness to move through the greatest obstacles. Beware of the tendency for some people to lean towards substance abuse, depression, and emotional instability. Consult the Internet for the times and locations for viewing this year's total Solar Eclipse, as many sights show a real-time view of this event

Mercury trine Jupiter (occurring July 7 – 12) This most favorable aspect brings good news of expansion and prosperity to those who are open to broadening their awareness. Ask and you shall have! Mercury in Leo trine Jupiter in Aries inspires ambitious and confident communication which can lead to career breakthroughs, adventure, great achievements, happiness and wellbeing. This is an excellent time to learn new skills which will improve one's livelihood and better one's outlook. Mercury brings news, while Jupiter brings wealth and prosperous change. Mercury trine Jupiter is often considered to be an advantageous time to advertise and put information out there, and to ask for a job or a loan. Look openly for opportunity when sharing information, and promote yourself and your capabilities. This aspect will reoccur November 4 with Mercury in Scorpio and Jupiter in Pisces.

July 12th Monday

Moon in Cancer / Leo	PDT	EDT
Moon sextile Saturn goes v/c	4:48 AM	7:48 AM
Moon enters Leo	5:54 AM	8:54 AM
Moon trine Uranus	6:48 AM	9:48 AM
Moon trine Jupiter	11:04 AM	2:04 PM
Moon conjunct Mercury	3:39 PM	6:39 PM

" If I am not, who will be? "

– Henry David Thoreau (born July 12, 1817)

Birthday: Buckminster Fuller 1895

Mood Watch: Early this morning, the Cancer Moon goes void-of-course for about an hour. Topsy-turvy feelings give way to a newly budding confidence. The waxing Leo Moon emerges to instill self-assured moods. Playful moods allow for jovial encounters with the youthfully waxing Leo Moon. If the lion does not sleep or play, his hunger leads him to the most serious venture of stalking. Keep your bellies full and your spirits light and there won't be much trouble keeping peace on the plains. Remember – cats are territorial. Energy at this time is upbeat and full of vigor and animal magnetism. Playful fun among friends and family is a source of amusement. Whenever possible, however, those who are inspired do not rely on others to provide them with entertainment. This is a good time to indulge in a favorite hobby or personal project. Be your own source of enlightenment.

July 13th Tuesday

Moon in Leo	PDT	EDT
Venus trine Pluto	10:55 AM	1:55 PM

" ...the Ego cannot be realized except through its opposition to the Non-Ego."

– Papus (Gérard Encausse) - born July 13, 1865

Birthday: John Dee 1527

Mood Watch: It's a Leo Moon day, bringing forth both the expression of playfulness and the need to keep life interesting. Leo Moon puts us in the mood to take on summertime practices with willful intentions. It also invites us to venture out into favorite hobbies, crafts, and gregarious kinds of fun.

Venus trine Pluto (occurring July 8 – 16) Venus trine Pluto is certainly exciting – with fate, power, love, and intensity at work! This aspect represents a love or fascination occurring with regard to the work of fate as well as power. Venus in Virgo emphasizes our love for cleanliness, purification, and good health practices, and while Venus is trine to Pluto, there is a strong appeal among the various generations, and among influential powers, to apply more care and effort to organize and implement greater health practices. Venus trine Pluto allows a breakthrough to occur for those who have trouble accepting the work of fate. This aspect allows loving energy to flow more easily between generations. Love triumphs over all, especially with Venus trine Pluto. This is a great time to let love cure the pain. This aspect last occurred on April 4, with Venus in Taurus.

July 14th Wednesday

Moon in Leo / Virgo	PDT	EDT
Moon opposite Neptune goes v/c	3:22 AM	6:22 AM
Moon enters Virgo	6:15 AM	9:15 AM
Moon trine Pluto	12:08 PM	3:08 PM
Moon conjunct Venus	2:14 PM	5:14 PM

Birthday: Bebe Buell 1953

Mood Watch: For a time during the early morning, the waxing Leo Moon goes void-of-course. Laziness and doubt eventually give way to our curiosities as the Moon enters Virgo. Waxing Moon in Virgo opens up our lines of communication, and encourages stamina, efficiency, order, and cleanliness. Cultural pursuits and stimulating conversations abound. This is a good time to get things done and to aid the body with nourishing and cleansing foods. Virgo Moon activities encourage resourcefulness and precision. Virgo Moon energy helps us to focus on our records, accounts, and important documents – and also emphasizes the importance of memory and logic.

July 15th Thursday

Moon in Virgo	PDT	EDT
Moon conjunct Mars	5:30 PM	8:30 PM
Moon sextile Sun	8:40 PM	11:40 PM

Birthday: Linda Ronstadt 1946

Mood Watch: The young waxing Virgo Moon brings our moods into a more practical and logical approach to the matters at hand. Virgo Moon is an excellent time to clean and organize. This Moon keeps us questioning and guessing, which also leads to the need to research our resources and find answers to rising concerns. Tonight's Moon conjunct Mars aspect is likely to bring masculine activity as well as the potential for heated emotions. This Virgo Moon is a good time to be gentle, discreet, careful, and accurate.

July 16th Friday

Moon in Virgo / Libra

	PDT	EDT
Moon conjunct Saturn goes v/c	6:45 AM	9:45 AM
Moon enters Libra	7:25 AM	10:25 AM
Moon opposite Uranus	8:19 AM	11:19 AM
Moon opposite Jupiter	12:59 PM	3:59 PM
Moon square Pluto	1:24 PM	4:24 PM
Sun trine Uranus begins (see July 23)		

Birthday: Ginger Rogers 1911

Mood Watch: For awhile this morning, the Virgo Moon goes void-of-course and while it is conjunct with Saturn, there may be a sense that time stands still, or that matters may seem out of control. Sure enough, as the Moon enters Libra, our moods are bound to cross over into a much more amicable and level headed quality. Waxing Libra Moon brings the potential for positive progress to be made among friends and with marital partners. This is a good time to review decisions that have to be made and to work towards making adjustments and compromises with others. Today will have its ups and downs as the Moon first opposes Uranus then Jupiter. Strong feelings bring out the continual desire to keep matters as balanced as possible. Moon square Pluto reminds us of the necessity to deal with the harsh realities of life. Libra Moon assists us to keep peace and friendship flowing. When the going gets tough, true friends stick together.

July 17th Saturday

Moon in Libra

	PDT	EDT
Moon sextile Mercury	7:36 AM	10:36 AM

Birthday: Vince Guaraldi 1928

Mood Watch: Thoughtful moods start off our day with Moon sextile Mercury. Today's Libra Moon activities emphasize the necessity for sound logic and clear objectives. We may want to investigate the feasibility of our plans. There is also a need for us to understand the current laws and rules of the situations we face. Leadership is emphasized on a Libra Moon day, and true leaders must be patient as well as convincing. Certainly no one can do absolutely everything alone, for without the corroboration of others, even the decisions of the most assertive leaders have no staying power. Libra Moon requires balanced thinking and acting, as well as benevolent and civilized approaches to creating harmony and camaraderie in the midst of carrying out our objectives.

July 18th Sunday
FIRST QUARTER MOON in LIBRA

Moon in Libra	PDT	EDT
Moon square Sun	3:11 AM	6:11 AM
Moon trine Neptune goes v/c	7:26 AM	10:26 AM
Moon enters Scorpio	10:42 AM	1:42 PM
Moon sextile Pluto	4:55 PM	7:55 PM
Sun sextile Saturn begins (see July 22)		

Birthday: Hunter S. Thompson 1937

Mood Watch: The Sun is in Cancer emphasizing activities of the home (the world of our feelings) and the need to preserve our emotional attachments; the **First Quarter Moon in Libra** (Moon square Sun) encourages us to harmonize with our partners and friends. This is the Moon which brings out a focus on the need to create balance in various relationships, particularly those of a close nature. Throughout this morning, it's time to make adjustments! Compromise is a two way street. There may also be some confusion since the Libra Moon will be void-of-course this morning, inspiring moods distracted by indecision. As the Moon enters Scorpio, our moods enter into a phase of dramatic awareness. Scorpio Moon puts us in touch with our passions. Sun in Cancer and Moon in Scorpio often create a somewhat watery and emotional kind of mood setting.

July 19th Monday

Moon in Scorpio	PDT	EDT
Moon sextile Venus	4:26 AM	7:26 AM
Moon square Mercury	7:40 PM	10:40 PM
Sun trine Jupiter begins	(see July 26)	
Mars conjunct Saturn begins (see July 31)		

Birthday: Arthur Rackham 1867

Mood Watch: The early morning Moon sextile Venus aspect brings pleasurable moods. We awaken to a Moon in Scorpio day, and this reminds us of the vital importance of living life without taking things for granted. Sometimes it is a brush with death, or a glance at something tragic that puts our encounters with monotony and the daily grind back into perspective. Scorpio Moon encourages us to take on great challenges with the courageous desire to overcome fear; sometimes it is through the act of acknowledging our trials and troubles that we can battle our weaknesses and triumph over our fears. Whatever will turn that around for us today, Scorpio Moon is there to allow us to face our doubts and fears through each step. Tonight's Moon square Mercury aspect is a good time to be cautious with words and wade patiently through complex thoughts.

July 20th Tuesday

Moon in Scorpio / Sagittarius	PDT	EDT
Moon sextile Mars	6:19 AM	9:19 AM
Moon trine Sun	1:07 PM	4:07 PM
Moon square Neptune	1:16 PM	4:16 PM
Moon sextile Saturn goes v/c	4:43 PM	7:43 PM

168

Moon enters Sagittarius	4:49 PM	7:49 PM	
Moon trine Uranus	5:43 PM	8:43 PM	
Moon trine Jupiter	11:07 PM	2:07 AM	(July 21)
Mars opposite Uranus begins (see July 30)			

Birthday: Carlos Santana 1947

Mood Watch: The Moon is in Scorpio for the first part of the day. Strong perceptions and psychic inclinations bring intense shifts to our moods. While Moon sextile Mars and Moon trine Sun bring an active, positive and upbeat start to the day, this afternoon's Moon square Neptune impedes our sense of spiritual harmony or self-assurance. As the Moon is sextile to Saturn, it also goes void-of-course for a very brief period. A somewhat serious frame of mind gives way to a distinctive change of moods. The Sagittarius Moon brings adventurous moods and urges a spirit of fascination, profound wonder, and insight.

July 21ˢᵗ Wednesday

Moon in Sagittarius	**PDT**	**EDT**
SATURN ENTERS LIBRA	8:10 AM	11:10 AM
Moon square Venus	4:42 PM	7:42 PM

Birthday: Ernest Hemingway 1899

Mood Watch: The waxing Moon in Sagittarius enlivens our moods with positive energy and it inspires travel and exploration. This is a time to set our priorities straight with a philosophical application of life's complexities. This is a time to build on our talents and skills, and we are drawn towards the need to explore and find opportunity wherever possible. Here we can reflect on our understanding of past events and transform them into a better picture of what the future holds.

Saturn enters Libra (Saturn in Libra: July 21, 2010 – Oct. 5, 2012) Saturn in Libra demands even-tempered and civil measures with regard to setting up perimeters and implementing rules. Approximately every 2 to 2.5 years, depending on the retrograde periods, Saturn enters a new zodiac sign. However, in this case, Saturn traverses through Libra, off and on, for an extended period of nearly three years, with the exception of the period of April 7 – July 21, 2010, when retrograde Saturn traveled back through the late degrees of Virgo. Saturn first entered Libra on October 29, 2009.

SATURN'S RECENT HISTORY IN VIRGO

During the time of Saturn in Virgo, September 2, 2007 – October 29, 2009, it has been important to recognize and to empower the structure of our economic condition and of the communications that have shaped our views in this realm. Focuses such as accounting, systems analysis, secretarial duties, and the apparent condition of the healthcare field have all been subject to Saturnian kinds of restriction. Virgo people will not deny the past couple of years have been a time of hard work for them, but also a time when their disciplines have allowed them to claim a greater sense of control over their lives. Take it easy, Virgo folks, and congratulations – this particular Saturn influence is now completed! Now the master of discipline and focus, Saturn, wends its way through the sign of Libra. In the next couple of years to come, lawful, deliberate, conciliatory, and diplomatic efforts will be the backbone of structure while Saturn is in Libra.

169

WHAT SATURN REPRESENTS

Saturn's influence represents the times in our lives when we take authority and responsibility for something. It represents commitment. Saturn is the planet which gives us the edge to proceed with clarity and focus. It is also our protection mechanism, our lock-and-key to the issues in our lives on which we choose to work, determining when and how these matters are to be unlocked, handled, and completed. Saturn represents those areas in life where we earnestly work to focus and concentrate our energies; it is where we manage and maintain some control.

Beginnings and endings occur when Saturnian experiences penetrate our lives. There is a hard edge to creating new disciplines as well as giving up old ones. Saturn reflects time constantly and doesn't skip a beat. Time waits for no one, not even Librans, so this is your time, Libra folks, to get your sense of timing in gear and to do what you do best.

HOW SATURN IN LIBRA AFFECTS LIBRANS

Saturn in Libra imposes greater responsibility and work on our Libra friends for the next couple of years. This may be the time for Librans to connect with their work and to use their talents to achieve goals that are important to them. Libra, the scales of justice, the diplomat, mediator, arbitrator, and peace maker will be put to the working test of setting up perimeters and territorial lines in an ever changing environment.

HOW SATURN IN LIBRA WORKS IN OUR SOCIETY

Discipline and the act of setting limits will now be emphasized in such Libra related things as the judicial system, law enforcement, and the world of marriage and marital relationships. Libra represents the development of structure through law, and the preservation of the power and unique qualities of cultural and artistic pursuits.

While Saturn is in Libra, many work contracts will be based on people's diplomacy skills and, their capabilities for harmonizing with others, as well as their tact in tight situations. One might expect that with Saturn in Libra, disciplinary measures and carefully planned teamwork will mean serious business for competitive companies.

SATURN'S SQUARING AND OPPOSING AFFECTS ON THE CARDINAL SIGNS OF THE ZODIAC:

Now the cardinal signs of the zodiac go into a disciplinary mode as Saturn goes through the cardinal sign of Libra. Cancers and Capricorns will experience Saturn's squaring affect to their natal Sun signs. They must learn to pace themselves and to be aware that Saturn squaring their natal Sun will bring career and work related tests, challenges, and difficulties. These people may have a great deal of doubt about their ability to identify with the work they are doing. Cancer and Capricorn people will need to be more focused on cleaning up unfinished business, solving repetitive problems, and they will endure tedious kinds of work. This is the time to face personal limitations and find a way to work with them or around them. It's an opportunity for these folks to gain a real sense of accomplishment and mastery over the inevitable challenges life brings.

Saturn in Libra will be opposing the cardinal sign of Aries, creating a more acute awareness of personal responsibilities on the part of our Aries friends. The work levels and disciplines in Aries' lives will be trying and overwhelming at times, and occasional bouts of exhaustion will inconvenience Aries. This is not a time for Aries folks to set themselves up with heavy commitments or workloads; the test of the days ahead will prove to be demanding enough while Uranus is in Aries (see May 27). Aries people must learn to pace themselves and, most of all, to be patient with their careers and work related focuses.

SATURN'S TRINE AFFECTS ON THE AIR SIGNS OF THE ZODIAC:

Saturn in the air sign of Libra will be trine to the other air signs of the zodiac, Aquarius and Gemini. This will activate and stimulate Aquarius and Gemini people's abilities to identify with the need for order and structure in their lives. They will experience a greater sense of ease in applying their work and creating more structure or discipline where they need it.

SATURN'S SEXTILE AFFECTS ON THE FIRE SIGNS – SAGITTARIUS AND LEO:

Sagittarius and Leo people are likely to experience more career or work opportunities, and get a better grasp on their personal disciplines, as Saturn goes through a sextile to their natal Sun signs. These people must act on their disciplines in order to find these opportunities and get results.

Libra says: "I BALANCE." While Saturn travels through Libra, structure and discipline, when applied to peacemaking in relationships, brings magnanimous results. Here, there is no room for Libra's ability to vacillate or to be indecisive. Here, it is patience, skill, persistence, and indefatigable management that will support grand feats of accomplishment for Libra.

LEO

Key Phrase: "I WILL"

Fixed Fire Sign

Ruling Planet: Sun

Symbol: The Majestic Lion

July 22nd through August 22nd

July 22nd Thursday
Moon in Sagittarius

	PDT	EDT	
Moon trine Mercury	11:26 AM	1:26 PM	
Sun enters Leo	3:21 PM	6:21 PM	
Moon square Mars	5:31 PM	8:31 PM	
Sun sextile Saturn	6:12 PM	9:12 PM	
Moon sextile Neptune goes v/c	9:51 PM	12:51 AM	(July 23)
Mercury opposite Neptune begins (see July 26)			

Birthday: Danny Glover 1946

Mood Watch: Moon trine Mercury brings positive thoughts and communications in the early part of the day. Sagittarius Moon inspires powerful visions and rich insights into the future. It is times like this which facilitate opening the portal to new adventure. As the Sun enters Leo, the Sagittarius Moon enlivens our outlook on summer, a time of travel and exploration. Tonight's Moon square Mars is a good time to be watchful about avoiding accidents as well as overly masculine energies. Much later tonight, Moon sextile Neptune brings spacey moods as the Moon goes void-of-course.

Sun enters Leo (Sun in Leo: July 22 – Aug. 22 PDT / 23 EDT) Leo, the sign ruled by the Sun, fills the season with strong, instinctive fervor and deep, fiery desire. Leo focuses on will, identity, truth, selfhood, integrity, pride, and strength. Yours is a lustful time of year, Leo, and your totem, the lion, is one of the most self-assured of the zodiac's symbols. Sun in Leo focuses our attention on Sun related frolic and play, outdoor activities for children and families, and the entire entertainment industry. This is the time for self-development and fulfillment. Leo says, "I Will," and it is important for a Leo to be expressive in the act of will. The Leo part within us must remember with a true affirmation of will we can have *anything* we want – we just can't have *everything*. Choose what is true to the self!

Sun sextile Saturn (occurring July 18 – 25) This occurrence of Sun sextile Saturn particularly affects those cusp born Cancer and Leo people celebrating birthdays between July 18 – 25, helping them focus their energy and disciplines with greater clarity throughout the year. As Saturn enters the sextile aspect to the natal Sun of these Cancer and Leo people, they will have a greater sense of making progress through discipline, and they may very well begin to see the rewards of their diligent labor in the coming year. This is only true, however, as long as they apply themselves to their work and maintain a vigilant and persistent effort to master personal discipline and training. Greater control comes with genuine effort. This aspect will reoccur on December 6, affecting the lives of some Sagittarians at that time.

July 23rd Friday

Moon in Sagittarius / Capricorn	PDT	EDT
Moon enters Capricorn	1:39 AM	4:39 AM
Moon square Saturn	1:55 AM	4:55 AM
Moon square Uranus	2:33 AM	5:33 AM
Sun trine Uranus	3:05 AM	6:05 AM
Jupiter goes retrograde	5:03 AM	8:03 AM
Moon square Jupiter	8:14 AM	11:14 AM
Moon conjunct Pluto	8:18 AM	11:18 AM
Uranus-square-Pluto-non-exact (see below)		

Birthday: Daniel Radcliffe 1989

Mood Watch: When there's work to be done, Capricorn Moon does not allow for a whole lot of emotional reaction time. We can make an effort to empower our goals and objectives of the season with serious applications of commitment and work. This is the time to get the physical and practical side of our life into working order, and to use our resources in ways that can improve our situation.

172

Sun trine Uranus (occurring July 16 – 26) This occurrence of Sun trine Uranus favorably affects our Cancer and Leo friends celebrating birthdays July 16 – 26. It puts the radical forces of Uranus in the favorable trine position to the natal Sun of these Cancer and Leo folks. This is the time for these birthday people to make the breakthrough. Don't hold back, birthday folks; chaos is here to stay for awhile, and the apparent madness occurring in your lives is there for a reason. Let the experience be positive as long as this aspect brings gifts. Expect restless desires for freedom and a heartfelt need to break out of your personal prison. These challenges are a necessary part of these folks' growth patterns, and the resultant changes are positive in nature, though on the surface they may seem harsh and overbearing. Freedom knocks loudly and the course of change for these people is inevitable in the next year. The trine aspect bestows gifts of triumph, and this could be a good time to let chaos be the force that brings freedom. This aspect will reoccur November 18, affecting the Scorpio birthday people of that time.

Jupiter goes retrograde (Jupiter retrograde: July 23 – Nov. 18) The planet of expansion and prosperity now begins to recede back through the degrees of the zodiac today through November 18. Jupiter in Aries (June 5 – Sept. 8/9) brings prosperity and expansion to such areas of life as new enterprises, exploration, initiation, and motivational training. This is a time when marketing strategies often employ the themes of new business, engineering, sportsmanship, and mechanical development. Jupiter retrograde is not the best time for the growth of large scale funds and investments, but it is a good time to meditate on – and to observe carefully – what truly makes us happy in the realms of fortune seeking. A clearer sense of growth will occur through internal processing and through personal skill development. While Jupiter is retrograde, it is important to apply wisdom and caution in the economic area of our lives, and in our livelihood, so we may see future growth. Although Jupiter in Aries represents new business, this is not necessarily the best time to invest in new business; however, creating new business incentives and meditating upon the direction of new business will be very revealing during Jupiter retrograde in Aries. On September 8/9 Jupiter will reenter Pisces and there may be some definitive signs of the need to let go of attachments and to take losses in stride. Remember – less is more. Let go of the old matter and build anew from a firm foundation.

Uranus-square-Pluto-non-exact (occurring May 6 – Aug. 11) Today Uranus and Pluto come within a few degrees of an exact square. This aspect is not your run-of-the-mill common occurrence! Oh no, this aspect has an irregular cycle of every 50 to 80 years, depending on the retrograde cycles of Uranus and Pluto. This major aspect involves two of the three outer planets, which are among the slowest moving in our solar system. Their interaction with each other affects *all* of humankind, bringing unfathomable – and unpredictable – acts of chaos and transformation and complex changes, usually of historical proportions. Last year we got the first glimpse (from June 7 – 23, 2009) of the affects of Uranus square Pluto, which takes years to develop, and will take a couple of more years to reach its ominous peak. Take note: Uranus square Pluto is temporarily showing itself for the second time this century, and the events during this occurrence period, May 6 through August

11, will provide some major clues for the types of dramatic changes we can expect to encounter over the next decade.

Uranus is the outer planet that represents revolution, chaos, explosive energy, and big changes. Pluto is known as the underworld god, the one who tests and evaluates the stability of all things, and where there is weakness, Pluto removes or annihilates weakness with illness, famine, decay, and putrefaction. Pluto purifies or cleans away that which is dead and gone. Where Pluto traverses, permanent change occurs. Out of this transformation, an entirely different perspective will affect our understanding of how things work on the physical plane. In the square position, these two planets are a force to be reckoned with – and then some.

Uranus in Aries square Pluto in Capricorn brings explosive new beginnings and a highly disciplined world of industrious transformation. False starts will go up in smoke as fast as old institutions will crumble. Competition is stiff in the world at large. This is the time of hard work towards establishing the happy medium of systems that must work for the next generations to come. The square aspect represents the stumbling blocks – as well as the stepping stones – to overcome complexity, destruction, and the struggles of life.

This aspect last occurred in the early 1930s (the classic depression), and it won't return, after this next phase, until the early 2070s. On April 8, 2011, this aspect begins occurring again, and on July 9, 2011, Uranus square Pluto *almost* reaches an exact peak, within one degree of an orbital square, but Uranus goes retrograde at that time, and no such exact square will occur. Despite this, the signs of the times are unable to hide while the mighty Uranus-square-Pluto-non-exact debacle continues through the year 2011. The exact peak occurrence dates for Uranus square Pluto are June 24, 2012, September 19, 2012, May 20, 2013, November 1, 2013, April 21, 2014, and March 17, 2015. When it's all over, very little will ever seem the same; Uranus square Pluto guarantees the most radical kind of transformation for all. This is the time to start paying attention to the signs.

July 24th Saturday

Full Moon Eve

Moon in Capricorn	PDT	EDT	
Moon trine Venus	8:12 AM	11:12 AM	
Jupiter square Pluto	9:28 PM	12:28 AM	(July 25)

Birthday: Emelia Earhart 1897

Mood Watch: Our moods are often quite elated with the heavily waxing Moon in Capricorn. At the same time, a serious push to control overwhelming moodiness creates an interesting dichotomy of feeling – very full, but not allowing enough time or effort to accurately express or feel it. That's the way Capricorn Moon works. It impresses upon us the need to fit a whole lot of experience and emotional wonder into a very limited space. This is a time to beware of the tendency to feel just plain overwhelmed, usually caused by a heavy work load, or if there is simply much too much going on. Today and tomorrow, soothing pool dips and baths, as well as comforting spa treatments may be just the ticket to easing Full Moon tension.

174

Jupiter square Pluto (occurring May 28 – Sept. 10) The newly retrograde Jupiter (see yesterday) now squares off to the power mongering Pluto, which also happens to be retrograde. This aspect last occurred on August 6, 2004, and it usually happens every six years. Jupiter represents expansion, prosperity, and social advancement, – to name a few – while Pluto represents transformation, power, and fate. This aspect is likely to bring an economic shift that, for some, may seem rather hellish. We began to feel a taste of this in May when this aspect began. Strong power plays are at work on the international market at this time. Jupiter square Pluto brings the difficulty of facing up to the economic haunts and crises of previous generations. There are likely to be struggles regarding inheritance. Jupiter in Aries is square to Pluto in Capricorn. New enterprises will be in conflict with institutional powers. Beware of the potential for large scale deception in business. Once again, the powers that be are likely to exhibit too much greed. Through this aspect, there will probably be many sacrifices, and there will be many power struggles over the fortunes that are made. Avoid heavy gambling, new credit lines, risky and hasty expenditures, and expect a few rounds of difficult transformation with regard to economics over this tricky period of Jupiter square Pluto. There is a great effort going on between generations to secure a prosperous future. This aspect reaches its peak twice – today, and again on August 2, before dissipating by September 10.

July 25th Sunday

FULL MOON in AQUARIUS

Moon in Capricorn / Aquarius	PDT	EDT
Moon trine Mars goes v/c	9:19 AM	12:19 PM
Moon enters Aquarius	12:39 PM	3:39 PM
Moon trine Saturn	1:19 PM	4:19 PM
Moon sextile Uranus	1:29 PM	4:29 PM
Moon opposite Sun	6:36 PM	9:36 PM
Moon sextile Jupiter	7:24 PM	10:24 PM
Mercury trine Pluto begins (see July 30)		
Mars opposite Jupiter begins (see August 3)		
Mars square Pluto begins (see August 3)		

Birthday: Maxfield Parrish 1870

Mood Watch: The day begins with the vibrant energy of Moon trine Mars as the Moon also goes void-of-course. The void Capricorn Moon is likely to bring serious and determined moods stifled by idleness or uncertainty. As the Moon enters Aquarius, our moods will be more inclined to seek some knowledgeable solutions to labor intensive troubles. The **Full Moon in Aquarius** (Moon opposite Sun) enlivens our senses with the need to apply clarity and definition. The mood of the day is likely to be blanketed in bizarre and unusual occurrences, and it's often focused on modern technological breakthroughs and inventions. People may seem idealistic and generous in some respects of this lunar expression, or out-of-hand and downright unrealistic in others. This is a good time to investigate, play around with ideas, seek answers, invent, reinvent, and celebrate knowledge.

July 26th Monday

Moon in Aquarius

	PDT	EDT
Mercury opposite Neptune	3:03 AM	6:03 AM
Sun trine Jupiter	4:30 AM	7:30 AM
SATURN OPPOSITE URANUS	10:06 AM	1:06 PM

" If you are going to let the fear of poverty govern your life... your reward will be that you will eat, but you will not live. "
— George Bernard Shaw (born this day, July 26, 1856)

Birthday: Mick Jagger 1943

Mood Watch: The all encompassing Full Moon energy from yesterday is still going strong. The Aquarius Moon brings rebellious moods, and there is often a need to break out of routines and to find solutions to old problems. Once we've worked our way through the various duties, more exciting ideas and interesting thoughts will occupy our minds. The summertime Aquarius Moon is an excellent time to explore innovative outdoor activities and new or spontaneous types of leisurely hobbies.

Mercury opposite Neptune (occurring July 22 – 28) Mercury opposite Neptune makes us acutely aware of discussions concerning religious beliefs. Beliefs go beyond the physical to the metaphysical realms, where information is accessed and spiritual fortification occurs. It is wisest to be clear on one's own beliefs, and not to put oneself in a position of having to expose or defend those beliefs before a pack of merciless critics. Spiritual growth and enlightenment are not easy things to relay in conversation, and during this aspect it may seem particularly overwhelming for some folks to try to communicate effectively – or to comprehend what others are trying to communicate about spiritual matters. This aspect occurs once this year.

Sun trine Jupiter (occurring July 19 – 29) This aspect brings those Cancer and Leo people celebrating a birthday from July 19 – 29 to a favorable natal solar position with relation to Jupiter. This will be a time of gifts and expansion for these birthday folks, and there are good times ahead for them in the coming year. This aspect will bring a better sense of what it means to expand and attain one's personal desire. Be sure to take the time right now, birthday people, to enjoy and appreciate life, which will definitely improve for you, despite other trials you may be facing. This aspect brings the gift of joy, so make use of it and be sure to look for the silver lining in your life! Sun trine Jupiter will reoccur November 15 with the Sun in Scorpio, affecting the Scorpio birthday people of that time.

Saturn opposite Uranus (occurring March 10 – Aug. 20) Today, Saturn is in Libra opposite Uranus in Aries at the zero degree mark. This means that these two monstrous influences will both be on the cusps of Virgo/Libra (Saturn) and Pisces/Aries (Uranus). Explosive endings and new beginnings are on the rise. Saturn in Libra (see July 21) brings the necessity for balance, law, and order. Meanwhile, Uranus in Aries (see May 27) brings radical new enterprises. For a recap on the amazing story of this long winded and powerfully effective aspect, *see April 26* when it last reached its peak.

176

July 27th Tuesday

Moon in Aquarius	PDT	EDT
Mercury enters Virgo	2:43 PM	5:43 PM
Moon conjunct Neptune goes v/c	8:46 PM	11:46 PM

Birthday: E.A. Wallis Budge 1857

Mood Watch: Eccentricity and ingenuity abound to keep our moods interesting and unpredictable. This is a good time to look for the loopholes in daily routines, and to look for an innovative way to see things differently. Acts of stupidity are particularly annoying; stick with the smart people! Spacey moods are likely to shroud the atmosphere as the Moon goes void-of-course this evening.

Mercury enters Virgo (Mercury in Virgo: July 27 – Oct. 3) Mercury will go retrograde from August 20 – Sept. 12, and that is why Mercury will remain in Virgo for a longer cycle than usual. Virgo is a most advantageous place for Mercury – the place where it both rules and is exalted. Mercury in Virgo brings clarity to our plan for the coming events of autumn. It also puts the focus of talk on such issues as computers, budgets, systems analysis, harvesting, accounting, filing, and organizing. Mercury in Virgo brings out the skeptical and analytical side of every argument and topic of discussion, keeping us on our toes. Overall, this is a great time for communications, research, and strategic planning. For more information on Mercury retrograde through the sign of Virgo, see the introduction on *Mercury retrograde periods.*

July 28th Wednesday

Moon in Aquarius / Pisces	PDT	EDT
Moon enters Pisces	1:00 AM	4:00 AM
Moon opposite Mercury	2:18 AM	5:18 AM
Moon sextile Pluto	7:43 AM	10:43 AM

Birthday: Beatrix Potter 1866

Mood Watch: Waning Pisces Moon carries us through the day with particularly dreamy, psychic, and artistic moods, and there may be a tendency towards escapism and fantasy. Pisces Moon gives no boundaries to the scope of the feelings. The imagination is strong, and emotions are absorbed from all around while our feelings are also busy addressing all of the post full moon changes. Throughout the day, the Moon in Pisces brings imaginative, poetic and deeply feminine images to the forefront of our emotional awareness.

July 29th Thursday

Moon in Pisces	PDT	EDT
Mars enters Libra	4:46 PM	7:46 PM
Moon opposite Venus goes v/c	8:43 PM	11:43 PM

Birthday: Stanley Kunitz 1905

Mood Watch: This is a good time to focus on creativity, and to enhance the mood by enjoying art, music and recreational activities. A water sign Moon in the heat of summer is an important time to keep flowers and shrubs well watered. A waning Pisces Moon often brings the potential for substance abuse or drunkenness.

Tonight's void-of-course Moon occurs as the Moon opposes Venus; strong desires for pleasure may be thwarted by weak intentions or tiredness.

Mars enters Libra (Mars in Libra: July 29 – Sept. 14) Mars in Libra now focuses more heat on the necessity for harmony in relationships. Heated energy will be directed to law related matters – particularly domestic disputes. Mars in Libra is often considered a detrimental position for the planet, especially given that Mars, the planet of war, is in the sign opposite to Aries, the place it rules. Libra folks will have an abundance of hot energy during this time, and will be quick to settle matters to the full extent of the law – matters that may disrupt the Libra's personal sense of harmony. Beware Libra people; with Mars in your sign, you may also be susceptible to fevers, accidents, or temper tantrums. Remember Mars represents activity; don't waste this energy with indecision. Now is the time to work towards making peace. When discord seems evident among loved ones, it is best to try to defuse and creatively redirect anger before irrational actions become a source of regret. Look for the signs of relationship trouble, anticipate trouble before it happens, and actively divert potential trouble – these are some of the best ways to manage the Mars-in-Libra days. It may be best, though difficult, to be a careful observer, and to withhold judgments about relationships right now.

July 30th Friday

Moon in Pisces / Aries	PDT	EDT
Mercury trine Pluto	3:04 AM	6:04 AM
Mars opposite Uranus	6:30 AM	9:30 AM
Moon enters Aries	1:42 PM	4:42 PM
Moon conjunct Uranus	2:22 PM	5:22 PM
Moon opposite Mars	2:48 PM	5:48 PM
Moon opposite Saturn	3:16 PM	6:16 PM
Moon square Pluto	8:16 PM	11:16 PM
Moon conjunct Jupiter	8:20 PM	11:20 PM

" If you think you can or you think you can't, you are right. "
– Henry Ford (1863 – 1947)

Birthday: Henry Ford 1863

Mood Watch: This morning's Moon in Pisces is void-of-course, and our moods may seem somewhat lazy, spacey, and uncertain at times. Delays and minor setbacks will be the theme of the early part of the day, but as the Moon enters Aries, our moods will become much more integral, interactive, and forthright. Hot lunar aspects bring rebellion, struggle, pressure, and serious moods. Aries Moon brings out self-awareness and self-assertiveness, and focuses our attention on pushing forward with force and vigor, and with strength and intent.

Mercury trine Pluto (occurring July 25 – Aug. 1) Mercury in Virgo trine Pluto in Capricorn brings the message of hope. Mercury in Virgo gives a very methodical, discriminating and meticulous expression to our methods of communication. Mercury trine Pluto brings greater definition to the meaning of fate, and allows us to more easily communicate about the power struggles occurring collectively around the world. Mercury is the communications tower that transmits information. Pluto's disruptive energy is focusing our attention on such issues as contagious diseases, senseless crime, misunderstandings between cultures, facing up to addiction, national debt, and many other painful realities. This is a good time to express encouraging words and reinforce the troubled people of our world with a sense of hope. This aspect last occurred April 6, May 3, May 19, and finally it will undergo one last (non-exact) appearance on September 12.

Mars opposite Uranus (occurring July 20 – Aug. 4) This aspect puts the fiery Mars in Libra into the acutely aware position to the radical and explosive power of Uranus in Aries. The potential for harsh action is very strong with this aspect, and we may encounter such travesties as explosions, the fires of war backfiring, rampant building and forest fires, and atrocious hate crimes against minorities and underdogs. Fiery violence is just a matter of course with this aspect. Rebellion and revolts are due to occur at an expedited rate. There is intensity in the air concerning our relationships (Mars in Libra) and the need to find independence and freedom (Uranus in Aries). Take caution regarding risky undertakings that may rock the boat of fiery activity. Those who are affected by this aspect are likely to be stir-crazy and in strong need of a revolution or revolt. Anger and frustration can be stifling at times, causing the need for freedom and a definite breakthrough. Fortunately, this opposition only occurs once this year.

July 31st Saturday

Moon in Aries	**PDT**	**EDT**
Mars conjunct Saturn	1:07 AM	4:07 AM
Moon trine Sun	6:13 AM	9:13 AM

Birthday: J.K. Rowling 1965

Mood Watch: The early morning aspect of Moon trine Sun allows us to make a smooth transition into the tasks and duties of the day. The Sun and Moon are now in fire signs, and this is a great time to be creative and enjoy outdoor activities. It's also an especially important time to keep watch over the potential for starting forest fires during this hot and dry season of the year in many parts of North America. Aries Moon reminds us to build on self confidence and to seek opportunities.

Mars conjunct Saturn (occurring July 19 – Aug. 5) This conjunction unites the forces of action itself (Mars) with the diligence to take this action to the limit (Saturn). This is the perfect time to apply discipline. In the striking of forces in battle, this aspect often brings swift and abrupt endings. It is always important to pay attention to those aspects of one's life that are active and hold the potential for accidents. Keep the fire extinguisher on hand. Overall, when applying caution and discipline as a basis for constructive activity, Mars conjunct Saturn is an excellent time to put the all-important theory to practice. In fact, with Mars and Saturn in Libra, this is an ideal time to practice, practice, and practice until you get it precisely right, especially with regard to action which requires perfect timing. Mars is the fire of our actions being precisely contained and preserved by the crucible: Saturn. Saturn is there to teach us about our limitations, and our sense of control is exercised through applying discipline. With practice, we can call up great strength through our disciplines. This may be just the right starting point to get the lazy rear in gear, so to speak.

August 1ˢᵗ Sunday

Lammas / Lughnassad

Moon in Aries	**PDT**	**EDT**
Moon sextile Neptune goes v/c	8:53 PM	11:53 PM
Venus opposite Uranus begins (see August 7)		

Birthday: Jerry Garcia 1942

Mood Watch: The Aries Moon instills confidence and self-assurance in our moods. Today brings us to the solar holiday of *Lammas*, and we have now reached the halfway mark of summer. The word *Lammas* comes from the term loaf-mass and it traditionally represents the first harvest of corn. The Druids call this festival holiday Lughnasadh, a time dedicated to Lugh, the Celtic Sun god whose name means "shining one." Just as the first crops are cut, this time represents a sacrifice, for Lugh was killed, but he came back to life. After Summer Solstice (June 21) the Sun's light begins to die, and rebirth occurs at Winter Solstice (December 21). Lammas takes place when the crops are thirsty and the green traces of spring have long gone. The fields become strawlike and golden. The Green Man of spring (May 1/Beltane) has been transformed, and he now appears to us as a straw figure popularly known as The Wicker Man or Jack Straw. Although the Sun's light dies away, the life of the Sun is retained in the living harvest. Let unwanted worries and fears die with the Sun King, and reaffirm the picture of self with the promise of the life contained in the harvest of seeds. Collect seeds of wisdom and contemplate in the heart of summer what part of you must die, and what part must be sustained through the impending autumn and winter until it can be reborn at Solstice. Celebrate life in the bounty of the summer harvest.

August 2ⁿᵈ Monday

Civic Holiday, Provincial Day, Canada
LAST QUARTER MOON in TAURUS

Moon in Aries / Taurus	**PDT**	**EDT**	
Moon enters Taurus	1:14 AM	4:14 AM	
Moon trine Pluto	7:27 AM	10:27 AM	
Moon trine Mercury	3:42 PM	6:42 PM	
Moon square Sun	9:57 PM	12:57 AM	(August 3)
Jupiter square Pluto	9:19 PM	12:19 AM	(August 3)
Venus conjunct Saturn begins (see August 8)			

Birthday: Peter O'Toole 1932

Mood Watch: The Last Quarter Moon in Taurus (Moon square Sun) focuses the general course of our moods on creating some sense of order in our financial situations, and encourages the need for creature comforts and esthetically pleasing or luxurious surroundings. There is often a focus on cleaning up and/or selling various useful artifacts that have collected in our lives. The Last Quarter Taurus Moon frequently inspires the activities of yard sales, auctions and flea markets. This is a good time to transform one's atmosphere into a more useful and practical working order. Letting go of attachment to material things that have bogged one down with too much maintenance or disruptive costs may very well be the best move. Certain kinds of sacrifice produce some very remedial freedom.

Jupiter square Pluto (occurring May 28 – Sept. 10) Since May 28, Jupiter square Pluto has been causing major power struggles over rising new enterprises and fortunes. The work of the fates can sometimes be quite harsh. Some transformation processes can be exceptionally expensive. For a recap on the story of this major player, Jupiter square Pluto, *see July 24*, when it first reached its peak during this occurrence period.

August 3rd Tuesday

Moon in Taurus	PDT	EDT	
Mars opposite Jupiter	9:19 PM	12:19 AM	(August 4)
Mars square Pluto	9:58 PM	12:58 AM	(August 4)

Birthday: Tony Bennett 1926

Mood Watch: The waning Moon in Taurus brings to our moods a bullish determination to control those money related woes. This Moon activates our moods to handle material matters succinctly. Taurus Moon puts us in touch with the need for physical and sensual comforts, but today's waning Taurus Moon may seem to have a few bumps along the way with all of the Mars related activity (see Mars aspects below). Economic ups and downs have led us to days like today when the waning Taurus Moon reminds us to sort out financial quandaries and meet payment deadlines. It's a good day to apply some patience with regard to material affairs, and to take comfort in a hard day's effort. We must always remember to relax in the midst of the beauty of the season, despite life's complex trials. Taurus is a place of exaltation for the Moon. Beauty and pleasure are always there for us to enjoy despite the ongoing economic and material shifts of life.

Mars opposite Jupiter (occurring July 25 – Aug. 8) This seems to be the theme of so many aspects occurring this summer. Heated activities and those areas of life where we wage battles (Mars) are at odds with our economic welfare and outlook (Jupiter). Mars in Libra opposes Jupiter in Aries. This aspect may bring an escalation of court related squabbles over money. It also brings an abrupt awareness of economic oppression or shortcomings. Fortunes may be mishandled due to unanticipated or accidental circumstances. While Mars is opposed to Jupiter, active forces are diametrically opposed to expansive fortitude, and sometimes our anger is spurred due to a lack of flow or growth in our economic resources. On the other hand, initiatives, when activated, will quickly come up against overpowering market demands. The push to save, or initiate, certain kinds of markets could be overwhelming. This is a very busy and often perplexing time to attempt to excel in business endeavors, especially in actively trading markets. While Mars is opposing Jupiter it is wise to remember that when you're roused to anger, you must take heed not to "bite the hand that feeds you."

Mars square Pluto (occurring July 25 – Aug. 8) It doesn't help much that Mars opposite Jupiter is occurring during this aspect (see above), nor does it help that Jupiter is square Pluto (see yesterday), so it's no surprise that Mars is square to Pluto, which is perfectly in keeping with the rough themes of the times. Mars in Libra square Pluto in Capricorn brings recklessly domineering battles and attempts

181

for justice over the seemingly unchangeable realities of global power structures. Mars emphasizes all forms of action, while Pluto represents the transformational powers of destiny. These two planets in the square position spell out the potential for trouble with regard to our actions. Strong disputes and war related action between generations, and among those of different cultures, are likely to occur. This aspect does imply a more likely time for an attack from groups seeking to take power, but with such attacks there will be struggles. These actions against or conflicts with higher powers are likely to backfire – it is best not to bluff those of a higher or unanticipated authority at this time, as taking action in an attempt to create a transformation may be very dangerous. This may be a particularly difficult time to fight addiction, disease, and war related stress – it is also the most crucial time not to give up the fight. Thankfully, this is the only time this year we will have to endure Mars square Pluto.

August 4th Wednesday

Moon in Taurus / Gemini	PDT	EDT
Moon trine Venus	4:48 AM	7:48 AM
Moon square Neptune goes v/c	5:43 AM	8:43 AM
Moon enters Gemini	9:55 AM	12:55 PM
Moon sextile Uranus	10:19 AM	1:19 PM
Moon trine Saturn	12:08 PM	3:08 PM
Moon sextile Jupiter	3:37 PM	6:37 PM
Moon trine Mars	4:34 PM	7:34 PM
Venus opposite Jupiter begins (see August 9)		
Venus square Pluto begins (see August 9)		
Venus conjunct Mars begins (see August 20)		

Birthday: Barack Obama 1961

Mood Watch: The moods of the day begin somewhat lazily with the waning Moon void-of-course in Taurus. As the Moon enters Gemini, the laziness quickly subsides as our moods become preoccupied with a myriad of details. Today's lunar aspects are largely very promising and upbeat. President Obama greets his forty-ninth birthday today with the Moon in Gemini, which just happens to be where his natal Moon is positioned. The Gemini Moon gives Mr. Obama the impetus to explore many possibilities and situations while keeping a keen eye on the dual affects of certain types of emotional responses. People with Gemini Moon often have mixed feelings about controversial matters, and they are keen on the necessity to talk matters through until some common ground is met. Sun in Leo and Moon in Gemini is generally a very positive time to seek playfulness and friendship.

August 5th Thursday

Moon in Gemini	PDT	EDT
Moon square Mercury	4:22 AM	7:22 AM
Moon sextile Sun	9:33 AM	12:33 PM

Birthday: Neil Armstrong 1930

Mood Watch: This waning Gemini Moon is here to help us get our thoughts and communications more evenly aligned. The Moon in Gemini reminds us how to mediate, interpret, deliberate, and negotiate in all those areas of life where discernment is needed most. Later in the day, Moon square Mercury brings moods challenged by recklessness communications and complex subjects. Gemini Moon brings a restless or nervous time for some people, and they must remember to feed the brain selectively and not to get distracted by disruptive and nonproductive chatter.

♌

August 6ᵗʰ Friday

Moon in Gemini / Cancer	PDT	EDT	
Moon trine Neptune	10:49 AM	1:49 PM	
Moon square Venus goes v/c	2:20 PM	5:20 PM	
Moon enters Cancer	2:51 PM	5:51 PM	
Moon square Uranus	3:08 PM	6:08 PM	
Moon square Saturn	5:17 PM	8:17 PM	
Moon square Jupiter	7:59 PM	10:59 PM	
Moon opposite Pluto	8:09 PM	11:09 PM	
Venus enters Libra	8:47 PM	11:47 PM	
Moon square Mars	11:25 PM	2:25 AM	(August 7)

Birthday: Lucille Ball 1911

Mood Watch: Throughout the morning, our Gemini Moon moods bring dreamy thoughtfulness with the Moon trine Neptune. Later, as the Moon squares Venus and then goes void-of-course, our moods are burdened by fickleness, indecision, and struggles to attract the things we want. Soon enough, the Moon in Cancer alters our moods with the need to adapt to the feelings beginning to surface. Cancer Moon puts us in touch with our feelings, and while the Moon squares to Uranus, Saturn, and Jupiter, our feelings may seem particularly disrupted by life's numerous complexities. Tough lunar aspects on a waning Cancer Moon day can easily create worrisome scenarios. Moon opposite Pluto and Moon square Mars further complicate our sense of security by reminding us of the price of hardship. Angry, fearful, or oppressed feelings must not enslave us – they are to be used as a gauge to warn and protect us, and to test our strength and intellect. This is a time to pace ourselves and to plan on providing nurturing foods and a comforting atmosphere whenever possible.

Venus enters Libra (Venus in Libra: August 6 – Sept. 8) It's all about to happen with Venus – a slew of activity – four Venus aspects in a row (see the *Overview* list of aspects for August). Today, Venus enters Libra, and the course of love, magnetism, affection and feminine perception begins to focus on harmonizing and balancing relationships, marriages, and friendships. Venus in Libra stimulates our Libra friends with a strong sense of affection, and of focusing our love relationships towards the goal of creating a more harmonized and balanced state of being. Venus is at home in Libra, and brings out a love of libraries, of scholarly works, and there is a greater attraction to large bodies of information. Venus in Libra emphasizes the love of books, education, law and order, friends and loved ones, and particularly a love and desire for balance wherever possible. As for the delicacy of love matters, in order to settle on the best choices and decisions possible, Libra strives hard to apply a great wealth of knowledge, common law, history, and helpful information with regard to relationships. Attraction is a mystery; Libra seeks to decode the mystery. Due to Venus' retrograde cycle (Oct. 8 – Nov. 18), it will return to Libra again this year from November 7 – 29.

August 7ᵗʰ Saturday

Moon in Cancer	PDT	EDT
Venus opposite Uranus	12:58 AM	3:58 AM
Moon sextile Mercury goes v/c	11:44 AM	2:44 PM

Birthday: Alan Leo 1860

Mood Watch: The Moon wanes in Cancer, and the only significant lunar aspect of the day, Moon sextile Mercury, brings a great deal of talk and a long void-of-course Moon phase. Waning Moon is the time to work through and let go of negative feelings, but we must first experience these feelings before disposing of them. The Moon is all about moods, and when the Moon is in her native sign, Cancer, there is a tendency for all scopes of mood to be richly felt. The void-of-course Cancer Moon continues throughout the day and into the evening; this is a recipe for spacey, withdrawn, and possibly even grumpy moods. Try not to let your worries get the best of you, and remember, moodiness is inevitable with the void-of-course Cancer Moon.

Venus opposite Uranus (occurring Aug. 1 – 9) Venus in Libra opposite Uranus in Aries brings many possibilities while Venus and Uranus counteract each other at the equinoxes of the zodiac. The polarity of Libra and Aries tests the harmony of relationships. The balance of love is challenged by unusual enterprises and radical warfare. Conflict may surface as love relationships are tested by fundamental differences over extraneous new developments and extraordinary circumstances. On the up side, exciting and unusual kinds of pleasure bring radical new awareness. On the down side, this type of love is explosive in nature, creating radical obsessions – some healthy and some not. Although they are often short lived, this aspect allows for unusual, exciting, and torrid love affairs. This is a good time for artists to make breakthroughs and for eccentric expressions of affection. Issues of freedom are likely to be raised in love related disputes. No matter how you look at it, issues of love are surely being activated with a broadening sense of awareness. This is the only time this aspect will occur this year.

August 8ᵗʰ Sunday

Moon in Cancer / Leo	PDT	EDT	
Venus conjunct Saturn	10:23 AM	1:23 PM	
Moon enters Leo	4:24 PM	7:24 PM	
Moon trine Uranus	4:35 PM	7:35 PM	
Moon sextile Saturn	7:01 PM	10:01 PM	
Moon sextile Venus	7:36 PM	10:36 PM	
Moon trine Jupiter	9:06 PM	12:06 AM	(August 9)

Birthday: Dustin Hoffman 1937

Mood Watch: The waning Moon in the sign of the crab continues to be void-of-course after yesterday's disruptively long void-of-course lunar phase. You may notice that people are compelled to complain and nag a lot about the state of affairs.

184

As the Moon enters Leo and then becomes trine to Uranus, rebellious and playful moods take us out of our bothersome stupor. After some timely adjustments, our moods are regenerated by an evening of promising and uplifting lunar aspects. Tonight is a good time to enjoy some entertainment.

Venus conjunct Saturn (occurring Aug. 2 – 11) Venus and Saturn are conjunct in Libra at the one degree mark, which makes it the cusp of Virgo and Libra. This creates subtly affectionate, communicative, and serious bonding between loved ones. This conjunction brings a favorable time to apply discipline in the arts and in love related matters. Venus conjunct Saturn represents our commitment and responsibility to the people and things we love and care about. It may also indicate there is a strong, timely quality about love matters taking place, or that love matters are undergoing a restriction, or possibly even closure of some kind. Abrupt endings may also factor in, given that Venus is currently opposing the explosive influence, Uranus (see yesterday, Venus opposite Uranus). This conjunction of Venus and Saturn can go either way on the positive-negative scale, since the loving attraction of Venus can be either encouraged or thwarted by the responsible, serious, and limiting discipline of Saturn's energy. This is the only time Venus will be conjunct with Saturn this year.

August 9th Monday
NEW MOON in LEO
Moon in Leo

	PDT	EDT	
Moon sextile Mars	2:39 AM	5:39 AM	
Venus opposite Jupiter	4:40 PM	7:40 PM	
Moon conjunct Sun	8:07 PM	11:07 PM	
Venus square Pluto	9:05 PM	12:05 AM	(August 10)

Birthday: Sam Elliott 1944

Mood Watch: The **New Moon in Leo** (Moon conjunct Sun) is a time of personal discovery. Leo is the optimist, and the New Leo Moon brings positive new perspectives to personal goals, as well as inspiring a fresh outlook on one's image. Some may be strongly touched by the need to get a new lease on life. The desire for the latest fashion and a focus on hair is commonplace for this sort of mood setting. A new pattern of positive self-image and dignity can be created while the old beastly pattern will have to be tempered and corrected. Image comes from within and is generated by the sheer magnitude of one's will. Everyone has room to grow if they take the time to apply self-worth, self-respect, and discipline. Leo also represents family and friends, and this may be just the time to initiate a new lease on an old friendship, or to enjoy a favorite hobby with the family.

Venus opposite Jupiter (occurring Aug. 4 – 12) First, Venus enters Libra on August 6, then, it opposes Uranus and conjuncts with Saturn (see the past couple of days). Now, the planet of love and attraction, Venus, opposes the planet of joy and prosperity, Jupiter. First, it's radical circumstances (Uranus), then it's serious limitations (Saturn), now it's the quality of life and money (Jupiter). Next, love and power struggles (see below, Venus square Pluto). Love and arts are undergoing the tests and trials of fortune. Venus in Libra brings a love for harmony and balance in relationships. Meanwhile, Jupiter in Aries focuses on the need for enterprising advancement and self-actualized fulfillment. It also focuses on the funding of charities, and those areas of our lives where we share common goals for society and our human rights. Venus opposite Jupiter brings on a significant awareness of the dynamics of attraction and wealth. During this aspect, many folks will find themselves torn between the need to focus on the self versus the need to help the less fortunate of our communities. Custody battles are hard fought under these circumstances. The process of overcoming personal loss requires a great deal of effort to attain the healing power of love. Money related tests and troubles in relationships are often a factor under this aspect. Venus opposite Jupiter increases awareness of the need for joy in relationships. This is the only time this aspect will occur this year.

Venus square Pluto (occurring Aug. 4 – 12) Venus in Libra is square Pluto in Capricorn. The diplomatic, peaceable, cooperative and naturally harmonious side of our affections (Venus in Libra) is likely to take a pretty good beating, while a seemingly major transformation is occurring on a physical level (Pluto in Capricorn). Our concepts of beauty may be challenged as the corruption of superpowers prompts action which threatens or alters the beauty and pleasure in our lives. Venus square Pluto usually involves such difficulties as loss or death of a loved one, the obstacles of rejection, and general oppression for those aspects of life to which we are undeniably attached and which we hold dear. If something of this nature is occurring for you, it is best to recognize that love will triumph in every dimension, despite the pain of separation, or the disease and strife of the beloved. Be both strong and gentle in matters of love. Let the obstacles of love's pain become the building blocks of a better outlook, and a stronger love will supersede these current trials of the heart. This aspect is a little more merciful with Venus in its home sign, Libra; that is, it's much more merciful than it was earlier this year, with Venus in the detrimental position of Aries on March 11.

August 10th Tuesday

Moon in Leo / Virgo

	PDT	EDT
Moon opposite Neptune goes v/c	12:09 PM	3:09 PM
Moon enters Virgo	4:01 PM	7:01 PM
Moon trine Pluto	8:51 PM	11:51 PM

Birthday: Antonio Banderas 1960

Mood Watch: Gregarious and playful moods make this a pleasant morning with the Moon newly waxing in Leo. However, this afternoon, as the Moon opposes Neptune and goes void-of-course, our moods are likely to turn spacey and many folks will seem easily distracted. Tender egos are easy to tread on when the Moon is void-of-course in Leo. Some folks will be mulling over the process of internalizing and perfecting self image. A sense of integrity and pride are enhanced through careful self-development, and it is times like this when the balance and imbalances of the self become clear to those who are bothering to notice. People who are more confident and self-assured do not need to force themselves on others for approval. Lions roar for many reasons, but for now, mostly just to be heard. This may serve

186

as a good time to listen to the beast within. This evening's Moon in Virgo puts our moods into a more practical and logical approach to the matters at hand.

August 11ᵗʰ Wednesday

Moon in Virgo	PDT	EDT
Moon conjunct Mercury goes v/c	5:03 PM	8:03 PM

Birthday: Alex Haley 1921

Mood Watch: While the youthfully waxing Moon is in Virgo, cautious and attentive attitudes pervade the atmosphere. Virgo Moon brings a general attitude of cautious resourcefulness, and we often lean towards the more practical method of satisfying our needs. Tonight, Moon conjunct Mercury brings talkative moods, but since the Moon goes void-of-course, many folks will stop to doubt or question, and to reassess the necessity of doing things correctly before much more is potentially done incorrectly. In the midst of the evening's mishaps, the sharpest sense of humor is often found in life's silly – or simple – mistakes. The worst mistakes can be avoided through the wisdom of caution and discernment.

August 12ᵗʰ Thursday

Moon in Virgo / Libra	PDT	EDT
Moon enters Libra	3:43 PM	6:43 PM
Moon opposite Uranus	3:46 PM	6:46 PM
Moon conjunct Saturn	7:01 PM	10:01 PM
Moon opposite Jupiter	8:06 PM	11:06 PM
Moon square Pluto	8:38 PM	11:38 PM

Birthday: Madame H. P. Blavatsky 1831

Mood Watch:: The Virgo Moon is void-of-course as we start the day, and it will remain so for several hours. Beware of the tendency for our moods to be full of doubt, skepticism, or criticism. Also be aware of the tendency for some folks to feel depressed. By the time the Moon enters Libra, our moods will enter into a much more balanced perspective. We may find that we are feeling somewhat rebellious with the Moon opposite Uranus, and many folks will seem restless at this point. Later, Moon conjunct Saturn brings serious expressions of mood. Tonight's Moon opposite Jupiter encourages our need to excel and to share our enthusiasm with others. Later, Moon square Pluto is anticipated to bring some dramatic emotional shifts. The Libra Moon is a time to work on harmonizing with others, and to empower the act of applying logic by keeping a cool head.

August 13ᵗʰ Friday

Moon in Libra	PDT	EDT
Moon conjunct Venus	1:59 AM	4:59 AM
Moon conjunct Mars	6:21 AM	9:21 AM
URANUS ENTERS PISCES	8:35 PM	11:35 PM

Birthday: Alfred Hitchcock 1899

Mood Watch: Waxing Libra Moon focuses our moods on the need to create harmony and beauty in our lives, and to get on with the necessity to create some order with our sense of progress. Friends and partners often become the highlights of our focuses during the waxing Libra Moon. This may be a good time to initiate a new friendship or rediscover a sense of newness with an old friend.

Why is **Friday the 13TH** considered such a bad omen? Friday the 13TH in October of the year 1307 was a really bad day in the life of Jacques DeMolay, fearless leader of the (notorious) Knights Templar. By sundown on that fateful day nearly all the Knights Templar throughout France were seized and thrown into dungeons. Thousands of men who were at one time considered nobles had their properties seized, and many suffered torture and inhumane conditions. The French King and the Pope conspired against the Templars to plunder their wealth; the Templars were then discarded as heretics and banned from the power they had held for so long. Seven years after the Friday the 13TH incident, DeMolay was executed. The fall of the Templars left such a bitter mark on the soul of Europe that Friday the 13TH has held a notorious reputation. Friday the 13TH is still considered unlucky, however, there are some people who think of thirteen as an auspicious number, and to them this day is considered to be a lucky time. These people naturally tend to have a better experience of this day, by virtue of their more positive outlook. On a positive note, the Knights Templar remain a fascination and a fraternally honored memory to this day. Perhaps their fortunes will yet revive.

Uranus enters Pisces (Uranus in Pisces: Aug. 13, 2010 – March 11, 2011) Uranus takes several years to pass through a zodiac sign. Since March 2003, Uranus has been in Pisces creating radical change in our belief structures. This past spring Uranus entered Aries for the first time (see May 27). Today the retrograde Uranus re-enters Pisces for the final phase of its travels there, and it will not re-enter Aries until March 11, 2011.

Uranus in Pisces brought storms to our institutions and how we view them. During this time, our consciousness was awakened to examine our belief systems and spiritual lifestyles. Chaos (Uranus) moves through the mutable water sign (Pisces) and challenges our beliefs and our sense of spiritual freedom. Uranus in Pisces brought an explosion of creative art and computer programs to blow our minds. Uranus in Pisces made the most of such Piscean expressions of behavior as addiction, escapism, and unconventional forms of worship. Over this time of Uranus in Pisces, new and radical fascinations and expressions were explored in the form of art, poetry, movie making, plays, and music. Those who treasure their beliefs as in intricate part of their lifestyle are likely to see great change and challenge in their spiritual life. This may not seem like a time of great change in our beliefs, but that's exactly what Uranus has been busily doing since March 2003. It's time to reexamine what we believe and where we're going, especially since radical new changes have begun to unfold through our recent initial phase of Uranus in Aries (May 27 – Aug. 13). This is a good time to become clear about beliefs.

August 14th Saturday

Moon in Libra / Scorpio

	PDT	EDT
Moon sextile Sun	3:06 AM	6:06 AM
Moon trine Neptune goes v/c	1:06 PM	4:06 PM

Moon enters Scorpio	5:27 PM	8:27 PM	
Moon sextile Pluto	10:37 PM	1:37 AM	(August 15)
Sun opposite Neptune begins (see August 20)			

ℒ

Birthday: Halle Berry 1966

Mood Watch: Waxing Libra Moon is an excellent time to kick back with a friend or partner and enjoy the lazy Leo sun energy of summertime. Friendship is highlighted this afternoon and this is a good time to enjoy artful and cultural endeavors. The Libra Moon also goes void-of-course this afternoon, avoid getting into domestic disputes. No big deal – just a few extra adjustments will have to be made in order to keep the atmosphere of our moods balanced. Later, the Scorpio Moon intensity works like a warning system as it tests our ability to cope with harsh realities. No fear – sometimes Scorpio Moons are just plain creative and energizing fun, and sometimes they open our senses to the deeper and more profound side of life.

August 15ᵗʰ Sunday
Moon in Scorpio
No Exact Aspects

Birthday: Oscar Peterson 1925

Mood Watch: The Moon has a way of being in the right place at the right time when it comes to checking the astrological temperature of our moods. Today's waxing Scorpio Moon teaches us how to cope with pressures. Scorpio says: "I create," or "I desire." This is a good time to create an understanding that works for you, and to place your hopes on your heart's desire, no matter how dire or exciting life's predicaments may seem. Sun in Leo and Moon in Scorpio is the time to conquer adversity, improve self-image, and to work on personal power, inner strength, and confidence.

August 16ᵗʰ Monday
FIRST QUARTER MOON in SCORPIO
Moon in Scorpio / Sagittarius	PDT	EDT	
Moon sextile Mercury	1:11 AM	4:11 AM	
Moon square Sun	11:15 AM	2:15 PM	
JUPITER OPPOSITE SATURN	1:43 PM	4:43 PM	
Moon square Neptune	5:47 PM	8:47 PM	
Moon trine Uranus goes v/c	10:25 PM	1:25 AM	(August 17)
Moon enters Sagittarius	10:34 PM	1:34 AM	(August 17)

Birthday: Madonna 1958

Mood Watch: The **First Quarter Moon in Scorpio** (Moon square Sun) arouses our moods in deep and impassioned ways. Throughout today, this waxing quarter Moon of Scorpio persists to bring our moods to a strange and intense level of existence. Get in touch with your creative and imaginative side and celebrate your passion.

Jupiter opposite Saturn (occurring April 25 – Aug. 31) Jupiter in Aries opposes Saturn in Libra at the two degree mark. This aspect last reached its peak on May 22 when Jupiter was in Pisces and Saturn was in Virgo. Now this heralding aspect, which represents economic change at an expedited rate, emphasizes an even greater level of change. Jupiter in Aries brings new enterprises, competitive business, and fiery economic transformation (see Jupiter enters Aries, June 5). Saturn in Libra emphasizes the necessity to put some balance into our disciplines and to implement stringent laws and guidelines (see Saturn enters Libra, July 21). Jupiter opposite Saturn requires a commitment to labor and the performance of difficult work to win the attainment and satisfaction of our social and economic needs. For the full story of Jupiter opposite Saturn, *see May 22*, when it first reached its peak during this four month long occurrence period.

August 17th Tuesday

Moon in Sagittarius	PDT	EDT
Moon trine Jupiter	2:59 AM	5:59 AM
Moon sextile Saturn	3:10 AM	6:10 AM
Moon sextile Venus	6:56 PM	9:56 PM
Moon sextile Mars	8:42 PM	11:42 PM

Birthday: Robert DeNiro 1943

Mood Watch: Positive lunar aspects make this a very good day. Sun in Leo and Moon in Sagittarius bring an outgoing, aspiring, and promising outlook. Moods are backed by an energetic and enthusiastic spirit. Lively, resilient, and athletic types of energy abound. Inspired perspectives help to uplift the overall mood, and this is a great time to spread hope, good cheer, and positive vibrations. Put some life force into each step. Harness the good vibrations.

August 18th Wednesday

Moon in Sagittarius	PDT	EDT	
Moon square Mercury	9:50 AM	12:50 PM	
Moon trine Sun	11:57 PM	2:57 AM	(August 19)

Birthday: Roman Polanski 1933

Mood Watch: The morning may bring a number of complex details into play as the Moon square Mercury complicates our thinking processes as well as our communications. In just a couple of days, Mercury will go retrograde (see August 20) and our communications will become considerably more multifaceted. This may be the time to focus on scheduling, organization, and preparation for the next few weeks to come. Be sure to incorporate contingency plans while wading through the complexities of the dwindling summer days. The Sun and Moon are both in fire signs today, igniting creative and energetic expressions. Moon in Sagittarius is a great time to travel.

August 19th Thursday

Moon in Sagittarius / Capricorn	PDT	EDT
Moon sextile Neptune	2:07 AM	5:07 AM
Moon square Uranus goes v/c	6:58 AM	9:58 AM
Moon enters Capricorn	7:18 AM	10:18 AM
Moon square Jupiter	11:35 AM	2:35 PM

190

Moon square Saturn	12:39 PM	3:39 PM
Moon conjunct Pluto	1:02 PM	4:02 PM
Sun trine Pluto begins (see August 25)		

♌

Birthday: Bill Clinton 1946

Mood Watch: Chaotic moods kick off this Thursday morning with the Moon going void-of-course as it squares to Uranus. Soon enough, the Moon enters Capricorn, and our moods will be much more prone to take control. The waxing Capricorn Moon is a time when many folks tend to mask their feelings. As the Moon squares to Jupiter, people may seem somewhat withdrawn and considerably less generous than usual. This afternoon's Moon square Saturn could bring some very complicated moods, and people may seem especially stern about focusing their energies with serious intent. As the Moon conjuncts with Pluto dramatic moods unfold. As a general rule, Capricorn Moon is a good time to stay busy and to avoid unnecessary melodrama.

August 20th Friday

Moon in Capricorn	**PDT**	**EDT**
Sun opposite Neptune	3:06 AM	6:06 AM
Moon square Venus	9:45 AM	12:45 PM
Moon square Mars	9:49 AM	12:49 PM
Venus conjunct Mars	11:49 AM	2:49 PM
Mercury goes retrograde	12:59 PM	3:59 PM
Moon trine Mercury	8:45 PM	11:45 PM

Birthday: H.P. Lovecraft 1890

Mood Watch: Moon in Capricorn demands a firm guard on the emotional side of our moods. Sound, resourceful and earnest labor will be the emphasis of the day. This morning the Moon is square to Venus, and then it squares to Mars; we may find that it will seem difficult to attract the things – or the kind of attention – we desire, or to muster up the kind of energy it takes to get motivated. A keen focus and serious determination to get things done makes the afternoon an excellent time to complete tasks and make some progress. This evening's Moon trine Mercury will aid our communication process despite Mercury retrograde (see below), and this will be a good time to adjust to the changes in the air.

Sun opposite Neptune (occurring Aug. 14 – 23) This occurrence of Sun opposite Neptune especially affects Leo and cusp born Virgo people celebrating birthdays from August 14 – 23. Neptune in opposition to these folks' natal Sun brings a strong awareness of Spirit, the spiritual path, and the acknowledgment of one's beliefs. The challenge facing these birthday folks is to confront and overcome all disruptive personal doubts that cause them to question the practice of believing. These people will be imminently aware this year of the vast shifts in spiritual beliefs, and they may feel quite overwhelmed by the confusion and fluctuations of their own spiritual awareness. This is no surprise – it is occurring for numerous people at this time – our birthday friends will just experience it more directly. Seek your favorite sanctuary and tune into Spirit.

Venus conjunct Mars (occurring Aug. 4 – Oct. 8) This conjunction brings together the feminine and the masculine in the sign of Libra. Venus conjunct Mars in Libra brings activity in relationships, proposals of marriage, and it brings masculine and feminine counterparts together in a harmonious way. This conjunction puts us in touch with the power of love in action and active attraction. Here, we are easily seduced by love. This may serve as a good time to express love ardently and sincerely, and to receive love just as well. This is also a good time for an individual to get in touch with both the masculine and feminine aspects of the self, and to create peace between those active and passive parts of the personality. Venus and Mars conjunct in Libra will bring a strong interest in such Libra-like interests as research, books, literature, marriage, partnership, friendships, and social endeavors. This is a time of integration between the feminine and masculine forces – it is best done in stride and with care. Masculine expression has less of a chance here, while Mars is in the detrimental place of Libra (see July 29). However, Venus in Libra (see Aug. 6) is the home for the pioneer of love, soothing the feminine approach to love with a great deal more grace and tact. Empower love relationships with the greatest respect. During this occurrence phase, this conjunction will reach another peak on October 3, with Venus and Mars in Scorpio.

Mercury goes retrograde (Mercury retrograde: Aug. 20 – Sept. 12) Hold on to your thinking caps – for the next few weeks (until Sept. 12), Mercury will be retrograde in one of the primary places it rules, Virgo. Mercury retrograde in Virgo is likely to bring disruption to our attempts to accurately analyze matters, and there are likely to be numerous misunderstandings over all kinds of data. Be on the lookout fo r frequent bouts of dyslexia, and other communication mistakes, particularly in such Virgo related activities as research, analytical sciences, health matters, accounting, and overall communications. During this time it will be best to attempt communications more than once or twice, and to be persistent as well as patient. At first it may be difficult to sit through everyone's excuses and misinformation, but eventually there will be a logical explanation to Mercury related setbacks. For more information on Mercury retrograde, see the section in the introduction about *Mercury retrograde periods.*

August 21st Saturday

Moon in Capricorn / Aquarius	PDT	EDT	
SATURN SQUARE PLUTO	3:15 AM	6:15 AM	
Moon sextile Uranus goes v/c	6:08 PM	9:08 PM	
Moon enters Aquarius	6:38 PM	9:38 PM	
Moon sextile Jupiter	10:37 PM	1:37 AM	(August 22)

Birthday: William "Count" Basie 1904

Mood Watch: A somewhat nondescript quality of mood fills the air. If anything *would* describe it, we would have to say the mood is serious. The waxing Capricorn Moon takes us through the day with serious and determined moods which are often focused on the accomplishment of goals and major tasks. Tonight, Moon sextile Uranus brings moods inspired by original thinking and unusual inventions. The Capricorn Moon goes void-of-course at this point in the evening, and then swiftly enters Aquarius. Innovative thoughts inspire us tonight with the Moon in Aquarius.

192

Saturn square Pluto (occurring June 21 – Sept. 14) This aspect has been occurring for nearly a year, although we did have a temporary break from it this past spring. This very serious and highly influential aspect is reaching its peak for the second time this year, for a review on what's going on, *see January 31.*

VIRGO

Key Phrase: " I ANALYZE "

Mutable Earth Sign

Ruling Planet: Mercury

Symbol: The Virgin

August 22nd through

September 22nd

August 22nd Sunday
Moon in Aquarius

	PDT	EDT	
Moon trine Saturn	12:42 AM	3:42 AM	
Sun enters Virgo	10:26 PM	1:26 AM	(August 23)

Birthday: John Lee Hooker 1917

Mood Watch: Our desires for freedom and equality are tested at different stages of our human experience. The mortal self is limited, but what he or she leaves behind is a reflection of the immortal soul which does not die. What we leave behind is not always seen; it is sometimes heard or spoken. It may be a simple concept, motto, or idea that is passed on. Our contributions to others may be received and perceived in many gifted ways. The energy of the Aquarius Moon inspires our desire to leave something behind that will benefit others.

Sun enters Virgo (Sun in Virgo: Aug. 22/23 – Sept. 22) Virgo's key phrase is, "I analyze," and the pragmatic spirit of Virgo examines all avenues of life. It is just like Virgo to pick everything apart, detail by detail, and yet Virgo strives to get as much of an overview of the whole picture as possible. Virgo questions, Virgo doubts, and Virgo demands proof. The Mercury ruled mutable sign of earth is keen, sharp-witted, and not so quick to believe any sort of random information, unless it's painstakingly researched by some reputable sources. Virgo will question the source every time. Virgos are famous for their ability to count, calculate, and measure everything that must be accounted for, which is why Virgo is chosen to watch over the vital and bountiful harvest season.

August 23rd Monday

Full Moon Eve

Moon in Aquarius	**PDT**	**EDT**
Moon trine Mars	1:16 AM	4:16 AM
Moon trine Venus	3:00 AM	6:00 AM

Birthday: Barbara Eden 1934

Mood Watch: The first full day and night of the Sun in Virgo are set to be illuminated by a Full Moon Eve. Sun in Virgo and Moon in Aquarius bring all styles of human expression. The spirit of this strongly waxing Aquarius Moon reminds us to learn from our mistakes and to add to our knowledge from our experiences of life. Be a contributor in some vast or tiny way, and oddly, eventually, your mark will resonate through time, like that piece of wisdom someone once told you years ago that still sticks with you. This is a good time to celebrate the love of humankind and to enjoy the company of good friends. Aquarius Moon brings the potential for technological breakthroughs and great feats of accomplishment in the world of invention.

August 24th Tuesday

FULL MOON in PISCES

Moon in Aquarius / Pisces	**PDT**	**EDT**
Moon conjunct Neptune goes v/c	1:29 AM	4:29 AM
Moon enters Pisces	7:11 AM	10:11 AM
Moon opposite Sun	10:04 AM	1:04 PM
Moon sextile Pluto	1:02 PM	4:02 PM

Birthday: Stephen Fry 1957

Mood Watch: The **Full Moon in Pisces** (Moon opposite Sun) brings out the psychic in everyone. People can be very sensitive, and as a result, some people express themselves in very artistic or perhaps nonsensical ways. Enchantment sets the stage for Full Pisces Moon activity early in the day. Dance, music, and art are often activities of the Full Pisces Moon. Imaginations will run wild today and anything is possible. Pisces says: "I believe," and while the Moon is full in Pisces, it is vitally important to carry our beliefs wisely, as destructive tendencies may bring us down if we're not careful. This will also be a time to watch out for low self-esteem or substance abuse.

August 25th Wednesday

Moon in Pisces	**PDT**	**EDT**	
Moon opposite Mercury	7:04 PM	10:04 PM	
Sun trine Pluto	10:12 PM	1:12 AM	(August 26)

Birthday: Elvis Costello 1954

Mood Watch: The Sun is in Virgo and the Moon is in Pisces on this post-full Moon day. Pisces is anatomically represented by the feet, and symbolically represents what we stand for, while the opposite sign, Virgo, is attributed to the intestines and symbolically represents what we don't stand for – that which we have assimilated and choose to eliminate. This polarity experience is a refinement, or purification process, which gives us the edge to move past illusions and to understand what we truly stand for. This is a time to shed illusions and reaffirm beliefs. Uranus is a strong and dynamic force which has been in Pisces since March 2003, with the exception of this year's brief interlude of Uranus in Aries (May 27 – Aug. 13, 2010). Uranus will remain in Pisces until March 2011. Overall, a great shakeup in our belief structures has radically changed what we stand for in the passing days of Uranus in Pisces. For a review on Uranus in Pisces, see August 13.

Sun trine Pluto (occurring Aug. 19- 29) Positive, life-altering changes are occurring in the lives of Leo and Virgo cusp born people celebrating birthdays this year from August 19 – 29 . They are currently undergoing the favorable trine aspect of Pluto to their natal Sun, bringing out experiences that involve transformation and encounters with greater powers and fate. Have no fear; this is a time to get in touch with your power, birthday Leos and Virgos! Pluto moves slowly in our cosmos, and powerful encounters that seem deadly or harsh are actually a necessary part of the process. Matters involving fate can be positive, and the trine aspect does represent a gift being bestowed – however unlikely it may seem. Be grateful this trine brings power issues into your life in a more positive fashion, leading to positive transformation. Finding out how to benefit from this power is a big part of discovering Pluto's gifts. This aspect last occurred April 25, affecting some of the Aries/Taurus cusp born folks.

August 26th Thursday

Moon in Pisces / Aries

	PDT	EDT	
Moon conjunct Uranus goes v/c	6:59 PM	9:59 PM	
Moon enters Aries	7:50 PM	10:50 PM	
Moon conjunct Jupiter	10:50 PM	1:50 AM	(August 27)

Birthday: Brandford Marsalis 1960

Mood Watch: A dreamy, rather psychic expression of awareness takes place with Moon in Pisces. Throughout the day moods remain somewhat spacey, exceedingly clairvoyant, and quite artistic and full of belief, prayer, and meditation. The Pisces Moon, although now waning, remains in essence very full. This, for some, may be an extremely emotional time requiring the spontaneous release of emotional expression. Be aware of the tendency towards escapism and of people seeking to indulge their fantasy world. Tonight's Moon conjunct Uranus brings chaotic moods as the Moon swiftly enters Aries. The Moon in Aries activates our moods with zeal. Waning Aries Moon is a good time to get in touch with the need to release anger or anxiety. A sporting effort to drop unproductive grudges brings relief.

August 27th Friday

Moon in Aries

	PDT	EDT
Moon square Pluto	1:35 AM	4:35 AM
Moon opposite Saturn	3:02 AM	6:02 AM

Birthday: Paul "Pee-wee Herman" Reubens 1952

Mood Watch: Aries Moon doesn't mess around with our moods – in fact, it demands succinct and direct reporting, so here goes… Today's lunar aspects occur in the earliest hours of the morning and the tone of them has a bit of a nightmarish quality. Moon square Pluto and Moon opposite Saturn delve into our need to face difficult twists of fate – and hardships – in a timely and serious manner. Nightmares aside, throughout the day the Aries Moon sails confidently into the open houses of the zodiac, putting us in touch with our own, individual integral character development process.

August 28th Saturday

Moon in Aries	PDT	EDT
Moon opposite Mars	9:08 AM	12:08 PM
Moon opposite Venus	1:54 PM	4:54 PM
Venus trine Neptune begins (see September 4)		

Birthday: Jack Black 1969

Mood Watch: Today's waning Moon in Aries sets the tone for many people to push their way through traffic and shopping lines, focusing on themselves and their own interests. While some are assured they know exactly what they want, others seem baffled at the tenacity and the fortitude that goes behind the push and drive of selfish desires. The Moon opposes Mars today, and later it opposes Venus; from anguish to desire, the passion of our moods is enduring in its fortitude. This is indeed a time when selfhood is touched upon, and our general moods are based on our own personal needs, as well as those pushy or powerful enough to come first! Avoid butting heads, since it's very easy to do on a waning Aries Moon.

August 29th Sunday

Moon in Aries / Taurus	PDT	EDT
Moon sextile Neptune goes v/c	1:46 AM	4:46 AM
Moon enters Taurus	7:36 AM	10:36 AM
Moon trine Pluto	1:10 PM	4:10 PM
Moon trine Sun	8:39 PM	11:39 PM

Birthday: Michael Jackson 1958

Mood Watch: The early morning urge to get up and go may be compromised by the void-of-course Aries Moon. However, soon enough the Moon enters Taurus, and a very sensible quality of interaction begins to affect our moods. This Taurus Moon Sunday with the Moon trine Pluto brings favorable healing, consoling, and regenerative themes. A calming atmosphere with beautiful surroundings will enhance our Taurus Moon moods. The Taurus Moon and Virgo Sun bring practical, earthy, and reasonable moods and vibrations.

August 30th Monday

Moon in Taurus	PDT	EDT
Moon trine Mercury	11:38 AM	2:38 PM

Birthday: Warren Buffett 1930

Mood Watch: As we enter this Taurus Moon day with the Moon trine Mercury, many of us may be marveling at the multiple misunderstandings that are going around while Mercury has been retrograde (August 20 – Sept. 12). Moon trine Mercury assists us to correct communication errors. Taurus Moon puts us in touch with earthly beauty. This may also be a time when we feel somewhat lazy and in need of a calming environment. Waning Taurus Moon often brings on lazy moods and the strong desire to just plain relax!

August 31st Tuesday

Moon in Taurus / Gemini	PDT	EDT
Moon square Neptune	11:38 AM	2:38 PM
Moon sextile Uranus goes v/c	4:12 PM	7:12 PM
Moon enters Gemini	5:20 PM	8:20 PM
Moon sextile Jupiter	7:08 PM	10:08 PM
Sun conjunct Mercury begins (see September 3)		
Mars trine Neptune begins (see September 9)		

Birthday: Richard Gere 1949

Mood Watch: The Moon wanes in Taurus, and the spirit of the day begins to focus on the need to get grounded, to become more sensible, and to get on with taking care of practical needs. We may find that we are not especially in tune spiritually while Moon square Neptune occurs. Sun in Virgo and Moon in Taurus is a great time to combine healthy foods with an exercise routine in a relaxing setting. Later today Moon sextile Uranus brings spontaneity geared towards breaking up routines. The Moon goes void-of-course for awhile and our attention span may diminish noticeably. As the Moon enters Gemini, our moods become thought oriented and outgoing – particularly as Moon sextile Jupiter occurs. Positive evening moods bring a quality ending to the day and an optimistic closing to the month.

September 1st Wednesday

LAST QUARTER MOON in GEMINI

Moon in Gemini	PDT	EDT
Moon trine Saturn	1:04 AM	4:04 AM
Moon square Sun	10:20 AM	1:20 PM
Moon square Mercury	4:16 PM	7:16 PM

Birthday: Edgar Rice Burroughs 1875

Mood Watch: The **Last Quarter Moon in Gemini** (Moon square Sun) brings talkative moods and informative interaction. That said, we must not forget Mercury is retrograde in Virgo (Aug. 20 – Sept. 12). People will have a lot on their minds today and intellectual pursuits are emphasized, but without carefully considered plans and an affirmation of schedules and appointments, one mislaid detail can set off a whirlwind of misinformation. Later today, Moon square Mercury becomes a particularly sensitive time to sort out complex details and to accurately communicate complicated information. Once the hubbub of details over this busy new month has been settled, this is the time to enjoy word games, puzzles, and casual conversations. Mercury may be retrograde, but we can still have fun!

September 2nd Thursday

Moon in Gemini / Cancer	PDT	EDT	
Moon trine Mars	9:28 AM	12:28 PM	
Moon trine Venus	3:45 PM	6:45 PM	
Moon trine Neptune	6:25 PM	9:25 PM	
Moon square Uranus goes v/c	10:38 PM	1:38 AM	(September 3)
Moon enters Cancer	11:51 PM	2:51 AM	(September 3)

Birthday: Billy Preston 1946

Mood Watch: There may be a lot of details to cover in this early part of a busy month, and today's waning Gemini Moon will assist us to put our priorities in order. Moon trine Mars will influence us to take action in positive ways. Later today, Moon trine Venus brings kind and loving energy. This evening, Moon trine Neptune inspires tranquil, calming, and spiritually uplifting moods. Overall, today's positive lunar aspects bring optimism and good cheer. Later this evening the Moon squares with Uranus and then goes void-of-course; this the time to call it a night, but bear in mind that chaotic feelings may cause restlessness. As the Moon enters Cancer, the need for emotional release becomes apparent.

September 3rd Friday

Moon in Cancer	PDT	EDT
Moon square Jupiter	1:04 AM	4:04 AM
Moon opposite Pluto	4:46 AM	7:46 AM
Sun conjunct Mercury	5:34 AM	8:34 AM
Moon square Saturn	7:33 AM	10:33 AM
Moon sextile Mercury	5:55 PM	8:55 PM
Moon sextile Sun	7:43 PM	10:43 PM

Birthday: Kitty Carlisle Hart 1914

Mood Watch: Mother Moon returns to her home turf in Cancer. It is time to address those feelings which are surfacing now. It's time to nurture through reassurance, to unload the emotional baggage, and to banish and clear the home and the heart of unwarranted fears and restraints.

Sun conjunct Mercury (occurring Aug. 31 – Sept. 4) This conjunction will create a much more thoughtful, communicative and expressive year ahead for those Virgo folks celebrating birthdays August 31 – Sept. 4. This is your time (birthday Virgo) to record ideas, relay important messages, and pay close attention to your imaginative thoughts as they are touched by Mercury, creating the urge to speak and be heard. Birthday Cancer, your thoughts will reveal a great deal about who you are, now and in the year to come.

September 4th Saturday

Moon in Cancer	PDT	EDT	
Venus trine Neptune	10:11 AM	1:11 PM	
Moon square Mars	3:48 PM	6:48 PM	
Moon square Venus	10:16 PM	1:16 AM	(September 5)

Birthday: Liz Greene 1946

Mood Watch: There are some definite changes in the air as the celestial shifts of the past few months have affected us strongly. The Moon is waning in Cancer, and this puts us in touch with what we are feeling about all these changes. Although the sun still touches our skin warmly on its daily course, it seems to emit considerably less warmth as the final days of summer season unfold. Cancer Moon gets us thinking about household security and stability. This is the time to secure the home by winter proofing outdoor items and preparing for autumn. Domestic hobbies and home cooking adventures often appeal to us on Cancer Moon.

Venus trine Neptune (occurring Aug. 28 – Sept. 8) Venus in Libra trine Neptune in Aquarius enhances spiritual love. This aspect brings well balanced and generous kinds of love into harmony with a very ingenious kind of spiritual expression. It delivers a calmness and tranquility that are vitally needed, and there is a greater potential to create a spiritually enhanced atmosphere. Wherever there is spiritual turmoil, Venus trine Neptune helps to ease our woes with a support network of feminine kindness. Visiting or meditating upon sacred places and favorite sanctuaries brings visions and inner wisdom. Peaceful, pleasurable, and spiritual love is possible with this aspect, which last occurred on May 18 with Venus in Gemini. It will also return within a two degree orb (non-exact) on November 23.

September 5th Sunday

Moon in Cancer / Leo

	PDT	EDT
Moon trine Uranus goes v/c	1:30 AM	4:30 AM
Moon enters Leo	2:46 AM	5:46 AM
Moon trine Jupiter	3:30 AM	6:30 AM
Moon sextile Saturn	10:22 AM	1:22 PM

Mercury-trine-Pluto-non-exact begins (see September 12)

Birthday: Freddie Mercury 1946

Mood Watch: It's a Leo Moon day, bringing forth the expression of playfulness and the need to keep life interesting and entertaining, particularly after all the emotional purging of the recent phase of the Cancer Moon. Leo Moon instills the need to get the most out of this late summer, and to indulge the senses in something delicious, appeasing, and completely satisfying. Do something good for yourself today! Leo Moon also reminds us of the need for affection in our lives; compliments will go a long way today. Some of the busiest weeks of the year are about to unfold; nonetheless, the Leo Moon on a holiday weekend will be classically reminiscent of summer's leisurely pleasures and recreational delights. *Carpe diem* – or as they say, make hay while the sun shines!

September 6th Monday

Labor Day, USA / Labour Day, Canada

Moon in Leo

	PDT	EDT	
Moon sextile Mars	6:37 PM	9:37 PM	
Moon opposite Neptune	9:51 PM	12:51 AM	(September 7)

Venus sextile Pluto begins (see September 12)

Birthday: Roger Waters 1943

Mood Watch: The waning Leo Moon keeps us active and inclined towards introspective desires and needs. Leo Moon puts a swagger into our step. This time emphasizes such Leo-like things as family, friends, and personal hobbies. Sun in Virgo and Moon in Leo call us to find a practical outlet for creative skills, public recognition, encouragement and appreciation. Tonight's Moon sextile Mars brings strong urges to activate the things that have been our minds. Later tonight, Moon opposite Neptune awakens our spiritual nature and impresses upon us the need to apply our faith.

September 7th Tuesday

Moon in Leo / Virgo	PDT	EDT
Moon sextile Venus goes v/c	1:16 AM	4:16 AM
Moon enters Virgo	2:53 AM	5:53 AM
Moon trine Pluto	7:17 AM	10:17 AM
Moon conjunct Mercury	2:13 PM	5:13 PM

Birthday: Buddy Holly 1936

Mood Watch: The Moon wanes darkly in the Mercury ruled sign, Virgo, and Mercury is currently retrograde (Aug. 20 – Sept. 12). There is a great deal of complexity at work. While the retrograde Mercury travels through Virgo, it would not be surprising if people's communication skills seem melancholic, indifferent, skeptical, or confused. This is a good time to try to encourage others to keep a stiff upper lip, to fight depression, and to battle doubt and disparity with hope and non-judgmental parity. Desperate people really need help today, and this is the time to take them seriously. Meanwhile, don't despair yourself; recognize this dark time for what it is and allow the dark shadow to pass over you, not through you. It's always darkest just before the New Moon. The balsamic phase of the pending New Moon brings insight and wisdom.

September 8th Wednesday
NEW MOON in VIRGO

Moon in Virgo	PDT	EDT	
Moon conjunct Sun	3:29 AM	6:29 AM	
Venus enters Scorpio	8:44 AM	11:44 AM	
JUPITER ENTERS PISCES	9:49 PM	12:49 AM	(September 9)

Birthday: Peter Sellers 1925

Mood Watch: The **New Moon in Virgo** (Moon conjunct Sun) invites us to start all over again with the development process of our feelings. This Moon calls to us to apply enthused methods of discernment, a new way of analyzing, and to apply caution. How about a new way of accounting or applying health practices? Finding fresh resources is often a common practice during the New Virgo Moon. This is the time to organize and prepare for the autumn season, a time when making adjustments is essential. New Virgo Moon assists us to prepare for the changes that occur in the physical world. This is the time of the harvest, and this Moon will assist us to make the most of this fruitful time with thrifty ingenuity.

Venus enters Scorpio (Venus in Scorpio: Sept. 8 – Nov. 7) Venus, which influences love, beauty, art, and attraction, now moves through Scorpio, bringing out deep and passionate levels of love's expression. We may feel preoccupied with themes of birth, sex, death and rebirth, and transformation. Magnetism runs strong with Venus in Scorpio, and love affairs are often torrid and well hidden. Sometimes the dark side of our love and our hidden fears surface while Venus is in Scorpio; this forces us to come clean about these feelings, and to take strong measures to ensure the power of our love. Venus is in detriment in the sign of Scorpio. This may be a time to work out anxiety, fear, mourning, and emotional stress relating to love. Love with passion is an empowering thing, but it is wise to ensure the experience does not hinder the wellbeing of those who are close to you. The intensity of Scorpio love can sometimes overwhelm loved ones. Love shines best when it is mutually expressed. Venus will be retrograde this autumn (Oct. 8 – Nov. 18), and it will reenter Libra on November 7. Venus reenters Scorpio on November 29 and remains in Scorpio throughout the year.

Jupiter enters Pisces (Jupiter in Pisces: Sept. 8/9 – Jan. 22, 2011) New enterprises are going through a backtracking process. Today the retrograde planet Jupiter reenters Pisces. Jupiter first entered Pisces this year in January and it swiftly moved forward into Aries on June 5/6. For a recap on this epic story of the planet of prosperity's traversal through Pisces, *see January 17.*

September 9th Thursday

Moon in Virgo / Libra	PDT	EDT
Moon opposite Uranus	12:35 AM	3:35 AM
Moon opposite Jupiter goes v/c	1:59 AM	4:59 AM
Moon enters Libra	2:01 AM	5:01 AM
Moon square Pluto	6:25 AM	9:25 AM
Moon conjunct Saturn	10:09 AM	1:09 PM
Mars trine Neptune	6:15 PM	9:15 PM

Birthday: Hugh Grant 1960

Mood Watch: A newly waxing Libra Moon allows us to approach the day with an open and informed mind. We will need to support each other today and to work together as a team while we additionally double check the facts during this Mercury retrograde time (Aug. 20 – Sept. 12). The dark phase of the Moon is past, and it's time to build on a more balanced and amicable bond of trust with the Moon in Libra. Now our moods have entered into the need for cooperation and teamwork. As we work together, it will become quickly apparent what we must do. This is the perfect time to commence the art of making decisions.

Mars trine Neptune (occurring Aug. 31 – Sept. 14) Mars in Libra is trine to Neptune in Aquarius. Actions taken to create balance will be well received, especially with regards to the necessity of upholding our faith in humanity. This will be an active time of obtaining spiritual gifts and helpful guidelines from the spirit world. Mars guarantees activities will occur, and with Neptune in the trine position, these activities will be favorably stirred up with spiritual and psychic awareness. Mars trine Neptune is an ideal time to initiate creative and imaginative spiritual practices; it's a good time to empower the personal outlook and spiritual wellbeing. This is the only time this aspect will occur this year.

September 10ᵗʰ Friday

Moon in Libra

	PDT	EDT	
Moon trine Neptune	8:57 PM	11:57 PM	
Moon conjunct Mars goes v/c	10:16 PM	1:16 AM	(September 11)
Mercury-sextile-Venus-non-exact begins (see September 16)			
Venus conjunct Mars begins (see October 3)			

Birthday: Dan "Homer Simpson" Castellaneta 1958

Mood Watch: It's a waxing Libra Moon day with the Sun in Virgo, and our moods and outlook on life are starting to look much more fall-like. With the exception of those places where heat waves are still occurring, we are much less likely to be preoccupied with summer related activities today. Libra Moon inspires the need to explore and enjoy fine company, epicurean delights, things of beauty, and some crowd pleasing social pleasures. This evening's Moon trine Neptune inspires tranquil moods and spiritually enhancing visions. Finally, Moon conjunct Mars brings an aggressive intent to our moods as the Moon goes void-of-course. All the while, Libra Moon reminds us of the need to strive for balance, to attempt harmony and peace, and to share life's joy with others.

September 11ᵗʰ Saturday

Moon in Libra / Scorpio

	PDT	EDT
Moon enters Scorpio	2:22 AM	5:22 AM
Moon conjunct Venus	5:54 AM	8:54 AM
Moon sextile Pluto	6:59 AM	9:59 AM
Moon sextile Mercury	11:29 AM	2:29 PM

Birthday: D.H. Lawrence 1885

Mood Watch: The waxing Scorpio Moon sets the tone of mood with a sense of urgency and drama. Scorpio Moon opens up such rich emotional issues as birth, sex, death, and transformation. Regenerative forces are at work to bring forth change and adjustment. Scorpio Moon often guides us through challenges and teaches us about stabilizing our emotional core in the midst of handling intensity or stress. Moon in Scorpio, a fixed water sign, reminds us that the psyche requires house cleaning now and then. When this occurs, we need to face our fears and to confront worry or paranoia with brave certainty. This Scorpio Moon is a good time to focus on healing the heart.

September 12ᵗʰ Sunday

Grandparent's Day

Moon in Scorpio

	PDT	EDT	
Venus sextile Pluto	3:43 AM	6:43 AM	
Moon sextile Sun	12:07 PM	3:07 PM	
Mercury goes direct	4:09 PM	7:09 PM	
Moon square Neptune	11:58 PM	2:58 AM	(September 13)
Mercury-trine-Pluto-non-exact (see below)			

202

Mars sextile Pluto begins (see September 18)

Birthday: Maria Muldaur 1943

♍

Mood Watch: Instinctive urges and intuitive observations are running strongly now. Scorpio Moon reminds us that life is a struggle in the process of coming and going, from a state of the impermanent to the permanent, and back again. On some level, we are reminded of the significance of certain events in our life, and how those events have shaped us through the year. Sometimes change occurs faster than we are able to process. Scorpio Moon is a vital and swift processor of emotional expression. It is through this course of action that we are able to work through an extraordinary buildup of awareness and pressure. Scorpio Moon helps us to find creative ways to accept those unfathomable mysteries of life's twists of fate, which deeply affect us all from time to time.

Venus sextile Pluto (occurring Sept. 6 – 15) Venus is in Scorpio focusing on the need for swift, passionate, attentive, and urgent responses in love matters. Pluto is in Capricorn changing the structure of power, fate, and career advancement. This aspect is most useful for those who command an element of love and passion for their work or career, and it allows them to optimize beauty in the course of their efforts. Opportunity knocks, and here, true beauty bridges the gap between generations. Venus sextile Pluto may bring exceptional breakthroughs in relationships. Sometimes this aspect helps us to recognize the devotion of our loved ones, to see the acceptance of the difficulty and hardship that comes with their devotion. Now is a good time to recognize and acknowledge their efforts. This aspect may allow someone to find true love by virtue of an unexpected twist of fate. This aspect last occurred February 14. It will reoccur on November 1, and again on December 8.

Mercury goes direct (Mercury direct: Sept. 12 – Dec. 10) Since August 20, Mercury has been retrograde in the sign of Virgo, commonly causing communication glitches and confusion when relaying information. Mercury retrograde in Virgo caused important information and data to undergo a tailspin. Now we can breathe a greatly needed sigh of relief as Mercury, the planet governing the realms of communication, becomes stationary and will soon begin to move forward. Take note that our faculties and manner of communicating will definitely improve within the next few days. Although perhaps not today, when the stationary Mercury often freezes communication efforts, but very soon our communications will run more smoothly; this will be a good time to begin clearing up various misunderstandings occurring over the past few weeks. For more information on this recently completed phase of Mercury retrograde, see August 20. For more on Mercury retrograde patterns throughout this year, see the introduction on *Mercury retrograde periods.*

Mercury-trine-Pluto-non-exact (occurring Sept. 5 – 15) Mercury in Virgo trine Pluto in Capricorn is occurring now. This could be the year for us to receive a lot of beneficial news from the world's superpowers, as this aspect is occurring for the fifth time this year! Due to Mercury's most recent retrograde cycle which is now ending, this particular cycle of Mercury trine Pluto doesn't reach an exact peak, however it does still have an affect on us from September 5 – 15. For a recap on the story of Mercury in Virgo trine Pluto in Capricorn, *see July 30*, when it last

203

reached its peak before Mercury was retrograde.

September 13th Monday

Moon in Scorpio / Sagittarius	PDT	EDT	
Moon trine Uranus	3:58 AM	6:58 AM	
Moon trine Jupiter goes v/c	4:53 AM	7:53 AM	
Moon enters Sagittarius	5:52 AM	8:52 AM	
Moon square Mercury	3:39 PM	6:39 PM	
Moon sextile Saturn	4:02 PM	7:02 PM	
Pluto goes direct	9:37 PM	12:37 AM	(September 14)

Birthday: Jacqueline Bisset 1944

Mood Watch: Liberating and auspicious dreams awaken our senses to the dawn of a new day as Moon trine Uranus and Moon trine Jupiter bring a lighting bolt of positive and charged moods. The waxing Scorpio Moon goes void-of-course and, for an hour in the early morning, trouble may strike those who are unsuspecting. As morning progresses, the Moon enters Sagittarius, and while the final weeks of summer wind to a close, the general moods of this day and night are winding up with a fiery fervor. Our moods now shift towards a restless inquisitiveness and visionary awareness as the Sagittarius Moon waxes. Moon square Mercury reminds us of the complications which have come with the past few weeks of Mercury retrograde (Aug. 20 – Sept. 12). We are now in the early stages of the forward moving Mercury; this is the time to make corrections and affirmations, to fine-tooth-comb the entanglements of the missed engagements and misunderstandings of the past few weeks. Moon sextile Saturn will give us the incentive to stay focused and to be diligent in our ways. While the Sagittarius Moon inspires us to be creative, it also shows us how to build on positive energies.

Pluto goes direct (Pluto direct: Sept. 13, 2010 – April 8, 2011) After the long – but common – retrograde period of Pluto (April 6 – September 13), the planet of transformation now moves into a smooth, direct pattern for the rest of the year. Since April 6, Pluto has been going back through the earliest degrees of Capricorn. Now that it is direct, with Pluto at the two degree mark of Capricorn, we can better acknowledge the evolution of humankind's condition in order to survive and adapt to the challenges that are occurring on planet Earth. This transformation emphasizes consciousness, without which we would not be. This is not a time to take life for granted; rather, it is a time to participate in making life better by consciously transforming fear into determination and despair into belief in oneself. Pluto in Capricorn (since 2008) inspires a new journey where we build a new world for ourselves and for the generations to come.

September 14th Tuesday
FIRST QUARTER MOON in SAGITTARIUS

Moon in Sagittarius	PDT	EDT	
Mars enters Scorpio	3:37 PM	6:37 PM	
Moon square Sun	10:51 PM	1:51 AM	(September 15)

Birthday: Sam Neill 1947

204

Mood Watch: The **First Quarter Moon in Sagittarius** (Moon square Sun) allows our moods to be adaptable and responsive to the situations that arise. Likely interests include sports events, adventure, vision quests, and philosophical perspectives. While the Virgo Sun reminds us to budget our resources for the changing season ahead, the Sagittarius Moon reminds us to reach out there while the brilliant beauty of summer is still occurring. Adventure and hope abound. Sagittarius says: "I see" – make use of the vision and take the time to *see beyond.*

Mars enters Scorpio (Mars in Scorpio: Sept. 14 – Oct. 27) Mars in Scorpio brings a very passionate and daring edge to our activities. In Scorpio, the execution of activity (Mars) is done with precision and intense clarity. Mars in Scorpio often brings out aggressive acts in people, but not necessarily ones that are cruel or destructive. When tension builds, it is often best to channel aggressive impulses into sports or outdoor activities. Scorpio people will have a lot of extra energy and strength, perhaps even anger or fever, as Mars connects with their natal Sun. Scorpios, use this extra energy constructively.

September 15th Wednesday

Moon in Sagittarius / Capricorn	PDT	EDT	
Moon sextile Neptune	7:01 AM	10:01 AM	
Moon square Uranus	11:18 AM	2:18 PM	
Moon square Jupiter goes v/c	11:52 AM	2:52 PM	
Moon enters Capricorn	1:30 PM	4:30 PM	
Moon sextile Mars	2:44 PM	5:44 PM	
Moon conjunct Pluto	6:52 PM	9:52 PM	
Moon sextile Venus	11:53 PM	2:53 AM	(September 16)
Sun opposite Jupiter begins (see September 21)			
Sun opposite Uranus begins (see September 21)			

Birthday: Tommy Lee Jones 1946

Mood Watch: A waxing Moon in Sagittarius brings out the adventurous side of our moods Curious and explorative thoughts captivate our moods, particularly while the influence of Moon sextile Neptune entices our imagination and our insightful. However, Moon square Uranus brings tyrannical moods, and there may be a lot of chaotic or unsettled feelings going around. As Moon square Jupiter occurs, the Moon also goes void-of-course and this could be costly, as many folks will be thrown off by a complex dispersion of energies. For awhile during the afternoon, it may seem difficult for us to get our bearings and to maintain a sense of staying on course. No fear! Discoveries made at this time will open us up to a richer perspective on life. A different perspective may just be what is needed in order to carry our energies over into the swiftly changing force of the pending season. By afternoon, the Moon enters Capricorn, and a serious work pace picks up the tempo of the day. Moon sextile Mars brings a strong masculine drive to our energy. Moon conjunct Pluto intensifies our moods. Much later, Moon sextile Venus eases our moods into a potentially pleasurable dream world.

September 16th Thursday

Moon in Capricorn

	PDT	EDT
Moon square Saturn	12:59 AM	3:59 AM
Moon trine Mercury	1:36 AM	4:36 AM
Mercury-sextile-Venus-non-exact (see below)		

Birthday: B. B. King 1925

Mood Watch: The Capricorn Moon atmosphere gives our moods a cool and calm composure in which to focus our energies, and also helps us to control our various levels of progress with greater concentration. Capricorn Moon and Virgo Sun bring a nose-to-the-grindstone sensibility to our moods; a serious, determined, down-to-earth effort to get things accomplished will bring a lot of progress. Decisive, clear, and direct interactions with others will make this a good time to get some business done.

Mercury-sextile-Venus-non-exact (occurring Sept. 10 – 20) Mercury sextile Venus now comes within a couple of degrees of an exact sextile aspect. However, all too quickly, it begins to dissipate before it gets a chance to reach its peak. Nonetheless, the affects of Mercury sextile Venus are active. Mercury is in Virgo, bringing talk about health matters, and other practical kinds of focuses, to the forefront of our discussions. Venus is in Libra, bringing the need for loving balance in relationships. This is a good time to seek opportunity with regard to the healthy welfare of the people and things we love. This aspect came into a non-exact position back on May 29 when Mercury was in Taurus and Venus was in Cancer. It will reach an actual peak on two other occasions this year – first, December 1 with Mercury in Capricorn and Venus in Scorpio, and secondly, December 10 while Mercury is retrograde.

September 17th Friday

Moon in Capricorn

	PDT	EDT	
Moon trine Sun	2:19 PM	5:19 PM	
Moon sextile Uranus	10:04 PM	1:04 AM	(September 18)
Moon sextile Jupiter goes v/c	10:13 PM	1:13 AM	(September 18)

Birthday: John Ritter 1948

Mood Watch:: Forethought and brazen effort are the model cornerstones of every project while the Sun is in Virgo with the Moon in Capricorn. The persistent drive of the waxing Capricorn Moon energy is an excellent way to wrap up the work week. Moon in Capricorn provides our moods with a steady resolution to meet important goals and make progress with work – both domestic types of work as well as career related focuses. This is good time to make some headway with the serious matters in our lives that need attention. The waxing Capricorn Moon spells out a big focus on business, getting organized, prioritizing, goal setting, management and development of finances and resources. There is so much to do on the physical plane!

September 18th Saturday

♍

Yom Kippur

Moon in Capricorn / Aquarius

	PDT	EDT
Moon enters Aquarius	12:35 AM	3:35 AM
Moon square Mars	5:23 AM	8:23 AM
Moon trine Saturn	1:08 PM	4:08 PM
Moon square Venus	2:37 PM	5:37 PM
JUPITER CONJUNCT URANUS	6:03 PM	9:03 PM
Mars sextile Pluto	7:47 PM	10:47 PM

Birthday: Greta Garbo 1905

Mood Watch: Moon in Aquarius waxes strongly as it brings a focus on knowledge and learning new skills. This is a time of fairs, social endeavors, conventions, as well as philanthropic and fund raising events. Aquarius Moon puts us in touch with our human side, particularly with the ups and downs in today's lunar aspects. While we often fall back on the awareness that we are simply human, the waxing Aquarius Moon also puts us in touch with the fact that we are – sometimes – super-human or extraordinary. Reaching out to others in a brotherly or sisterly fashion enhances our chances of being extraordinary. Keep your eyes and ears peeled for the unique opportunity to experience – or perpetrate – a human gesture that is nothing shy of astonishing! After all, the auspicious arrival of Jupiter conjunct Uranus is often astonishing in itself (see below).

Jupiter conjunct Uranus (occurring April 25 – Oct. 27) Today's peak conjunction of Jupiter and Uranus occurs at the 28 degree mark of Pisces. This conjunction brings the illusion of prosperity. For many, there is no illusion; prosperity is a hard earned commodity. This aspect tests our faith and our dreams, and it demands a revolutionary process of rebuilding our economic future. For the full explanation of this amazing conjunction which last reached its peak in the spring, *see June 8.*

Mars sextile Pluto (occurring Sept. 12 – 21) Mars, the planet of action is in a favorable position to Pluto, the planet of the generations. Mars in Scorpio sextile to Pluto in Capricorn brings the opportunity for powerful and swift action. This is a superb time to take up activities with people of a different culture, or with someone who is of a different level of maturity or experience. This is also potentially a good time to reconcile differences. Those who are not in accordance with others at this time are likely to stand out – quite obviously. This may be a beneficial aspect for successfully recuperating from an illness. Mars represents the masculine push of our personal lives, the area where we activate our will, strength, and vitality; this brings opportunity, optimism, and the added boost to face otherwise tense situations and predicaments. The activities of Mars sextile Pluto will teach us about hardships and what we can learn from other generations.

September 19th Sunday

Rosh Hashana

Moon in Aquarius

No Exact Aspects
Sun square Pluto begins (see September 25)

207

Birthday: Leslie "Twiggy" Lawson 1949

Mood Watch: The general mood on this Aquarius Moon day is positive, outgoing, and eccentric. Thoughts and ideas will be unusual and inspired. This is a good time to enjoy social outings and appreciate the late summer with our most inspired friends and comrades. Human rights issues or debates are taking place all the time, and it is often the Aquarius Moon influence that gives us the chance to collectively share special human interests and promote humanitarian causes. This is also a good time to work on finding solutions to pressing problems. Let the ingenuity and insightfulness of this Aquarius Moon time guide you to find some brilliant answers.

September 20th Monday

Moon in Aquarius / Pisces	PDT	EDT	
Moon conjunct Neptune goes v/c	6:08 AM	9:08 AM	
Moon enters Pisces	1:15 PM	4:15 PM	
Moon sextile Pluto	6:55 PM	9:55 PM	
Moon trine Mars	9:45 PM	12:45 AM	(September 21)

Birthday: Ferdinand "Jelly Roll" Morton 1885

Mood Watch: Technical problems? Are there social idiosyncrasies and entanglements? Has humanitarian decency gone out the door? Are those who are pretending to know just making the problem worse? Relax, it's only the void-of-course Moon in Aquarius. Much of the early part of today's chaos will involve accepting that this is a time to engage in a learning process. Some must learn to listen, others must learn to keep the politics out of the personal realm, and some folks must learn to simply be more patient when the system isn't working for them. Setbacks of the void-of-course Aquarius Moon are often based around issues of knowledge and know-how. The mistakes we make are a component of our learning process. Take this time to learn from these mistakes. As the Moon enters Pisces, our moods will become less oriented towards making mistakes and more oriented towards intuitive awareness. Although it may not seem logically sound, the Pisces Moon is usually the best time to rely on instinct.

September 21st Tuesday

Moon in Pisces	PDT	EDT
Sun opposite Jupiter	4:35 AM	7:35 AM
Moon trine Venus	6:22 AM	9:22 AM
Sun opposite Uranus	9:58 AM	12:58 PM
Moon opposite Mercury	11:42 AM	2:42 PM

Birthday: H.G. Wells 1866

Mood Watch: The last day of summer is upon us as autumn draws near, and the Moon is in Pisces, the last sign of the zodiac. Today's Moon in Pisces will draw many people to the heart of their beliefs and needs. The waxing Pisces Moon reminds us to keep a close check on addictive tendencies that, for some people, will require careful monitoring. Our moods will have a mystical quality to them, and our interactions with each other will seem emotionally vibrant. The waxing

Pisces Moon brings out our artistic side, as well as our intuition.

Sun opposite Jupiter (occurring Sept. 15 – 23) Virgo and Libra birthday people, celebrating birthdays from September 15 – 23, are experiencing the opposition of Jupiter to their natal Sun. This brings an acute awareness of the shifts in personal economic conditions, for better or worse. There is a strong personal acknowledgment, or perhaps an obsession, at work to obtain a sense of wealth, joy, and wellbeing. Use your best techniques, birthday folks, to persevere through financial trials. Governing your expenditures with wisdom instead of impetuosity will assuredly bring you around to the place you know you need to be. This aspect only occurs once this year.

Sun opposite Uranus (occurring Sept. 15 – 24) This occurrence of Sun opposite Uranus particularly affects Virgo and cusp born Libras celebrating birthdays September 15 – 24. The opposition of Uranus creates an acute awareness of the revolutionary forces in one's life. There will undoubtedly be a lot of chaos, and the challenge (in part) may be to accept the rebel within you, and to persevere through the drastic and edgy discord. This is the time to go with the flow of unusual and unpredictable occurrences. It's also a good time to learn the Tao of chaos, and to understand that this awakening force is enlivening a sense of freedom. The only alternatives are to break through, or to break down if one resists. Survival counts; use your senses and your sensibilities well but do not resist the forces of great change. In its opposition to Virgo and Libra, Uranus will both challenge and strengthen our Virgo and Libra (birthday) friends to live a life of freedom. We are beginning to come to the end of the cycle of Uranus in Pisces, and this is also the end of the Uranus opposition to Virgo. This aspect has been annually teaching Virgo people the value in allowing for a greater range of possibilities. In the years to come, it will be certain Libra people's turn to ride the big waves of chaos. This will be an exciting and, at times, exhausting year ahead for these birthday folks.

LIBRA

Key Phrase: "I BALANCE"

Cardinal Air Sign

Ruling Planet: Venus

Symbol: The Scales

September 22nd through October 22nd

September 22nd Wednesday

Full Moon Eve

Autumnal Equinox

Moon in Pisces	PDT	EDT	
Sun enters Libra	8:09 PM	11:09 PM	
Moon conjunct Jupiter	10:05 PM	1:05 AM	(September 23)
Moon conjunct Uranus goes v/c	10:51 PM	1:51 AM	(September 23)

"Act passionately; think rationally; be Thyself."
- Liber Librae (The Book of Balance) of The Equinox series, 1909

Birthday: Joan Jett 1960

Mood Watch: The Pisces Moon highlights the need for a strong spiritual exchange among people. This can be done with music, chanting, spellbinding fragrances, enchanting elixirs, and with artistry and charismatic charm. Tonight's Moon conjunct Jupiter aspect brings optimism and hope. However, later tonight the Moon conjunct Uranus aspect produces explosive moods as the Moon goes void-of-course. Rebellious tendencies are likely to lead to an out-and-out revolt if our desires for freedom are not appeased. A restless energy comes with the pending Full Aries Moon, set to take place early a.m. Thursday (tomorrow).

Sun enters Libra (Sun in Libra: Sept. 22 – Oct. 22) It's the magical time of Autumnal Equinox. This time of year calls to us to reach out to one another and to create a support system of helpful friends to prepare for the busy season ahead and the darker and colder days yet to come. The Sun now enters Libra, a Venus ruled sign that focuses our attention on the power of teamwork and partnership. The key phrase for Libra is, "I balance," and the key to Libra's happiness comes with a sense of balance. Another factor to take into account for our Libran friends is the perpetual state of adjustment required to meet that balance. Libra could therefore easily say, "I adjust." The cornucopia of life is full of expressions of harmony and beauty. Libra focuses on libraries and accesses data and knowledge, particularly in the area of law. May this new autumn season be pleasurable and fruitful for you and all your loved ones!

September 23rd Thursday

FULL MOON in ARIES

Moon in Pisces / Aries	PDT	EDT
Moon enters Aries	1:48 AM	4:48 AM
Moon opposite Sun	2:16 AM	5:16 AM
Moon square Pluto	7:24 AM	10:24 AM
Moon opposite Saturn	3:31 PM	6:31 PM
Sun conjunct Saturn begins (see September 30)		

Birthday: Ray Charles 1930

Mood Watch: The **Full Moon in Aries** (Moon opposite Sun) reaches its peak in the earliest hours of the morning and, despite the fact that its fullness is maximized before sunrise, the momentum of its influences charges our spirits with an extra dose of energy. All the high pomp and hype of this time comes to a crescendo and is marked with the burning and willful force of Aries Moon activity. A warrior spirit touches us all, particularly with regard to the personal challenges in our lives. Be prepared for headstrong attitudes and potential rudeness. Avoid hastiness and impetuosity. There will also be a great deal of confidence, enthusiasm, and a pioneering spirit. This is a good time to celebrate and to enjoy the fruits of our labors. The Full Aries Moon occurs today with the Moon at the zero degree mark of Aries. On October 22, the Full Aries Moon will occur for a second time this year, when the Moon is nearly out of Aries at the 29 degree mark.

September 24th Friday
Moon in Aries
  No Exact Aspects

Birthday: Jim Henson 1936

Mood Watch: For some, this post-Full Moon in Aries period may seem like a restless and impatient time. There is a competitive air increasing in many folks. This is a good time to take initiative with autumn projects that need to be started. While the spirit of Aries Moon may seem relentless to some, the necessity to forge the will with precision and expertise brings an improved sense of wellbeing. Taking action towards personal goals is the most natural way to channel this hard driving energy of Aries. As the impetuous edge and straightforward tenacity of our moods begins to dissipate, we may begin to settle into a steady, far less hurried pace. All the while, the cardinal fire heat of strong intent and the drive that urges us onward is ever present throughout the day.

September 25th Saturday

Moon in Aries / Taurus	PDT	EDT
Moon sextile Neptune goes v/c	6:11 AM	9:11 AM
Moon enters Taurus	1:17 PM	4:17 PM
Sun square Pluto	5:25 PM	8:25 PM
Moon trine Pluto	6:48 PM	9:48 PM

Birthday: Christopher Reeve 1952

Mood Watch: This morning, the Aries Moon goes void-of-course as it reaches the sextile position to Neptune. Spacey moods are swiftly followed by impatience, irritation, and intolerance. It may be best to avoid direct confrontations until the Moon settles into Taurus this afternoon. The Taurus Moon wanes with the Sun in Libra. Late this afternoon, thrifty and constructive shopping efforts will yield satisfying results. Waning Taurus Moon is a good time to handle finances succinctly, and to seek beauty and pleasure in practical and affordable ways.

Sun square Pluto (occurring Sept. 19 – 28) This occurrence of Sun square Pluto particularly affects those Virgo and Libra people celebrating birthdays from September 19 – 28. For them, Pluto squaring their natal Sun brings disruptive changes and many challenges to overcome, such as the pain of loss and the severity of transformation. These tests often involve illness, irreparable damage, and dramatic life and death changes. This is the time to persevere through the obstacles of hardship. The hardships that are taking place now will resurface again in time, and that necessitates finding methods of release and of attitude adjustment in order to survive the anxiety and stress. Take it one day at a time, and do not let fear and worry rule you, birthday folks. Move steadily through the required transformation, as stagnation and fear will only bring extended suffering. Pluto tests are hard, but not impossible. This aspect last occurred on March 25, affecting the Pisces/Aries birthday people of that time.

September 26th Sunday

Moon in Taurus	PDT	EDT
Moon opposite Mars	4:27 AM	7:27 AM
Moon opposite Venus	10:24 AM	1:24 PM

Birthday: George Gershwin 1898

Mood Watch: Hot and active emotions erupt at the earliest hour of the morning with Moon opposite Mars. Fortunately, the Taurus Moon energy will influence us to hold our ground and although, at first, there may be some resistance or stubbornness of mood, this is effectively remedied by today's most endearing lunar aspect, Moon opposite Venus. We are compelled by our wants and desires, and our moods are inspired by the things we love. This is a time to spread affection and connect with loved ones. It is also a time to evaluate what matters, and what is valuable. The waning Taurus Moon brings on a cool Sunday pace of rummaging through piles of material goods at late September garage sales. What we put off doing all summer now needs to be addressed, particularly in the material part of our world. Taurus Moon preoccupies us with our need for beauty, security, and the desire to make our surroundings comfortable, neat, and sound. Moon in Taurus reminds us of our imminently pressing needs.

September 27th Monday

Moon in Taurus / Gemini	PDT	EDT	
Moon trine Mercury	2:38 AM	5:38 AM	
Moon square Neptune	4:12 PM	7:12 PM	
Moon sextile Jupiter	6:27 PM	9:27 PM	
Moon sextile Uranus goes v/c	8:02 PM	11:02 PM	
Moon enters Gemini	11:11 PM	2:11 AM	(September 28)

Birthday: Gwyneth Paltrow 1972

Mood Watch: The Sun and Moon are both in signs ruled by Venus. Sun in Libra and Moon in Taurus bring balance, admiration, and beauty. Taurus is a place of exaltation for the Moon. Beauty and pleasure are always there for us to enjoy despite the ongoing economic and material shifts of life. Today will have its ups and downs. Moon square Neptune produces skepticism, doubt, and challenging circumstances with regard to our spiritual comfort zones. However, Moon sextile Jupiter brings a sense of hope, luck, and opportunity. Optimism and charm create a graceful evening of comforts until Moon sextile Uranus occurs, and the Moon also goes void-of-course. Chaotic feelings could reduce our sense of confidence. For a few hours in the evening, the void-of-course Taurus Moon generates introverted moods, stubbornness, and laziness. Later, Moon in Gemini brings thoughtful reverie.

212

September 28th Tuesday

Ω

Moon in Gemini

	PDT	EDT
Moon trine Sun	9:26 AM	12:26 PM
Moon trine Saturn	1:15 PM	4:15 PM
Mercury opposite Jupiter begins (see October 1)		
Mercury opposite Uranus begins (see October 2)		

Birthday: Brigitte Bardot 1934

Mood Watch: The waning Gemini Moon helps us to get a handle on the busy pace of this new season. The primary objective of the day will be to push past superfluous and unimportant details and to focus on what's important. Sun in Libra and Moon in Gemini bring a need for intelligent and stimulating interaction with others. This is a good time to plan, organize, and research. It is also a great time to catch up on correspondences. A lot can be learned today. Why not choose some interesting people to interact with and to get some helpful ideas? Everyone needs support. Give a little, inquire, and learn something!

September 29th Wednesday

Moon in Gemini

	PDT	EDT
Moon square Mercury	7:29 PM	10:29 PM

Birthday: Madeline Kahn 1942

Mood Watch: Sun in Libra and Moon in Gemini focus our morning energies on the need for intelligence, logic and adaptability. This is an interesting time of intellectual pursuits, witty humor, and congenial interaction – strategize and socialize! Tonight's only lunar aspect, Moon square Mercury, interferes with our desire to pay attention and concentrate on the message, leading to communications that are prone towards argument. Nevertheless, this is still an overall good day to engage in teamwork, focus on research, and to make inquiries.

September 30th Thursday

LAST QUARTER MOON in CANCER

Moon in Gemini / Cancer

	PDT	EDT
Moon trine Neptune	12:01 AM	3:01 AM
Moon square Jupiter	1:42 AM	4:42 AM
Moon square Uranus goes v/c	3:35 AM	6:35 AM
Moon enters Cancer	6:46 AM	9:46 AM
Moon opposite Pluto	11:53 AM	2:53 PM
Sun conjunct Saturn	5:41 PM	8:41 PM
Moon square Saturn	8:39 PM	11:39 PM
Moon square Sun	8:51 PM	11:51 PM

Birthday: Truman Capote 1924

Mood Watch: The Gemini Moon is void-of-course this morning, and we may be caught up in a confusing round of early morning mixed feelings. However, our emotions will become much clearer to us as the Moon enters Cancer. This is the day of the **Last Quarter Moon in Cancer** (Moon square Sun). The emotional concerns surfacing now require that extra bit of nurturing and understanding.

Feelings must surface at times throughout the day. There are some challenging lunar aspects which are poised to give us some emotional turmoil. This is a good time to practice patience and to lend a listening ear. However, don't get caught up in allowing others to bend your ear if you feel like they are being manipulative or wasting your precious time. In group situations, it is wise to be patient, and to practice a kind and cool composure.

Sun conjunct Saturn (occurring Sept. 23 – Oct. 4) This occurrence of Sun conjunct Saturn especially affects those Libra people celebrating birthdays September 23 – October 4. These birthday people are being reminded to take charge of their lives more responsibly, and to recognize the importance of their limitations. This year, it may be best for these birthday Libras to incorporate a balanced lifestyle by applying routines that contribute to their sense of harmony. Maybe it's time for an overhaul, Libra – at least until certain areas of your life become more comfortable again. Saturn is urging you to connect with a sound dose of responsibility that fits your lifestyle and energy level. This may be the time to tune into your sensibilities and make some serious decisions that you've needed to make. Don't be so hard on yourself, Libra; reward yourself throughout this year with each measure of your progress – it's good for the soul. Make up for lost time, and apply some self-love and nurturing to your renewed self-discipline. Hang in there and keep up the work, birthday folks, and don't be so glum; the tedious work in which you are now immersed will bring you genuine rewards later on.

October 1st Friday

Moon in Cancer

	PDT	EDT
Moon trine Mars	2:38 AM	5:38 AM
Moon trine Venus	4:49 AM	7:49 AM
Mercury opposite Jupiter	3:35 PM	6:35 PM
Mercury square Pluto begins (see October 4)		

Birthday: Isaac Bonewits 1949

Mood Watch: The Cancer Moon wanes while positive lunar aspects shower us with hope in the earliest hours of the morning. Cancer Moon drives our emotions to the surface and allows us to review them, particularly since our feelings are always in a state of change. This is a time when our feelings don't lie, unless we've mastered the art of rejecting the truth. Let the feelings flow and then let them go. Don't hold on to guilt, fear, or worries – release them! You'll feel a whole lot better once you do. If you're feeling good, and don't experience the necessity to go through this drill, consider yourself fortunate this time. Next time, the Cancer Moon will put you through this again, and if you are good at embracing the truth, then you're certainly evolving. If not, it's back to the drill. Cancer Moon is not all that complicated!

Mercury opposite Jupiter (occurring Sept. 28 – Oct. 3) Mercury in Virgo is opposite to Jupiter in Pisces, bringing overwhelming scrutiny and astute observations about the mysterious and dream-like qualities of our aspirations and hopes for the economic future. We may find ourselves bartering for things that cannot be sold. An economic shift brings notable financial or political awareness, and the incessant chatter which fills the airwaves has a further effect on the sharp

214

movements occurring in the stock market. This aspect also focuses news on the opulent lifestyles of the rich and famous, as people find themselves unable to stop talking about their financial situation or their need for advancement, a raise, or an income. Wealth is highlighted, and there is considerable debate as to what wealth really represents. Most of the time wealth is an illusion, and people really don't know what they're talking about when they make assumptions about the apparent wellbeing of others. As class separation continues, it is a time of acute concern in this realm. This short-lived aspect only occurs once this year.

♎

October 2nd Saturday

Moon in Cancer / Leo	PDT	EDT
Moon trine Jupiter	6:06 AM	9:06 AM
Mercury opposite Uranus	7:23 AM	10:23 AM
Moon trine Uranus	8:13 AM	11:13 AM
Moon sextile Mercury goes v/c	8:20 AM	11:20 AM
Moon enters Leo	11:21 AM	2:21 PM

" Freedom is a two-edged sword of which one edge is liberty and the other responsibility..."
– Jack Parsons (born October 2, 1914)

Birthday: Arthur Edward Waite 1857

Mood Watch: This is the year of the *Metal* Tiger (*see Feb. 14*), and today is the birthday of a famous Metal Tiger, Groucho Marx (born in 1890), the wittiest of the notorious Marx Brothers. As a colorful spirited Libra, Groucho loved attention, crowds, and a swanky backdrop to accompany his brazen prowess and vaudeville style. He was a genius at taking a gloomy atmosphere and turning it into a joyous occasion. If your morning seems to start out moody, uncertain, or lethargic with the void-of-course Moon in Cancer, you can rely on this afternoon's Leo Moon to kick the spirit of the day into high gear. Here in the year of the wildcat Tiger, the Leo Moon insures that our moods will be open to humor, curiosity, and playfulness as the day progresses. We may, however, also find a strong air of mayhem, chaos, and confusion, with Mercury opposite Uranus (see below), but this quality of atmosphere is also a prime example of the Marx Brother's most endearing tactics in the name of fun. Free spirited action has its price. Be sure to think wisely before launching a cannonball statement.

Mercury opposite Uranus (occurring Sept. 28 – Oct. 3) Mercury in Virgo opposes Uranus in Pisces. Explosive events under discussion are testing our ability to trust or be convinced. Many will approve openly but will still maintain a healthy dose of skepticism. Ideas may seem bigger than life, and talk seems to focus on concepts which have not been fully grasped, but appear to be presented with assured confidence. Shocking or liberating statements tend to come out with this aspect. There is an acute awareness of the need to speak out for freedom, and the dialogue may appear sharp; radical and sometimes vulgar language may erupt. Outrageous claims and verbal presumptions made at this time may bring fiery or irrational flare-ups in discussion groups and chat rooms. This is a really good time to watch your mouth. Fortunately, this is the only time this aspect occurs this year.

215

October 3rd Sunday

Moon in Leo	PDT	EDT
Moon sextile Saturn	12:52 AM	3:52 AM
Moon sextile Sun	4:25 AM	7:25 AM
Mercury enters Libra	8:03 AM	11:03 AM
Moon square Mars	8:38 AM	11:38 AM
Moon square Venus	8:52 AM	11:52 AM
Venus conjunct Mars	2:55 PM	5:55 PM

Birthday: Chubby Checker 1941

Mood Watch: The waning Leo Moon brings playful and feisty moods. The onslaught of emotional ups and downs during the past couple of days has come to a close. If you're still holding onto stuff, the waning Leo Moon is a good time to lean on friends and family, or to work on bettering your personal needs. No one knows you better than you do, and if someone does, perhaps it's time you paid some more attention to yourself. The waning Leo Moon makes us introspective. This is a bold move for a sign such as Leo, as it usually tends to project outwardly.

Mercury enters Libra (Mercury in Libra: Oct. 3 – 20) Mercury in Libra aligns us with diplomacy, tact, and the need to connect with friends and loved ones. Libra is the cardinal autumn sign that emphasizes balance and adjustment. Today through October 20, Mercury in Libra will bring a focus on harmonizing with others and preparing for the pending change of the seasons. This is a good time for people to communicate by gathering important information, as our decision making process kicks into high gear.

Venus conjunct Mars (occurring Aug. 4 – Oct. 8) Venus and Mars have maintained a very close orbital conjunction since August 4, and this conjunction last reached its peak on August 20 in the sign of Libra. Today's conjunction takes place in Scorpio, bringing love and action into a much more passionate light. Here, we are easily seduced by love in the most gripping and compelling way. Venus and Mars conjunct in Scorpio emphasizes the need to act in a loving way towards life's most important events, especially such Scorpio-like events as birth, death, and regenerative forces to aid in the healing of wounds. For more information on the work of Venus conjunct Mars, *see August 20* when it first occurred this year in the sign of Libra.

October 4th Monday

Moon in Leo / Virgo	PDT	EDT	
Moon opposite Neptune goes v/c	6:52 AM	9:52 AM	
Moon enters Virgo	1:00 PM	4:00 PM	
Moon trine Pluto	5:40 PM	8:40 PM	
Mercury square Pluto	11:08 PM	2:08 AM	(October 5)

Mercury conjunct Saturn begins (see October 8)

Birthday: Susan Sarandon 1946

Mood Watch: The Leo Moon reminds us of our need for creature comforts, inspiration, and optimism. However, the void-of-course Leo Moon disrupts our sense of individuality and identity. As we search for self-confidence and the personal cutting edge that's needed to get the morning rolling, we are surrounded by others who are also preoccupied with identity and personal needs. Consequently, not much gets done this morning. Later this afternoon, the Moon enters Virgo. Waning Virgo Moon activity stresses the need to prepare and organize for the colder months ahead. There is a strong emphasis on making decisions and preparing schedules. The Virgo Moon also emphasizes the need for good health practices and proper physical hygiene.

Mercury square Pluto (occurring Oct. 1 – 6) Mercury in Libra is square to Pluto in Capricorn. Attempts at communicating the need for balance may be difficult with regard to dominant powers that are fatefully at work creating permanent changes that will affect the generations to come. Procrastinating and vacillating thoughts make it especially difficult to communicate with those of another generation, or to discuss hardships and matters of fate in a constructive manner. This is a particularly hard time to deal with burdensome issues and discuss them in a manner that relieves tension. Mercury square Pluto often brings harsh and sometimes fatal news. Talk revolves around the corruption of superpowers. This may be an especially difficult time to discuss matters involving permanent change. This aspect last occurred on March 20 with Mercury in Aries.

October 5th Tuesday

Moon in Virgo	PDT	EDT
Moon sextile Venus	10:00 AM	1:00 PM
Moon sextile Mars	11:41 AM	2:41 PM

Birthday: Kate Winslet 1975

Mood Watch: The Moon wanes in Virgo. This is a time when we tend to become technical, critical, meticulous, and in need of some organization. When the Moon is in the Mercury-ruled sign of Virgo, it's a good time to clean up, apply some extra physical care and hygiene, and to take precautions not to catch other people's cold and flu viruses. Fall season is slipping into the more challenging periods of wet, stormy, and cold days here in North America. The Virgo Moon gives us the wherewithal to prepare for and handle the obstacles of this time.

October 6th Wednesday

Moon in Virgo / Libra	PDT	EDT	
Moon opposite Jupiter	7:11 AM	10:11 AM	
Moon opposite Uranus goes v/c	9:42 AM	12:42 PM	
Moon enters Libra	12:52 PM	3:52 PM	
Moon square Pluto	5:29 PM	8:29 PM	
Moon conjunct Mercury	11:08 PM	2:08 PM	(October 7)

Birthday: George Westinghouse 1846

Mood Watch: Moon opposite Jupiter brings high hopes in the early hours. Moon opposite Uranus leads to a void-of-course lunar phase in the early part of the day. Skepticism abounds and there may be a tendency for people to overanalyze their feelings. Finally, the Moon enters Libra and we have now reached the dark phase of the lunar cycle. Change is definitively in the air. The Sun and Moon are both in Libra. This is the time to deliberate and to examine the best course of action to create a balance. Libra says: "I balance," and there is no point in waiting for the imbalances of your life to bring you down; take measures to secure a firm sense of stability.

October 7th Thursday

NEW MOON in LIBRA

Moon in Libra	PDT	EDT
Moon conjunct Saturn	2:24 AM	5:24 AM
Moon conjunct Sun	11:45 AM	2:45 PM

Birthday: John Cougar Mellencamp 1951

Mood Watch: The **New Moon in Libra** (Moon conjunct Sun) is a time of reaffirming and harmonizing our relationships with friends and partners, as well as a time of initiating friendships while autumn activities create a fresh working environment for many people. New rules also set the standard for how to create a more harmonious environment in the days of autumn. This Moon places an emphasis on laws, the courts, the litigation process, custody battles, and the like. Justice comes when there is peace, but this is not always found in the courts. The rest of the world will pretty much do what it has always done since the beginning of time, and not all matters are individually controllable. In order to begin anew, the New Libra Moon reminds us to seek peace within.

October 8th Friday

Moon in Libra / Scorpio	PDT	EDT
Venus goes retrograde	12:06 AM	3:06 AM
Mercury conjunct Saturn	4:35 AM	7:35 AM
Moon trine Neptune goes v/c	6:37 AM	9:37 AM
Moon enters Scorpio	12:52 PM	3:52 PM
Moon sextile Pluto	5:40 PM	8:40 PM
Sun conjunct Mercury begins (see October 16)		

Birthday: Jesse Jackson 1941

Mood Watch: The newly waxing Libra Moon goes void-of-course this morning, and for awhile it may be difficult to effectively make decisions. Spacey moods keep us groping for clarity of thought. This afternoon as the Moon enters Scorpio, our moods will become considerably more perceptive and keen. Scorpio Moon is often a time for a renewal, or a sharpening, of the senses. For many people, a new perspective emerges, and there is a better understanding of the transformation processes occurring in their lives. Sun in Libra with Moon in Scorpio is a time to make adjustments and to fearlessly move through life's changes in order to get to the place that we desire most.

Venus goes retrograde (Venus retrograde: Oct. 8 – Nov. 18) Today the planet of love and magnetism, Venus, begins the retrograde process at the thirteen degree mark of Scorpio. While Venus is retrograde in Scorpio, the expression of love and beauty is internalized with deep-seated and passionate levels of interplay. Love related activities tend to be dramatically pursued, or they can be obsessively internalized. Scorpio is a detrimental position for Venus to begin with, and while Venus is retrograde in Scorpio, the internal processes of our love related focuses may undergo episodes of jealousy or competition. Those who struggle with their own sense of self-love may have a difficult time with this retrograde period. Venus brings a yearning for affection, pleasure, beauty, and for the things we love. If we cannot identify with who we are and love ourselves unconditionally, then we are likely to attract people and things to ourselves that cause conflict and confrontation. It is important to maintain and respect the source from which love flows, to recognize true love for what it is, as well as maintaining a love and respect for yourself and your personal needs. The retrograde Venus will reenter the tail end of Libra on November 7, emphasizing the need for balance in love related matters. Hang in there, lovers, Venus retrograde in Scorpio and Libra will be teaching us about the importance of not trying to control our love pursuits and pleasures, but simply to learn to enjoy what comes our way by attracting it to us naturally and without a struggle. True control comes from within, and the retrograde Venus helps us to internalize our understanding of love relationships altogether.

Mercury conjunct Saturn (occurring Oct. 4 – 10) Mercury conjunct Saturn will bring talk about the need to put an end to the useless or unwanted components of our lives. It will focus our thoughts on the areas of life that have reached limitations, or where timely new beginnings – or endings – are occurring. When occurring in Libra, this conjunction implies that strong rules or guidelines will be established with regard to social conduct, court cases, and relationships. There is a discerning quality at work with Mercury conjunct Saturn, making this conjunction a very good one for speakers and writers to inspire, initiate and capture vital thoughts. News concerning the end of a cycle is likely to occur. Examples include retirement announcements, job loss, and possibly even the news of a notable death. Overall, Mercury conjunct Saturn tends to bring out a strong tone of seriousness in communications. There is a restriction, a discipline, a carefully considered emphasis of thoughts placed on our communications; it's a serious intent to get the word across in no uncertain terms. There is the strong implication at work that we must be seriously responsible for what we say, particularly around authority and in official public statements. "Anything you say can and will be used against you..." This is the only time this conjunction of Mercury and Saturn will occur this year.

October 9th Saturday

Moon in Scorpio

	PDT	EDT
Moon conjunct Venus	10:35 AM	1:35 PM
Moon conjunct Mars	5:06 PM	8:06 PM

Birthday: John Lennon 1940

Mood Watch: The newly waxing Moon in Scorpio brings the need for warmth, acceptance, mental relaxation, and objectivity. Perhaps it would be wise to engage in some physical exertion in order to defuse emotional intensity. Some definite rest will be needed for those who have been feeling sick or run down. This is no time to push the envelope. Today's Moon conjunct Venus brings the potential for gentle, kind and loving moods. Later today, Moon conjunct Mars activates our moods with the need to work through various types of aggression. The Scorpio Moon connects us with our passions and puts an emphasis on the things that seem to matter most.

October 10ᵗʰ Sunday

Moon in Scorpio / Sagittarius	PDT	EDT
Moon trine Jupiter	8:10 AM	11:10 AM
Moon square Neptune	8:28 AM	11:28 AM
Moon trine Uranus goes v/c	11:28 AM	2:28 PM
Moon enters Sagittarius	3:09 PM	6:09 PM

Birthday: Thelonious Monk 1917

Mood Watch: This morning's Moon trine Jupiter brings a sense of joy and prosperity. Scorpio Moon is filled with possibilities, and with this comes exiting ways to handle life. Also this morning, Moon square Neptune opens up harsh sentiments or doubts. The Scorpio Moon goes void-of-course as Moon trine Uranus occurs. Our rebellious tendencies will bring reckless chaos and distraction, but it's all in good fun. However, the Moon also goes void-of-course for a number of hours. Intense subjects and cruel intentions are things to be monitored. Also, beware of vindictiveness and thievery this afternoon. Emotional interactions may be somewhat dramatic. Later, as the Moon enters Sagittarius, optimism and enthusiasm inspire friendly and uplifting moods.

October 11ᵗʰ Monday

Columbus Day, USA / Thanksgiving Day, Canada

Moon in Sagittarius	PDT	EDT
Moon sextile Saturn	7:01 AM	10:01 AM
Moon sextile Mercury	5:31 PM	8:31 PM

" Of course, America had often been discovered before Columbus, but it had always been hushed up. "
— Oscar Wilde (1854 – 1900)

Birthday: Eleanor Roosevelt 1884

Mood Watch: Moon sextile Saturn gives us the opportunity to get focused, organized, and disciplined this morning. As a general rule, the waxing Sagittarius Moon brings hopefulness and optimism to our moods. Sun in Libra and Moon in Sagittarius bring balance and expansion. A new point of view can change everything. Change is always occurring, but it is best experienced when a positive outlook is applied. Don't wait for all this good stuff to come to you; here's your chance to make it happen! Explore, enjoy, and be merry! This evening's Moon sextile Mercury is an excellent time to reach out and touch someone.

October 12ᵗʰ Tuesday

Ω

Moon in Sagittarius / Capricorn	PDT	EDT	
Moon sextile Sun	12:45 AM	3:45 AM	
Moon square Jupiter	1:16 PM	4:16 PM	
Moon sextile Neptune	2:00 PM	5:00 PM	
Moon square Uranus goes v/c	5:08 PM	8:08 PM	
Moon enters Capricorn	9:17 PM	12:17 AM	(October 13)

" *Every intentional act is a Magical Act* " – Aleister Crowley (1875 – 1947)

Birthday: Aleister Crowley 1875

Mood Watch: Enthusiastic moods will brighten our outlook as the waxing Sagittarius Moon invites us to explore all avenues of possibility. If we are astute and willing to watch for the signs, a vision can be magnified with a positive affirmation. Empower and perfect the vision! For awhile, this might not seem possible while the Moon squares to Jupiter, a time when some folks might seem less than generous. As Moon sextile Neptune occurs, our spirits have the potential to become uplifted. Sun in Libra and Moon in Sagittarius provide an opportunity to live by example, and to apply the old motto, "think globally, act locally." Sagittarius Moon invites us to share our visions with the global community. For some hours this evening, the Sagittarius Moon will be void-of-course – guard against getting lost or thrown off track. The Sagittarius Moon instigates very spacey moods when it's void-of-course. Later, the Capricorn Moon brings pragmatic, serious, and grounded moods.

October 13ᵗʰ Wednesday

Moon in Capricorn	PDT	EDT	
Moon conjunct Pluto	2:57 AM	5:57 AM	
Moon square Saturn	2:59 PM	5:59 PM	
Moon sextile Venus	9:10 PM	12:10 AM	(October 14)
Sun trine Neptune begins (see October 19)			
Mars trine Jupiter begins (see October 20)			
Mars square Neptune begins (see October 22)			

Birthday: Paul Simon 1941

Mood Watch: Capricorn Moon reminds us that the important things in life are worth taking seriously, and those are the things we must try to stabilize in the midst of disruption. This Moon puts us in touch with our sense of ambition and the determination to accomplish things. Capricorn says, "I Use," and this is a good time to recognize the functionality and usefulness of various things and people in your life. Concentration, effort and the application of skill brings a sense of reward to our moods. Tonight's Moon sextile Venus is a good time to count your blessings and to seek simple pleasures.

October 14ᵗʰ Thursday
FIRST QUARTER MOON in CAPRICORN

Moon in Capricorn	PDT	EDT	
Moon square Mercury	10:57 AM	1:57 PM	
Moon sextile Mars	12:33 PM	3:33 PM	
Moon square Sun	2:28 PM	5:28 PM	
Moon sextile Jupiter	10:22 PM	1:22 AM	(October 15)
Mercury trine Neptune begins (see October 18)			

Birthday: e e cummings 1894

Mood Watch: The **First Quarter Moon in Capricorn** (Moon square Sun) strongly emphasizes the need for serious labor. Some staunch determination is required despite today's challenging lunar aspects. There is a steadily mounting concern to achieve a notable level of accomplishment or completion in projects, particularly after the slow progress of the earlier part of the day. The harvest ripens and the physical labor force of the world is hard at work. People's moods are greatly moved by the acknowledgement of merits. The need to hunt for a steady job, a marketing edge, or a secure investment keeps us vigilant and focused. Punctuality in business is stressed. Some may feel isolated by constant work and no play. No one likes feeling rushed, particularly when high standards must be met.

October 15ᵗʰ Friday

Moon in Capricorn / Aquarius	PDT	EDT
Moon sextile Uranus goes v/c	2:49 AM	5:49 AM
Moon enters Aquarius	7:24 AM	10:24 AM

Birthday: P.G. Wodehouse 1881

Mood Watch: For awhile in the morning, there will be some spacey moods as many people will discover that it is somewhat difficult to concentrate with the Moon void-of-course in Capricorn. As the Moon enters Aquarius, our moods shift over into a much more intelligent level of output. The Sun is in Libra, the Moon is in Aquarius and this is a time of officiating over and clarifying the terms of our life with education, law, documentation, and research. A busy shuffle rustles through the halls of large institutions. Waxing Aquarius Moon puts the spotlight on such focuses as science, charities and humanitarian based causes and issues. Unusual and unconventional people are spurred towards exposing their creative genius. The general mood is outgoing and eccentric. Moon in Aquarius brings on a full day of inspired moods and openness towards learning and exploring new views of the people around us. Aquarius Moon focuses our moods on seeking knowledge as well as innovative and unusual avenues of thought.

October 16ᵗʰ Saturday

Moon in Aquarius	PDT	EDT
Moon trine Saturn	2:40 AM	5:40 AM
Moon square Venus	7:09 AM	10:09 AM
Sun conjunct Mercury	6:04 PM	9:04 PM
Mars trine Uranus begins (see October 24)		

Birthday: Oscar Wilde 1854

Mood Watch: We are living in the Age of Aquarius, and every month the Aquarius Moon reminds us more and more of our social development, as well as the challenges we must confront in the world of science and technology, whose presence grows more ominous with time. Today, our moods are encouraged to face the issues of humanity, raising questions about ourselves and our conduct in the world. Knowledge and how we use it are the keys to discovering how to perfect our personal approaches to the new millennium.

Sun conjunct Mercury (occurring Oct. 8 – 21) This conjunction will create a much more thoughtful, communicative and expressive year ahead for those Libra folks celebrating birthdays Oct. 8 – 21. This is your time (birthday Libras) to record ideas, relay important messages, and pay close attention to your imaginative thoughts as they are touched by Mercury, creating the urge to speak and be heard. Birthday people, your thoughts will reveal a great deal about who you are, now and in the year to come.

October 17ᵗʰ Sunday

Moon in Aquarius / Pisces	PDT	EDT
Moon square Mars	4:17 AM	7:17 AM
Moon trine Sun	7:58 AM	10:58 AM
Moon trine Mercury	8:55 AM	11:55 AM
Moon conjunct Neptune goes v/c	11:48 AM	2:48 PM
Moon enters Pisces	7:52 PM	10:52 PM

Birthday: Rita Hayworth 1918

Mood Watch: With the exception of Moon square Mars, most of our morning moods are upbeat and positive. Moon square Mars sometimes creates conflict, and it may be difficult to get motivated at first. As some more positive lunar aspects occur, the Aquarius Moon keeps us determined and interested in life. Morning will be the best time to get things done. As the Moon goes void-of-course, spacey, lazy, and some not so brilliant moods occur. The overall consensus is that this is not likely to be a particularly high performance day. Much later, as the Moon enters Pisces, our moods shift to a deeper, more emotional level of output. Tonight's Moon in Pisces will draw many people to the heart of their beliefs and needs. The waxing Pisces Moon reminds us to keep a close check on addictive tendencies, which for some people will require careful monitoring. Pisces Moon brings on a mystical time of strong psychic inclinations and a wide range of emotional expressions.

October 18ᵗʰ Monday

Moon in Pisces	PDT	EDT
Moon sextile Pluto	2:07 AM	5:07 AM
Mercury trine Neptune	5:03 AM	8:03 AM
Moon trine Venus	6:02 PM	9:02 PM

Birthday: Chuck Berry 1926

Mood Watch: Today our moods drift into and out of a series of flowing and changing images and impressions. As the Moon travels through Pisces, a mystical and timeless element of perception captivates our moods. Bubbly, artistic, enchanting, and dreamy moments allow us to access some hidden sanctuary where the soulful or prayerful part of ourselves is revealed.

Mercury trine Neptune (occurring October 14 – 19) Mercury in Libra trine Neptune in Aquarius brings diplomacy in speech, and it also brings intuitive and uplifting knowledge. Communicate about spiritual needs with helpful counsel and receive gifts of renewed faith in your own beliefs. Recognize that some messages are there to spiritually uplift you. This aspect last occurred June 24 with Mercury in Gemini.

October 19th Tuesday

Moon in Pisces	PDT	EDT	
Sun trine Neptune	5:18 AM	8:18 AM	
Moon trine Mars	8:47 PM	11:47 PM	
Moon conjunct Jupiter	10:14 PM	1:14 AM	(October 20)

Birthday: John Lithgow 1945

Mood Watch: Bubbly and happy spirits bring creative and intuitive expressions of mood. The waxing Pisces Moon is an excellent time to work on dreams, skill development, and artistic projects. Positive lunar aspects occur in the evening, however, this entire day holds promise and there could be some very pleasant delights coming our way. Pisces Moon puts us in touch with the things we believe. This is a splendid time to dream and to use the imagination.

Sun trine Neptune (occurring Oct. 13 – 22) This occurrence of Sun trine Neptune particularly affects those Libra and Scorpio people celebrating birthdays October 13 – 22. These birthday folks are experiencing the favorable trine aspect of Neptune to their natal Sun. This brings gifts of spiritual encounters and awareness, as well as a calming effect on one's life. It also serves as a good time (particularly for these birthday folks) to seek visions, apply prayer and meditation, and to explore spiritual avenues and beliefs that are being presented. This aspect last occurred June 19 with the Sun in Gemini.

October 20th Wednesday

Moon in Pisces / Aries	PDT	EDT
Moon conjunct Uranus goes v/c	3:25 AM	6:25 AM
Moon enters Aries	8:24 AM	11:24 AM
Mercury enters Scorpio	2:18 PM	5:18 PM
Moon square Pluto	2:38 PM	5:38 PM
Mars trine Jupiter	6:41 PM	9:41 PM
Mercury sextile Pluto begins (see October 22)		

Birthday: Viggo Mortensen 1958

Mood Watch: Early this morning, the waxing Pisces Moon goes void-of-course, our moods will be especially spacey, and many may find that they are somewhat uncoordinated at first. However, as the Moon enters Aries everything changes. The strongly waxing Aries Moon brings motivated moods, and many folks will become much more on the ball by afternoon. Moon square Pluto tends to force us to acknowledge the unpleasant and harsh realities of life. The Aries Moon gives us the wherewithal to do what we must do. Fortunately, Mars trine Jupiter will help to inspire us (see below).

Mercury enters Scorpio (Mercury in Scorpio: Oct. 20 – Nov. 8) Mercury in Scorpio is often a time when communications are veiled in secrecy, and talk revolves around matters of intensity and sensitivity. Passionate issues are communicated with creativity and intuition. This is also a time to be aware that a sharp tongue may easily cause a violent or challenging reaction. It is through this medium of Mercury in the sign of Scorpio that the expression of communications is seemingly fearless, obstinate, reckless, and passionate. From indecent babble to the subtle perfection of clear articulation, discussions frequently deliver a powerful punch. Not only our words but also our appearance, mannerisms and attitudes all send out the message of who we are. The mask we choose for the grand masquerade of autumn's darkening days teaches us much about ourselves.

Mars trine Jupiter (occurring Oct. 13 – 24) Mars is in Scorpio activating a strong focus on such life altering activities as birth, death, and transformation. Jupiter is in Pisces, expanding our sense of growth through the enhancement of our faith, through the arts, and through dreams that help us tap into our expansive potential. This is the most auspicious time to take action to develop and learn extraordinary types of skills. This aspect brings an all-around emphasis on the power of success. Act on opportunities as they arise, and set visions and dreams into a feasible plan that holds the potential for favorable actions to occur. Mars activates and stirs action in this direction, while Jupiter represents not only economy and advancement, but our sense of philosophic and visionary awareness as well. For some people this aspect brings gifts of inheritance; for most of us it brings opportunities for growth. Mars trine Jupiter allows us to activate a stronger, more intelligent grasp of our domain, and gives many folks the extra energy and spark to boost their sense of achievement. This most favorable aspect only occurs once this year, so it will be best to take advantage while the action is potent.

October 21ˢᵗ Thursday

Full Moon Eve

Moon in Aries

	PDT	EDT
Moon opposite Saturn	4:45 AM	7:45 AM

Birthday: Dizzy Gillespie 1917

Mood Watch: It's the last full day of Sun in Libra. High hopes and strong ambition overcome our moods as Moon opposite Saturn brings a demanding start to the day. Serious and concentrated moods will inspire us to apply some effort and discipline. The Aries Moon is almost full and the spirit of the day is energetic. Aries initiates, and very rarely finishes the task as the spirit of cardinal fire burns through to the next stage of life, leaving in its path unfinished business and a creative or impulsive course of action, which often brings new light to a situation. This almost Full Moon in Aries is a restless and impatient time for some. There is a competitive air building for many folks. This is a good time to take initiative with autumn projects that need to be started up at this time.

SCORPIO

Key Phrase: " I CREATE " or "I DESIRE"

Fixed Water Sign

Ruling Planet: Pluto

Symbol(s): The Scorpion,

The Eagle, and The Phoenix

October 22nd through

November 2nnd

October 22nd Friday
FULL MOON in ARIES

Moon in Aries / Taurus	PDT	EDT
Sun enters Scorpio	5:35 AM	8:35 AM
Mars square Neptune	8:34 AM	11:34 AM
Moon sextile Neptune	11:40 AM	2:40 PM
Mercury sextile Pluto	12:38 PM	3:38 PM
Moon opposite Sun goes v/c	6:36 PM	9:36 PM
Moon enters Taurus	7:30 PM	10:30 PM
Mercury conjunct Venus begins (see October 25)		
Sun sextile Pluto begins (see October 26)		

Birthday: Timothy Leary 1920

Mood Watch: For the second time this year, since September 23, the **Full Aries Moon** (Moon opposite Sun) reaches its peak. The Full Aries Moon initiates rich, vibrant feelings. In everyone is a warrior spirit, inspiring the confidence and fortitude to persevere through the endless tests of life, especially the challenging tests of selfhood. For some this is a restless and impatient time, and in many circles of life there will be a strong competitive spirit. Strength and vitality are blessings that Aries Moon energy allows us to tap into, helping us handle the mounting tasks of autumn in preparation for the pending storms of the season – a good time to take initiative with autumn projects. While the spirit of Aries Moon may seem relentless to some, taking action to complete personal goals is the most natural way to channel this hard driving energy of Aries Moon. Happy Full Moon, and be careful not to burn yourself out today. Tonight's Moon in Taurus will bring energy that it stable, sensible, and down to earth. This is a good time to enjoy comfortable and casual pleasures.

Sun enters Scorpio (Sun in Scorpio: Oct. 22 – Nov. 22) This time of year, like the Scorpio personality, creates an air of mystery and mysticism. This is a time when people are more likely to focus on their hidden agendas and their need to get in touch with their own passion. Scorpio focuses our attention on the most important events of life: birth, sex, death and regeneration or transformation, as this sign is ruled by the underworld god known as Pluto. Scorpio represents the powers

226

of hidden meaning, the need for secrecy, and the deeper psychologically ensnaring struggles with the self-destructive nature of humans and beasts. The totem of ♏ the sign of Scorpio is classically the desert arachnid known as the scorpion. The scorpion sting can kill; this is the violent or criminal side of the Scorpio personality. There are other totems – the Eagle and the Phoenix. These higher aspects of the Scorpio personality relate to the eagle's ability to observe from very far away, and see a larger and more objective picture of life while noting all the details essential to life itself. The Phoenix totem represents the ability to rise above the burning rays of the sun as a transformed and enlightened being. Pushing through and surviving the perilous difficulties and dangers of life is practically a personality trait of the sign of Scorpio. The Scorpio archetype demands some respect. Scorpios are often stereotyped for having a desire to live richly and often dangerously. There is always the vast and more esoteric version, too – the way of spirit, the mystical and spiritual path, or the acknowledgment of one's own truth.

Mars square Neptune (occurring Oct. 13 – 26) Mars is in Scorpio and Neptune is in Aquarius; there may be a dramatic disruption that intrudes on or impedes our spiritual level of experience. Martial forces are bursting through temples, belief systems, and holy moments. Active aggression occurs around spiritual groups and religious institutions, often targeting the belief systems of others. Mariners at sea may run into challenging storms. This aspect also brings the potential for accidents and temper tantrums, especially with regard to opinions about substance abuse and sacred matters. It is important not to get so wrapped up in the spiritual side of things that physical world realities, such as fire, are overlooked. Angry outbursts are likely to affect sacred land or the personal territory of spiritual sentiment. While Mars square Neptune occurs, it is best to anticipate confrontations concerning moral or spiritual issues. As this aspect passes, it will be easier to put spiritual beliefs and practices back on course without much conflict or interference. Meanwhile, stay aware and ready to deal with whatever comes along. This is the only time this aspect will occur this year.

Mercury sextile Pluto (occurring Oct. 20 – 23) This aspect brings an opportunity for us to get the message across to people in strong positions of power and authority. Mercury is in Scorpio, focusing discussions on matters of birth, sex, death, and transformation. Pluto in Capricorn is forcing us to acknowledge our resources and to use them wisely. Mass media may well be entranced by news concerning world superpowers and/or challenging power issues. This is an opportunistic time to reach out to those of another generation and make an attempt to communicate something vital. This aspect last occurred on March 4 with Mercury in Pisces.

October 23rd Saturday

Moon in Taurus	PDT	EDT
Moon sextile Pluto	1:39 AM	4:39 AM
Moon opposite Mercury	3:36 AM	6:36 AM
Moon opposite Venus	12:06 PM	3:06 PM

Birthday: Nicholas Stuart Gray 1922

Mood Watch: Waning Taurus Moon is a good time to handle finances succinctly and to seek beauty and pleasure in practical and comfortable ways. Today's lunar aspects have some challenging qualities, but the Taurus Moon, which now wanes but is still fairly full, encourages us to enjoy life. After all the hubbub of the high intensity full lunar energy, many folks will want to relax today. The waning Taurus Moon urges us to get back to practicalities. For the more ambitious types among us, this is a good time for cleaning, shopping, and beautifying one's surroundings. Taurus Moon emphasizes the need to get a handle on the physical world.

October 24ᵗʰ Sunday

Moon in Taurus	PDT	EDT	
Mars trine Uranus	7:56 AM	10:56 AM	
Moon sextile Jupiter	6:27 PM	9:27 PM	
Moon square Neptune	9:10 PM	12:10 AM	(October 25)
Moon sextile Uranus	11:49 PM	2:49 AM	(October 25)

Birthday: Kevin Kline 1947

Mood Watch: Sun in Scorpio and Moon in Taurus bring strong desires for sensual pleasures and comforting delights. The Taurus Moon keeps us focused on simple pleasures as well. Autumn is a time of beauty and the Taurus Moon stresses our need to enjoy the beauty and to make the most of it.

Mars trine Uranus (occurring Oct. 16 – 28) Mars in Scorpio trine Uranus in Pisces brings heated activities concerning very sensitive emotional matters and the radical tendencies that are seen in art and spiritual practices. It is through this aspect that positive emotional breakthroughs may occur. Be careful what you stand for or you'll fall for anything in this atmosphere of active yet favorable destruction. This is a good time to tackle the breakdown of unwanted barriers that stifle the human spirit from evolving in chosen ways. Mars trine Uranus is bound to create fire somewhere and the heat can be worked to our advantage. In the triumph mode, Mars trine Uranus creates fireworks of celebration, and there is a certain sense of truly being alive with regard to the demand for spiritual freedom and rights, and the need to bring an artistic form of relief to those who have experienced the challenge of emotional and spiritual battles. This aspect came close to occurring (non-exact) on March 15, with Mars in Leo, on the Cusp of Cancer/Leo, trine Uranus in Pisces, on the cusp of Pisces/Aries.

October 25ᵗʰ Monday

Moon in Taurus / Gemini	PDT	EDT
Moon opposite Mars goes v/c	12:48 AM	3:48 AM
Moon enters Gemini	4:48 AM	7:48 AM
Mercury conjunct Venus	6:17 AM	9:17 AM
Sun conjunct Venus begins (see October 28)		
Venus sextile Pluto begins (see November 1)		

" When I work, I relax. Doing nothing... makes me tired. " – Pablo Picasso (1881 – 1973)

Birthday: Pablo Picasso 1881

Mood Watch: For the earliest morning risers among us, the void-of-course Taurus Moon brings lazy and somewhat tired moods. This all changes swiftly when the Moon enters Gemini. This Moon touches on our curiosities and our investigative qualities. Many folks will be active with their communications. Waning Gemini Moon also keeps us introspectively thoughtful. This is a good time to work towards getting organized, and to become well informed in order to meet the busy tasks and events of the week ahead.

Mercury conjunct Venus (occurring Oct. 22 – 26) Today's conjunction of Mercury and Venus takes place in the invigorating and transformative realm of Scorpio. This is often a time when intimate and loving thoughts are shared with ardent and dramatic affection. With this conjunction, loving gestures are usually very intense and passionate. There may be a tendency for love-related communication to seem somewhat instinctual, clairvoyant – and possibly – suspicious, or jealous. However it manifests, the need to communicate our desires is definitely present. This conjunction last occurred on January 5 in Capricorn. It will also came very close to occurring March 26 – April 11, reaching its closest (non-exact) position to the conjunction on April 6.

October 26ᵗʰ Tuesday

Moon in Gemini	PDT	EDT
Moon trine Saturn	12:59 AM	3:59 AM
Sun sextile Pluto	12:00 PM	3:00 PM

Birthday: Hillary Rodham Clinton 1947

Mood Watch: Gemini Moon keeps us questioning, sorting, and fussing over the details of life. Thinking matters through and exploring a wide range of details gives adaptability and flexibility to our outlook. Communicating, investigating, and examining our choices will help us to think through our situations.

Sun sextile Pluto (occurring Oct. 22 – 28) The Sun, now just a few degrees into Scorpio, is sextile Pluto, which is newly in Capricorn since 2008. This brings opportunities that appear both vast and demanding to Libra and Scorpio cusp born people who are celebrating birthdays October 22 – 28. These birthday people are experiencing the sextile aspect of their natal sun to Pluto, giving them opportunities to take charge, to step into positions of power, and to accept and embrace permanent change in their lives. These are powerful transformations which provide opportunities to embody what has been learned from the personal trials of the past. Go thee forth and conquer, master Librans and Scorpions! Persist with diligence to resolve the conflicts of your life with self-respect and assurance. Your time to triumph is always available when your will to achieve is balanced by knowledge and hard work. This holds true for all signs of the zodiac. This aspect last occurred on February 23 with the Sun in Pisces, affecting some of the Pisceans experiencing birthdays around that time.

October 27th Wednesday

Moon in Gemini / Cancer	PDT	EDT	
Moon square Jupiter	1:54 AM	4:54 AM	
Moon trine Neptune	4:51 AM	7:51 AM	
Moon square Uranus goes v/c	7:18 AM	10:18 AM	
Moon enters Cancer	12:15 PM	3:15 PM	
Moon opposite Pluto	6:11 PM	9:11 PM	
Moon trine Sun	8:34 PM	11:34 PM	
Moon trine Venus	11:03 PM	2:03 AM	(October 28)
Mars enters Sagittarius	11:47 PM	2:47 AM	(October 28)

Birthday: Pablo Picasso 1881

Mood Watch: Nervous and anxious moods erupt as the waning Gemini Moon squares to Uranus and then goes void-of-course. This morning's events might not go so smoothly, particularly if there are a lot of things to do on our plates. This is a good time to try to take it easy, and it's an especially important time to limit one's caffeine intake. Forgetfulness, delays, information overload, and chaotic scenarios may make the early part of the day a trying time for some folks. As the Moon enters Cancer, various kinds of emotional expressions strike our moods. The waning Cancer Moon taps us into our true feelings and allows us to nurture and care for ourselves – as well as others – more genuinely. Cancer Moon is a good time to make the home more inviting and to enjoy domestic bliss.

Mars enters Sagittarius (Mars in Sagittarius: Oct. 27 – Dec. 7) While Mars travels through Sagittarius, Sagittarian people are likely to apply some extra energy to creative and outgoing projects – they will be feeling the heat of Mars activity in their lives. Mars is a fiery influence, and Sagittarius serves this energy very well as a mutable fire sign. Philosophers, athletes and travelers are particularly open to generating vast amounts of output and energy as the force of Mars activates the Sagittarian perspective. When in Sagittarius, Mars has stirred up our viewpoints over areas where the god of war has stepped beyond the usual bounds. Mars forces us to take some course of action, even if the course of action is the *choice* of inaction, at which point new vistas of understanding will evolve, and the warrior within will begin to take shape. Mars, the king of action, does not have to apply war-like activity all the time, as it simply represents the energy and strength necessary to take action. Sagittarius says, *"I see."* Perhaps we can actively take hold of a vision, a picture or a philosophy that can be manifested through our actions towards a positive, more balanced approach to what we hope to create for ourselves in the future. Mars means business in Sagittarius, and this is not the time to actively close our eyes – this is the time to open our eyes to the activities taking place around us.

October 28th Thursday

Moon in Cancer	PDT	EDT
Moon square Saturn	8:13 AM	11:13 AM
Moon trine Mercury	11:07 AM	2:07 PM
Sun conjunct Venus	6:10 PM	9:10 PM

Birthday: Bill Gates 1955

230

Mood Watch: Sun in Scorpio with Moon in Cancer is generally a very elusive, watery, emotional, and instinctual time. An emotional emphasis seems to jump out of every form of interaction, even the casual kinds. Mother Moon is at home in Cancer, and many folks associate the home with mother. The archetypical mother focuses on nourishment, contentment, comfort, and safety. Where these are not, the motherly instinct tends to gnaw at the subconscious part of the soul. It beckons us to show care and compassion.

Sun conjunct Venus (occurring Oct. 25 – 30) The Sun and Venus are conjunct in Scorpio. This conjunction particularly affects the love lives of those Scorpio people celebrating birthdays from October 25 – 30. These birthday folks are being filled with the need to have or to express love as best as they can, and this is the year for them to address the love matters in their lives. There is an attraction which draws us to beauty, romance, and love when Venus connects with the natal solar degrees. The issue of love is unavoidable, and these birthday folks' love needs become evident whether they wish to acknowledge them or not. It is through the attraction magnet of Venus that the personality (Sun sign) is assured of that with which they choose to identify, be affected by, and attracted to. Sometimes sheer magnetism is unavoidable and an event or relationship cannot be chosen – it just happens. This can encompass not only love matters, but also other areas such as the arts, aesthetics or appreciation of beauty. This conjunction last occurred January 11, affecting the birthday Capricorns of December 17, 2009 – January 24, 2010.

October 29th Friday

Moon in Cancer / Leo

	PDT	EDT
Moon trine Jupiter	7:27 AM	10:27 AM
Moon trine Uranus goes v/c	12:47 PM	3:47 PM
Moon enters Leo	5:39 PM	8:39 PM
Moon trine Mars	7:55 PM	10:55 PM

Birthday: Kate Jackson 1948

Mood Watch: Optimism springs to our hearts as Moon trine Jupiter brings hope, enthusiasm, and generous moods. The waning Cancer Moon allows us to share our emotions openly, and to sort through the ebb and flow of our ups and downs. The Moon reflects on our emotional cycles. The important thing to remember always with the emotional realm is to keep the energy flowing. That said, there's no denying that today's long void-of-course Cancer Moon might make this a somewhat melancholic day. This is no time to allow worry or fear to rule one's condition. There's nothing wrong with being emotional, but it's best not to spread sadness or pain. The brave Mother Moon teaches us how to feel what we're feeling and to let go of it. Don't hold on to bad stuff! Tonight's Leo Moon will change things around, as it inspires optimism and courage. Tonight is a good time to enjoy some entertainment with friends and to brush off this emotional day with some genuine lightheartedness.

October 30th Saturday
LAST QUARTER MOON in LEO

		PDT	EDT	
Moon	square Venus	1:48 AM	4:48 AM	
Moon	square Sun	5:45 AM	8:45 AM	
Moon	sextile Saturn	1:14 PM	4:14 PM	
Moon	square Mercury	10:11 PM	1:11 AM	(October 31)

Birthday: Ezra Pound 1885

Mood Watch: Today, people will want to be entertained and to get their minds on enjoying life. We now come to the Last Quarter Moon in Leo (Moon square Sun). When the Moon is waning in Leo, it urges us to take special care of ourselves as well as the children in our life. Projects of interest are sometimes considered children, too. If there is a hobby of special interest to you, take the time to brighten and enliven this work which represents your own talent and self-reflection. Throughout the working (or playing) day, jokes will fly, toys will be admired, and moods will reflect childlike frolic and revel. If you're serious about not being distracted by such playfulness, perhaps a quiet workspace is the key. If you must work with others, allow the frivolity to flow; the work will get done, but the child in everyone has to play now and then.

October 31st Sunday
All Hallows (Halloween) / Samhain / Witches' New Year
Moon in Leo / Virgo

	PDT	EDT
Moon opposite Neptune goes v/c	2:00 PM	5:00 PM
Moon enters Virgo	8:52 PM	11:52 PM
Mercury trine Jupiter begins (see November 4)		

Birthday: Dan Rather 1931

Mood Watch: Leo Moon is an excellent Moon to get into the mood for masquerading and Halloween frolic. However, as the Moon opposes Neptune and then goes void-of-course, we might find that we are somewhat spacey and uncertain about our former inspirations. An overwhelming depth of spirit carries us through the day despite the lack of organization and precision that comes with the void-of-course Moon time. As the Moon enters Virgo, our moods will become considerably more communicative and interactive. Virgo Moon allows us to cut through the bull and see things as they truly are. That could be interesting on a Halloween night!

Happy Halloween! Happy Witches' New Year! The slumber of the plant and animal world will deepen, and the crops and seeds of the fields will take their rest with the promise of returning as new growth in the spring. This is the time to honor the dead and invite the beloved spirits of our ancestors to join in our celebrations. Some believe from sunset until dawn, the spirits of our deceased loved ones are able to roam the earth and converse with the living. This is a particularly important time to speak aloud the names of those who have passed away (especially within the past year) and to honor them with the food, drink and song they enjoyed during their lifetime; following old traditions will awaken the memories of these loved ones. Don't forget to set a token plate of food and drink aside at mealtime in their honor.

232

November 1st Monday

All Saints Day / Day of the Dead

Moon in Virgo	PDT	EDT
Moon square Mars	1:44 AM	4:44 AM
Moon trine Pluto	2:29 AM	5:29 AM
Moon sextile Venus	2:39 AM	5:39 AM
Venus sextile Pluto	6:37 AM	9:37 AM
Moon sextile Sun	12:15 PM	3:15 PM

Birthday: Larry Flynt 1942

Mood Watch: Virgo Moon, on the first of the month, is a good time to access resources, take inventory, and to review accounts. The waning Virgo Moon also appeals to our need for caution. Virgo taps into our disbelieving or questioning nature. We are reminded that we need to tend to those basic but important health practices that keep us safe from harm. The Sun in Scorpio with the waning Moon in Virgo brings out our guarded, suspicious, and skeptical qualities. In a world full of the dangers of illness – or possible death – we are often reminded to use safe hygiene practices, and to handle foods with a thorough and meticulous cleaning process. The energies of the waning Virgo Moon emphasize our need to apply sensible precautionary measures wherever there is the potential for danger.

The *Day of the Dead* is celebrated on November 1st in Mexico and by enthusiasts of the Mayan and Aztec cultures. Colorful altars with decorative skulls, photos of the dead, and symbols of death all adorn the streets and villages. This is a classic time to honor the dead.

Venus sextile Pluto (occurring Oct. 25 – Nov. 4) Opportunity knocks, and here true beauty bridges the gap between generations. This aspect first occurred this year on February 14. For a recap on the story of today's reoccurring aspect, Venus in Scorpio sextile Pluto in Capricorn, *see September 12*. This aspect will also repeat for the fourth time this year on December 8.

November 2nd Tuesday

Election Day, USA

Moon in Virgo / Libra	PDT	EDT	
Moon sextile Mercury	6:18 AM	9:18 AM	
Moon opposite Jupiter	12:23 PM	3:23 PM	
Moon opposite Uranus goes v/c	5:36 PM	8:36 PM	
Moon enters Libra	10:19 PM	1:19 AM	(November 3)
Mercury square Neptune begins (see November 5)			
Mercury trine Uranus begins (see November 6)			

Birthday: k.d. lang 1961

Mood Watch: This morning brings curious and inquisitive moods as the Virgo Moon reaches the sextile position to Mercury. The waning Virgo Moon brings subtle, keen, and sometimes, prudent – or guarded – attitudes. Today, people will be playing their cards close to their chest, and they may appear somewhat reluctant to bluff. As the Moon opposes Jupiter, life may seem to be especially expensive, and our tendencies to overextend our energies, or our resources, may be more prevalent during this time. This evening's Moon opposite Uranus will be a period of conflicting or chaotic messages, particularly since the Moon goes void-of-course at this point. Radical breakthroughs can occur this evening. As the Moon enters Libra, our moods are focused on the need for peace and forgiveness.

November 3rd Wednesday

Moon in Libra	PDT	EDT
Moon square Pluto	3:54 AM	6:54 AM
Moon sextile Mars	5:38 AM	8:38 AM
Moon conjunct Saturn	5:33 PM	8:33 PM

Birthday: Benvenuto Cellini 1500

Mood Watch: Waning Libra Moon focuses our moods on the need for balance in our lives. Relationships that need mending at this time require structure and some ground rules in order to generate trust. Waning Libra Moon sometimes confronts us with our imbalances. This is a superb time to focus on the areas of life that have been put off the longest. For whatever reason, something important has been swept under the carpet; now's the time to shake the fabric and vacuum away the ancient stardust. The world turns and it also travels through space. There is no reason to avoid the old matter, for you, too, must revolve and change for the better. If something old is still haunting you, this means it's still important to you, and it's still unresolved. Face it now, while the core of those old dust bunnies can still be recognized. Libra Moon is a great time to consolidate lost friendships, make peace, and clear the air.

November 4th Thursday

Moon in Libra / Scorpio	PDT	EDT	
Mercury trine Jupiter	2:45 PM	5:45 PM	
Moon trine Neptune goes v/c	4:33 PM	7:33 PM	
Moon enters Scorpio	11:16 PM	2:16 AM	(November 5)
Venus-trine-Neptune-non-exact begins (see November 23)			

Birthday: Will Rogers 1879

Mood Watch: Today's Libra Moon wanes darkly and there may be some pensive qualities to our moods. The cardinal nature of the Libra Moon compels us to seek level ground. The Libra Moon is an instigator for our attempts at making logical and intelligent decisions. However, as the Moon goes void-of-course this evening, it is likely that many of us will venture off the beaten track despite our need to remain centered. For most of the evening, progress is slowed down by a persistent drive to get things just right. The act of weighing and measuring, judging and deliberating, as well as the attempt to balance out the situations that arise will probably become more of an ordeal than a practical process. Void Libra Moons commonly bring indecision. As the Moon enters Scorpio, there will be a deeper perception of the various situations of life. A darkly waning Scorpio Moon, also known as the *balsamic* phase of the Moon, brings strong emotional depth.

Mercury trine Jupiter (occurring Oct. 31 – Nov. 6) Mercury gets the message out there, the trine aspect brings gifts and positive breakthroughs, and Jupiter brings prosperity. This most favorable aspect brings good news of expansion and prosperity to those who are open to broadening their awareness. Ask and you shall have! Mercury in Scorpio trine Jupiter in Pisces brings profound communications which can lead to a gold mine of happiness and wellbeing. Since Jupiter is in Pisces, this is a favorable time to launch fundraisers for charities. It's an excellent time to learn new skills which will improve one's livelihood and better one's outlook. This is also a great time for salespeople to make sales, and for people to advertise and put information out there. For some folks, Mercury trine Jupiter is an advantageous time to ask for a job or a loan, or to provide a service which may have a bearing on a potential promotion. Look openly for opportunity when sharing information, and promote yourself and your capabilities. This aspect last occurred on July 11 with Mercury in Leo and Jupiter in Aries.

November 5th Friday
NEW MOON in SCORPIO - *Hecate's Moon*

	PDT	EDT	
Moon conjunct Venus	1:24 AM	4:24 AM	
Moon sextile Pluto	4:59 AM	7:59 AM	
Moon conjunct Sun	9:52 PM	12:52 AM	(November 6)
Mercury square Neptune	11:44 PM	2:44 AM	(November 6)

Birthday: Tilda Swinton 1961

Mood Watch: The **New Moon in Scorpio** (Moon conjunct Sun) marks the regenerative point of the New Moon – and the sign of Scorpio just happens to represent the phenomenon of regenerative force and transformation. The New Moon in Scorpio focuses on a rebirthing process for our emotional body, and this is the time when we are sure to address the proverbial skeletons in our emotional closet. New Moon in Scorpio encourages us to regenerate our hopes while transforming our fears into a courageous and renewed outlook for ourselves. This is the time to take bold steps to defeat undesirable emotional patterns and fear mechanisms. New Scorpio Moon casts new light on our ability to overcome pain and suffering.

Hecate's Moon: Hecate is the Wiccan goddess of the underworld who leads us through death towards a cycle of rebirth. She guides the lost souls to their final destiny, and can be called on at this time to guide those who have passed on, especially those who have met their end in a demeaning and challenged way, such as violent death or suicide. Hecate cures the ills that surround death.

Mercury square Neptune (occurring Nov. 2 – 7) Hecate's Moon is a very good time to apply some extra caution with this aspect. It often brings a struggle to communicate with regard to the spirit world and human spirituality. Efforts to explain our beliefs may be especially challenging. Neptune is in Aquarius, stirring up issues around human divinity and humanity's beliefs in this confusing and changing period of the dawning age. While Mercury in Scorpio is squaring Neptune, dramatic types of thought will be generated, particularly with respect to issues that concern divine experience (birth, sex, death); relaying this information may seem all the more difficult with this aspect. Anticipate religion related arguments and disputes. Deep subjects must not be treated lightly while Mercury squares Neptune. This aspect last occurred on June 9 with Mercury in Taurus.

November 6ᵗʰ Saturday

Moon in Scorpio	PDT	EDT
Moon trine Jupiter	2:47 PM	5:47 PM
Mercury trine Uranus	5:14 PM	8:14 PM
Moon square Neptune	6:28 PM	9:28 PM
Moon trine Uranus	8:22 PM	11:22 PM
Moon conjunct Mercury goes v/c	8:45 PM	11:45 PM
Neptune goes direct	11:05 PM	1:05 AM **EST** (Nov. 7)

Birthday: Maria Shriver 1955

Mood Watch: The Moon is still dark, still new, although now waxing in Scorpio. This is a time for renewal and for many, a place to come to terms with the transformations occurring in their lives. There is an initiation process of the soul taking place for those who are open to rebirth. Mystery and intrigue ring strongly throughout the day. New Moon in Scorpio is a splendid time to drop late autumn seeds expected to rise next spring. There are also seeds of dreams and seeds of the heart. This could be the day to accomplish something new, something that feels right.

Daylight Saving Time ends tomorrow. Don't forget to turn all clocks and timepieces **back** one hour this evening before hitting the sack. Tomorrow we begin Standard Time; at 2:00 a.m. on November 7ᵗʰ Daylight Saving Time ends coast to coast in North America.

Mercury trine Uranus (occurring Nov. 2 – 8) Mercury in Scorpio is trine to Uranus in Pisces. This combination stirs up an intelligent, compelling and awakening thought process, one that is usually well defined. This is a good time to record your thoughts and delight in brilliant thinking and information. Much of this brilliant thinking may seem like propaganda or information with a radical twist. Catch phrases, radical concept statements and ideas are often born under this aspect. Sensationalism, or matters of censorship, may be emphasized. Mercury in Scorpio dredges up important topics such as birth, sex, death, and the regenerative force realized through overcoming illness. Uranus is in Pisces, creating radical change in areas of addiction, the arts, music, psychology, and religion. This aspect last occurred July 6 – 11, reaching its peak on July 9 with Mercury in Cancer.

Neptune goes direct (Neptune direct: Nov. 6/7, 2010 – June 6, 2011) Neptune resumes a direct-moving course after five months (since May 31) of being retrograde. This will regenerate our spiritual and intuitive work and facilitate our development. Neptune is in Aquarius, influencing the flow of the Aquarian age and the evolutionary processes of belief systems. Neptune is the master of illusion, while Aquarius demands scientific proof. As Neptune proceeds further into Aquarius, we will learn to achieve a higher and freer sense of spiritual awareness – a sense that something divine is occurring, even though it cannot be explained in mortal terms. Since the late 20ᵗʰ century, Neptune has been in Aquarius filling our belief systems with a great deal of knowledge, and by April 2011, the planet of spiritual peace and serenity returns to its home base in Pisces, where our spiritual experience is infused with adaptable and inspiring believability. Neptune's calming and forgiving nature will help us to let go of malicious and non-productive thoughts, and will melt away cold-heartedness. A good meditation, when sincerely applied, helps to discharge our emotional baggage. Frequently invoke the spiritually uplifting meditations that work for you. This practice will lead you to a positive and regenerative place in your own spiritual evolution. Neptune moving direct allows us to move freely forward, using divine wisdom and our spiritual aspirations as guides.

November 7th Sunday
DAYLIGHT SAVING TIME ENDS
Turn clocks back one hour at 2:00 a.m.

Moon in Scorpio / Sagittarius			EST	
Moon enters Sagittarius	1:28 AM	PDT	3:28 AM	
Moon conjunct Mars	1:43 PM	PST	4:43 PM	
Venus enters Libra	7:06 PM	PST	10:06 PM	
Moon sextile Saturn	9:48 PM	PST	12:48 AM	(November 8)

Birthday: Joni Mitchell 1943

Mood Watch: Daylight Saving Time begins, an extra hour is gained, and for those who would rather rise to the occasion than take the extra hour of sleep, there is one more hour of daylight to explore and make discoveries on this Sagittarius Moon morning. The newly waxing Moon in Sagittarius brings optimism and an outgoing spirit. The feeling of renewed hope is upon us. This is a good time to engage in philosophical conversation and to share ideas. This Moon enlivens our moods towards a congenial, cooperative and flexible expression of service. Keep an eye out for opportunity. Exploration and a little bit of risk taking is highlighted. This is a time when our moods are more prone to consider possibilities and alternatives. Good food, travel, plays, and research are all strong Sagittarius Moon focuses.

Venus enters Libra (Venus in Libra: Nov. 7 – 29) We are all attracted to the need for balance these days. As autumn continues, our nesting instincts grow deeper, and relationships that aren't stable enough to undergo the responsibilities and tests of winter are likely to break off, as Venus in Libra strives to apply diplomacy as tactfully as possible. Due to the fact that Venus is currently retrograde (Oct. 8 – Nov. 18), it is now returning to the tail end of Libra. For more information on Venus in Libra, *see August 6*, when it first entered Libra this year.

November 8th Monday

Moon in Sagittarius	PST	EST	
Mercury enters Sagittarius	3:43 PM	6:43 PM	
Moon square Jupiter	6:03 PM	9:03 PM	
Moon sextile Neptune	10:10 PM	1:10 AM	(November 9)
Mars sextile Saturn begins (see November 14)			

Birthday: Bonnie Raitt 1949

Mood Watch: The young crescent Moon waxes in Sagittarius. No planets are currently traveling through the spring and summer signs of the zodiac. Daylight Saving time has taken affect and these are the darkening days of autumn. We have traveled beyond the scope of our deep rooted feelings with the Sun in Scorpio and the Moon in Sagittarius. The Sagittarius Moon teaches us to look beyond. This Moon puts the adaptable and mutable fire into the soul of our moods. It activates our desires to hold a shining beacon – or torch – of hope, confidence, and light. Scorpio teaches us about resilience, regenerative force, and transformation. The Sagittarius Moon inspires the conscientious expansion of our dreams and visions, generating optimism, versatility, and exploration. Tonight's Moon square Jupiter brings moods that might complicate or inhibit our expansive capabilities. Moon sextile Neptune brings the potential for a cool, calm composure.

Mercury enters Sagittarius (Mercury in Sagittarius: Nov. 8 – 30) Mercury, the planet of communication, information, and news is traveling through Sagittarius. New perspectives are bound to come up. News is always more philosophical and visionary when Mercury is in this sign. Word travels fast and further than expected. Sagittarius is the challenging "detrimental" place for Mercury, and this is a time when Mercury's greatest weapon – words – are best communicated with carefully considered diplomacy. People will be increasingly curious to know what is happening in the world, and to be more aware of global perspectives. Mercury in Sagittarius offers an opportunity to share your vision of a better world with others, and also brings adventure to the world of communications. Mercury will go retrograde (Dec. 10 – 29) causing the planet of communications to begin its second cycle in Sagittarius (Dec. 18, 2010 – Jan. 13, 2011). For more information on Mercury retrograde in Sagittarius, see the section in the introduction about *Mercury retrograde periods.*

November 9th Tuesday

Moon in Sagittarius / Capricorn	PST	EST
Moon square Uranus	12:05 AM	3:05 AM
Moon sextile Venus goes v/c	4:35 AM	7:35 AM
Moon enters Capricorn	5:37 AM	8:37 AM
Moon conjunct Pluto	12:15 PM	3:15 PM
Sun trine Jupiter begins (see November 15)		

Birthday: Carl Sagan 1934

Mood Watch: This morning the Moon enters Capricorn, and many folks will appear industrious and serious about getting to work on their plans and goals.

Capricorn is the achiever; therefore, not only do we wish to get grounded, now we are aspiring to climb some higher ground. Capricorn Moon brings focus and determination into the spirit of the day. Moon conjunct Pluto puts us in touch with issues of destiny and permanent change. This Moon reminds us that the important things in life are worth taking seriously, and those are the things we must try to stabilize in the midst of disruption. Capricorn Moon gives us the wherewithal to take care of business.

♏

November 10th Wednesday

Moon in Capricorn	PST	EST
Moon square Saturn	4:57 AM	7:57 AM
Moon sextile Sun	4:16 PM	7:16 PM

Birthday: Theophrastus Paracelsus 1493

Mood Watch:: Early this morning, Moon square Saturn brings a challenging time to get motivated and to stay focused. The morning may begin slowly, but, steady-does-it for the tortoise who outruns the overconfident rabbit in the day's race. Stumbling blocks are inevitably an incentive to try harder. The waxing Capricorn Moon inspires the need for diligent effort and determination. Moon sextile Sun sets the tone of our moods based on the seasonal changes around us. Despite many kinds of distractions, Capricorn Moon brings moods that are not easily swayed away from the original intent or purpose. This is a good time to utilize the powers of concentration.

November 11th Thursday

Veteran's Day, USA / Remembrance Day, Canada

Moon in Capricorn / Aquarius	PST	EST
Moon sextile Jupiter	2:04 AM	5:04 AM
Moon sextile Uranus	8:31 AM	11:31 AM
Moon square Venus goes v/c	11:57 AM	2:57 PM
Moon enters Aquarius	2:32 PM	5:32 PM
Mercury conjunct Mars begins (see November 20)		

" Say what you will about the sweet mystery of unquestioning faith. I consider the capacity for it terrifying. "
— Kurt Vonnegut, Jr. (born Nov. 11, 1922)

Birthday: Antero Alli 1952

Mood Watch: Astrologer and film maker, Antero Alli, would tell you that his own "astrological ethos does not agree with the notion of the physical planets governing or influencing our earthbound fates." On many levels he is quite right. We are stronger and more in control of our destiny than we give ourselves credit for, yet even Mr. Alli uses astrology to determine certain factors about his experiences, others, and the conditions that surround him. Among astrologers in general, there is a strong agreement with this notion that we are subject to various qualities and conditions of our outcome due to planetary shifts and lunar energies. It's a Capricorn Moon morning, and Capricorns are often among the most skeptical about astrology. Today, the Capricorn Moon is void-of-course for nearly three hours, and this is classically considered a time when we are vulnerable or weak in our work capacity. Laziness and slowness of production are often observed around this time. Absentmindedness or insensitivity may also be a sign of the void-of-course Capricorn Moon. Frankly, I, Annie Bones, am still somewhat divided on this phenomenon of astrological conditions governing our fates. Following certain preordained rules, I observe the energies like a weather forecaster – sometimes the forecast is not accurate, but most of the time it appears to have some punch. It's up to you to decide what *you* think. You are always the judge – not the victim – of what you read or predict about the stars. This evening's Moon in Aquarius is a superb time to measure the results of your observations about today's void-of-course Capricorn Moon.

November 12ᵗʰ Friday

Moon in Aquarius	PST	EST
Moon sextile Mercury	12:21 AM	3:21 AM
Moon sextile Mars	12:50 PM	3:50 PM
Moon trine Saturn	3:50 PM	6:50 PM
Sun square Neptune begins (see November 18)		

Birthday: Auguste Rodin 1840

Mood Watch: Waxing Aquarius Moon inspires us to take on mounting tasks with brilliance and admirable confidence. It's an active day of positive lunar aspects. Moon in Aquarius reminds us to apply ourselves in a thoughtful and knowledge-able manner, and to handle the challenges of this time with attentive awareness and ingenuity. This is a good time to work on innovative ideas and projects, and to experiment. Aquarius influence emphasizes reaching out towards a body of light and information which will benefit everyone. The Moon in Aquarius changes our concepts, ideas, and work ethics as we begin to see how much easier we can make life and our workload through an innovative approach to our work. Aquarius calls for the need to break through outmoded methods of achieving progress, and sets the precedent of what we accept as fixed scientific knowledge.

November 13ᵗʰ Saturday

FIRST QUARTER MOON in AQUARIUS

Moon in Aquarius	PST	EST	
Moon square Sun	8:38 AM	11:38 AM	
Moon conjunct Neptune	6:10 PM	9:10 PM	
Moon trine Venus goes v/c	10:33 PM	1:33 AM	(November 14)
Sun trine Uranus begins (see November 18)			

Birthday: Whoopi Goldberg 1955

Mood Watch: We have now reached the **First Quarter Moon in Aquarius** (Moon square Sun). Waxing Aquarius Moon puts the spotlight on eccentric and unusual breakthroughs of humankind. Controversial subjects are strongly at work. At this time we are often aware of great shifts of energy, and change in conscious-ness. The Aquarius Moon will assist our moods to meet and formally address humanity's newest challenges. Whenever we take strides to improve our world, the ramifications of our actions – and our experiments – are not always fully realized, but now we're taking broader measures to consider the impact our actions have on the environment. Aquarius Moon directs our attention to the vitally important focuses of humanity.

November 14ᵗʰ Sunday

Moon in Aquarius / Pisces	PST	EST	
Moon enters Pisces	2:25 AM	5:25 AM	
Moon sextile Pluto	9:57 AM	12:57 PM	
Moon square Mercury	8:59 PM	11:59 PM	
Mars sextile Saturn	9:57 PM	12:57 AM	(November 15)
Mercury sextile Saturn begins (see November 17)			

Birthday: Claude Monet 1840

Mood Watch: A dreamy, tranquil, and interchangeably moody reverie fills the atmosphere. The Moon in Pisces allows us to get more easily in touch with our intuition, our dreams, and our beliefs. Sun in Scorpio and Moon in Pisces often bring deeply penetrating wet weather; a watery, rainy, cloudy, snowy, and all around damp cast to the North American landscape brings misty moods. Hot delicious drinks bring comfort to the soul.

Mars sextile Saturn (occurring Nov. 8 – 18) Mars in Sagittarius sextile Saturn in Libra is an active time for travel, sports, and philosophical endeavors, particularly in the realm of careers and setting goals. During this aspect, actions create opportunities, provided there is an application of discipline and timing. Those who are affected by this aspect may feel noticed now. Diligently practice your favorite sport, especially those physical activities that demand precision and perfect timing. Offensive and defensive forces tend to work harmoniously with this aspect. Movement and the application of energy (Mars), plus responsibility and awareness of limitation (Saturn) allow the timely qualities of completion and new beginnings to occur. This would be the time to end a bad habit or to work to accomplish a goal. This aspect last occurred February 2 – March 30, reaching two peaks, one on February 15, and the other on March 22.

November 15ᵗʰ Monday

Moon in Pisces	PST	EST
Moon square Mars	5:14 AM	8:14 AM
Sun trine Jupiter	3:44 PM	6:44 PM

Birthday: Georgia O'Keeffe 1887

Mood Watch: Early this morning, Moon square Mars brings the potential for accidents, anger, or frustration, but the morning is young and it will soon pass. The waxing Pisces Moon brings creative, imaginative, and artistic moods. Fantasy and ceremonial traditions are often the draw of attention. Pisces Moon is a good occasion to reaffirm one's sense of faith and spiritual purpose. This is a good point to build on dreams and personal talents. Sun in Scorpio with Moon in Pisces is a particularly psychic time for our moods, when our secrets are perceived and revealed through thin veils of light.

Sun trine Jupiter (occurring Nov. 9 – 18) Scorpio people celebrating a birthday from November 9 – 18 are undergoing a favorable natal solar position with relation to Jupiter. This will be a time of gifts and expansion for these birthday folks, and there are good times ahead for them in the coming year. This aspect will bring a better sense of what it means to expand and attain one's personal desire. Be sure to take the time right now, Scorpio birthday people, to enjoy and appreciate life, which will definitely improve for you, despite other trials that you may be facing. Sun trine Jupiter brings the gift of joy, so make use of it and be sure to look for the silver lining in your life! This aspect last occurred July 26, affecting some of the Cancer and Leo birthday folks of that time.

November 16ᵗʰ Tuesday

Moon in Pisces / Aries	PST	EST	
Moon conjunct Jupiter	1:55 AM	4:55 AM	
Moon trine Saturn	2:52 AM	5:52 AM	
Moon conjunct Uranus goes v/c	8:36 AM	11:36 AM	
Moon enters Aries	2:59 PM	5:59 PM	
Moon square Pluto	10:34 PM	1:34 AM	(November 17)

Birthday: Diana Krall 1964

Mood Watch: The first lunar aspects of the day occur overnight and bring positive and tranquil dreams. However, Moon conjunct Uranus kicks off the morning with a chaotic trip to nowhere. This entire day with its void-of-course Moon in Pisces gives us illusive, uncertain, and spacey moods, classically bringing a great deal of confusion and making people easily distracted or persuaded. Heavy issues in our lives keep us preoccupied, overwhelmed, full of concern, hope, and prayer. The long and short of it is that many people are busily trying to escape from harsh realities. There is a tendency to indulge in addictive substances, pain-killers, or fantasy. Soothing art and music are among the most creative ways to ease the overrun senses. Later today, the Moon enters Aries and a defiant spirit of needing to take charge sets the tone for our moods. Aries Moon brings the spirit of spring season to our moods. There is an enterprising new hope on the horizon. Later, Moon square Pluto is a good time to avoid trouble and to attempt to get some rest.

November 17ᵗʰ Wednesday

Moon in Aries	PST	EST	
Moon trine Mercury	5:25 PM	8:25 PM	
Moon opposite Saturn	5:30 PM	8:30 PM	
Mercury sextile Saturn	6:08 PM	9:08 PM	
Moon trine Mars	9:14 PM	12:14 AM	(November 18)

Birthday: Israel Regardie 1907

Mood Watch: The waxing Moon in the Mars-ruled sign, Aries, brings out the spirit of the warrior. Aries declares: "I Am", and the spirit is proud. This is a good time to get in touch with new sources of inspiration, and to exercise independence, confidence, and originality. Sun in Scorpio and Moon in Aries bring an enterprising spirit that is courageous and unstoppable.

Mercury sextile Saturn (occurring Nov. 14 – 19) Mercury in Sagittarius is sextile to Saturn in Libra. Philosophical viewpoints bring the potential for opportunities when it comes to applying judicial disciplines and the rules and regulations of the courts. Opportunities are now available to assist us in communicating vital information in a more organized and pragmatic fashion. This aspect gives people an opportunity to learn essential lessons concerning boundaries, limitations, responsibilities and timely completion. It's a favorable aspect to discuss where to set up boundaries and how to implement security systems, and to teach people about handling responsibilities and disciplines. This aspect last occurred July 8 with Mercury in Cancer and Saturn in Virgo. It will also begin to occur on December 26 when Mercury is retrograde, and it will come within three orbital degrees of this sextile aspect on December 29 (non-exact), where it will begin to dissipate due to Mercury ending its retrograde cycle on that day.

November 18ᵗʰ Thursday

Moon in Aries	PST	EST	
Sun square Neptune	1:53 AM	4:53 AM	
Jupiter goes direct	8:54 AM	11:54 AM	
Venus goes direct	1:18 PM	4:18 PM	
Moon sextile Neptune	6:14 PM	9:14 PM	
Moon opposite Venus goes v/c	9:32 PM	12:32 AM	(November 19)
Sun trine Uranus	9:56 PM	12:56 AM	(November 19)

Birthday: William Schwenck Gilbert 1836

Mood Watch: The Moon is in Aries, the Sun is in Scorpio; there was a time when the planet Mars was attributed to both Aries and Scorpio. Mars has to do with raising energy and many folks will be doing this very thing today. Depending on the kind of atmosphere we have chosen, Aries Moon can create a very defensive or offensive quality of mood. Dominant moves and plays on others are a direct result of the competitive aggression typical of a strongly waxing Aries Moon. As a general rule, it's the same old story of wants and needs: to get ahead, to act on those higher impulses, to stir up some incentive among workers, to be self-expressive and reliant, to become motivated by success, to curb the temper when tested by challenges and, at the very least, to harness energy as it is required.

Sun square Neptune (occurring Nov. 12 – 21) This occurrence of Sun square Neptune especially affects Scorpio people who are celebrating birthdays November 12 – 21. Neptune in the square position to these birthday folks' natal Sun brings a sense of obstacles getting in the way of Spirit or the acknowledgement of spiritual beliefs. The challenge for these Scorpio birthday folks is to overcome the interfering doubts and confrontations. This especially applies to overcoming those extremely dangerous and destructive addictive tendencies. Remember, Scorpio, spiritual lessons do not have to be life threatening! Over the next year, there will undoubtedly be some spiritual adjustments, and perhaps a change of belief is required. This aspect last occurred on May 19, affecting the lives and beliefs of some of our Taurus and early born Gemini friends.

Jupiter goes direct (Jupiter direct: Nov. 18, 2010 – Aug. 29, 2011) Since July 23, Jupiter has been retrograde in the signs Aries and Pisces. Let us celebrate as

243

the planet Jupiter moves forward! Jupiter represents skill, fortune, luck, wealth, expansion, wellbeing, and joviality; it's also associated with advancement, prosperity, opportunity, fulfillment, and inheritance. The process of Jupiter retrograde is sometimes difficult for systems, and for the predictability of economic growth, such as business and market control. Jupiter engages one with a sense of happiness and fulfillment. Now that Jupiter goes direct, advancement goes from an internalized process to an externalized process, which is how Jupiter operates best.

Venus goes direct (Venus direct: Nov. 18, 2010 – May 15, 2012) Since October 8, Venus has been retrograde through the signs Scorpio and Libra. This has probably been creating many difficulties and challenges in the love lives of those born at the cusps of Scorpio/Libra. It is not only our love lives or our affections and attractions that are affected by Venus; beauty, art, and aesthetics are impacted as well. Today Venus in the late degrees of Libra goes direct, bringing a forward moving sense of faith and harmony in our relationships. Now that Venus is direct, expressions of affection and love matters can be begin to move forward with much more clarity and certainty.

Sun trine Uranus (occurring Nov. 13 – 21) This occurrence of Sun trine Uranus favorably affects our Scorpio friends celebrating birthdays November 13 – 21. It puts the radical forces of Uranus in the favorable trine position to their natal Sun. It is time for these people to make a breakthrough. Don't hold back, birthday people; chaos is here to stay for awhile. Let the experience be positive as long as this aspect brings gifts. Expect restless desires for freedom and the need to break out of your personal prison. Freedom knocks loudly, and the course of change is inevitable in the coming year. Change is necessary for growth. These influential changes are positive in nature, though on the surface they may seem harsh. Birthday people, the apparent madness occurring in your life is there for a reason. You will find a clearer picture in the long run by keeping up the good fight to preserve your inspiration, intelligence, and Scorpio passion. The trine aspect gives gifts of triumph, and this may be a good time to let chaos be the force that brings freedom. This aspect last occurred July 23, affecting some of the birthday Cancer and Leo folks of that time.

November 19th Friday

Moon in Aries / Taurus	PST	EST
Moon enters Taurus	2:05 AM	5:05 AM
Moon trine Pluto	9:31 AM	12:31 PM

Birthday: Larry King 1933

Mood Watch: A great deal of energy is building up at this time and we are on the brink of change. Between yesterday's long list of celestial events and tomorrow's bullish Full Moon Eve, today's Taurus Moon emphasizes the need to get a handle on the physical world and the most pragmatic things necessary to simplify and beautify our lives. As the last days of Scorpio touch on our instinctual urges to stay on top of important matters, the exalted Taurus Moon inspires beauty, sensuality, opulence, wealth, and taste. Quality, value, and style are accentuated. If beauty is in the eye of the beholder, anyone can find it. This is the time when we easily recognize beauty and splendor. Today's Moon trine Pluto is a good time to work on healing emotional wounds.

November 20ᵗʰ Saturday

Full Moon Eve

Moon in Taurus

	PST	EST	
Mercury conjunct Mars	10:35 AM	1:35 PM	
Moon sextile Jupiter	10:41 PM	1:41 AM	(November 21)
Mercury square Jupiter begins (see November 25)			
Mars square Jupiter begins (see November 29)			

Birthday: Joe Biden 1942

Mood Watch: The Moon is in Taurus on this Full Moon Eve, but the Moon will reach its peak fullness in Gemini, early in the day tomorrow. Nonetheless, this nearly Full Taurus Moon focuses our energies on such Taurus-like things as finances, accounting, valuables, gift shopping, decorating, and on the other end of the scale – lazing about in the lap of leisure. There is an active hopefulness in our aspirations and goals. The Taurus Moon brings positive, grounded, and pleasant moods, particularly wherever there is an effort to improve the appearance and functionality of our daily lives.

Mercury conjunct Mars (occurring Nov. 11 – Dec. 15) This conjunction brings the forces of communication (Mercury) together with the forces of action (Mars). This is not a very good time to bluff, especially with regard to travels or philosophical subjects while the two planets are in Sagittarius. This aspect brings words and deeds together, and in this case, the greatest action occurs with communication and is empowered in the expression of the message. This is an excellent time to get others motivated through speech. This may be a time of angry words being spoken. Some might say the best way to win an argument is to begin by being right; taking this approach during this time is likely to win you favors but not friendship. Take caution with your words; if they are intended to incite a battle, this is the time to put on your boxing gloves. Note: due to Mercury retrograde (Dec. 10 – 18), this conjunction will continue for longer than usual, and Mercury will be conjunct with Mars at the cusp of Sagittarius and Capricorn. On December 13, this conjunction will repeat again with both planets in Capricorn.

November 21ˢᵗ Sunday

FULL MOON in GEMINI

Moon in Taurus / Gemini

	PST	EST
Moon square Neptune	3:16 AM	6:16 AM
Moon sextile Uranus	4:45 AM	7:45 AM
Moon opposite Sun goes v/c	9:26 AM	12:26 PM
Moon enters Gemini	10:46 AM	1:46 PM

Birthday: Goldie Hawn 1945

Mood Watch: The **Full Moon in Gemini** (Moon opposite Sun) often brings moods that may seem overwhelmed by mutable thoughts just when we are trying to make decisions. This Gemini Moon, in all of its glorious fullness, brings amazing talk, speeches, mind games, and intellectual pursuits. People may tend

245

to babble senselessly, and very few are able to keep their minds on what they're doing, thinking, or feeling for very long. Ideally, this is a good time astrologically to pace oneself and relax the mind at various intervals. It may also be a time when our minds are relentlessly active and difficult to calm or ease. Full Moon in Gemini goes straight to charging our nervous systems, and we quickly discover that quieting down or easing an overworked nervous system takes some extra time after it has been running at top speed. Take it easy on the caffeine and sugar.

SAGITTARIUS

Key Phrase: "I SEE" or
" I PERCEIVE "
Mutable Fire Sign
Ruling Planet: Jupiter
Symbol: The Centaur
November 22nd through
December 21st

November 22nd Monday

Moon in Gemini	PST	EST	
Sun enters Sagittarius	2:14 AM	5:14 AM	
Moon trine Saturn	12:03 PM	3:03 PM	
Moon opposite Mars	9:21 PM	12:21 AM	(November 23)

Birthday: Jamie Lee Curtis 1958

Mood Watch: The waning Gemini Moon is still rather full as it directs our attention to a number of things at once. Filing, recording, inquiring, text messaging, twittering, and letter writing are highly emphasized activities during a Gemini Moon. Today's Moon trine Saturn creates a focus on time sensitive work projects. Tonight's Moon opposite Mars brings active temperaments. Moon in Gemini is an important time to guard the nervous system from taxing substances such as caffeine and sugar. It is also a good time to stimulate the mind with interesting and educational source materials.

Sun enters Sagittarius (Sun in Sagittarius: Nov. 22 – Dec. 21) Sun in Sagittarius represents the final laps of autumn and the shortest days of the solar year. The Sagittarius expression, "I see," opens our eyes to some new discoveries during this time. This mutable fire sign achieves visionary awareness by reaching out into the world of possibilities, the stars, and beyond. The Sagittarius time of year

246

– often thought of as being early winter – is actually still fall season, and sees to the closing of autumn by putting to sleep the last of the restless foliage in preparation for the pending winter's great slumber. Sun in Sagittarius days bring a focus on prosperity. Jupiter is the ruling planet of Sagittarius and inspires Sagittarians to excel, expand, and prosper. As the holidays begin and the Christmas season unfurls, the pressure to consume elaborate foods and purchase gifts, while keeping the great economic wheel turning, can be monumental for absolutely everyone. We are often required to pull together an outstanding number of social events and personal expenditures. The concept of prosperity has been tested to the extremes each time this season unfolds; it is, therefore, very important to get back to the basics of what one identifies as prosperous. The true challenge for many of us will be met when we finally reach out towards the higher vision of what prosperity really means. Sun in Sagittarius serves as a good time to direct the forces of vision and inspiration towards attaining a sense of wealth and wellbeing.

November 23rd Tuesday

Moon in Gemini / Cancer	PST	EST
Moon opposite Mercury	12:24 AM	3:24 AM
Moon square Jupiter	5:39 AM	8:39 AM
Moon trine Neptune	10:03 AM	1:03 PM
Moon square Uranus	11:23 AM	2:23 PM
Moon trine Venus goes v/c	1:55 PM	4:55 PM
Moon enters Cancer	5:15 PM	8:15 PM

Venus-trine-Neptune-non-exact (see below)
Mercury square Uranus begins (see November 27)

Birthday: Harpo Marx 1888

Mood Watch: The waning Gemini Moon brings pensive and curious moods. This morning's Moon square Jupiter may bring some complications with our efforts to expand, succeed, or travel. A little later, Moon trine Neptune brings a brief time of relaxed and inspired moods. As Moon square Uranus occurs, chaos gets out of hand and there are a lot of details to take in at once. This afternoon's Moon trine Venus brings pleasant distractions, and a myriad of scattered facts and disorganized figures will require a bit of backtracking. The Gemini Moon brings a busy mind, and this past phase of the Gemini Moon has been especially busy. This evening we can all fall back on the reliability of Cancer Moon. It always puts us in touch with how we feel.

Venus-trine-Neptune-non-exact (occurring Nov. 4 – 26) Due to the retrograde motion of these two planets at the beginning of this month, today is as close as we come, within two orbital degrees, to the Venus trine Neptune aspect. Venus and Neptune are now moving in a direct pattern and although this aspect will not reach its peak, it has been in full swing since the beginning of the month. For a recap on the story of Venus in Libra trine Neptune in Aquarius, *see September 4* when it last occurred.

November 24ᵗʰ Wednesday

Moon in Cancer

	PST	EST
Moon opposite Pluto	12:23 AM	3:23 AM
Moon square Saturn	6:04 PM	9:04 PM
Mercury sextile Neptune begins (see November 27)		

Birthday: Scott Joplin 1868

Mood Watch: Moon in Cancer emphasizes the need for a homey atmosphere and a safe and cozy realm to explore one's feelings. When in doubt, take a bath, or pamper yourself with whatever works to create a calming and soothing affect. For those working people that don't have time for such luxuries, acknowledge that moodiness and emotional traffic is a standard Cancer Moon influence. This evening's Moon square Saturn may bring a time when few will tolerate interruptions, poor workmanship, or the inability to concentrate. Irritability is often a symptom of not being loved, understood, or properly cared for. Wherever there is an attempt to remedy and undo these insufficiencies, there will be a grateful and welcomed response. Cancer Moon is the best time for some gentle, motherly, care.

November 25ᵗʰ Thursday

Thanksgiving Day, USA

Moon in Cancer / Leo

	PST	EST	
Mercury square Jupiter	6:18 AM	9:18 AM	
Moon trine Jupiter	10:50 AM	1:50 PM	
Moon trine Uranus	4:18 PM	7:18 PM	
Moon square Venus goes v/c	7:43 PM	10:43 PM	
Moon enters Leo	10:02 PM	1:02 AM	(November 26)
Mars square Uranus begins (see December 3)			

Birthday: Paul Desmond 1924

Mood Watch: The Moon is waning in Cancer and our moods are geared toward caring for and nurturing the tender parts of our being. The depth of our emotional experience can be felt, and today is the time to comfort, ease, and pamper the heart. A warming drink of something delicious and a nurturing and homey Thanksgiving dinner can be uplifting, however, people can be especially emotional during a Cancer Moon, and we must be careful not to tread on their sensitive areas without their consent. In the face of adversity, a caring companion's listening ear does wonders. Since the Moon will go void-of-course tonight, an early dinner would be the best plan. Beware of the tendency for people to be moody and emotional over seemingly small or insignificant things. Later, Moon in Leo brings strong urges for entertainment, family support, or plain and simple relaxation.

Mercury square Jupiter (occurring Nov. 20 – 27) Mercury in Sagittarius is square to Jupiter in Pisces. Philosophical conversations are likely to complicate our cultural activities. With this aspect it is best to beware of negative views that discourage prosperous growth, as deceptive words, lies – and even the truth – are easily misconstrued on a much larger scale. During this aspect, it may be best to hold off on a job request, asking for a raise, or signing any binding contracts concerning long term investment and payment schedules. It may be an especially difficult time to communicate during travels, and it may be best to double check travel schedules. This aspect has a tendency to create expensive misunderstandings when it comes to large scale investments. This may also be a difficult time to raise money for charities. Dig harder and investigate more thoroughly the details associated with long term investments. This aspect last occurred on June 26 when Mercury was in Cancer and Jupiter was in Aries. Due to the next phase of Mercury retrograde (Dec. 10 – 29), this aspect will also reoccur on December 21.

November 26th Friday

Moon in Leo	PST	EST	
Moon trine Sun	5:14 AM	8:14 AM	
Moon sextile Saturn	10:35 PM	1:35 AM	(November 27)
Mercury sextile Venus begins (see December 1)			

Birthday: Tina Turner 1939

Mood Watch: The waning Moon is in Leo and our moods are drawn to the need for warmth, affection, and reassurance. The waning Moon in Leo puts us in touch with our domain – that place where we rule. Self-image is reviewed from this plateau and fills us with questions. Are we satisfied with our chosen lifestyle? Can we maintain and live up to our choices in life? Are self-worth and respect present? Take the time to enhance your self-image with a positive affirmation. Leo Moon puts people in touch with their personal needs. The positive lunar aspects of today will give us what we need to succeed.

November 27th Saturday

Moon in Leo	PST	EST
Mercury sextile Neptune	5:13 AM	8:13 AM
Moon trine Mars	12:33 PM	3:33 PM
Mercury square Uranus	6:27 PM	9:27 PM
Moon opposite Neptune	6:48 PM	9:48 PM
Moon trine Mercury	8:04 PM	11:04 PM
Mars sextile Neptune begins (see December 2)		

Birthday: Jimi Hendrix 1942

Mood Watch: Today's lunar aspects are promising as they bring an interest in personal hobbies, family endeavors, and leisurely activities. There will be a lot of activity, in fact, as people are inclined to move about with an outgoing and engaging spirit. The Sun and Moon are in fire signs, and this brings creativity and excitement. This Leo Moon inspires us to seek light, comfort, and warmth.

Mercury sextile Neptune (occurring Nov. 24 – 28) Mercury in Sagittarius sextile Neptune in Aquarius reassures us that communicating our philosophies and our beliefs also empowers our belief in humanity. This is an opportunistic time to cautiously attempt communication with regard to beliefs and spiritual matters. Mercury is in Sagittarius placing a philosophical emphasis of talk on such Neptune related subjects as spiritual growth, guidance, and inspiration. Take this opportunity to transmute thoughts and beliefs into a workable understanding and to share it with others in a way that encourages them. Prayers, channeling, and spells are all very effective with Mercury sextile Neptune. This aspect last occurred on March 31 with Mercury in Aries. Due to Mercury's final retrograde period this year (Dec. 10 – 29), this aspect will also return on December 20.

Mercury square Uranus (occurring Nov. 23 – 30) Mercury in Sagittarius square the retrograde Uranus in Pisces creates explosive mental states and causes some people to speak abrasively or to promote overly radical ideas. Tact and diplomacy are likely to go right out the door when religion is discussed. Communications and philosophical debates may come up against unusual or explosive viewpoints. Spiritual harmony is always best achieved when we exercise discretion. This really is a time to watch what you say: communications have the potential to shake matters up considerably. This aspect last occurred on June 25 with Mercury in Cancer and Uranus in Aries. It will reoccur on December 20 with Mercury retrograde in Sagittarius and Uranus in Pisces.

November 28ᵗʰ Sunday
LAST QUARTER MOON in VIRGO

Moon in Leo / Virgo	PST	EST
Moon sextile Venus goes v/c	12:29 AM	3:29 AM
Moon enters Virgo	1:34 AM	4:34 AM
Moon trine Pluto	8:37 AM	11:37 AM
Moon square Sun	12:36 PM	3:36 PM

" One thought fills immensity."   – William Blake (1757 – 1827)

Birthday: William Blake 1757

Mood Watch: The Last Quarter Moon in Virgo (Moon square Sun) calls for the release of doubt. These are the days of Sun in Sagittarius; applying the vision of how one wants to see their future-self is not an easy task, especially if poisonous and debilitating addictions are involved. However, the Sagittarian outlook often projects selfhood in an outward fashion in order to envision the demands of an expanding spirit. That same Sagittarian awareness is just as capable of traveling inward and perceiving the needs of the inner self. Let the doubts and fears of your life be flushed away at this time so that, through clarity, you may achieve the benefits of your visionary picture of health, wealth, and wellbeing.

November 29ᵗʰ Monday

Moon in Virgo	PST	EST	
Mars square Jupiter	6:50 AM	9:50 AM	
Venus enters Scorpio	4:31 PM	7:31 PM	
Moon opposite Jupiter	5:40 PM	8:40 PM	
Moon square Mars	6:15 PM	9:15 PM	
Moon opposite Uranus	10:40 PM	1:40 AM	(November 30)
Mercury conjunct Pluto begins (see December 5)			

Birthday: C.S. Lewis 1898

Mood Watch: The Moon wanes in Virgo where a cautious quality of moods leads us to be more discerning, courteous, and relatively tactful. Virgo Moon churns our curious juices and gets us in the mood to investigate and examine the possibilities.

Today's lunar aspects are gruesome, and it is advisable to conserve energies and to tread lightly through the challenges that are presented. The waning Virgo Moon guides us through our doubts. Prudent sensibility will have its rewards.

Mars square Jupiter (occurring Nov. 20 – Dec. 3) With this aspect various activities are met with the obstacles of economic oppression and shortfall. This is a very difficult time to excel in business endeavors, especially in actively trading markets. This aspect warns us that there will be trouble when approaching the job market aggressively. Trying to make progress using headstrong attitudes and unwarranted self-confidence might impede progress. This aspect brings no-nonsense demands or increases in our workload. Mars in Sagittarius suggests the need for aggressive business tactics in foreign markets and in banking adjustments, which are likely to become expensive while Mars is square to Jupiter. Additionally, travel expenses may be particularly high. Jupiter is in Pisces, focusing on the expansion of wealth through the endowment of the arts and through religious organizations. The square aspect of these two planets creates a challenging dynamic in the struggle to grow economically. Expect to work a lot harder and perhaps a lot longer in order to smooth the rough edges of the financial empire while Mars in Sagittarius squares Jupiter in Pisces. Fortunately, this is the only time Mars square Jupiter occurs this year.

Venus enters Scorpio (Venus in Scorpio: Nov. 29, 2010 – Jan. 7, 2011) Venus has already been in Scorpio this year. It was retrograde this autumn (Oct. 8 – Nov. 18), and consequently, it entered Libra on November 7. Today Venus re-enters Scorpio on for the second time. For a recap on the story of Venus in Scorpio, see *September 8*, when it first entered Scorpio this year.

November 30ᵗʰ Tuesday

Moon in Virgo / Libra	PST	EST
Moon square Mercury goes v/c	3:16 AM	6:16 AM
Moon enters Libra	4:16 AM	7:16 AM
Moon square Pluto	11:22 AM	2:22 PM
Mercury enters Capricorn	4:11 PM	7:11 PM
Moon sextile Sun	7:02 PM	10:02 PM
Venus sextile Pluto begins (see December 8)		

Birthday: Mark Twain 1835

Mood Watch: Early this morning the waning Virgo Moon goes void-of-course and one hour later it enters Libra. The Libra Moon helps us to create harmony among friends. Of course, there will be a lot of weighing and balancing the pros and cons of our relations with others, but overall, Libra Moon guides us to make adjustments, and to be more tolerant than usual with our friends and loved ones. Midday may bring a certain degree of melodrama with Moon square Pluto. Later in the day, our moods will improve as we come closer and closer to establishing some balance in our lives.

Mercury enters Capricorn (Mercury in Capricorn: Nov. 30 – Dec. 18) While Mercury travels through Capricorn, communications tend to be more serious and to the point, although not necessarily less complex. In negotiations, there is an emphasis on enterprise. While this versatile planet goes through Capricorn, our realms of communications have a determined and persistent quality of expression, like a demanding voice waiting to be heard and received with hospitality. Mercury will be retrograde in Capricorn from December 10 – 18; this could bring miscommunications over large scale contracts, issues of control and time restraints. Communication is one of the tools of survival, and this is an important time to use those skills wisely and sensibly.

December 1st Wednesday

Moon in Libra	PST	EST	
Moon conjunct Saturn	4:48 AM	7:48 AM	
Mercury sextile Venus	8:39 AM	11:39 AM	
Moon sextile Mars	11:30 PM	2:30 AM	(December 2)

Birthday: Lou Rawls 1933

Mood Watch: The waning Libra Moon preoccupies our moods with a serious focus on marital partners and important relationships, particularly this morning as Moon conjunct Saturn highlights our need for balance in those places where it is seriously required. Libra Moon emphasizes such focuses as libraries, teaching, research, intellectual pursuits, law and justice. This serves as a good time to apply ourselves to assist others and to create harmony among loved ones.

Mercury sextile Venus (occurring Nov. 26 – Dec. 12) Mercury in Capricorn sextile Venus in Scorpio teaches us of the necessity to speak up succinctly and plainly for our needs, particularly for passionate and essential kinds of love and affection. This aspect focuses talk and discussion on the things in life we are most attracted to and touched by. The sextile aspect of Mercury to Venus brings hope and good possibilities for our love needs. This is a good time to speak up for the things and the people of our lives – those things and people whom we treasure. This aspect occurred twice this year, on May 29 and September 16, although neither time did those aspects reach an exact peak. It will also reach an exact peak one more time, on December 10 with Mercury retrograde.

December 2nd Thursday

Chanukah begins (ends December 9)

Moon in Libra / Scorpio	PST	EST
Moon trine Neptune goes v/c	12:08 AM	3:08 AM
Moon enters Scorpio	6:44 AM	9:44 AM
Moon conjunct Venus	8:43 AM	11:43 AM
Moon sextile Mercury	9:39 AM	12:39 PM
Mars sextile Neptune	11:38 AM	2:38 PM
Moon sextile Pluto	2:00 PM	5:00 PM
Sun sextile Saturn begins (see December 6)		

Birthday: Gianni Versace 1946.

Mood Watch: The early morning Libra Moon is void-of-course, and this often leads to confused or indecisive moods. As the Moon enters Scorpio, the morning energy will shift into high gear. Moon conjunct Venus brings passion, special interests, and the intrigue of beauty and excitement. Moon sextile Mercury brings the potential for significant information, or there may be a notable swiftness of energy when sharing communications. The Scorpio Moon energy drives us, and with encouraging moods, it will also give us the stamina to carry through extreme conditions. Moon sextile Pluto brings the potential for a successful and powerful step forward.

Mars sextile Neptune (occurring Nov. 27 – Dec. 5) Mars in Sagittarius is sextile to Neptune in Aquarius. Personal initiative – when taken – brings the potential for a spiritual awakening in humanity. Mars sextile Neptune is a splendid time to *act* on our *beliefs*. This aspect brings the vitality of Mars' energy into a favorable position with the spirit-awakening influence of Neptune. This is a place where we can safely dump our anger and can potentially make a connection with a spiritual healing process. Those who act on their visions and on the ceremonies of their particular belief systems will have an opportunity to connect with a very profound spiritual experience. This aspect makes the active work of artists, poets, and musicians into unique and very powerful statements about being in an endowed and sacred state of awareness. Mars is active and masculine, while Neptune has a very nebulous and passive guise that affects our deeper inner sense of beliefs and spirit. When these two planets are placed in a favorable position to each other, personal spiritual breakthroughs can be made. This is the only time this aspect occurs this year.

December 3rd Friday

Moon in Scorpio

	PST	EST
Mars square Uranus	6:00 AM	9:00 AM
Moon trine Jupiter	11:28 PM	2:28 AM (December 4)

Birthday: Brendan Fraser 1968

Mood Watch: For some the smell and sensation of cold is in the air. Nothing drives the Scorpio Moon experience into some form of recognizable existence more viably than the element of intensity. If it doesn't come in the form of a cold snap or a great snow, it may be something more close to the passionate centers of one's sojourn. Intensity can be seen on the faces of a passing crowd. It can be felt in the attitude of others. It may dwell within, and lingers in an unexplainable fashion. It may be so subtle that a floating bubble moves unscathed near a raging fire, but what's so subtle about that? However simple or complex the circumstances, Scorpio Moon has a hold on the imagination. Today Mars is in a square to Uranus (see below), and there is very rarely a quality of subtlety to that. There is always some form of intensity occurring that a darkly waning Scorpio Moon will most assuredly put us in touch with in inexplicable ways. Brace yourself and pace yourself.

Mars square Uranus (occurring Nov. 25 – Dec. 7) Mars square Uranus is sometimes tyrannical, and is never an aspect to be underestimated. Masculine fortitude and the enigmatic force of chaos are in an especially volatile and difficult phase of expression when Mars is square to Uranus. This aspect was suspiciously present when the December 26, 2004 tsunami tidal wave disaster of the century swept the Indian Ocean. Today, Mars is in Sagittarius and, while it squares to Uranus, the resulting tensions may cause extensive damage in the forces of offensive and defensive action. While Uranus is in Pisces, chaos abounds in the sacred territory of our beliefs. The events of Mars square Uranus do not always predictably yield natural disasters, but unfortunately they are often the catalyst for difficult human trials and tension. This aspect is like a pressure cooker; it may seem dormant at first, but if not carefully handled, the aftermath can be a real mess! It is wise to completely avoid extremely risky undertakings that may rock the boat of fiery activity during Mars square Uranus. This is no time to step into the eye of the storm! Fortunately, this is the only time this aspect will occur this year.

December 4th Saturday

Moon in Scorpio / Sagittarius

	PST	EST
Moon square Neptune	3:17 AM	6:17 AM
Moon trine Uranus goes v/c	4:13 AM	7:13 AM
Moon enters Sagittarius	10:00 AM	1:00 PM

Birthday: Tyra Banks 1973

Mood Watch: The Scorpio Moon goes void-of-course early this morning, and for many hours there will be a lingering intensity to our moods. Beware of the possibility of thievery or mischief. There are likely to be some delays and setbacks. As the Moon enters Sagittarius a strong, philosophical, optimism strikes our moods. The Moon will reach the new mark tomorrow, but for now, deep, profound, and exhilarating visions may be found in the shadows of our moods. This is a good time to internalize personal visions and to picture the things that will bring joy and happiness to you. Although we strive to save energy, the attraction of lights has the greatest appeal on New Moon eve in the dark days of late autumn. There are many way to use light conservatively.

December 5th Sunday

NEW MOON in SAGITTARIUS

Moon in Sagittarius

	PST	EST
Moon conjunct Sun	9:36 AM	12:36 PM
Moon sextile Saturn	12:16 PM	3:16 PM
Mercury conjunct Pluto	5:22 PM	8:22 PM
Uranus goes direct	5:50 PM	8:50 PM
Mars conjunct Pluto begins (see December 13)		

Birthday: Robert Hand 1942

Mood Watch: The **New Moon in Sagittarius** (Moon conjunct Sun) inspires us to look at life in a whole new way. Early in the day a hopeful outlook is felt strongly as the Moon reaches the new mark. New Moon in Sagittarius encourages us to start exercise programs, look into original philosophies, and to explore new territory in our lives. Sagittarius says, "I see," so vision and insight are the primary incentives to explore fresh ground. Today is a good day to optimistically look ahead and get in touch with an innovative vision for the coming month and year.

Mercury conjunct Pluto (occurring Nov. 29 – Dec. 16) Mercury conjunct Pluto raises issues of power. The areas of our lives that have required challenge, struggle, sacrifice and transformation now bring us to a place where we can talk about them.

With Mercury and Pluto in Capricorn, a very strong sense of duty is instilled in the delivery of messages. This is a time when people instinctively know their own fate. Mercury conjunct Pluto in Capricorn allows us to voice our hardships, and to contemplate and deliberate over the powerful occurrences that challenge and change our lives. There will be a great deal of intensity in our conversations at this time, especially with regard to the fate of the world and our ongoing efforts to end hardship and suffering. This conjunction also occurred Jan. 8 – 20 (*see Jan. 15*) but it never actually reached an exact peak during that time. It will also repeat on December 13, when Mercury is retrograde (Dec. 10 – 29).

Uranus goes direct (Uranus direct: Dec. 5, 2010 – July 12, 2011) Since July 5, Uranus, known for stirring up calamity, has been retrograde. Now the planet of chaos and rebellion moves steadily forward at the twenty six degree mark of Pisces, awakening the spiritual needs of humanity, perhaps even inspiring break-throughs in human rights, or promoting creativity in art and music. The work of radical and revolutionary forces resumes course as Uranus moves direct until July, 2011. We all feel the need to break out of oppressing conditions of life. As Uranus moves forward, the volatile quality of its work demands the utmost intelligence and knowledge as each level of urgency is unveiled. Uranus is the ruler of Aquarius and teaches us to seek higher levels of intelligence through unusual, brilliant, and open minded measures. The next time the urge for unabashed rebellion makes you kick up your heels, remember to kindle the light of love for humankind's wisdom. This is, after all, the Age of Aquarius.

December 6th Monday

Moon in Sagittarius / Capricorn	PST	EST	
Moon square Jupiter	4:27 AM	7:27 AM	
Moon sextile Neptune	8:18 AM	11:18 AM	
Moon square Uranus	9:13 AM	12:13 PM	
Moon conjunct Mars goes v/c	1:47 PM	4:47 PM	
Moon enters Capricorn	3:16 PM	6:16 PM	
Moon sextile Venus	9:54 PM	12:54 AM	(December 7)
Moon conjunct Pluto	11:25 PM	2:25 AM	(December 7)
Sun sextile Saturn	11:59 PM	2:59 AM	(December 7)

Birthday: Dion Fortune 1890

Mood Watch: The newly waxing Sagittarius Moon brings hope, despite the ups and downs of today's lunar aspects. Pensive moods give birth to rich insights. However, for awhile in the afternoon, the Sagittarius Moon goes void-of-course, and it's a time to beware of the potential for accidents and to anticipate traffic delays. As the Moon enters Capricorn, our moods are geared towards the necessity to stay focused, to concentrate, and to stay on track. The newly waxing Capricorn Moon brings determination.

Sun sextile Saturn (occurring Dec. 2 – 9) This occurrence of Sun sextile Saturn particularly affects Sagittarius people celebrating birthdays December 2 – 9, helping them focus their energy and discipline with greater clarity throughout this year. As Saturn traverses the sextile aspect to the natal Sun of these Sagittarius people, there is a sense of making progress through discipline, and they may very

255

well begin to see the rewards of their diligent labor in the coming year. This is only true as long as they apply themselves to their work, and maintain a vigilant and persistent effort to master personal discipline and training. Greater control comes with genuine effort. This aspect last occurred on July 22, presenting better opportunities and allowing more control in the lives of some Cancer and Leo folks.

December 7th Tuesday

Moon in Capricorn	PST	EST
Moon conjunct Mercury	12:41 AM	3:41 AM
Mars enters Capricorn	3:48 PM	6:48 PM
Moon square Saturn	7:17 PM	10:17 PM

Birthday: Tom Waits 1949

Mood Watch: *Tom Waits* for no one on a Moon in Capricorn day, and time is of the essence. The newly waxing Capricorn Moon encourages us to stay on track and to take matters very seriously, and in a guarded fashion. People may seem very intent on making things happen and doing the work. However, this evening's Moon square Saturn may bring a somewhat trying and difficult time to complete projects or to stay focused. The Capricorn Moon phase often puts a lot of demands on our sense of control and limitation. It's important to know when to work and when to stop. Waxing Capricorn Moon is a good time to create realistic goals and objectives.

Mars enters Capricorn (Mars in Capricorn: Dec. 7, 2010 – Jan. 15, 2011) Now the planet Mars, known to many as "the god of war," is in the sign of Capricorn. The main thrust of activities will be inspired by the industrious push of Capricornian persistence. Mars in Capricorn is the place where it's exalted. Activities will shift towards dynamic, ambitious and enterprising endeavors. With Mars in Capricorn, a sense of duty is instilled. Activities, if successfully managed, will produce long lasting results. This is *not* a good time to create enemies; the inherent difficulties will also produce long lasting results, and long standing enemies are not a good thing to have when trying to create a sense of forward moving progress. The last time Mars was in Capricorn was December 26, 2008 to February 4, 2009, when the US inaugurated the newly elected President who began weathering the first open signs of a global financial crisis. Large industries, including the automobile industry, pleaded for bailouts from the government. No one could deny at that point that the economy had fallen off a cliff, as Warren Buffet had suggested. Mars deals with action, Capricorn deals with the usefulness of industry. The conservative Capricorn goat squarely took action and booted superfluous hired employees right off that cliff and, consequently, raised the unemployment level in America to alarming rates.

Mars shakes up commerce in Capricorn, and since it's the god of war, we have learned a lot about its exalted activities when in Capricorn. Mars was in Capricorn January 16 – February 25, 2007, when US Democrats regained a legislative majority, but their initial attempts to pull troops out of Iraq failed. At that point in time, people began to really understand what an enormous mission and expense troop withdrawal from Iraq involves. Before that, during February through March 2005, Mars in Capricorn also brought a difficult time for our ruthlessly warring planet, with exceptionally high casualty rates in Iraq. Before that, Mars entered Capricorn in March 2003, when the US war on Iraq officially began. Interestingly enough, the time Mars entered Capricorn before that was the week of September 11th, 2001. It appears that here in the beginning of the 21st century, the guns of war are activated in no uncertain terms when Mars is in Capricorn. As is the nature of Capricorn, this is a time for vigilance, diligence, and perseverance.

December 8th Wednesday

Moon in Capricorn / Aquarius	PST	EST	
Venus sextile Pluto	8:18 AM	11:18 AM	
Moon sextile Jupiter	12:22 PM	3:22 PM	
Moon sextile Uranus goes v/c	5:07 PM	8:07 PM	
Moon enters Aquarius	11:31 PM	2:31 AM	(December 9)

Birthday: David Carradine 1936

Mood Watch:: T'is the season to be busy! Our workload may seem colossal – no fear – the Capricorn Moon is here to assist us to get the work done. A determined attitude is carried with certainty throughout the day. This evening, as the Capricorn Moon goes void-of-course, a lazy quality of mood enters the picture. People may seem spacey, disinterested, or preoccupied. It may be best to complete the better part of your workload in the daytime – as a general rule, not much gets done during the void-of-course Capricorn Moon.

Venus sextile Pluto (occurring Nov. 30 – Dec. 11) Opportunity knocks, and here true beauty bridges the gap between generations. Four times this aspect takes place this year! It first occurred on February 14, when Venus was in Pisces. It occurred last on November 1, with Venus in Scorpio. For a recap on the story of the currently reoccurring Venus in Scorpio sextile Pluto in Capricorn, see September 12.

December 9th Thursday

Moon in Aquarius	PST	EST
Moon square Venus	9:31 AM	12:31 PM

Birthday: John Milton 1608

Mood Watch: Sun in Sagittarius and waxing Moon in Aquarius generally bring insightful, brilliant, and inspired incentives and moods. That said, it must be noted the only aspect of the day is not necessarily upbeat. We begin the day with Moon square Venus, and our moods may be disrupted by a lack of pleasant feelings. We may be challenged in our attempts to get closer to the things we love. The Aquarius Moon puts us in touch with our feelings about people and humanity, and in particular, the systems by which we operate. Many of our systems are changing at an alarming rate, and the Aquarius Moon gives us the motivation to learn, teach, experiment, and to observe with an open mind.

December 10th Friday

Moon in Aquarius	PST	EST
Mercury goes retrograde	4:05 AM	7:05 AM
Moon trine Saturn	5:29 AM	8:29 AM
Moon sextile Sun	12:02 PM	3:02 PM
Mercury sextile Venus	12:49 PM	3:49 PM
Sun square Jupiter begins (see December 16)		

Birthday: Emily Dickinson 1830

Mood Watch: Progressive, open-minded, and truthful attitudes will keep us inspired during the waxing Aquarius Moon. Aquarius calls for the need to break through outmoded methods of achieving progress, and sets the precedent of what we accept as fixed scientific knowledge. Astrologically we are now under the influence of Mercury retrograde (see below), and it is important to get a clear picture of holiday season plans. Simple solutions are the best, and it would be wise to reiterate daily plans with everyone who needs to stay informed.

Mercury goes retrograde (Mercury retrograde: Dec. 10 – 29) Just in time for the holidays! Mercury goes retrograde today in Capricorn; it will travel back to the later degrees of Sagittarius (see Mercury enters Sagittarius, Dec. 18) before going direct at the 19 degree mark of Sagittarius on December 29. Mercury retrograde in the cardinal earth sign, Capricorn, is likely to bring a number of communication mishaps over building contracts, corporate mergers, and in matters with regard to authority and control. A real test of everyone's patience occurs; this leaves us susceptible to arguments and confusion over who's in control, and over the means, methods, and issues of control. On December 18, Mercury enters Sagittarius, the final half of Mercury retrograde. While Mercury is retrograde in Sagittarius (Dec. 10 – 29) we can expect to see a lot of frustration with regard to communications mishaps and misunderstandings over travel, travel schedules, delayed forms of transportation, and with regard to exploration, as well as philosophical viewpoints. Expect to repeat yourself more than once or twice, and to be persistent as well as patient during this time. This may not be the best time to engage in tender subjects over the holidays. For more information on Mercury retrograde, see the section in the introduction about *Mercury retrograde periods.*

Mercury sextile Venus (Nov. 26 – Dec. 12) Mercury in Capricorn sextile Venus in Scorpio teaches us of the necessity to speak up succinctly and plainly for our needs, particularly for passionate and essential kinds of love and affection. However, it may be difficult to get the message across very eloquently while Mercury is currently in a stationary position and about to go retrograde (see above). With persistent effort to relay the message effectively, Mercury sextile Venus is there to assist us to take the opportunity to speak up for love, and the things we cherish, whenever necessary. This aspect last occurred on December 1 when Mercury was direct. It also occurred on May 29 and September 16, although neither time did those aspects reach an exact peak.

December 11th Saturday

Moon in Aquarius / Pisces	PST	EST	
Moon conjunct Neptune goes v/c	3:09 AM	6:09 AM	
Moon enters Pisces	10:41 AM	1:41 PM	
Moon sextile Mars	4:50 PM	7:50 PM	
Moon sextile Pluto	7:58 PM	10:58 PM	
Moon sextile Mercury	10:03 PM	1:03 AM	(December 12)

Birthday: John Kerry 1943

Mood Watch: This morning will be somewhat spacey, and some folks may appear thoughtless while the Moon is void-of-course in Aquarius. Mercury is officially retrograde (see yesterday) and it may seem particularly difficult to get adjusted to communication errors during the first few days of the Mercury retrograde phase. As the Moon enters Pisces, strong psychic inclinations occur among people, and this may be a good opportunity to rely on intuition in order to effectively read between the lines. Positive lunar aspects make this a promising day. This is a good time to reflect upon the troubled part of our spirits with beautiful crafts, creative projects, and sweet, cheerful, uplifting music.

December 12th Sunday

Moon in Pisces	PST	EST
Moon trine Venus	12:39 AM	3:39 AM
Sun square Uranus begins (see December 18)		

Birthday: Frank Sinatra 1915

Mood Watch:: The Moon enters Pisces, and our moods are filled with artistic flair and great enthusiasm. Crafts, a musical atmosphere, and creative endeavors call out to us during the waxing Pisces Moon. Effervescent drinks and a festive holiday surrounding will enliven the imagination. Meditative moods also give us a relaxed and comforted feeling. Psychic awareness is strong today. This is a good time to recharge the spiritual batteries with some activity that puts us in touch with our divinity.

December 13th Monday

FIRST QUARTER MOON in PISCES

Moon in Pisces / Aries	PST	EST	
Moon square Sun	5:58 AM	8:58 AM	
Moon conjunct Jupiter	12:16 PM	3:16 PM	
Moon conjunct Uranus goes v/c	4:34 PM	7:34 PM	
Mercury conjunct Pluto	7:58 PM	10:58 PM	
Mercury conjunct Mars	8:06 PM	11:06 PM	
Mars conjunct Pluto	8:15 PM	11:15 PM	
Moon enters Aries	11:15 PM	2:15 AM	(December 14)

Birthday: Dick Van Dyke 1925

Mood Watch: The **First Quarter Moon in Pisces** (Moon square Sun) often brings our hearts and minds to a peaceful place. A spacey, dreamy sort of consciousness leads to strong psychic awareness. While the first quarter Moon is in Pisces, calming music, art, and poetry will fill us with inspiration, intuition, and hope.

Unhappy people are likely to turn to intoxicants to escape their troubles. Deep meditation and spiritual practices will empower the imagination. However, this may not be your typical First Quarter Pisces Moon. Since Mars is conjunct with Pluto and Mercury is also hovering close by in a conjunction with both Mars and Pluto (see below), we are in for an extraordinary period of abrupt energies. These energies will bring a swarm of media attention. In this case, the Pisces Moon will act as a highly sophisticated intuitive detection system. That which you are sensing today will reveal especially powerful indications of what is going on. Use your intuition attentively. Observe cautiously and strive as best you may to ease the senses whenever they seem to be overloaded. Much later tonight, as the Moon enters Aries, a much more militant and defensive quality of mood is likely to emerge.

Mercury conjunct Pluto (occurring Nov. 29 – Dec. 16) Due to Mercury retrograde (Dec. 10 – 29), this conjunction is reaching its peak for the second time this year. Take note that while Mercury is retrograde in Capricorn, issues of power, struggle, and sacrifice will be difficult to discuss and relay in a way that is easily understood. For more information on Mercury conjunct Pluto in Capricorn, *see December 5.*

Mercury conjunct Mars (occurring Nov. 11 – Dec. 15) Today the retrograde Mercury is conjunct with Mars in Capricorn. This means a definite punch in the face when the wrong thing is said about a serious matter. Mars is also conjunct with Pluto today, creating the potential for some very shaky war related activity in the world. Now is the time to proceed with absolute caution and vigilance. Stay on the defense for awhile. For more information on Mercury conjunct Mars, see November 20, when this conjunction first reached its peak this year.

Mars conjunct Pluto (occurring Dec. 5 – 17) This conjunction is not terribly uncommon, as it is likely to occur at least once every couple of years. However, while these two planets are aligning in the sign of Capricorn for the first time in our lives, we may expect to see a higher than average level of conflict occurring on the planet. Mars is notoriously brutal while traveling through relentless Capricorn. As for the phenomenon of Pluto in Capricorn (2008 – 2023), it has certainly shown its tenacity in this early period of being in this cardinal sign.

December 14th Tuesday

Moon in Aries	PST	EST
Moon square Mercury	7:58 AM	10:58 AM
Moon square Pluto	8:42 AM	11:42 AM
Moon square Mars	9:31 AM	12:31 PM
Sun sextile Neptune begins (see December 18)		

" *It was not just the Church that resisted the heliocentrism of Copernicus.* " – *Tycho Brahe (born this day, Dec. 14, 1546)*

Birthday: Nostradamus 1503

Mood Watch: Today's square aspects of the Aries Moon to Mercury, Pluto, and Mars suggest that our moods will have a great deal of complexity to process and handle. Events being what they are, we all have a job to do. The Aries Moon being what it is, reminds us of the need to venture forth courageously. Today we will need to muster our strength, stamina, and wherewithal to face the current conditions of life. Nostradamus had no qualms about predicting the world's tragedies with ominous candor, but he wasn't very adept at applying respectability, trust, and dependability amongst his comrades. In fact, many of his fraternal associates considered him an absolute traitor. Those who do not conduct themselves in an honorable fashion are likely to be at the hub of destruction and mayhem. The positive cannot exist without the negative. The key to negativity, or conflict, is to keep it flowing. Don't dwell for very long in the fatalist mental plane where Nostradamus chose to live his life. There are far better ways to make a name for yourself.

December 15ᵗʰ Wednesday

Moon in Aries	PST	EST	
Moon opposite Saturn	6:43 AM	9:43 AM	
Moon trine Sun	11:31 PM	2:31 AM	(December 16)

Birthday: Don Johnson 1949

Mood Watch: The Moon opposes Saturn on this Aries Moon morning, and with this comes the sense that there is all too much work to be done. The need to concentrate and stay on top of responsibilities might seem somewhat oppressive at first, but as the day progresses, the spirit of the waxing Aries Moon will get us through. Aries Moon fills the day with hustling and bustling moods. This is a time to do things for the self as well as for others. As ever, Aries Moon moods often preoccupy us with the need to stand out and be on top, to notice who is in control of situations and just how they're handling it. There is an eagerness or sometimes aggression present at times, yet overall there is youthful inspiration and a drive to get things started.

December 16ᵗʰ Thursday

Moon in Aries / Taurus	PST	EST
Moon sextile Neptune goes v/c	3:40 AM	6:40 AM
Moon enters Taurus	10:49 AM	1:49 PM
Sun square Jupiter	1:47 PM	4:47 PM
Moon trine Mercury	2:51 PM	5:51 PM
Moon trine Pluto	8:05 PM	11:05 PM
Mercury square Uranus begins (see December 20)		

Birthday: Ludwig van Beethoven 1770

Mood Watch: Hasty or overly ambitious moods will get you nowhere this morning as the void-of-course Aries Moon tends to put a damper on our efforts, particularly while Mercury is retrograde (Dec. 10 – 29), creating a less than ideal working atmosphere. People may seem impatient, headstrong, and aggressive this morning, but they aren't necessarily on the ball. As the Moon enters Taurus, practicality and sensibility will come to the rescue. Many folks will be more inspired to think about material matters, especially now that the holiday season is upon us. Waxing Moon in Taurus is a good time to get on with practical matters and to focus on acquiring

261

the goods necessary to get us through this holiday season. This afternoon's Moon trine Mercury aspect is ideal for reiterating plans and reviewing communication efforts. Taurus Moon is an excellent time to seek beauty.

Sun square Jupiter (occurring Dec. 10 – 19) This occurrence of Sun square Jupiter will particularly affect those Sagittarius people celebrating birthdays December 10 – 19. This aspect creates difficulties and obstacles to the personal joy and prosperous welfare of these birthday folks. Getting ahead financially or just staying on top of current trends or financial shifts may be personally challenging right now, requiring persistence and determination. Sagittarius folks who are doing well financially may find this aspect is challenging their sense of what makes them happy, or that advancement in the world brings too much complexity and requires a lot of management. Though not all Sagittarians are living as prosperously as they may desire, they do have the ability to come through this and be much better for it. Obstacles create challenges, but do not necessarily dictate an end to efforts to improve our welfare. It is the Sagittarius personality (Sun) that is being challenged (square aspect) in matters of advancement (Jupiter), requiring them to make do with less assistance than they had anticipated. This may be a time to redefine and redirect personal goals. These birthday folks must reexamine what truly brings prosperity for them in their lives. This aspect last occurred June 23 affecting some of the birthday Gemini and Cancer folks of that time.

December 17th Friday

Moon in Taurus	PST	EST
Moon trine Mars	12:33 AM	3:33 AM
Moon opposite Venus	7:48 AM	10:48 AM
Sun conjunct Mercury begins (see December 19)		
Mercury sextile Neptune begins (see December 20)		
Mercury square Jupiter begins (see December 21)		

Birthday: Arthur Fiedler 1894

Mood Watch: The Taurus Moon focuses our attention on the matter of having or not having what we need to get by. Of course, there is also the matter of what we *want* in order to make the holidays festive. Money management and money related issues are very prevalent in these times, especially when the Moon is in Taurus. The drive to shop and buy can be overwhelming. Taurus Moon brings an earthy and stubborn determination to get things done right. Sensible buyers do not waste their energy on overpriced gifts. Quality and value are important. Simple and practical gifts are a time honored tradition. The strongly waxing Taurus Moon also sets the stage for a lot of concern with regard to the handling of valuables and goods. There is a strong emphasis building up at this time on the need to transport all those backbreaking material goods. This physical work of schlepping them is unavoidable. Slowly and steadily, let the Taurus bull's consummate pace keep the labor from being overtaxing.

December 18ᵗʰ Saturday

Moon in Taurus / Gemini	PST	EST
Sun sextile Neptune	2:29 AM	5:29 AM
Mercury enters Sagittarius	6:52 AM	9:52 AM
Moon sextile Jupiter	10:22 AM	1:22 PM
Sun square Uranus	10:47 AM	1:47 PM
Moon square Neptune	12:57 PM	3:57 PM
Moon sextile Uranus goes v/c	1:35 PM	4:35 PM
Moon enters Gemini	7:38 PM	10:38 PM

Birthday: Keith Richards 1943

Mood Watch: Today's advice: stay ahead of the crowd! If that's not possible, try to enjoy the beauties of your adventures. A superb Moon, the exalted Taurus Moon, is sextile to Jupiter, and it's an uplifting, adventurous, optimistic way to begin the day. Morning is a good time to develop and seek the vision of fortune that will make today successful. This afternoon's Moon square Neptune may be a time when our faith is tested. Beware of the tendency for many folks to become easily hypnotized by time-wasting illusions of wealth. Do not become ensnared by laziness or complacency. This short-lived spell of spacey moods is quickly altered as Moon sextile Uranus brings abruptly spontaneous and periodically chaotic moods. At this point, the Moon goes void-of-course, and our ability to concentrate may be compromised by numerous distractions. It's too busy out there and delays are unavoidable. The void-of-course Taurus Moon is the best time to relax – don't stress, do the best you can, and take it at an easy pace! Tonight's Moon in Gemini will bring thoughtful moods, helping to process the complexities of the day.

Sun sextile Neptune (occurring Dec. 14 – 20) This occurrence of Sun sextile Neptune creates an opportunistic time for those Sagittarius people celebrating birthdays from December 14 – 20. These Sagittarius folks are experiencing an opportunity to awaken in the realm of spirituality and creativity. There is an awareness of the self that goes deep here, and these birthday people are likely to appear distracted and difficult to reach while this phenomenon of great depth is occurring. This will be your year, birthday folks, to explore personal opportunities of spiritual growth. It may be a time to get away from it all, and find a sanctuary in which to meditate and open up to some valuable answers to old questions. These folks are in a place that gives them an opportunity to better understand the work of their path, but this is probably only true if they act on their own intuitive sensibilities, without the influences of others. That shouldn't be too hard for the adventurous, open-minded, and outgoing Sagittarius natures among us. This will be your year (Sagittarius birthday people) to enhance and strengthen your intuition and primal instincts by tapping into them while they are easily available. This may also be the time to overcome addictions and disruptive patterns. This aspect last occurred on April 18, when the Sun was in Aries, affecting the cusp born Aries and Taurus people of that time.

Mercury enters Sagittarius (Mercury in Sagittarius: Dec. 18, 2010 – Jan. 13, 2011) Due Mercury retrograde (Dec. 10 – 29), it is currently entering Sagittarius for the second time this year. Mercury retrograde in Sagittarius during the holiday season is bound to bring a number of communication mix-ups when it comes to travel schedules, travel plans, and misunderstandings with regard to travel. For a recap on the story of how Mercury in Sagittarius affects our communications, *see November 8*, when Mercury first entered Sagittarius.

Sun square Uranus (occurring Dec. 12 – 21) This occurrence of Sun square Uranus particularly affects Sagittarius and Solstice born Capricorn people celebrating birthdays December 12 – 21. The square of Uranus in Aquarius to these birthday folks' natal Sun brings about challenging events and a strong dose of unrestrained chaos. This may be the year for you birthday people to surrender to those aspects of life that are truly out of your control, and to concentrate more rationally on those facets of life over which you do have control. Sometimes the aftermath of Uranus's influence is an improvement, but with the square aspect at work, it is likely these people will feel personally challenged. It is important to understand that some types of personal challenges are best left alone, while others must be confronted directly without causing destructive damage, particularly to the self. On the other hand, birthday folks, if your life has no foundation, there is no point in holding onto the illusion of stability at this juncture of your sojourn. This aspect will pass, and it is vital not to give this rapid change too much resistance, lest you be bound to the reversals of trying to fight chaos with logic at a time when resistance is futile. Matters will settle down in due time; try to be detached from chaotic events as they occur, and the outcome will seem less costly. If you need it, project the picture of peace and it will be there for you at the other end. This aspect last occurred June 21 when the Sun was just entering Cancer.

December 19th Sunday

Moon in Gemini PST EST
Sun conjunct Mercury 5:22 PM 8:22 PM

Birthday: Criss Angel 1967

Mood Watch: The Full Moon in Gemini energy is upon us, and our moods are easily affected by our busy thoughts. Gemini Moon focuses our attention on discussions, sales details, security details, parking details, secretarial chores, postal chores, invitations and greeting cards, and an endless trail of necessary details. It doesn't help that Mercury is retrograde (Dec. 10 – 29), and our communications are just as challenged as our busy moods. Everywhere you turn, someone will have something to say about their current predicaments. It may be wise to take deep breaths along the way today, and to take all these busy details in stride. There is an increasingly ominous quality of mood about to be added to the weight of our lunar influences. The Moon is heavily waxing and this upcoming Full Gemini Moon (see Dec. 21) will also bring a total lunar eclipse.

Sun conjunct Mercury (occurring Dec. 17 – 20) This conjunction will create a much more thoughtful, communicative and expressive year ahead for those Sagittarius folks celebrating birthdays December 17 – 20. This is your time (birthday Sagittarians) to record ideas, relay important messages, and pay close attention to your imaginative thoughts as they are touched by Mercury, creating the urge to speak and be heard. Birthday people, your thoughts will reveal a great deal about who you are, now and in the year to come.

264

December 20th Monday

Full Moon Eve

Moon in Gemini

	PST	EST	
Moon trine Saturn	12:40 AM	3:40 AM	
Mercury square Uranus	3:30 PM	6:30 PM	
Moon square Jupiter	5:01 PM	8:01 PM	
Moon trine Neptune	7:08 PM	10:08 PM	
Moon opposite Mercury	7:19 PM	10:19 PM	
Moon square Uranus	7:42 PM	10:42 PM	
Mercury sextile Neptune	9:03 PM	12:03 AM	(December 21)
Sun conjunct Pluto begins (see December 26)			
Mars square Saturn begins (see December 29)			

Birthday: Uri Geller 1946

Mood Watch: Ready or not, here it comes! This long day of lunar aspects on the Full Gemini Moon Eve is bound to bring a wave of excitement, complexity, and bountiful mixed feelings. Tomorrow's Total Lunar Eclipse in Gemini is building a lot of energy today. What we are likely to observe, with this Total Eclipse of the Moon in Gemini, is the sense that the important – or necessary – details of life may not appear to be going our way. At times, annoying, mean or negative people may have some affect on the shadowy emotional subtleties of this Gemini Lunar Eclipse atmosphere. Trifling details, particularly of other people's lives, may be part of today's annoyances. Coarse or sly behavior, coupled with subtle bouts of cruelty and oppression may also be prevalent. Failing, giving up, and also being nagged, mocked, or ignored may send some folks into a reckless frenzy. The death of prominent people may be notable around this time. A Gemini Ecliptic Moon also influences hurricanes, wind storms, thunder and lighting.

Tonight's almost Full Moon, set to take place in the earliest hours tomorrow, will be spectacular. However, it comes and goes all too quickly, and what we are experiencing today is the stressful build up of a strong, energy demanding Gemini Moon. Be sure to SEE TOMORROW – Total Lunar Eclipse in Gemini. Late tonight, check out the Total Eclipse; consult the World Wide Web for the times and locations for viewing this year's event as some web sites show a real-time view.

Mercury square Uranus (occurring Dec. 16 – 22) Mercury is retrograde (from Dec. 10 – 29) in Sagittarius, and it is currently square to Uranus in Pisces. This brings chaotic talk and discussions. Confusion over chaos is especially disruptive while Mercury is retrograde. For a recap on the story of this aspect, now occurring for the third time this year, *see November 27* when it last occurred.

Mercury sextile Neptune (occurring Dec. 17 – 22) Due to Mercury's final retrograde period now occurring (Dec. 10 – 29), this aspect currently takes place for the third time this year. The retrograde Mercury in Sagittarius sextile Neptune in Aquarius brings the potential for spiritual enhancement in the relaying of messages – just don't expect the symbolic language of the spiritual to make a whole lot of sense! For a recap on the story of Mercury sextile Neptune, see November 27 when it last occurred.

CAPRICORN

Key Phrase: " I USE "
Cardinal Earth Sign
Ruling Planet: Saturn
Symbol: The Goat
December 21st, 2010 through
January 20th, 2011

December 21st Tuesday

Winter Solstice
FULL MOON in GEMINI – Lunar Eclipse

Moon in Gemini / Cancer	PST	EST
Moon opposite Sun goes v/c	12:12 AM	3:12 AM
Moon enters Cancer	1:23 AM	4:23 AM
Moon opposite Pluto	9:59 AM	12:59 PM
Sun enters Capricorn	3:38 PM	6:38 PM
Mercury square Jupiter	4:59 PM	7:59 PM
Moon opposite Mars	8:05 PM	11:05 PM

Birthday: Frank Zappa 1940

Mood Watch: The first lunar aspect of the day occurred in the wee small hours, and with it came the peak of the **Full Gemini Moon** (Moon opposite Sun). This peak brings the crescendo of an intense Full Gemini Moon expression, the **Total Lunar Eclipse**. A lunar eclipse occurs when the Earth moves between the moon and the sun, blocking the light that reflects off the moon's surface back to Earth. Darkness is the key, as there tends to be the common belief that the casting of a shadow upon the Moon brings darker than average moods. This may be especially true with the compounding element of today's winter solstice; the notorious shortest and, consequently, darkest day of the year. Some view this as mere superstition, while others may base this belief on their personal experiences. By the time most people in North America have awakened, the Lunar Eclipse will have already passed. The Moon will be in Cancer today, and our moods will be primed for the inevitable shift from autumn to winter. This is a good time to attempt to recover from the immense amount of energy that has just been discharged. Today's parade of astrological events indicates that it will take awhile to get settled after all the Full Moon excitement.

Sun enters Capricorn (Sun in Capricorn: Dec. 21, 2010 – Jan. 20, 2011) Spark up the lights – it's **Winter Solstice**! Today the Sun King returns from the ashes of the longest night. This is the time of Saturn-ruled Capricorn. Sun in Capricorn is the time to step into success. Jack Frost is nipping at our heels, but the Sun King returns! The lengthening days of the Sun are finally here and a new season and cycle begins. The symbol of Capricorn is the mountain goat. The Capricorn goat consciousness is revealed to us through the high and lofty heights the goat commands. No mountain is too high for the true archetypal Capricorn, and the focus of this season is always placed on accomplishing the highest of goals and achievements. The working pace for the New Year is established here. Capricorn energy emphasizes corporate growth, the creation and maintenance of institutions, construction and development, and the use and control of industrial services and equipment. Many outstanding Capricorns are devoted to their careers and lifestyles with unyielding tenacity. Capricorn days of the Sun are splendid times to focus on goals, and to discipline one's nature to make daily tasks add up to something worth accomplishing. Although tedious and often predictable, the Capricorn nature makes sure the job is done – and done well.

Mercury square Jupiter (occurring Dec. 17 – 24) Be especially careful to communicate well during travels. Mercury retrograde in Sagittarius may be the cause of travel delays and communication mix-ups. Be sure double check travel schedules and communicate backup plans. This aspect is occurring for the third time this year. For a recap on the story of Mercury in Sagittarius square Jupiter in Pisces, *see November 25* when it last occurred.

December 22nd Wednesday

Moon in Cancer	PST	EST	
Moon trine Venus	3:04 AM	6:04 AM	
Moon square Saturn	5:19 AM	8:19 AM	
Moon trine Jupiter	9:10 PM	12:10 AM	(December 23)
Moon trine Uranus goes v/c	11:24 PM	2:24 AM	(December 23)

Birthday: Lady Bird Johnson 1912

Mood Watch: Today, "home is where the heart is" with the Moon in Cancer. This place gives us an edge, the ability to bend the forces of the universe in our own particular way to suit our emotional needs. Many of us will be hoping to get some extra rest after all of the exciting Full Moon energy over the past couple of days. It is in this special, homelike environment we can drop our societal pretenses and express how we really feel. It is essential that we find some sort of emotional outlet. The healthy home environment or place of the heart is a place of refuge that nurtures, soothes, protects and reassures. Cancer Moon is an essential time to be nurturing and caring with those who need it most.

December 23rd Thursday

Moon in Cancer / Leo	PST	EST
Moon enters Leo	4:51 AM	7:51 AM

Birthday: Harry Shearer 1943

Mood Watch: Early this morning, the void-of-course Cancer Moon brings unsettled emotions, but that swiftly changes as the Moon enters Leo. Although it wanes, the Leo Moon is still somewhat full, and our energy is easily directed at children, family, and pets. Leo Moon brings an interest in personal hobbies, family endeavors, and leisurely activities. The Sun and Moon are in fire signs and this brings creativity, excitement, and an engaging spirit. Holiday entertainment will do well today as many folks are strongly inclined to seek amusement on a Leo Moon day. The waning Leo Moon is a good time to get in touch with things that warm the heart and uplift the spirit.

December 24th Friday

Christmas Eve

Moon in Leo	PST	EST
Moon sextile Saturn	8:15 AM	11:15 AM
Moon square Venus	9:09 AM	12:09 PM
Moon trine Mercury	5:44 PM	8:44 PM

"Tradition is a guide and not a jailer."
— W. Somerset Maugham (1874 – 1965)

Birthday: Howard Hughes 1905

Mood Watch: Leo Moon is an excellent lunar expression for Christmas Eve. This time emphasizes the endearing influences of family and friends. There is a cool sense of being in control as Moon sextile Saturn brings the potential for us to apply some keen concentration efforts. However, Moon square Venus may put a damper on our efforts to come closer to the things that attract us. This may be a difficult time with loved ones, but fortunately, the morning is the only time we'll need to weather tricky moods. Tonight's Moon trine Mercury is an excellent time to talk matters through and work towards correcting the communication misunderstandings that have occurred during this Mercury retrograde period (Dec. 10 – 29). The best way to win stardom is to win the hearts of loved ones. Leo Moon is a good time to concentrate on keeping family and friends feeling loved and cared for.

Santa Claus is coming. Do you believe? In the eighteenth century his name appeared in the American press as "St. A Clause," but we got to know the fully Americanized version of this northern dwelling Dutch-American elf by his name, "Saint Nick" in the classic 1823 poem, "The Night Before Christmas" by Clement Clarke Moore.

December 25th Saturday

Christmas

Moon in Leo / Virgo	PST	EST
Moon opposite Neptune goes v/c	1:27 AM	4:27 AM
Moon enters Virgo	7:15 AM	10:15 AM
Moon trine Sun	1:55 PM	4:55 PM
Moon trine Pluto	3:47 PM	6:47 PM

" The trick is in what one emphasizes. We either make ourselves miserable, or we make ourselves happy. The amount of work is the same. " – Carlos Castaneda (1925 – 1998)

Birthday: Carlos Castaneda 1925

Mood Watch: In the earliest morning hours, the Leo Moon is void-of-course. Some

268

folks may appear grumpy or slow to get adjusted to the day. Some may awaken ♑
to the void-of-course waning Leo Moon overload, complete with such things as
an identity crisis, personal dissatisfaction, or high demands for attention. The
energy changes as the Moon enters Virgo, and our moods will become a lot more
observant this morning. Sun in Capricorn and Moon in Virgo bring a very earthy
tone to this Christmas day. The Virgo Moon brings dignified, simple, and curious
qualities to our moods. Practicality and convenience are in high demand. Purity
and simplicity will have the most impact on our Virgo Moon moods. Anything too
complex would take too long to digestion. Speaking of digest, Virgo anatomically
rules *the intestines*. Therefore, it is very important to maintain some good common
sense when eating holiday foods. Stick to a reasonable, balanced, and digestible
intake of foods and liquids. Virgo Moon brings out the need to clean up, organize,
and tend to health matters. The Mercury-ruled Virgo also influences our need to
make connections, to stop and question, and to learn from interesting topics and
discussions. *Have a very Merry Christmas!*

December 26th Sunday

Boxing Day
Moon in Virgo

	PST	EST
Moon trine Mars	7:04 AM	10:04 AM
Moon sextile Venus	2:49 PM	5:49 PM
Sun conjunct Pluto	5:04 PM	8:04 PM
Moon square Mercury	5:36 PM	8:36 PM

Mercury-sextile-Saturn-non-exact begins (see December 29)

Birthday: Henry Miller 1891

Mood Watch: Prudent resourcefulness comes in handy during waning Virgo
Moon. Sun in Capricorn with Moon in Virgo is a good time to get organized and
to purge the world around us of all its physical clutter. This is the time to communicate and to clean up. Once we have conquered our duties and purified the energy
around us through Moon trine Mars, relaxing and pleasant moods will carry us
through the day with Moon sextile Venus. Tonight's Moon square Mercury may
be a particularly difficult time to relay information easily, or in a way that it will
be easily understood. Remember to apply prudence – if it doesn't need to be discussed, tonight isn't necessarily the best time. This Virgo Moon holds the potential
to bring a lot of nervous feelings over unnecessary misunderstandings. No worries
– it will all be sorted out by the next time the Moon is in Virgo.

Sun conjunct Pluto (occurring Dec. 20 – 29) This occurrence of Sun conjunct
Pluto strongly affects late born Sagittarians and early born Capricorns – most specifically, those who are celebrating birthdays December 20 – 29. These Sagittarius/
Capricorn birthday folks will experience challenges of mind-altering proportions.
Sun conjunct Pluto affects the core of the personality, and diminishes those parts
of the self which are weak and no longer viable. Pluto's energy melds with the
personality to bring out the strongest points of one's character, the very best that
one can muster. Pluto removes all impurities by transforming the old self through
unpredictable trials. Take this opportunity to make some personal breakthroughs,

birthday folks, and find your power! Learn to harness your power willingly and responsibly while great transformation is occurring in your life.

December 27ᵗʰ Monday

LAST QUARTER MOON in LIBRA

Moon in Virgo / Libra	PST	EST
Moon opposite Jupiter	2:49 AM	5:49 AM
Moon opposite Uranus goes v/c	4:20 AM	7:20 AM
Moon enters Libra	9:38 AM	12:38 PM
Moon square Pluto	6:24 PM	9:24 PM
Moon square Sun	8:18 PM	11:18 PM

Venus trine Jupiter begins (peaks Jan. 4, 2011 / ends Jan. 7, 2011 – see June 15)

Birthday: Gérard Depardieu 1948

Mood Watch: The Moon in Virgo goes void-of-course early this morning, and there may be a tendency towards delays caused by doubt or skepticism. On the more positive side, we could say that our thoroughness and caution are the cause of lengthy endeavors. As the Moon enters Libra, our moods begin to soften into a more objective quality of expression. **Last Quarter Moon in Libra** (Moon square Sun) reminds us of the need to continue working on the imbalances in our relationships, much of which is probably caused by Mercury retrograde (Dec.10 – 29). Libra's adage is simple: "I balance." This is the time to let the emotional pressure be released, and to handle matters with friends and loved ones carefully and congenially. The Last Quarter Moon aspect confirms the need to make amends with others and unite peacefully. If some aspect of your connection to a friend or loved one disrupts your sense of peace, reach within for the answers. A balanced response will follow, but don't expect instant answers. Today's confusion will make a whole lot more sense by the New Year.

December 28ᵗʰ Tuesday

Moon in Libra	PST	EST
Moon square Mars	12:42 PM	3:42 PM
Moon conjunct Saturn	1:40 PM	4:40 PM
Moon sextile Mercury	7:11 PM	10:11 PM

Venus trine Uranus begins (occurs on Jan. 4, 2011 – see June 14)
Venus square Neptune begins (occurs on Jan. 4, 2011 – see April 23)

Birthday: Denzel Washington 1954

Mood Watch: Moon in Libra focuses our moods on the importance of teamwork and the interaction of our friends and loved ones. Friendships and partners play big roles on days like today. Be careful not to get caught up in too many balancing acts in order to please everyone. Today's Moon square Mars is likely to lead to conflict. Moon conjunct Saturn is ideal to concentrate on work and the completion process. Moon sextile Mercury brings a potentially good time to communicate and reiterate plans. Tomorrow Mercury will go direct, but we must be vigilant with our communication efforts for a few more days. Above all, Libra Moon emphasizes the need to make adjustments for the sake of balance.

December 29th Wednesday

⛑

Moon in Libra / Scorpio	PST	EST	
Moon trine Neptune goes v/c	7:05 AM	10:05 AM	
Mars square Saturn	7:28 AM	10:28 AM	
Moon enters Scorpio	12:50 PM	3:50 PM	
Moon sextile Pluto	9:56 PM	12:56 AM	(December 30)
Mercury goes direct	11:21 PM	2:21 AM	(December 30)
Mercury-sextile-Saturn-non-exact (see below)			

Birthday: Jude Law 1972

Mood Watch: The Libra Moon focuses on our need for harmony, but as the Moon goes void-of-course, we tend to become indecisive, and for awhile during the day, there will be a lot of delays due to indecisiveness. As the Moon enters Scorpio, we tend to become withdrawn and perhaps a little secretive. Waning Scorpio Moon brings out our mysterious side. People are often a great deal more perceptive and psychic on Scorpio Moon days. The waning Scorpio Moon is a good time to focus on safe, therapeutic, methods of emotional release.

Mars square Saturn (occurring Dec. 20, 2010 – Jan. 1, 2011) This is a difficult aspect for the holiday season. Mars is in Capricorn and Saturn is in Libra; competition is very stiff as independent companies take a beating in actively trading markets. There may be a large struggle to change the nature of bankruptcy rules between large companies and the banks. In general, this aspect brings abrupt endings. It is also known for creating confrontations between offensive and defensive forces, and is usually not a good time to start a new enterprise. When deploying forces in battle, this aspect often brings fiery and sometimes tragic endings. It is wise to proceed with extra caution. This may be an especially difficult time to muster the strength to finish up projects, or to end affairs amicably. Hang in there; it won't be long before this aspect passes. Fortunately, this is the only time that Mars will square Saturn this year.

Mercury goes direct (Mercury direct: Dec. 29, 2010 – March 30, 2011) Since December 10, Mercury has been retrograde in the sign of Sagittarius, commonly causing communication mix-ups particularly with regard to travel arrangements, travel schedules, and travel delays. Now we can breathe a greatly needed sigh of relief as Mercury, the planet governing the realms of communication, becomes stationary and will soon begin to move forward. Take note that our faculties and manner of communicating will definitely improve within the next few days. Although perhaps not today – when the stationary Mercury often freezes communication efforts – but very soon our communications will run more smoothly; this will be a good time to begin clearing up various misunderstandings that have occurred over the past few weeks. For more information on this recently completed phase of Mercury retrograde, see December 10. For more on Mercury retrograde patterns throughout this year, see the introduction on *Mercury retrograde periods.*

Mercury-sextile-Saturn-non-exact (occurring Dec. 26, 2010 – Jan. 2, 2011) Retrograde Mercury in Sagittarius now comes within three orbital degrees of the sextile aspect to Saturn in Libra, but this is as close as it comes to reaching the peak. Nonetheless, this aspect is in full swing emphasizing the necessity to speak out on important topics and to complete our workload judiciously. For an explanation of how this aspect works, see *November 17* when it last occurred.

December 30th Thursday

Moon in Scorpio	PST	EST
Moon sextile Sun	3:50 AM	6:50 AM
Moon sextile Mars	7:39 PM	10:39 PM

Birthday: Tiger Woods 1975

Mood Watch: The spirit of Scorpio Moon gives us the awareness of deeper, more subtle levels of emotional interplay. The Pluto ruled sign of Scorpio puts us in touch with transformation. Our emotional field is now undergoing a transformational process that allows us to work through all kinds of emotional entanglements. This Moon gives us the courage to live life as passionately and freely as possible.

December 31st Friday

Moon in Scorpio / Sagittarius	PST	EST
Moon conjunct Venus	5:11 AM	8:11 AM
Moon trine Jupiter	11:11 AM	2:11 PM
Moon square Neptune	11:33 AM	2:33 PM
Moon trine Uranus goes v/c	11:57 AM	2:57 PM
Moon enters Sagittarius	5:22 PM	8:22 PM

Birthday: Noel Tyl 1936

Mood Watch: The final day of the year comes to us with the waning Moon in Scorpio, a Moon that is often described as intense and powerful. Moon conjunct Venus brings loving energy first thing this morning. Moon trine Jupiter inspires positive, optimistic, and prosperous feelings. Moon square Neptune puts obstacles between our feelings and our beliefs. Moon trine Uranus brings liberating feelings, but the Moon also goes void-of-course, so we may end up beings somewhat withdrawn, or overwhelmed by all the unnecessary mini-dramas that create delays and contingencies. After a somewhat impatient day of trying to get the day's tasks in order, the Moon enters Sagittarius. The old year ends and a New Year begins with the Moon in Sagittarius. This is the Moon that calls to our visions and our ability to look beyond. This is a great time to empower the personal outlook with a philosophy that works.

Cheers to All! Bright Blessings, And Happy New Year!

Ephemeris 2010 Noon GMT
Longitudes based on Greenwich Mean Time (GMT) at Noon

JANUARY 2010

Date	☉	☽	☿	♀	♂	♃	♄	♅	♆	♇
1	10♑57	20♋46	18♑28	08♑28	18♌44	26♒27	04♎31	23♓06	24♒35	03♑19
2	11 58	05♌50	17 R 18	09 44	18 R 34	26 39	04 32	23 07	24 37	03 21
3	12 59	20 49	16 02	10 59	18 23	26 52	04 33	23 09	24 39	03 23
4	14 01	05♍34	14 43	12 15	18 11	27 04	04 34	23 10	24 41	03 26
5	15 02	20 00	13 21	13 30	17 59	27 16	04 35	23 12	24 43	03 28
6	16 03	04♎05	12 02	14 46	17 45	27 29	04 36	23 14	24 44	03 30
7	17 04	17 46	10 45	16 01	17 31	27 42	04 37	23 16	24 46	03 32
8	18 05	01♏05	09 35	17 17	17 16	27 54	04 37	23 18	24 48	03 34
9	19 06	14 05	08 32	18 32	17 01	28 07	04 38	23 19	24 50	03 36
10	20 07	26 46	07 38	19 48	16 45	28 20	04 38	23 21	24 52	03 38
11	21 09	09♐13	06 54	21 03	16 27	28 33	04 38	23 23	24 54	03 40
12	22 10	21 28	06 19	22 19	16 10	28 46	04 39	23 25	24 56	03 43
13	23 11	03♑33	05 54	23 34	15 51	28 59	04 39	23 27	24 58	03 45
14	24 12	15 31	05 39	24 50	15 32	29 12	04 R 39	23 29	25 00	03 47
15	25 13	27 23	05 33	26 05	15 13	29 25	04♎38	23 32	25 02	03 49
16	26 14	09♒12	05 D 35	27 21	14 52	29 38	04 38	23 34	25 04	03 51
17	27 15	21 00	05♑46	28 36	14 32	29 52	04 38	23 36	25 06	03 53
18	28 17	02♓48	06 04	29 51	14 10	00♓05	04 37	23 38	25 08	03 55
19	29 18	14 41	06 28	01♒07	13 49	00 18	04 37	23 40	25 10	03 57
20	00♒19	26 40	06 59	02 22	13 26	00 32	04 36	23 43	25 12	03 59
21	01 20	08♈49	07 35	03 38	13 04	00 45	04 35	23 45	25 15	04 01
22	02 21	21 13	08 16	04 53	12 41	00 59	04 34	23 48	25 17	04 03
23	03 22	03♉55	09 02	06 08	12 18	01 13	04 33	23 50	25 19	04 05
24	04 23	16 58	09 52	07 24	11 54	01 26	04 32	23 52	25 21	04 07
25	05 24	00♊27	10 45	08 39	11 31	01 40	04 31	23 55	25 23	04 09
26	06 25	14 23	11 42	09 55	11 07	01 54	04 30	23 58	25 25	04 11
27	07 26	28 46	12 42	11 10	10 43	02 07	04 28	24 00	25 27	04 13
28	08 27	13♋32	13 45	12 25	10 19	02 21	04 27	24 03	25 30	04 14
29	09 28	28 37	14 50	13 41	09 55	02 35	04 25	24 05	25 32	04 16
30	10 29	13♌52	15 57	14 56	09 31	02 49	04 23	24 08	25 34	04 18
31	11 30	29 07	17 07	16 11	09 07	03 03	04 22	24 11	25 36	04 20

FEBRUARY 2010

Date	☉	☽	☿	♀	♂	♃	♄	♅	♆	♇
1	12♒30	14♍12	18♑18	17♒27	08♌43	03♓17	04♎20	24♓13	25♒39	04♑22
2	13 31	28 58	19 32	18 42	08 R 20	03 31	04 R 18	24 16	25 41	04 24
3	14 32	13♎19	20 47	19 57	07 56	03 45	04 15	24 19	25 43	04 25
4	15 33	27 12	22 03	21 12	07 33	03 59	04 13	24 22	25 45	04 27
5	16 34	10♏37	23 21	22 28	07 10	04 13	04 11	24 25	25 48	04 29
6	17 35	23 37	24 40	23 43	06 47	04 28	04 08	24 28	25 50	04 31
7	18 35	06♐14	26 01	24 58	06 25	04 42	04 06	24 31	25 52	04 32
8	19 36	18 33	27 23	26 13	06 03	04 56	04 03	24 33	25 54	04 34
9	20 37	00♑38	28 46	27 29	05 42	05 10	04 01	24 36	25 57	04 36
10	21 38	12 33	00♒10	28 44	05 21	05 25	03 58	24 39	25 59	04 37
11	22 38	24 23	01 35	29 59	05 00	05 39	03 55	24 42	26 01	04 39
12	23 39	06♒11	03 01	01♓14	04 41	05 53	03 52	24 45	26 03	04 40
13	24 40	17 58	04 28	02 29	04 21	06 08	03 49	24 49	26 06	04 42
14	25 40	29 48	05 56	03 44	04 03	06 22	03 46	24 52	26 08	04 44
15	26 41	11♓42	07 26	05 00	03 45	06 36	03 43	24 55	26 10	04 45
16	27 42	23 42	08 56	06 15	03 27	06 51	03 39	24 58	26 13	04 47
17	28 42	05♈49	10 27	07 30	03 11	07 05	03 36	25 01	26 15	04 48
18	29 43	18 05	11 59	08 45	02 55	07 20	03 32	25 04	26 17	04 50
19	00♓43	00♉34	13 32	10 00	02 39	07 34	03 29	25 07	26 19	04 51
20	01 44	13 16	15 05	11 15	02 25	07 48	03 25	25 11	26 22	04 52
21	02 44	26 16	16 40	12 30	02 11	08 03	03 22	25 14	26 24	04 54

FEBRUARY 2010 (Cont'd)

Date	☉	☽	☿	♀	♂	♃	♄	♅	♆	♇
22	03♓45	09♊35	18♒16	13♓45	01♌58	08♓17	03♎18	25♓17	26♒26	04♑55
23	04 45	23 18	19 53	15 00	01 R 46	08 32	03 R 14	25 20	26 28	04 56
24	05 46	07♋24	21 30	16 15	01 35	08 46	03 10	25 24	26 31	04 58
25	06 46	21 54	23 09	17 30	01 24	09 01	03 06	25 27	26 33	04 59
26	07 46	06♌45	24 48	18 45	01 14	09 15	03 02	25 30	26 35	05 00
27	08 47	21 51	26 29	20 00	01 05	09 30	02 58	25 33	26 37	05 01
28	09 47	07♍03	28 11	21 14	00 57	09 44	02 54	25 37	26 40	05 02

MARCH 2010

Date	☉	☽	☿	♀	♂	♃	♄	♅	♆	♇
1	10♓47	22♍11	29♒53	22♓29	00♌49	09♓59	02♎50	25♓40	26♒42	05♑04
2	11 47	07♎05	01♓37	23 44	00 R 43	10 13	02 R 46	25 43	26 44	05 05
3	12 47	21 37	03 22	24 59	00 37	10 28	02 42	25 47	26 46	05 06
4	13 47	05♏41	05 07	26 14	00 32	10 42	02 37	25 50	26 49	05 07
5	14 48	19 16	06 54	27 28	00 27	10 57	02 33	25 54	26 51	05 08
6	15 48	02♐22	08 42	28 43	00 24	11 11	02 28	25 57	26 53	05 09
7	16 48	15 02	10 31	29 58	00 21	11 26	02 24	26 00	26 55	05 10
8	17 48	27 21	12 21	01♈12	00 19	11 40	02 20	26 04	26 57	05 11
9	18 48	09♑24	14 12	02 27	00 18	11 55	02 15	26 07	26 59	05 12
10	19 48	21 17	16 05	03 42	00 17	12 09	02 11	26 11	27 02	05 13
11	20 48	03♒05	17 58	04 56	00 D 17	12 24	02 06	26 14	27 04	05 14
12	21 48	14 51	19 52	06 11	00♌18	12 38	02 01	26 17	27 06	05 14
13	22 47	26 40	21 48	07 25	00 20	12 52	01 57	26 21	27 08	05 15
14	23 47	08♓34	23 44	08 40	00 22	13 07	01 52	26 24	27 10	05 16
15	24 47	20 36	25 42	09 54	00 25	13 21	01 47	26 28	27 12	05 17
16	25 47	02♈47	27 40	11 09	00 29	13 35	01 43	26 31	27 14	05 17
17	26 47	15 07	29 39	12 23	00 34	13 50	01 38	26 35	27 16	05 18
18	27 46	27 38	01♈38	13 38	00 39	14 04	01 33	26 38	27 18	05 19
19	28 46	10♉19	03 38	14 52	00 45	14 18	01 29	26 41	27 20	05 19
20	29 46	23 13	05 38	16 07	00 51	14 33	01 24	26 45	27 22	05 20
21	00♈45	06♊19	07 39	17 21	00 58	14 47	01 19	26 48	27 24	05 20
22	01 45	19 39	09 39	18 35	01 06	15 01	01 14	26 52	27 26	05 21
23	02 44	03♋16	11 39	19 49	01 14	15 15	01 10	26 55	27 28	05 21
24	03 44	17 11	13 38	21 04	01 23	15 29	01 05	26 59	27 30	05 22
25	04 43	01♌24	15 36	22 18	01 33	15 44	01 00	27 02	27 32	05 22
26	05 43	15 54	17 32	23 32	01 43	15 58	00 56	27 05	27 34	05 23
27	06 42	00♍38	19 27	24 46	01 53	16 12	00 51	27 09	27 36	05 23
28	07 42	15 31	21 20	26 00	02 05	16 26	00 46	27 12	27 38	05 23
29	08 41	00♎24	23 10	27 14	02 16	16 40	00 42	27 16	27 40	05 24
30	09 40	15 08	24 57	28 28	02 29	16 54	00 37	27 19	27 41	05 24
31	10 39	29 35	26 40	29 42	02 41	17 07	00 32	27 22	27 43	05 24

APRIL 2010

Date	☉	☽	☿	♀	♂	♃	♄	♅	♆	♇
1	11♈39	13♏39	28♈20	00♉56	02♌55	17♓21	00♎28	27♓26	27♒45	05♑24
2	12 38	27 17	29 55	02 10	03 08	17 35	00 R 23	27 29	27 47	05 24
3	13 37	10♐27	01♉26	03 24	03 23	17 49	00 19	27 32	27 48	05 25
4	14 36	23 11	02 52	04 38	03 37	18 03	00 14	27 36	27 50	05 25
5	15 35	05♑34	04 13	05 52	03 53	18 16	00 10	27 39	27 52	05 25
6	16 34	17 40	05 28	07 06	04 08	18 30	00 05	27 42	27 54	05 25
7	17 33	29 34	06 38	08 19	04 24	18 44	00 01	27 45	27 55	05 R 25
8	18 32	11♒23	07 42	09 33	04 41	18 57	29♍56	27 49	27 57	05♑25
9	19 31	23 11	08 40	10 47	04 58	19 11	29 52	27 52	27 58	05 25
10	20 30	05♓03	09 32	12 00	05 15	19 24	29 48	27 55	28 00	05 25
11	21 29	17 03	10 17	13 14	05 33	19 38	29 44	27 58	28 02	05 24
12	22 28	29 13	10 57	14 28	05 51	19 51	29 39	28 02	28 03	05 24

APRIL 2010 (Cont'd)

Date	☉	☽	☿	♀	♂	♃	♄	♅	♆	♇
13	23♈27	11♈36	11♉29	15♉41	06♌10	20♓04	29♍35	28♓05	28♒05	05♑24
14	24 26	24 12	11 56	16 55	06 28	20 17	29 R 31	28 08	28 06	05 R 24
15	25 24	07♉00	12 15	18 08	06 48	20 31	29 27	28 11	28 07	05 24
16	26 23	20 02	12 29	19 21	07 07	20 44	29 23	28 14	28 09	05 23
17	27 22	03♊14	12 36	20 35	07 28	20 57	29 19	28 17	28 10	05 23
18	28 21	16 38	12 R 37	21 48	07 48	21 10	29 15	28 21	28 12	05 23
19	29 19	00♋12	12♉32	23 02	08 09	21 23	29 12	28 24	28 13	05 22
20	00♉18	13 56	12 22	24 15	08 30	21 36	29 08	28 27	28 14	05 22
21	01 16	27 50	12 06	25 28	08 51	21 48	29 04	28 30	28 16	05 21
22	02 15	11♌55	11 45	26 41	09 13	22 01	29 01	28 33	28 17	05 21
23	03 13	26 10	11 19	27 54	09 35	22 14	28 57	28 36	28 18	05 21
24	04 12	10♍33	10 50	29 07	09 57	22 26	28 54	28 39	28 19	05 20
25	05 10	25 00	10 17	00♊21	10 20	22 39	28 51	28 41	28 20	05 19
26	06 09	09♎27	09 41	01 34	10 43	22 51	28 47	28 44	28 22	05 19
27	07 07	23 48	09 04	02 47	11 06	23 04	28 44	28 47	28 23	05 18
28	08 05	07♏55	08 25	03 59	11 30	23 16	28 41	28 50	28 24	05 18
29	09 04	21 45	07 45	05 12	11 54	23 28	28 38	28 53	28 25	05 17
30	10 02	05♐14	07 05	06 25	12 18	23 40	28 35	28 56	28 26	05 16

MAY 2010

Date	☉	☽	☿	♀	♂	♃	♄	♅	♆	♇
1	11♉00	18♐19	06♉27	07♊38	12♌42	23♓53	28♍32	28♓58	28♒27	05♑16
2	11 58	01♑02	05 R 49	08 51	13 06	24 05	28 R 29	29 01	28 28	05 R 15
3	12 57	13 26	05 14	10 03	13 31	24 16	28 27	29 04	28 29	05 14
4	13 55	25 34	04 42	11 16	13 56	24 28	28 24	29 07	28 30	05 13
5	14 53	07♒31	04 12	12 29	14 22	24 40	28 21	29 09	28 30	05 13
6	15 51	19 21	03 46	13 41	14 47	24 52	28 19	29 12	28 31	05 12
7	16 49	01♓12	03 24	14 54	15 13	25 03	28 17	29 14	28 32	05 11
8	17 47	13 06	03 06	16 06	15 39	25 15	28 14	29 17	28 33	05 10
9	18 45	25 10	02 53	17 19	16 05	25 26	28 12	29 19	28 34	05 09
10	19 43	07♈27	02 44	18 31	16 32	25 37	28 10	29 22	28 34	05 08
11	20 41	19 59	02 40	19 43	16 58	25 49	28 08	29 24	28 35	05 07
12	21 39	02 48	02 D 40	20 56	17 25	26 00	28 06	29 27	28 36	05 06
13	22 37	15 54	02♉45	22 08	17 52	26 11	28 05	29 29	28 36	05 05
14	23 35	29 16	02 54	23 20	18 20	26 22	28 03	29 31	28 37	05 04
15	24 33	12♊52	03 08	24 32	18 47	26 32	28 01	29 34	28 37	05 03
16	25 31	26 40	03 27	25 44	19 15	26 43	28 00	29 36	28 38	05 02
17	26 29	10♋36	03 50	26 56	19 43	26 54	27 58	29 38	28 38	05 01
18	27 27	24 39	04 17	28 08	20 11	27 04	27 57	29 40	28 39	05 00
19	28 24	08♌46	04 49	29 20	20 39	27 15	27 56	29 43	28 39	04 59
20	29 22	22 55	05 24	00♋32	21 07	27 25	27 55	29 45	28 40	04 57
21	00♊20	07♍06	06 03	01 44	21 36	27 35	27 54	29 47	28 40	04 56
22	01 17	21 16	06 46	02 56	22 05	27 45	27 53	29 49	28 40	04 55
23	02 15	05♎23	07 33	04 07	22 34	27 55	27 52	29 51	28 41	04 54
24	03 13	19 24	08 23	05 19	23 03	28 05	27 51	29 53	28 41	04 53
25	04 10	03♏17	09 17	06 31	23 32	28 15	27 51	29 55	28 41	04 51
26	05 08	16 58	10 14	07 42	24 02	28 24	27 50	29 57	28 41	04 50
27	06 06	00♐24	11 15	08 54	24 31	28 34	27 50	29 58	28 41	04 49
28	07 03	13 34	12 18	10 05	25 01	28 43	27 50	00♈00	28 41	04 47
29	08 01	26 26	13 25	11 16	25 31	28 52	27 50	00 02	28 42	04 46
30	08 58	09♑01	14 34	12 28	26 01	29 01	27♍49	00 04	28 42	04 45
31	09 56	21 20	15 47	13 39	26 31	29 10	27 D 49	00 05	28 42	04 43

JUNE 2010

Date	☉	☽	☿	♀	♂	♃	♄	♅	♆	♇
1	10♊53	03♒26	17♉02	14♋50	27♌02	29♓19	27♍50	00♈07	28♒42	04♑42
2	11 51	15 23	18 20	16 01	27 32	29 28	27 50	00 09	28 R 42	04 R 41
3	12 48	27 15	19 42	17 12	28 03	29 36	27 50	00 10	28 42	04 39

JUNE 2010 (Cont'd)

Date	☉	☽	☿	♀	♂	♃	♄	♅	♆	♇
4	13♊46	09♓06	21♉06	18♋23	28♌34	29♓45	27♍51	00♈12	28♒41	04♑38
5	14 43	21 02	22 32	19 34	29 05	29 53	27 51	00 13	28 R 41	04 R 37
6	15 41	03♈07	24 02	20 45	29 36	00♈01	27 52	00 15	28 41	04 35
7	16 38	15 26	25 34	21 56	00♍07	00 09	27 52	00 16	28 41	04 34
8	17 35	28 02	27 08	23 06	00 38	00 17	27 53	00 17	28 41	04 32
9	18 33	10♉58	28 46	24 17	01 10	00 25	27 54	00 18	28 40	04 31
10	19 30	24 15	00♊26	25 27	01 42	00 33	27 55	00 20	28 40	04 29
11	20 28	07♊53	02 09	26 38	02 13	00 40	27 56	00 21	28 40	04 28
12	21 25	21 50	03 54	27 48	02 45	00 48	27 58	00 22	28 39	04 26
13	22 22	06♋02	05 42	28 59	03 17	00 55	27 59	00 23	28 39	04 25
14	23 20	20 25	07 33	00♌09	03 49	01 02	28 01	00 24	28 39	04 23
15	24 17	04♌53	09 26	01 19	04 22	01 09	28 02	00 25	28 38	04 22
16	25 14	19 22	11 21	02 29	04 54	01 15	28 04	00 26	28 38	04 20
17	26 12	03♍47	13 19	03 39	05 26	01 22	28 05	00 27	28 37	04 19
18	27 09	18 05	15 19	04 49	05 59	01 28	28 07	00 28	28 37	04 17
19	28 06	02♎12	17 21	05 59	06 32	01 35	28 09	00 29	28 36	04 16
20	29 04	16 09	19 25	07 08	07 05	01 41	28 11	00 29	28 35	04 14
21	00♋01	29 52	21 31	08 18	07 38	01 47	28 13	00 30	28 35	04 13
22	00 58	13♏22	23 39	09 28	08 11	01 53	28 16	00 31	28 34	04 11
23	01 55	26 37	25 47	10 37	08 44	01 58	28 18	00 31	28 33	04 10
24	02 52	09♐39	27 57	11 46	09 17	02 04	28 20	00 32	28 33	04 08
25	03 50	22 27	00♋08	12 56	09 50	02 09	28 23	00 32	28 32	04 07
26	04 47	05♑01	02 19	14 05	10 24	02 14	28 25	00 33	28 31	04 05
27	05 44	17 23	04 30	15 14	10 57	02 19	28 28	00 33	28 30	04 04
28	06 41	29 33	06 41	16 23	11 31	02 24	28 31	00 34	28 30	04 02
29	07 38	11♒35	08 52	17 31	12 05	02 28	28 34	00 34	28 29	04 00
30	08 36	23 29	11 02	18 40	12 39	02 33	28 37	00 34	28 28	03 59

JULY 2010

Date	☉	☽	☿	♀	♂	♃	♄	♅	♆	♇
1	09♋33	05♓21	13♋11	19♌49	13♍13	02♈37	28♍40	00♈35	28♒27	03♑57
2	10 30	17 12	15 20	20 57	13 47	02 41	28 43	00 35	28 R 26	03 R 56
3	11 27	29 08	17 27	22 06	14 21	02 45	28 46	00 35	28 25	03 54
4	12 24	11♈12	19 33	23 14	14 55	02 49	28 50	00 35	28 24	03 53
5	13 22	23 29	21 37	24 22	15 30	02 52	28 53	00 35	28 23	03 51
6	14 19	06♉04	23 40	25 30	16 04	02 56	28 57	00 R 35	28 22	03 50
7	15 16	19 00	25 41	26 38	16 39	02 59	29 00	00♈35	28 21	03 48
8	16 13	02♊20	27 40	27 46	17 13	03 02	29 04	00 35	28 20	03 47
9	17 11	16 04	29 38	28 53	17 48	03 05	29 08	00 35	28 19	03 45
10	18 08	00♋13	01♌33	00♍01	18 23	03 07	29 11	00 34	28 18	03 44
11	19 05	14 42	03 27	01 08	18 58	03 10	29 15	00 34	28 16	03 42
12	20 02	29 26	05 19	02 15	19 33	03 12	29 19	00 34	28 15	03 41
13	21 00	14♌20	07 09	03 23	20 08	03 14	29 23	00 34	28 14	03 39
14	21 57	29 13	08 57	04 30	20 43	03 16	29 28	00 33	28 13	03 38
15	22 54	14♍00	10 43	05 36	21 18	03 17	29 32	00 33	28 12	03 37
16	23 51	28 33	12 27	06 43	21 54	03 19	29 36	00 32	28 10	03 35
17	24 49	12♎49	14 09	07 49	22 29	03 20	29 41	00 32	28 09	03 34
18	25 46	26 44	15 50	08 56	23 05	03 21	29 45	00 31	28 08	03 32
19	26 43	10♏19	17 28	10 02	23 41	03 22	29 50	00 30	28 06	03 31
20	27 40	23 35	19 05	11 08	24 16	03 23	29 54	00 30	28 05	03 30
21	28 38	06♐33	20 39	12 14	24 52	03 23	29 59	00 29	28 04	03 28
22	29 35	19 15	22 12	13 19	25 28	03 24	00♎04	00 28	28 02	03 27
23	00♌32	01♑43	23 43	14 25	26 04	03 24	00 08	00 27	28 01	03 26
24	01 29	14 01	25 12	15 30	26 40	03 R 24	00 13	00 27	28 00	03 24
25	02 27	26 09	26 39	16 35	27 16	03♈23	00 18	00 26	27 58	03 23
26	03 24	08♒11	28 04	17 40	27 52	03 23	00 23	00 25	27 57	03 22
27	04 21	20 06	29 27	18 45	28 29	03 22	00 29	00 24	27 55	03 20

JULY 2010 (Cont'd)

Date	☉	☽	☿	♀	♂	♃	♄	♅	♆	♇
28	05♌19	01♓58	00♍47	19♍49	29♎05	03♈21	00♎34	00♈23	27♒54	03♑19
29	06 16	13 49	02 06	20 53	29 42	03 R 20	00 39	00 R 22	27 R 52	03 R 18
30	07 13	25 41	03 23	21 57	00♎18	03 19	00 44	00 21	27 51	03 17
31	08 11	07♈37	04 37	23 01	00 55	03 17	00 50	00 19	27 49	03 15

AUGUST 2010

Date	☉	☽	☿	♀	♂	♃	♄	♅	♆	♇
1	09♌08	19♈41	05♍50	24♍05	01♎31	03♈16	00♎55	00♈18	27♒48	03♑14
2	10 05	01♉56	07 00	25 08	02 08	03 R 14	01 01	00 R 17	27 R 46	03 R 13
3	11 03	14 28	08 07	26 11	02 45	03 12	01 06	00 16	27 45	03 12
4	12 00	27 19	09 12	27 14	03 22	03 09	01 12	00 14	27 43	03 11
5	12 58	10♊34	10 15	28 16	03 59	03 07	01 18	00 13	27 42	03 10
6	13 55	24 15	11 15	29 19	04 36	03 04	01 23	00 12	27 40	03 09
7	14 53	08♋23	12 12	00♎21	05 13	03 02	01 29	00 10	27 38	03 08
8	15 50	22 57	13 06	01 22	05 51	02 59	01 35	00 09	27 37	03 07
9	16 48	07♌52	13 57	02 24	06 28	02 55	01 41	00 07	27 35	03 06
10	17 45	23 01	14 45	03 25	07 05	02 52	01 47	00 06	27 34	03 05
11	18 43	08♍13	15 29	04 26	07 43	02 48	01 53	00 04	27 32	03 04
12	19 41	23 20	16 10	05 27	08 20	02 45	01 59	00 02	27 30	03 03
13	20 38	08♎11	16 47	06 27	08 58	02 41	02 05	00 01	27 29	03 02
14	21 36	22 39	17 20	07 27	09 36	02 37	02 11	29♓59	27 27	03 01
15	22 33	06♏42	17 49	08 26	10 14	02 32	02 18	29 57	27 25	03 00
16	23 31	20 18	18 13	09 25	10 52	02 28	02 24	29 55	27 24	02 59
17	24 29	03♐29	18 33	10 24	11 30	02 23	02 30	29 54	27 22	02 58
18	25 27	16 18	18 48	11 23	12 08	02 18	02 37	29 52	27 21	02 58
19	26 24	28 49	18 58	12 21	12 46	02 13	02 43	29 50	27 19	02 57
20	27 22	11♑05	19 03	13 18	13 24	02 08	02 49	29 48	27 17	02 56
21	28 20	23 11	19 R 02	14 16	14 02	02 03	02 56	29 46	27 16	02 55
22	29 17	05♒09	18♍55	15 12	14 40	01 58	03 02	29 44	27 14	02 55
23	00♍15	17 03	18 43	16 09	15 19	01 52	03 09	29 42	27 12	02 54
24	01 13	28 55	18 24	17 04	15 57	01 46	03 16	29 40	27 11	02 53
25	02 11	10♓46	18 00	18 00	16 36	01 40	03 22	29 38	27 09	02 53
26	03 09	22 38	17 30	18 55	17 14	01 34	03 29	29 36	27 07	02 52
27	04 07	04♈34	16 55	19 49	17 53	01 28	03 36	29 34	27 06	02 52
28	05 05	16 33	16 14	20 43	18 32	01 22	03 43	29 32	27 04	02 51
29	06 03	28 41	15 28	21 36	19 11	01 15	03 49	29 30	27 03	02 51
30	07 01	10♉58	14 39	22 28	19 50	01 09	03 56	29 28	27 01	02 50
31	07 59	23 28	13 46	23 20	20 28	01 02	04 03	29 25	26 59	02 50

SEPTEMBER 2010

Date	☉	☽	☿	♀	♂	♃	♄	♅	♆	♇
1	08♍57	06♊15	12♍50	24♎12	21♎08	00♈55	04♎10	29♓23	26♒58	02♑49
2	09 55	19 24	11 R 53	25 03	21 47	00 R 48	04 17	29 R 21	26 R 56	02 R 49
3	10 53	02♋56	10 56	25 53	22 26	00 41	04 24	29 19	26 55	02 49
4	11 51	16 56	09 59	26 42	23 05	00 34	04 31	29 17	26 53	02 48
5	12 49	01♌22	09 05	27 31	23 44	00 27	04 38	29 14	26 51	02 48
6	13 47	16 12	08 14	28 19	24 24	00 20	04 45	29 12	26 50	02 48
7	14 46	01♍20	07 28	29 06	25 03	00 12	04 52	29 10	26 48	02 48
8	15 44	16 38	06 48	29 52	25 43	00 05	04 59	29 07	26 47	02 47
9	16 42	01♎53	06 15	00♏38	26 23	29♓57	05 07	29 05	26 45	02 47
10	17 40	16 55	05 49	01 23	27 02	29 50	05 14	29 03	26 44	02 47
11	18 39	01♏35	05 31	02 06	27 42	29 42	05 21	29 00	26 42	02 47
12	19 37	15 48	05 22	02 49	28 22	29 34	05 28	28 58	26 41	02 47
13	20 36	29 31	05 D 23	03 31	29 02	29 26	05 35	28 56	26 39	02 47
14	21 34	12♐44	05♍32	04 12	29 42	29 18	05 43	28 53	26 38	02 D 47
15	22 32	25 33	05 51	04 52	00♏22	29 11	05 50	28 51	26 36	02♑47
16	23 31	08♑00	06 19	05 30	01 02	29 03	05 57	28 48	26 35	02 47
17	24 29	20 11	06 56	06 08	01 42	28 55	06 04	28 46	26 34	02 47

SEPTEMBER 2010 (Cont'd)

Date	☉	☽	☿	♀	♂	♃	♄	♅	♆	♇
18	25♍28	02♒12	07♍42	06♏44	02♏22	28♓47	06≏12	28♓44	26♒32	02♑47
19	26 27	14 05	08 35	07 19	03 03	28 R 39	06 19	28 R 41	26 R 31	02 47
20	27 25	25 55	09 36	07 53	03 43	28 31	06 26	28 39	26 30	02 48
21	28 24	07♓46	10 44	08 25	04 24	28 23	06 34	28 36	26 28	02 48
22	29 22	19 39	11 59	08 56	05 04	28 15	06 41	28 34	26 27	02 48
23	00≏21	01♈36	13 19	09 26	05 45	28 07	06 48	28 32	26 26	02 48
24	01 20	13 38	14 44	09 54	06 25	27 59	06 56	28 29	26 24	02 49
25	02 19	25 47	16 14	10 20	07 06	27 51	07 03	28 27	26 23	02 49
26	03 17	08♉03	17 47	10 45	07 47	27 43	07 11	28 24	26 22	02 49
27	04 16	20 28	19 24	11 08	08 28	27 35	07 18	28 22	26 21	02 50
28	05 15	03♊04	21 04	11 29	09 09	27 27	07 25	28 20	26 19	02 50
29	06 14	15 54	22 45	11 49	09 50	27 19	07 33	28 17	26 18	02 51
30	07 13	29 01	24 29	12 06	10 31	27 11	07 40	28 15	26 17	02 51

OCTOBER 2010

Date	☉	☽	☿	♀	♂	♃	♄	♅	♆	♇
1	08≏12	12♋28	26♍14	12♏22	11♏12	27♓04	07≏48	28♓13	26♒16	02♑52
2	09 11	26 16	27 59	12 36	11 53	26 R 56	07 55	28 R 10	26 R 15	02 52
3	10 10	10♌29	29 46	12 47	12 35	26 48	08 02	28 08	26 14	02 53
4	11 09	25 04	01≏33	12 57	13 16	26 41	08 10	28 05	26 13	02 53
5	12 08	09♍57	03 20	13 05	13 57	26 33	08 17	28 03	26 12	02 54
6	13 07	25 02	05 07	13 10	14 39	26 26	08 25	28 01	26 11	02 55
7	14 07	10≏09	06 54	13 13	15 20	26 19	08 32	27 59	26 10	02 55
8	15 06	25 08	08 41	13 R 13	16 02	26 11	08 39	27 56	26 09	02 56
9	16 05	09♏50	10 28	13♏12	16 44	26 04	08 47	27 54	26 08	02 57
10	17 04	24 06	12 14	13 08	17 26	25 57	08 54	27 52	26 07	02 58
11	18 04	07♐54	13 59	13 01	18 07	25 50	09 01	27 50	26 06	02 58
12	19 03	21 13	15 44	12 52	18 49	25 44	09 09	27 47	26 05	02 59
13	20 02	04♑05	17 28	12 41	19 31	25 37	09 16	27 45	26 04	03 00
14	21 02	16 35	19 12	12 27	20 13	25 31	09 23	27 43	26 04	03 01
15	22 01	28 47	20 55	12 11	20 55	25 24	09 31	27 41	26 03	03 02
16	23 01	10♒47	22 38	11 53	21 38	25 18	09 38	27 39	26 02	03 03
17	24 00	22 40	24 20	11 32	22 20	25 12	09 45	27 37	26 02	03 04
18	25 00	04♓30	26 01	11 09	23 02	25 06	09 53	27 35	26 01	03 05
19	25 59	16 22	27 41	10 44	23 45	25 00	10 00	27 33	26 00	03 06
20	26 59	28 18	29 21	10 17	24 27	24 54	10 07	27 31	26 00	03 07
21	27 59	10♈21	01♏00	09 49	25 10	24 49	10 14	27 29	25 59	03 08
22	28 58	22 33	02 39	09 18	25 52	24 44	10 21	27 27	25 59	03 10
23	29 58	04♉54	04 17	08 46	26 35	24 38	10 28	27 25	25 58	03 11
24	00♏58	17 25	05 54	08 13	27 17	24 33	10 36	27 23	25 58	03 12
25	01 58	00♊06	07 31	07 38	28 00	24 29	10 43	27 21	25 57	03 13
26	02 57	12 58	09 07	07 03	28 43	24 24	10 50	27 19	25 57	03 14
27	03 57	26 01	10 43	06 27	29 26	24 19	10 57	27 17	25 56	03 16
28	04 57	09♋17	12 18	05 50	00♐09	24 15	11 04	27 16	25 56	03 17
29	05 57	22 47	13 53	05 13	00 52	24 11	11 11	27 14	25 56	03 18
30	06 57	06♌32	15 27	04 37	01 35	24 07	11 18	27 12	25 55	03 20
31	07 57	20 34	17 01	04 01	02 18	24 03	11 25	27 11	25 55	03 21

NOVEMBER 2010

Date	☉	☽	☿	♀	♂	♃	♄	♅	♆	♇
1	08♏57	04♍53	18♏34	03♏25	03♐01	24♓00	11≏31	27♓09	25♒55	03♑23
2	09 57	19 24	20 07	02 R 50	03 45	23 R 56	11 38	27 R 07	25 R 55	03 24
3	10 57	04≏06	21 39	02 16	04 28	23 53	11 45	27 06	25 55	03 25
4	11 57	18 50	23 12	01 44	05 11	23 50	11 52	27 04	25 54	03 27
5	12 57	03♏29	24 43	01 13	05 55	23 47	11 59	27 03	25 54	03 28
6	13 58	17 56	26 14	00 44	06 38	23 45	12 05	27 01	25 54	03 30
7	14 58	02♐03	27 45	00 16	07 22	23 42	12 12	27 00	25 D 54	03 32
8	15 58	15 48	29 16	29≏50	08 06	23 40	12 19	26 59	25♒54	03 33